The United Nations and Changing World Politics

The United Nations and Changing World Politics

Third Edition

Thomas G. Weiss
The CUNY Graduate Center

David P. Forsythe
University of Nebraska

Roger A. Coate
University of South Carolina

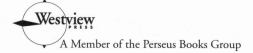

Westview
PRESS
A Member of the Perseus Books Group

Copyright © 2001 by Westview Press, A Member of the Perseus Books Group

Published in 2001 in the United States of America by Westview Press, 5500 Central Avenue, Boulder, Colorado 80301-2877, and in the United Kingdom by Westview Press, 12 Hid's Copse Road, Cumnor Hill, Oxford OX2 9JJ

Visit us on the World Wide Web at www.westviewpress.com

Library of Congress Cataloging-in-Publication Data
Weiss, Thomas George.
    The United Nations and changing world politics / Thomas G. Weiss, David P. Forsythe, and Roger A. Coate.—3rd ed.
        p.   cm.
    Includes bibliographical references and index.
    ISBN 0-8133-9750-2
    1. United Nations.   2. World politics—1989– .   I. Forsythe, David P., 1941– .   II. Coate, Roger A.   III. Title.

JZ4984.5 .W45   2000
341.23'1—dc21
                                                                                                00-043703

The paper used in this publication meets the requirements of the American National Standard for Permanence of Paper for Printed Library Materials Z39.48-1984.

EBC   02 03   10 9 8 7 6 5

Contents

Part Three   Building Peace Through Sustainable Development

Conclusion: Learning from Change   308

Tables and Illustrations

Tables

Figures

Photographs

Foreword to the Second Edition

Inis L. Claude, Jr.
Professor Emeritus, University of Virginia

Since the end of the Cold War, the United Nations has enjoyed—and suffered—a burst of unaccustomed prominence. The organization initially gained attention as sponsor of the successful effort to roll back Iraq's conquest of Kuwait. Euphoric expectations of a global collective security apparatus soon gave way to disillusionment as the United Nations became conspicuously involved in disasters in Somalia and Bosnia. In any case, the United Nations is no longer ignored and neglected; whether it is regarded with utopian idealism or with cynical disdain, it has achieved notable visibility.

The organization's revived prominence has continued largely because of the role it has undertaken in dealing with many of the crises that have erupted within states. We no longer hear the United Nations praised or scorned as a talkshop. Rather, evaluations of the organization now relate mainly to what it does, tries to do, or should do or to what it should be equipped to do as an operating agency in the field. The focus of international relations is no longer exclusively interstate but has become predominantly intrastate, and the most significant activity of the United Nations is no longer that occurring at headquarters but that taking place in trouble spots around the globe.

These changes intensify the need for serious study of the United Nations with a view to development of realistic and sophisticated understanding of the nature of the organization, its possibilities and limitations, its merits and defects, the promise that it holds, and the dangers that it poses. Above all, we need to examine the United Nations in its political context, regarding it as essentially an institutional framework within which states make decisions and allocate resources, arranging to do a variety of things with, to, for, and against each other. Americans, in particular, need to escape the illusion that the world organization is some gigantic "it," beneficent or sinister, and to realize that the United Nations is instead a "we"—ourselves and other states. States acting jointly as well as singly are primary members of the cast in the drama of international politics.

The authors of this volume are keenly aware of this reality. Whether they are writing about the use of the United Nations in operations relating to peace and security or its role in protecting human rights and responding to humanitarian needs or its programs in economic and environmental fields, they emphasize its political character. Wisely forgoing the effort to present a comprehensive history of the United Nations and related agencies, they concentrate on the areas in which the United Nations has recently been most actively engaged. In so doing, they illuminate the changes that are sweeping the world in the post–Cold War era and the responding changes in the character of the United Nations and in its agenda. Students who seek a thoughtful analysis of the multilateral aspects of today's international relations will find it here. The book effectively conveys the thoughts of three well-qualified scholars; even better, it informs and stimulates the reader to develop his or her own thinking on the subject. I stand by the proposition that I enunciated a generation ago: The United Nations has too many supporters and opponents and too few students. May their tribe increase!

Foreword to the Third Edition

Leon Gordenker
Professor Emeritus, Princeton University,
Center of International Studies

As this is written, soldiers wearing patches indicating participation in a mission for the United Nations have been taken captive in Sierra Leone. From Lebanon, where the Israeli military has just withdrawn from its so-called security zone, voices call for a strengthened presence by the United Nations to ensure tranquility. Ironically, for more than forty years, spokesmen on both sides of that border have often vilified UN activities, and on many occasions actions rendered peacekeeping ineffective. In New York, the five main nuclear powers complemented an existing nonproliferation treaty, worked out thirty years ago by the United Nations, by pledging to eliminate nuclear weapons. In Washington, renewed obstacles in the U.S. Senate to paying a financial obligation for UN membership ensures continuing penury for the organization to which almost every country of every conceivable size and capacity belongs. In Geneva, in meeting rooms that date back to the League of Nations, a gathering of experts on human rights pores over reports to the United Nations. The intrusiveness into national domains of their discussion would have made the nationalistic hair of old school diplomats stand up in shock. A covey of representatives from nongovernmental organizations intensely follows the proceedings for which they provide information. In East Timor, a UN mission offers help with the construction of a government.

On many a day during the last fifty-five years such a paragraph about UN activities could have been written. And, as now, it would have ignored more than it disclosed.

The United Nations, then, is a fact of our global life. To say so is not a defense of the organization, a claim about its worthiness, or a denunciation. It rather signals a need to understand this fact, to explain its boundaries, to fit it with other facts of contemporary life. This book, by three authors who have been close observers and students of, and participants in, several UN activities, fills that need.

The authors do not pretend to relate everything that could be known about the UN system. To begin with, UN history, spanning more than half a century, has been anything but fully compiled. And it is as complex as the world around it. Other parts of the story remain cloistered in inaccessible governmental and organizational archives.

The UN decisionmaking process includes some of the best and worst practices of international diplomacy and parliamentary procedure. Much of it consists of painstaking searches for agreement on texts on which representatives of many governments can agree. This effort involves speech making that can be incomprehensible to the untutored onlooker. Some of the keys to understanding can be found in the usually bland published documents prepared by international civil servants in the name of the UN Secretary-General. Outside the meeting rooms, guarded informal encounters, instructions from national capitals that remain secret, and sometimes flamboyant nationalistic demands complement the public proceedings.

The words that set out what is agreed, encoded in diplomatic language and the catch phrases of international law, themselves guarantee little. They have to be applied by governments, most of which, it is sad to admit, either routinely avoid giving them the fullest execution or do not have the means to do so. But words, as the Universal Declaration of Human Rights illustrates, can have lasting and even profound effects on what governments and their subjects do.

As the book suggests, no single theory provides a shortcut to understanding all of this. Some of the simpler theoretical approaches, much loved by muscle flexers, simply fail to explain much. Nor do analytical frameworks that strictly concentrate on national interests claims as seen from the perspectives of national capitals. Beyond the UN institutions, moreover, lies an increasingly complex, intertwined set of extragovernmental practices, organizations, and communications channels that help shape the UN agenda.

Instead of an encyclopedic approach or an abstract sketch, this book highlights three of the most important sectors of UN concern—peace and security, human rights, and sustainable development and environmental protection. As a result of digging deeply in those sectors, some of the main historical developments also emerge. Policy issues are clearly posed, the nature of the UN process comes into view. Some nuanced judgments about success and failure are drawn.

At the same time, the demand for a third edition of this book makes clear that as a totality the book admirably introduces its subject. Moreover, it opens doors to more enquiry. Why is the UN system so complex? How does it match and diverge from the actual world around it? Is it paralyzed by its own diplomatic culture? Can it be counted on to continue to develop? Can it, and should it, have a greater influence on international relations generally? What encourages that development and what holds it back? For that matter, is the very institutional form, built around the concept of national sovereignty and parliamentary and diplomatic procedures, increasingly obsolete in a world that each day less resembles that of 1945, when the UN was created?

If the responses to such questions remain uncertain, cause controversy, and seem beyond terse summaries, avoiding them will not make them disappear. They challenge imagination, bedevil statesmen, intrigue scholars, and ultimately condition our future as they have affected our past. In providing an analytical and historical framework for understanding where the UN has been, Weiss, Forsythe, and Coate provide the foundation for understanding where its future may lie.

Preface to the Third Edition

As the name implies, *The United Nations and Changing World Politics* is about the United Nations (UN) system and the role of the UN and its associated family of specialized agencies in global governance. Writing a preface for this third edition is both encouraging and discouraging. As authors we are delighted that so many colleagues and students have found it to be a useful book. In an age with ever-decreasing shelf lives for examinations of contemporary events, we also have been gratified to verify that our original analyses and structure held up well to subsequent events from 1994 through 2000. The three organizing themes in this volume—international peace and security, human rights and humanitarian action, and sustainable human development—continue to provide plenty of grist for analytical and policy mills of the post–post–Cold War world. It was of course necessary to update information and correct minor errors, but readers of the third edition will recognize much of its predecessors here.

At the same time, we can hardly be encouraged by the fortunes in the interim of the world organization itself and of multilateralism more generally. As discussed in the pages that follow, the United Nations has in many ways been on a decade-long roller-coaster ride, especially in the peace and security area. Moreover, at the turn of the century it continued to teeter on the brink of financial insolvency, with Washington leading the pack of deadbeats in arrears on payments.

We are not card-carrying members of the UN fan club, but we remain persuaded that something like the world organization would have to be created if the present one ceased to exist. Hence, we have endeavored first and foremost to capture the essence of the United Nations as a political organization caught in the struggle to make public policy through the exercise of power. We stress how representatives of member states and other actors seek to use UN symbols and procedures to shape policy. Those actors do not approach the UN only or even primarily in terms of peace and justice. They may give some attention to these abstract values, but they are primarily driven by their own values, needs, and interests. Indeed, a classic study of the UN and the great powers concludes that conceptions of immediate interests, not long-term and abstract concerns for peace and justice, have been the most important factor in shaping UN activities.[1]

Policymaking always involves power, understood as a synonym for influence. We also observe how UN structure and processes constrain the exercise of power. Hard power is coercion through manipulation of economic resources and through military force. Soft power is persuasion and pressure through words and symbolic acts. The central question for those interested in the United Nations is:

Who seeks what policy objective, using what power, and with what outcome? What occurs at the UN, to paraphrase Harold Lasswell, is about who governs across national boundaries and who gets what, when, how.[2]

Yet this approach to UN politics is misleading in one important way because the United Nations is about global governance without a world government, or about how transnational problems can be collectively managed in the absence of the "normal" attributes of government. These attributes include a true legislature, a single executive branch, an integrated court system, and, above all, a legitimate monopoly on the exercise of force. Our primary objective is to get students to understand the UN as part of the fabric of world politics.

We also wanted to capture the essence of public international law as an institution that exerts real influence on real political struggles. We emphasize that, like all public law, international law is not a technical subject independent of politics but rather part and parcel of world politics. International law is formulated through a political process, frequently centering on the United Nations. Consequently, international law interacts with world politics, sometimes shaping it greatly and sometimes only slightly or not at all.

Whatever its ultimate impact on a given policy or situation, international law is always present in UN proceedings. Indeed, the world organization is a construction of international law because the UN Charter is a multilateral treaty. The ever-present, often subtle, influence of international law is perhaps better understood by those who practice politics at the UN than by many academics observing the process from the outside. We want readers to understand how international law interacts with "pure" politics; how attention to international legal rules (reflecting formalized policy) interacts with subsequent considerations of policy and power.

Moreover, we want to stress the importance of history. The present and even the future have a history. When seemingly new issues arise, there is almost always a background to the issue that affects its management or disposition. Rather than providing a tabula rasa or constituting the "end of history,"[3] a phrase that was popular for a very brief moment, the end of the Cold War has permitted the brutal expression of historical grievances. So when the Security Council or General Assembly deals with an apparently new issue such as violence in the Balkans or humanitarian assistance in Somalia or how to pursue economic growth while protecting the environment in Brazil, the history of these issues exerts a pull. History does not necessarily determine the future, but history affects the future. The history of such issues as using force, coordinating assistance, or promoting sustainable development affects new policy decisions. We want readers to know the political and legal history of the UN so that present and future choices can be analyzed and debated against that background.

The notion of change has long bedeviled social scientists. We have found it easier to chart the past than to understand the full implications of current issues, or where policy decisions on those issues may take us in the future. Nevertheless, we want to try to say as much as we can about change in world politics and what this might mean for the future of the United Nations. We do not pretend to possess privileged knowledge of the future, but we do want to encourage and guide readers to look at several ways of understanding the political changes that drive events in the UN system.

In that context, we have endeavored to design this book so that it can be used in at least two ways. First, we want it to serve as a core text in college courses on international organization and the United Nations. Second, we want it to be useful as supplemental reading in other courses, such as international relations and international law. Thus we have sought to present the essentials of politics at the UN in three central arenas: security, human rights, and sustainable human development.

We selected these areas not only because of their intrinsic importance in world politics but also because the United Nations has had significant normative and operational impacts in all three of them. But we have not tried to write everything we know about the UN. For example, we have not discussed disarmament under security because, Iraq and North Korea aside, the UN has had few operational responsibilities in the area; such a discussion would dilute the emphasis on the concrete illustrations of significant military activities over the past half century. We want to keep the work short enough to be used as supplemental information in a variety of courses.

Each of us drafted a section of the book. Tom Weiss wrote and then updated the first draft on peace and security issues; Dave Forsythe did the same for the part on human rights and humanitarian affairs; and Roger Coate drafted the section on sustainable human development. Each of us then rewrote all sections so that pride of authorship could yield to collective judgment. This holds true for the introduction and conclusion as well. Our collaboration has, we hope, not only discouraged ill-informed and parochial points of view but produced a synergy and a better text than any one of us could have written on our own. Each of us had conducted original research and taught about the three crucial areas of UN activity that provide the central framework for this book: international peace and security, human rights and humanitarian law, and sustainable development. We have also spent considerable time working within, or consulting with, international organizations.

Four outside reviewers read the original manuscript of the first edition in 1993. Craig Murphy of Wellesley College and Lawrence Finkelstein, then at Northern Illinois University, are both recognized scholars of international organization and world politics; they provided comments through the cooperation of the International Organization Section of the International Studies Association. Two other readers, unknown to us, were provided by Westview Press. A discussion group focused on this manuscript at the annual meeting of the Academic Council on the United Nations System (ACUNS) held in Montreal during June 1993. The prepress manuscript was finalized by the staff of the Watson Institute at Brown University, working under a grant from ACUNS. Thus this book is in some ways a product of the International Studies Association and ACUNS, although only the authors are responsible for the final version. We acknowledge with gratitude the time and effort that others put into improving our work.

We would like to express our special gratitude to those staff members of our respective academic institutions who—with good humor and professionalism—assisted in the preparation of the various versions of the manuscript. Special thanks are in order for the first edition to Susan Costa, Mary Lhowe, and Melissa Phillips and for the second edition to Fred Fullerton and Laura Sadovnikoff. Without their help final texts would have been considerably slower in appearing and certainly less well presented. Another word of appreciation goes to those younger researchers who have helped at one stage or another in framing arguments, checking facts and endnotes, and prodding their mentors: Peter Breil, Christopher Brodhead, Cindy Collins, Paula L'Ecuyer, Jean Garrison, and Peter Söderholm. Thanks are also in order to Corinne Jiminez for her technical assistance.

The three of us are sympathetic to multilateral organizations in general, and to the United Nations in particular. We believe that the UN fits into a complicated world situation that does not often yield to unilateral undertakings. We believe that the first Clinton administration recognized this reality when initially describing its foreign policy as one that pursued "assertive multilateralism." Although it retreated from this rhetoric, it has been reluctant to act without collective approval and support. Madeleine Albright, secretary of state for the second Clinton administration but at the time of this quote U.S. Permanent Representative to the United Nations, stated clearly in 1993 what in fact remains valid today: "There will be many occasions when we need to bring pressure to bear on the belligerents of the post–Cold War period and use our influence to prevent ethnic and other regional conflicts from erupting. But usually we will not want to act alone—our stake will be limited and direct U.S. intervention unwise."[4]

We do not believe that such an orientation is accurately described as "Wilsonian idealism" or that it reflects uncritical support for world organizations. A preference for multilateral diplomacy is not idealistic at the start of the twenty-first century. On the contrary, unilateralists promoting an image of unbridled state control over events are the real utopians of the twenty-first century. We believe some scholars are helpful in referring to much of world politics as a scene of complex interdependence in which a vast array of issues require multilateral treatment largely through peaceful management.

In principle we believe that collectively endorsed policies within the confines of the UN Charter stand a better chance of being successful than others. We usually are suspicious of unilateral actions; we believe in the beneficial effects of channeling perceptions of national interests through the process of collective evaluation. Thus we do not endorse the view that states should use the UN framework only as a last resort or the view of those who would prefer to say of most situations, "Fortunately, the United Nations was not involved."[5] We believe that much damage has been done to world affairs by states that disregard the UN Charter and shun serious multilateral consultation, whether during the Cold War or after. Multilateral diplomacy can be complicated and messy, but much unilateral action can be dangerous and destructive. Jesse Helms's threat to withdraw from the UN stems from a series of illusions.[6]

Nevertheless, we point out the weaknesses of the UN system. We do not hesitate to discuss places where the organization has not measured up to reasonable expectations. After all, the UN is not a religion or a church. It is something not to be worshipped but to be critically analyzed. It is basically a political organization, even if it is affected by international law, and it is primarily affected by the foreign policies of member states. We believe that multilateral organizations reflect a world of many connections, but we also believe that constructive criticism of the United Nations is essential for a more peaceful, just, and prosperous world.

If we can get students to better understand the United Nations as a political organization, affected by international law, with its own history; if we can accurately portray the UN as greatly affected by basic changes in its political milieu; and if we can provide insights about what it has done and how these efforts might be improved in the future, we will have succeeded in this endeavor.

Each of the three substantive parts starts with an overview of basic ideas about the UN and that issue area (security, human rights, and sustainable human development). Each follows with a historical overview of how the UN has been involved in that issue area and a discussion on changes that might lead to improved UN performance. Current events until spring 2000 have been incorporated into the text. The cutoff for historical examples is December 1999. Each part situates the broader political changes driving events at the UN; the nature of these political changes appears prominently in both the introduction and the conclusion. At the end of the book we include suggestions for further reading to be used in conjunction with this text.

Thomas G. Weiss
David P. Forsythe
Roger A. Coate

Notes

1. John G. Stoessinger, *The United Nations and the Superpowers* (New York: Random House, 1966), p. 178.

2. Harold D. Lasswell, *Politics: Who Gets What, When, How* (New York: McGraw-Hill, 1936).

3. Francis Fukuyama, "The End of History," *The National Interest* 16 (1989), pp. 3–18; *The End of History and the Last Man* (New York: Free Press, 1992).

4. Quoted in the *Washington Post, National Weekly Edition,* June 21–27, 1993, p. 16.

5. Ernest W. Lefever, "Reining in the U.N.: Mistaking the Instrument for the Actor," *Foreign Affairs* 72, no. 3 (Summer 1993), p. 20.

6. Jesse Helms, "Saving the U.N.," *Foreign Affairs* 75, no. 5 (1996), pp. 2–7.

Acronyms

ACC	Administrative Committee on Coordination
ACP	African, Caribbean, and Pacific states
ACUNS	Academic Council on the United Nations System
ASCEND	Agenda of Science for Environment and Development into the Twenty-first Century
ASEAN	Association of Southeast Asian Nations
CAT	Committee Against Torture
CCMS	Committee on the Challenges of Modern Society
CCSQ	Consultative Committee on Substantive Questions
CEDAW	Committee on the Elimination of Discrimination Against Women
CERD	Committee on the Elimination of Racial Discrimination
CESCR	Committee on Economic, Social, and Cultural Rights
CIDIE	Committee of International Development Institutions on the Environment
CIS	Commonwealth of Independent States
CONGO	Conference on Non-Governmental Organizations in Consultative Status with ECOSOC
CRC	Committee on the Rights of the Child
CSCE	Conference on Security and Cooperation in Europe
CSD	Commission on Sustainable Development
CSO	Civil society organization
DESA	United Nations Department for Economic and Social Affairs
DHA	Department of Humanitarian Affairs
DOEM	Designated Officials for Environmental Matters
DOMREP	Mission of the Representative of the Secretary-General in the Dominican Republic
DPA	Department of Political Affairs
DPKO	Department of Peace-keeping Operations
DSR	Deputy special representative
EC	European Community
ECA	Economic Commission for Africa
ECAFE	Economic Commission for Asia and the Far East
ECE	Economic Commission for Europe
ECHA	Executive Committee for Humanitarian Affairs

ECLAC	Economic Commission for Latin America and the Caribbean
ECOMOG	Military Observer Group of the Economic Community of West African States
ECOSOC	Economic and Social Council
ECOWAS	Economic Community of West African States
EEC	European Economic Community
ELCI	Environment Liaison Centre International
EPTA	Expanded Program of Technical Assistance
ERC	Emergency relief coordinator
ESCAP	Economic and Social Commission for Asia and the Pacific
ESCWA	Economic and Social Commission for Western Asia
EU	European Union
FAO	Food and Agriculture Organization
FMLN	Frente Farabundo Martí para la Liberación Nacional (Farabundo Martí National Liberation Front)
G-7	Group of Seven
G-77	Group of 77
GATT	General Agreement on Tariffs and Trade
GCC	Gulf Cooperation Council
GEF	Global Environmental Facility
GPA	Global Programme on AIDS
GSDF	Global Sustainable Development Facility
HABITAT	UN Conference on Human Settlements
HDI	Human development index
HRC	Human Rights Committee
HRFOR	Human Rights Field Operation in Rwanda
IADB	Inter-American Defense Board
IAEA	International Atomic Energy Agency
IASC	Interagency standing committee
IBP	International Biological Programme
IBRD	International Bank for Reconstruction and Development (the World Bank)
ICAO	International Civil Aviation Organization
ICC	International Criminal Court
ICCAT	International Convention for the Conservation of Atlantic Tunas
ICJ	International Court of Justice
ICPD	International Conference on Population and Development
ICRC	International Committee of the Red Cross
ICSU	International Council of Scientific Unions
ICTFY	International Criminal Tribunal for the Former Yugoslavia
ICTR	International Criminal Tribunal for Rwanda
IDA	International Development Association

IDB	Inter-American Development Bank
IDP	Internally displaced person
IFAD	International Fund for Agricultural Development
IFC	International Facilitating Committee
IFC	International Finance Corporation
IFOR	Implementation Force (in the former Yugoslavia)
IGBP	International Geosphere-Biosphere Programme
IGO	Intergovernmental organization
ILO	International Labour Organisation
IMF	International Monetary Fund
IMO	International Maritime Organization
INSTRAW	International Research and Training Institute for the Advancement of Women
INTERFET	International Force in East Timor
IOC	International Oceanographic Commission
IPDC	International Programme for the Development of Communication
ISSC	International Social Science Council
ITU	International Telecommunications Union
IUCN	International Union for the Conservation of Nature and National Resources
JCGP	Joint Consultative Group on Policy
KFOR	Kosovo Force
KLA	Kosovo Liberation Army
LDCs	Least-developed countries
MAB	Man and the Biosphere
MFN	Most favored nation
MIGA	Multilateral Investment Guarantee Agency
MINURSO	UN Mission for the Referendum in Western Sahara
MNF	Multinational Force
MONUA	United Nations Observer Mission in Angola
MONUC	United Nations Observer Mission in the Democratic Republic of the Congo
MSC	Military Staff Committee
NAFTA	North American Free Trade Agreement
NAM	Non-Aligned Movement
NATO	North Atlantic Treaty Organization
NGO	Nongovernmental organization
NIEO	New International Economic Order
NWICO	New world information and communication order
OAS	Organization of American States
OAU	Organization of African Unity
OCHA	Office for the Coordination of Humanitarian Affairs

ODA	Overseas development assistance
OECD	Organization for Economic Cooperation and Development
OILPOL	International Convention for the Prevention of Pollution at Sea by Oil
OMS	Operational manual statement
ONUC	United Nations Operation in the Congo
ONUCA	United Nations Observer Group in Central America
ONUMOZ	United Nations Operation in Mozambique
ONUSAL	United Nations Observer Mission in El Salvador
ONUVEH	United Nations Observer Mission to Verify the Electoral Process in Haiti
ONUVEN	United Nations Observer Mission to Verify the Electoral Process in Nicaragua
OPEC	Organization of Petroleum Exporting Countries
OPPRC	International Convention on Oil Pollution Preparedness Response and Cooperation
ORCI	Office for Research and Collection of Information
OSCE	Organization on Security and Cooperation in Europe
PDD	Presidential decision directive
PLO	Palestine Liberation Organization
PrepCom	UNCHE Preparatory Committee
PVOs	Private voluntary organizations
RPG	Refugee Policy Group
RUF	Revolutionary United Front
SAARC	South Asian Association for Regional Cooperation
SADCC	Southern African Development Coordination Conference
SCOPE	Scientific Committee on Problems of the Environment
SHD	Sustainable human development
SMG	Senior management group
SRSG	Special representative of the Secretary-General
STABEX	Stabilization of Export Earnings
SUNFED	Special United Nations Fund for Economic Development
SU/TCDC	United Nations Special Unit for Technical Cooperation Among Developing Countries
SWAPO	South-West Africa People's Organization
TAC	Technical Assistance Committee
UDI	Unilateral Declaration of Independence
UNAIDS	Joint United Nations Programme on HIV/AIDS
UNAMET	United Nations Mission in East Timor
UNAMIR	United Nations Assistance Mission in Rwanda
UNAMSIL	United Nations Mission for Sierra Leone
UNASOG	United Nations Aouzou Strip Observer Group
UNAVEM	United Nations Angola Verification Mission

UNCAST	United Nations Conference on Applications of Science and Technology for the Benefit of Less Developed Areas
UNCDF	United Nations Capital Development Fund
UNCED	United Nations Conference on Environment and Development
UNCHE	United Nations Conference on the Human Environment
UNCHS	United Nations Center for Human Settlements (Habitat)
UNCITRAL	United Nations Commission on International Trade Law
UNCLOS	United Nations Conference on the Law of the Sea
UNCRO	United Nations Confidence Restoration Operation
UNCTAD	United Nations Conference on Trade and Development
UNDAF	United Nations Development Assistance Framework
UNDCP	United Nations International Drug Control Programme
UNDG	United Nations Development Group
UNDOF	United Nations Disengagement Observer Force
UNDP	United Nations Development Programme
UNDRO	United Nations Disaster Relief Office
UNEF	United Nations Emergency Force
UNEP	United Nations Environment Programme
UNESCO	United Nations Educational, Scientific and Cultural Organization
UNFCCC	United Nations Framework Convention on Climate Change
UNFDA	United Nations development assistance framework
UNFICYP	United Nations Peace-keeping Force in Cyprus
UNFPA	United Nations Population Fund (formerly Fund for Population Activities)
UNGA	United Nations General Assembly
UNGOMAP	United Nations Good Offices Mission in Afghanistan and Pakistan
UNHCHR	United Nations High Commissioner for Human Rights
UNHCR	United Nations High Commissioner for Refugees
UNICEF	United Nations Children's Fund
UNIDO	United Nations Industrial Development Organization
UNIFEM	United Nations Development Fund for Women
UNIFIL	United Nations Interim Force in Lebanon
UNIIMOG	United Nations Iran-Iraq Military Observer Group
UNIKOM	United Nations Iraq-Kuwait Observation Mission
UNIPOM	United Nations India-Pakistan Observation Mission
UNITA	National Union for the Total Independence of Angola
UNITAF	Unified Task Force (in Somalia)
UNITAR	United Nations Institute for Training and Research
UNMIBH	United Nations Mission in Bosnia and Herzegovina
UNMIG	United Nations Observer Mission in Georgia
UNMIH	United Nations Mission in Haiti

UNMIK	United Nations Interim Administration Mission in Kosovo
UNMOGIP	United Nations Military Observer Group in India and Pakistan
UNMOP	United Nations Mission of Observers in Prevlaka
UNMOT	United Nations Mission of Observers in Tajikistan
UNOGIL	United Nations Observer Group in Lebanon
UNOMIG	United Nations Observer Mission in Georgia
UNOMIL	United Nations Observer Mission in Liberia
UNOMSIL	United Nations Observer Mission in Sierra Leone
UNOMUR	United Nations Observer Mission in Uganda and Rwanda
UNOPS	United Nations Office for Project Services
UNOSOM	United Nations Operation in Somalia
UNPREDEP	United Nations Preventive Deployment Force
UNPROFOR	United Nations Protection Force (in the former Yugoslavia)
UNPSG	United Nations Civilian Police Support Group
UNRRA	United Nations Relief and Rehabilitation Administration
UNRWA	United Nations Relief and Works Agency
UNSF	United Nations Security Force
UNSMIH	United Nations Support Mission in Haiti
UNTAC	United Nations Transitional Authority in Cambodia
UNTAES	United Nations Transitional Administration for Eastern Slavonia, Baranja and Western Sirmium
UNTAET	United Nations Transitional Administration in East Timor
UNTAG	United Nations Transition Assistance Group in Namibia
UNTEA	United Nations Temporary Executive Authority
UNTSO	United Nations Truce Supervision Organization
UNU	United Nations University
UNV	United Nations Volunteers
UNYOM	United Nations Yemen Observation Mission
UPU	Universal Postal Union
USSR	Union of Soviet Socialist Republics
VOLAGS	Volunteer agencies
WCED	World Commission on Environment and Development
WCRP	World Climate Research Programme
WEU	Western European Union
WFP	World Food Programme
WHO	World Health Organization
WIPO	World Intellectual Property Organization
WMO	World Meteorological Organization
WRI	World Resources Institute
WTO	World Trade Organization
WWF	World Wide Fund for Nature

Introduction

The most casual observer of the international scene can see that the problem of world order has not been solved.

—Inis L. Claude, Jr., *Swords into Plowshares*

At the dawn of the twenty-first century even the most casual observer of international affairs is deeply affected by the notion of change. As the twentieth century began, global multilateral relations and universal international organizations were in their infancy. Experiments with international unions, conference diplomacy, and the expansion of multilateral relations beyond Europe remained fledgling. As the decades unfolded, so did universal multilateralism, albeit on the European state-system model. Challenged by the increasing lethality of warfare and the evolving associated norm of the illegality of launching aggressive war, the first great experiment with collective security—the League of Nations—was launched.

This experiment failed, but after the second great European war of the century became a global conflict, national governmental leaders once again began to search for a way to prevent it from happening again. Under the leadership of officials from the United States and Great Britain, a second great experiment in collective security was launched. This time, however, the collective security agreement was seen as part of a more comprehensive global arrangement in which the guarantees of collective security were linked to a series of international institutions aimed at promoting and fostering the social and economic conditions necessary for peace to prevail. Many of the social and economic elements of the postwar world order were, in fact, agreed on before the formal adoption of the UN Charter. The UN system was born plural and decentralized and was never intended to approximate a centralized unitary system. At the same time, the UN system was born from pragmatism and realism and not utopian idealism, as some would have us believe. A great war against fascism and irrationalism had just been fought and won; the price of a third great war during the twentieth century was simply viewed as too great—the nuclear era had begun.

In this first decade of the new century, it is difficult to conceive of a world without multilateralism. The national rulers of today began their attentiveness to world events when the United Nations was in the headlines and on the front pages of even local newspapers. UN officials were managing more than 20,000 troops in the old Belgian Congo (then Zaire and more recently once again the Congo) in the 1960s. Secretary-General Dag Hammarskjöld died while coping with that crisis, which almost caused the collapse of the world organization. UN diplomatic and military personnel have been deeply involved in Middle Eastern politics since the late 1940s in Palestine but especially in the 1956 Suez crisis and the 1967 Arab-Israeli War.

These officials then watched as their predecessors placed the United Nations on a back burner. For much of the 1970s and even more in the 1980s, major states often seemed to bypass the world organization. Some developing countries continued to look upon it as central to world politics, but both Washington and Moscow seemed to favor action outside the UN. Circles of opinion in the U.S. capital, both public and private, were particularly harsh in their criticisms of the organization in the 1980s. The first Reagan administration, and related think tanks like the Heritage Foundation, manifested a deep distrust of multilateral diplomacy. One Reagan official, Charles Lichenstein, assigned to the UN spoke publicly of "waving . . . a fond farewell as [the UN] sailed into the sunset."[1] Several U.S. allies also shied away from an organization whose "automatic" voting majorities, which were seemingly predictable, had shifted over the decades from being controlled by the United States to being dominated by developing countries. Even some of these developing countries, however, appeared at times to despair of an organization whose resolutions were not followed by commitment to action.

All parties then watched again while some participated as a marked change came over the organization in the wake of the collapse of communism from 1985 to 1991. Mikhail Gorbachev, then the first secretary of the Communist Party of the Soviet Union, called upon the UN in a September 1987 article in *Pravda* to play a more central role in world politics—as a cornerstone of global security. Then boldly, more boldly than any previous leader of a superpower, Gorbachev embraced the UN and its collective security mechanism as a cornerstone of Soviet security policy. The Reagan administration, the most unilateralist in modern American political history, responded cautiously. Nonetheless, by the end of the Bush administration, the United States had used the UN to a great extent in dealing with such major issues as the Iraqi invasion of Kuwait in 1990, although earlier it had bypassed the UN on other matters such as the invasion of Panama in 1989. By the mid-1990s, the UN was back again on the front pages and in the headlines—and on CNN as well!

Many in the South were cautious as the "two elephants," to paraphrase a popularly used analogy during that period, and their three Security Council permanent-member counterparts began to dance the dance of consensus, which led to an unprecedented use of the Security Council as a global security mechanism. In the years immediately following the end of the Cold War, there was a tremendous surge in UN peacekeeping and enforcement activities. In the short period from

1988 to 1993, there were substantially more UN military operations—over twenty new operations were launched—than during the entire first four decades of the world organization. Great euphoria reigned in prointernationalist circles in the United States just as great concern reigned in many smaller member states of the world organization.

The roller-coaster ride continued as the UN's peacekeeping and peace enforcement profile once again changed. The scope of the UN Security Council's business slowed greatly after the 1988–1993 period. In the next five years (until December 1998), sixteen peacekeeping operations were authorized. However, that number is misleading because seven were offshoots of previous missions. Of the remaining new operations, only the third UN Angola Verification Mission (UN-AVEM III) was of significant size (with 6,500 troops) and duration. Both the total number of UN blue helmets and the peacekeeping budget fell by two-thirds from 1994 to 1998, reflecting disillusionment in Somalia, Rwanda, and the Balkans.

In 1999, change set in again, effectively more than doubling the number of personnel involved. Major new missions were launched in Sierra Leone (6,260 military troops and observers), East Timor (9,150 troops and observers), and Kosovo (approximately 4,500 UN and partner organization personnel and civilian police). But the numbers of operations and personnel tell only part of the story. The missions in Kosovo, East Timor, and another smaller new operation, the UN Observer Mission in the Democratic Republic of the Congo (MONUC), represent a qualitatively different kind of operation. These operations are exceedingly complex and multidimensional. They are mandated the tasks of creating viable political and social institutions, rebuilding basic social and economic infrastructures, strengthening the rule of law and protecting human rights, and demobilizing former combatants and reintegrating them into society. Greatly expanding on earlier multidimensional operations, especially in El Salvador and Cambodia, the new efforts aimed to reconstitute viable states, an ambitious effort that critics referred to as "neocolonialism" but that Jarat Chopra has dubbed "peace-maintenance."[2]

At the same time, as discussed in Parts 2 and 3 of this book, the UN's roles in promoting humanitarian affairs and human rights and sustainable human development also have continued to evolve. The *Human Development Reports* of the UN Development Programme (UNDP) indicate that the world may be losing, not gaining, ground toward the objective of promoting sustainable human development. The 1996 report, for example, highlighted two "disturbing" findings:

Economic growth has been failing over much of the past fifteen years in about 100 countries, with almost a third of the world's people. And the links between growth and human development are failing for people in many countries with lopsided development—with either good growth but little human development or good human development but little or no growth.[3]

In 70 of those countries, average incomes in 1993 were less than they were in 1980. In 43 of those countries, average incomes were less than they had been in 1970. If the communications revolution is an engine of growth, the fact that the poorest 20 percent of the globe's countries contain only 0.2 percent of Internet users is startling. Clearly, the four development decades of the United Nations have not met with complete successes. Many poor countries have become ever more marginalized in the world economy, and global inequality continues to increase substantially.[4]

But these statistics tell only part of the story. Even in the peacekeeping arena, the character of UN operations has been changing. Less than 20 percent of the UN missions launched since 1988, for example, have been in response to interstate conflict, the type for which the founders of the world organization had planned. The majority of UN operations have been primarily intrastate. On all fronts, a great challenge has been launched against the foundations of the world organization and the legal concept of sovereignty. Antiquated notions of the inviolability and absolute character of state sovereignty have been called into question by new types of threats to international peace and security—as well as the sanctity of the notion of noninterference in the internal affairs of states.

When one sees highly publicized war crimes and other human rights abuses along with widespread poverty, malnutrition, environmental degradation, and resource depletions, the preeminent challenge to the future of the UN comes into sharper focus. The challenge of relevance in the UN system is linked to changing notions of sovereignty. Thus we should examine the legal concept of state sovereignty and its historical evolution.

The Legal Foundations of Sovereignty

Since about the middle of the seventeenth century, when the Peace of Westphalia (1648) essentially ended European religious wars, powerful political circles have accepted that the world should be divided into territorial states. Before that time there were dynastic empires, city-states, feudalistic orders, clans and tribes, churches, and a variety of other arrangements for organizing persons into broader groupings for problem solving. From about the middle of the fifteenth century to the middle of the seventeenth, the territorial state emerged, first in Europe and then elsewhere, as the basic unit of social organization that presumably commanded primary loyalty and was responsible at least for order, and eventually for justice and prosperity, within a state's boundaries. European rulers found the institution of the state useful and perpetuated its image; then politically aware persons outside the West adopted the notion of the state to resist domination by European states.

Even after 1648, however, many other groupings persisted. In Europe, Napoleon sought to substitute a French empire for several states as late as the nineteenth century, and European colonialism persisted in Africa until the 1970s (the Portuguese were the last Europeans to abandon their African colonies, in 1974, although South Africa controlled Namibia until 1992). Despite these exceptions and the persistence of clan, ethnic, and religious identities, most of those exercising power increasingly promoted the perception that the basic politicolegal unit of world affairs was the state: a governing system within a specific geographical area, with a stable (nonnomadic) population and a functioning and presumably independent government. The territorial state may have extraterritorial jurisdiction, such as control of maritime areas not technically owned by the state, but we leave that subject matter to advanced students of international law.

Frequently the territorial state is referred to as the "nation-state." This label is not totally false, but it can be misleading because nations and states are not the same. A nation is a people (a group of persons professing solidarity on the basis of language, religion, history, or some other bonding element) linked to a state. By definition, where there is a state there is a nation, but there may be several peoples within a state. For example, in Switzerland (officially the Helvetian Confederation), by definition there is the Swiss nation, but in reality there are four peoples linked to that state: the Swiss-Germans, the Swiss-French, the Swiss-Italians, and the Swiss-Romanisch. The confusing notion of a multinational state also has arisen along with a divided nation (East and West Germany between 1945 and 1989 and North and South Korea today) and states with irredentist claims (Serbia). In this sense the word "nation" refers to any grouping of people as well as to the totality of persons governed by a state. There is the state of Belgium; there is the nation of Belgians; and within Belgium there are the Flemish people (the Dutch speakers) and the Walloons (the French speakers), some of whom possibly may make claims to be an independent nation.

State Sovereignty

The emergence of the territorial state (a governing system for a specific territory with a stable population and a functioning government) was accompanied by the notion that the state was sovereign. Accordingly, the sovereignty of all other social groupings was legally subordinated to the sovereignty of the state. Political and legal theorists argued that sovereignty resided in territorial states' rulers; they had ultimate authority to make policy within a state's borders. Those who negotiated the two treaties making up the Peace of Westphalia wanted to stop the religious wars that had brought such destruction to Europe; they specified that whoever ruled a certain territory could determine the religion of that territory. Europeans further developed the ideas about state sovereignty. For example, Jean Bodin, a sixteenth-century French economics writer, thought the notion of sovereignty a useful argument on behalf of the monarchs of new states who were trying to suppress the power of feudal officials contesting the power of the emerging state rulers.

State sovereignty was thus an idea that arose in a particular place at a particular time. But it came to be widely accepted as European political influence spread around the world. It was an argument about legal rights but it was intended to affect power. All states were said to be sovereign equals, regardless of their actual "power"—meaning capability to control outcomes. They had the right to control policy within their jurisdictions even if they did not have the power to do it. Framed in the language of the abstract state, sovereignty enhanced the power of those persons making up the government that represented the state.

But if the territorial state, and the government that spoke for it, was sovereign within its boundaries, were there no outside rules and organizations with some authority over the state? Sovereignty arose as an idea designed to produce order, to stop violence between and within states over religious questions. But did state sovereignty become, on balance, an idea that guaranteed international disorder? Was it necessary to think of relations between and among states as anarchical— not in the sense of chaos but in the sense of interactions among equal sovereigns recognizing no higher rules and organizations?

The original versions of state sovereignty, coming as they did out of a Europe that was nominally Christian, emphasized external limits on monarchs by virtue of the "higher" norms of natural law. These monarchs were said to be the highest secular authorities, but they still were inferior to an external set of rules—at least from the viewpoint of political and religious theorists. But as Europe became more and more secular—which is to say, as the Catholic Church in Rome gave up its pretenses at territorial empire and increasingly emphasized the spiritual domain, at least in church dogma—the presumed restraints of natural law theory fell away. Thus the notion of state sovereignty came to represent absolute secular authority.

State sovereignty, originally designed to produce order and to buttress central authority within the state, led to negative external consequences, the main one being that central authority over global society and interstate relations was undermined. All territorial states came to be seen as equal in the sense of having ultimate authority to prescribe what "should be" in their jurisdictions. No outside rules and organizations were held to be superior to the state. Only those rules consented to, and only those organizations voluntarily accepted, could exist in interstate relations. This was the Westphalian system of world politics.

So interstate relations came to be conceived of as part of what political scientists often characterize as an "anarchical society." Individuals existed and were grouped into nations. Nations were governed by states. States had governments. Sovereignty was an attribute of states, but it was exercised by governments. What was frequently called national sovereignty was actually state sovereignty. Whether the persons of a nation were sovereign referred to whether the state derived its legitimacy ultimately from popular will. This latter issue was, presumably, an interior or domestic question for the state; foreign actors had no authority to pronounce on it. Once state sovereignty was accepted, external actors were not supposed to comment on national or popular sovereignty, since that was an internal matter for the sovereign state.

This notion of state sovereignty is a political-legal prism. It is a fact only in the sense that if it is accepted, it becomes part of the dominant psychology of an era—the same way slavery was accepted as part of the natural order of things in a previous era. The notion is not a material or physical fact, like energy or a doorknob. Since state sovereignty is not a material fact or necessity but an intellectual or social construct about who should have ultimate authority to make policy, there can be reasonable differences of opinion about it.

Indeed, there are differences—reasonable and otherwise—about who should govern in international society and world politics. Should the state, through its government, have the ultimate and absolute right to govern—regardless of all other considerations? Should regional intergovernmental organizations like the European Union (EU) have the ultimate say about proper policy within a state? Should local communities? Should the United Nations? Does the answer depend on what policy question one is addressing? Does the answer depend on how much suffering or destruction is occurring? Should state entities be given the first chance at managing a problem, but not ultimate authority if they fail to resolve it?

These are indeed the very questions that are being raised at the United Nations at the beginning of the twenty-first century. The state has disintegrated in the geographical area known as Somalia, which is to say that the governing system for the territory does not function. If there is no effective government to represent the state, should the UN be the organization ultimately responsible for ending disorder and starvation and helping to reestablish the state? Although the answer was no in the Horn of Africa at the beginning of the decade of the 1990s, it was affirmative at the end of the decade when the UN began to administer Kosovo and Timor. If disputes within a state, such as was the case in Bosnia and Herzegovina and between it and a smaller Yugoslavia (Serbia and Montenegro), lead to mass murder, mass migration, and mass misery, should the UN be ultimately responsible? Or, as was the controversial case in Kosovo, should another multilateral organization—to wit, NATO (North Atlantic Treaty Organization)—override claims by Serbia?

Governments act in the name of states to determine how to manage certain transnational problems. On occasion they have agreed to let an international organization have the ultimate say as to what should be done. For example, about thirty states in Europe, forming the Council of Europe, have created the European Convention on Human Rights. Under this treaty, the European Court of Human Rights has the ultimate say as to the correct interpretation of the convention, and it regularly issues judgments to states concerning the legality of their policies. If one starts, as do European governments, with the notion that their states are sovereign, then one should say that these states have used their sovereignty to create international bodies that restrict the authority of the state. Among these thirty states, the protection of human rights on a transnational basis is valued more highly than state independence. States have used their freedom to make policies that reduce their freedom. Initial sovereignty, linked to territory, has been used to restrict that sovereignty by means of an international body acting primarily on the basis of nonterritorial considerations.

This situation was not typical of interstate relations in the 1990s, and that is not likely to change in the foreseeable future. There are relatively few other examples of what is called "supranational" authority in world politics at the beginning of the new century. Although much noise arises in Washington about the powers of the World Trade Organization's (WTO) dispute panels to dictate policy to states, the authority is modest.

In any case most states, especially the newer ones that have achieved formal independence as a result of rapid decolonization since the 1950s, value state sovereignty more than supranational cooperation to improve security, protect human rights, or pursue sustainable development. Indeed, Edward Luck has pointed to American "exceptionalism" and traditional skepticism about inroads on its authority as every bit as ferocious as any Third World state.[5] There may be considerable international cooperation. But it usually falls short of being supranational and of giving an international organization the legal right to override state independence.

Moreover, several older states also highly value state sovereignty. The United States, for example, has neither ratified the InterAmerican Convention on Human Rights nor accepted the jurisdiction and authority of the InterAmerican Court of Human Rights. China, too, argues that only the state, not outside parties, can determine what is best for the Chinese people whether in the realm of security, human rights, or sustainable human development.

Nevertheless, as the peoples and states of the world become more interconnected materially and morally, demands increase for effective international management. As persons become not just interconnected but interdependent (meaning that their relations become sensitive), demands increase for international management at the expense of state sovereignty. That is to say, Americans are interconnected with Hondurans concerning trade in bananas; but Americans can do without Honduran bananas and not become very upset. At the same time, Americans were interdependent with Kuwaitis concerning trade in oil; this relationship was sensitive because its alteration would have caused a major disruption in American society. Because of interdependence involving sensitive relations, some issues that were formerly considered domestic or inconsequential have come to be redefined as international or significant because of the strength of transnational concern—of either a material or a moral nature.

The UN Security Council has determined that human rights repression in Iraq threatened international peace and security, that the breakdown of order within Somalia was a proper area for UN enforcement action, and that the humanitarian situation in Bosnia was such that all states and other actors were entitled to use "all measures necessary" to provide humanitarian assistance. Situations similar to these used to be considered within the domestic jurisdiction of states. But the situations inside Iraq, Somalia, and Bosnia—and more recently in Rwanda, Haiti, Albania, Kosovo, and East Timor—came to be redefined as proper international concerns, subject to action by the United Nations and other external actors. In all these cases the principle of state sovereignty yielded to a transnational demand for the effective treatment of pressing problems.

It is certainly true that in many parts of the world existing states are under pressure from within because a variety of groups—usually loosely called "ethnic," although they often are based on religious, linguistic, or other cultural characteristics—demand some form of sovereignty and self-determination. Many demands cause problems, but conflict is particularly pronounced when self-determination takes the form of a demand for a people's right to construct a new state. But in these cases the idea of accepting the territorial state as the basic unit of world politics is not at issue, at least in principle. What is at issue, and unfortunately fought over frequently, is which states and nations should be recognized. At one point, for example, Georgia was an internal province of the state known as the Union of Soviet Socialist Republics (USSR); at another time it became a national state. Since Georgian independence, some Ossetians have not been content to be a people within Georgia but wish to be a nation with their own state. Not far away, another former Soviet province, Chechnya, became part of another successor state, Russia, and began a bloody war to be recognized as more than autonomous after making a declaration of independent statehood without consultations; a reluctant Russia has recently decided to destroy Chechnya in order to save it from itself and for the Russian state. The issue is not whether to have territorial states but whether the state that is sovereign over a particular population or geographical area should be the former USSR, Georgia, or Ossetia in the first case and the former USSR, Russia, or Chechnya in the second.

The state may be simultaneously under attack from several quarters. Some believe that the managers of transnational corporations have a global vision, doing what is best for the company without much thought about state boundaries. Some observers write of the globalization of finance capital and the meshing of the perspectives of corporate executives, regardless of nationality. Some moralists may also give scant regard to national boundaries. Thus for either material or moral reasons, some observers may endorse a supranational approach to problem solving, but state sovereignty persists as a nonmaterial fact in the perceptions of most political elites. It is reaffirmed in principle at each annual meeting of the UN General Assembly. But state sovereignty, linked to the power and independence of those who govern in the name of the state, is not the only value in world politics. Other values include enhanced security, human rights, and sustainable human development. And there is, in fact, considerable debate about the precise meaning of all these social constructs.

Much of world politics consists of managing the contradictions between conceptions of state sovereignty, on the one hand, and the desire for improved security, human rights, and sustainable human development, on the other. These contradictions are not the only ones in world politics, and managing them is not the only pressing need, but they constitute a fault line that permeates much debate at the United Nations. Sovereignty versus other considerations is one of the leading issues—if not the leading issue—in changing world politics at the beginning of the twenty-first century. One scholar, looking especially at the UN, observes that "although the picture is blurred and in many places hard to decipher, there has been movement away from the decentralized system of respect for sovereignty and toward a more centralized system of decision that in some respects approaches being international governance."[6]

Changing Raisons d'État

Those who rule in the name of the state, basing their views on the principle of state sovereignty, have claimed the right to determine what norms and actions are needed in the national interest. What English speakers call "national interests" is perhaps better captured by what French speakers call *raisons d'état:* "reasons of state." It is fair to ask whether those who rule are primarily concerned about the interests of the nation, meaning the people they rule, or the interests of the state, meaning the government of the state, meaning their own interests.

Nomenclature aside, individuals acting in the name of a state display a variety of interests. Some scholars assume that state interests must of necessity come down on the side of state power and independence. This is frequently true. From a self-interested point of view, this may be rational. If we assume an anarchical international society without effective governing arrangements, it may seem rational to protect the independent power of the state. That power can then be used to secure "good things" for the nation.

It is provocative to inquire whether states—at least some of them, some of the time—may be coming to see their interests in fundamentally different ways. There is a question whether the growing interconnectedness and interdependence among governments and peoples is causing at least some states sometimes to seek more effective management of transnational problems at the expense of state separateness. No single national government, for example, is able unilaterally to solve the problem of the thinning ozone layer. In regard to this issue, states can secure their long-term interests in a healthy environment only through multilateral action. Such situations can lead to the adoption of shared norms, such as the Montreal Protocol, or to concrete action by an international organization such as the United Nations Environment Programme (UNEP). The result can create important legal and organizational restrictions on states.

States remain sovereign as an abstract principle, at least in the eyes of those who rule. But the operational application of sovereignty is another matter. Perceptions of *raisons d'état* cause state actors sometimes to subordinate state authority and independence to multilateral norms and procedures. This trend may be increasing.

In order to manage problems, state officials may increasingly agree to important principles, rules, and decisionmaking procedures featuring a cluster of different actors. The notion of an international regime has come into vogue as a way of describing this reality. An international regime is a set of principles, rules, and procedures for "governing," or managing, an issue. The norms (principles and rules) can be legal, diplomatic, informal, or even tacit. The procedures frequently include nongovernmental and intergovernmental organizations as well as states. World politics is frequently characterized by a network of different actors, all focusing on the same problem. Not infrequently, several parts of the UN system are involved in this network approach to problem solving.

There is, for example, an international refugee regime. The norms of managing refugee problems derive both from international law and from UN General Assembly resolutions, which are not immediately binding in international law, as well as from daily practice. The various actors involved in trying to apply these norms in concrete situations are states, nongovernmental organizations (NGOs) such as the American Refugee Committee, and different parts of the UN system such as the office of the UN High Commissioner for Refugees (UN-HCR).

States have determined that it is in their interest to coordinate policies to manage refugee problems. And they have constructed norms and organizations to pursue this goal. This application of *raisons d'état* may stem from moral or practical concerns—and most likely from some combination of the two. U.S. officials may want to help Cuban refugees because they are human beings victimized by communism, and because the United States wants to keep Fidel Castro from dumping mental patients and other undesirables on U.S. shores. Both viewpoints lead to use of the UNHCR to screen and interview Cuban immigrants to determine if individuals have either a well-founded fear of persecution or mental health problems and a criminal background.

At the beginning of the twenty-first century many states appear to be "learning" a new concept of *raisons d'état*—one that is conducive to an expansion in the authority, resources, and tasks of the United Nations. Given the impact of communications and other technologies, states may be in the process of learning that their own interests would be best served by greater international cooperation. Many state leaders learned from World War I that there was a need for the League of Nations to institute a cooling-off period so that states would not rush blindly into hugely destructive wars. State actors learned from World War II that a stronger world organization was needed, one with a security council that had the authority to make binding decisions to oppose calculated aggression and cope with other threats to the peace. Some state leaders subsequently learned and promoted the notion that peacekeeping was needed to respond to security crises during the Cold War so that armed disputes could be managed without triggering another world war.

States progressively adjusted their policies on security affairs, based on perceptions of interests, in ways that increased the importance of international organizations. The process was not a zero-sum game in which the state lost and the United Nations won. Rather, states won in the sense of greater barriers against armed attacks on them, and the UN won in the sense of being given more authority and tasks than the League of Nations once had.

Traditional international law considered resort to war to be within the sovereign competence of states. If state officials perceived that their interests justified force, it was used. But increasingly state authorities, not ivory-tower academics or pacifists, have agreed that changing patterns of warfare require international attempts to avoid or constrain force. Interest in peace and security has been combined with an interest in state authority, power, and independence. The result is international norms and organizations that continue to depend on state authority and power even as those norms and organizations try to restrain unwise, and eventually illegal, uses or threats of force.

State actors originally thought that their best interests were served by absolute sovereignty and complete freedom in the choice of policy. They learned that this was indeed a dangerous and frequently destructive situation. From the viewpoint of their own interests, limiting the recourse to and the process of force was highly desirable. That led to the part of international law called *jus ad bellum* (law regulating recourse to war) and also *jus in bello* (law regulating the process of war). Thus international laws and organizations developed to contribute to state welfare even as they limited state freedom.

Central questions now are: How far are state actors willing to go in this process of international cooperation? How far can they be nudged by intergovernmental organizations (IGOs), NGOs, and unorganized public opinion? Are state actors willing to do more than create modern versions of the League of Nations—international organizations without the authority and resources to play decisive roles in world politics? Are they willing to cede significant authority and resources, as in the European Union, so that international organizations can act apart from state control in ways that really make a difference across borders? Can public opinion, NGOs, and the independent or uninstructed personnel in IGOs generate enough influence on state authorities to produce important international organizations? Can the UN be more than a debating society and set of passive procedures?

The United Nations: Actor or Framework?

Many journalists and not a few other observers use phrases like "the UN failed" (to stop ethnic cleansing in the Balkans), or "the UN was successful" (in checking Iraqi aggression against Kuwait). This phraseology obscures a complex reality. The UN is most fundamentally an intergovernmental organization in which key decisions are made by governments representing states. The UN Charter may say initially, "We the peoples," but the legal members of the UN are states. The UN is also a broad and complex system of policymaking and administration in which some decisions are made by individuals who are not instructed by states. Nongovernmental organizations are also active—and sometimes influential—in this system.

When it is said that the Security Council decided to authorize force in Somalia or the Balkans, in reality representatives of fifteen states made the decision, acting as the Security Council according to the UN Charter. They may have been influenced by reports from the UN Secretary-General, who in theory and often in practice is independent from state control and is responsible only to the Charter. Nevertheless, state representatives decide. Moreover, to the extent that UN decisions involve force or economic resources, or considerable diplomatic pressure, these elements of UN action are, in effect, borrowed from member states. The same point is true for the General Assembly and all other UN bodies made up of states. States make most of the important decisions made in the name of the United Nations, however much they may be influenced, pressured, or educated by independent UN personnel or NGOs.

But authority—and influence flowing from it—may be delegated by IGO bodies to independent UN personnel. And the Charter confers some independent authority on the Secretary-General. For example, he may address the Security Council and indeed call it into session. He makes an annual report on the work of the organization to the General Assembly in which he can try to focus attention on certain problems and solutions. Moreover, certain UN organs are made up of independent persons, not state officials—for example, the UN Sub-Commission on Protection of Minorities. Some UN agencies have independent secretariats—for example, UNEP. Within the broad UN system, UN personnel may come to exercise some influence as independent actors not controlled by states. Their authority is not supranational, but their influence may be significant. Hence, they cannot tell states how to behave, but they may be able to induce states to behave in certain ways.

Once member states created the UNHCR, funded it, and authorized it to deliver humanitarian assistance in the Balkans, the high commissioner for refugees—in the 1993 crisis and throughout the 1990s Sadako Ogata—was able to direct great attention to the situation in Bosnia by ordering a suspension of that humanitarian assistance on her own authority. She succeeded in altering priorities, at least temporarily. She compelled the UN Secretary-General, state officials, and other policymakers to address the problem of interference with humanitarian assistance.

The United Nations is primarily an institutional funnel through which member states may channel their foreign policies. The UN Charter is the closest thing that we have to a global constitution. When state actors comply with the Charter and use UN procedures, their policies acquire the legitimacy that stems from international law. They also acquire the legitimacy that stems from collective political approval, the realization of which is one of the more important tasks performed by the UN. Normally, policies that are seen as legal and collectively approved are more likely than not to be successful. The stamp of legality and the weight of collective political approval may induce recalcitrant political authorities to accept a UN policy or program. It is better to have UN approval than otherwise.

In the pages that follow we speak mostly of decisions at the United Nations. We write of politics at or through the UN. We are careful to distinguish the UN as framework from the UN as actor. Most of the time the former rather than the latter situation obtains. Nevertheless, at times "the UN" is phraseology that refers to important behavior by independent persons representing the world organization. For example, in El Salvador in the early 1990s, UN Secretary-General Javier Pérez de Cuéllar and his representatives, especially his personal representative, Alvaro de Soto, played crucial roles in ameliorating the civil war. In places like El Salvador, the world organization's staff members have greatly affected decisions in the field and at headquarters concerning UN peacekeeping, mediation, and observation. The Appendix illustrates the components of the UN system as actors in the context of the UN as institutional setting. This appendix is relevant to all chapters in this book; the reader may wish to refer to it frequently.

It is also true that state foreign policy was important in El Salvador, both within the UN framework (for instance, via U.S. votes in the Security Council in favor of human rights and peace) and outside the UN system (for instance, U.S. unilateral commitments regarding foreign assistance). National reconciliation in El Salvador was advanced by states acting outside the UN, by state-controlled decisions within the UN, and by the independent actions of UN personnel. Moreover, the role of nongovernmental actors in El Salvador should not be minimized, including the decisions by the armed opposition (the Frente Farabundo Martí para la Liberación Nacional, or the FMLN), by local NGOs (churches and people's groups), and by external human rights and aid agencies. This tapestry of decisionmaking both circumscribes and energizes the United Nations, a theme that permeates this book.

One of the more interesting questions at the dawn of the twenty-first century is whether the growing demand for UN management of transnational problems will lead to greater or reduced willingness by member states to confer authority on the world organization's personnel and will transfer the resources necessary to resolve problems effectively. The options and processes are complex.

In Somalia in mid-1992, then UN Secretary-General Boutros Boutros-Ghali publicly pressured states to demonstrate the same concern for suffering in Somalia as they were showing for the "white-man's war" in the Balkans. Key states responded by using the Security Council to authorize all necessary means (including force) for the creation of a secure environment for the delivery of humanitarian assistance in Somalia. That use of force was effectively controlled first by the United States—which was more-or-less deputized to represent the Security Council. But the Unified Task Force (UNITAF) of soldiers in Somalia progressively became a more international force. Then, it was transformed into the first enforcement action truly controlled by UN personnel. To understand accurately "the UN" in Somalia, it is necessary over time to distinguish independent UN personnel, decisions made by states in the name of the UN, and decisions made by states outside the UN.

By and large, state decisions outside the United Nations affect what "the UN" is allowed to do, or how UN procedures and symbols are employed. President Bush's decision to commit U.S. ground troops in Somalia was the key to what followed. Only when that decision had been made in the White House could the Security Council proceed to authorize force and then actually facilitate the delivery of humanitarian assistance. However much the U.S. president may have been influenced by the UN Secretary-General or by reports from the communications media, it was a state decision outside the UN that constituted, for a given time span, the independent variable explaining what happened. In this sense the UN became the dependent variable—that is, the factor that came into play once President Bush decided to move forward.

In terms of a fundamental generalization, political factors outside the UN are primary and factors inside the UN are secondary. The end of the Cold War, indeed the end of the Soviet Union, primarily explained the renaissance of UN security activities that began in the late 1980s. It was not the Security Council that ended the Cold War. It was the end of the Cold War that allowed the Security Council to act with renewed consensus and commitment and vigor.

Once allowed to act, UN personnel and organs may independently influence states and other actors. What was once a secondary factor, dependent on state approval, may come to be a primary factor in the ongoing process to make and implement policies. Once member states' authorities decided to create an environmental program, UNEP came to exert some relatively independent influence—both in cleaning up the Mediterranean Sea and in coordinating scientific evidence about the need to protect the ozone layer.

In any event, state decisions about power and policy constitute the primary force driving events at the UN. When important states show a convergence in policy, "the UN" may be allowed to act in important ways. Without that political agreement, all parts of the UN system will be severely restricted in what they can accomplish. This has been true since 1945. The end of the Cold War has not altered this fundamental fact.

UN Politics

In the exercise of power needed to make and implement policies through the United Nations, states naturally seek allies. Academic and diplomatic observers have been prone to adopt generalizations about different political alliances, coalitions, or blocs within the United Nations. The countries of the West—that is, the Western industrialized democracies that are members of the Organization for Economic Cooperation and Development (OECD), sometimes joined by Israel—

frequently have been grouped as the First World. The "developing countries," basically all of the countries of Asia, Africa, and Latin America, have been examined under the rubric of the Third World, the South, the Non-Aligned Movement (NAM), or the Group of 77 (or G-77, for the original constellation of seventy-seven states, which has now grown to some 130 members). The "socialist countries," when the Soviet Union and its European allies existed, were also called the East and the Second World. The West and the East, in a curious bit of mathematical geography, were added together to constitute the North, or the developed countries, in juxtaposition to the South, or the developing countries.

Although they roughly correspond to the bulk of voting patterns during the Cold War, these distinctions have become less useful over time. Not only has the bloc of European socialist states and the Soviet Union ceased to exist, but also some of this terminology was in fact never accurate: Cuba was hardly nonaligned, and the socialist countries were developed in few ways beyond weaponry.

The end of the Cold War has allowed scholars, and especially diplomats, to begin to look more objectively at alliances within the United Nations, although many of the labels from the former era remain. For example, it is now quite common to point out that developing countries consist of a series of crosscutting alignments reflecting the heterogeneous character of their economies and ideologies.[7] In the past, it was politically more correct to speak of the Third World as if it were homogeneous, with little hesitation in grouping Singapore's and Chad's economies or Costa Rica's and North Korea's ideologies.

Only on a few issues—like emphasizing the importance of the General Assembly, where each state has one vote—do developing countries show common interests. In such instances, and in some other international forums, the North-South divide continues to be salient. Frequently developing countries subdivide according to the issue before the UN: between radicals and moderates, between Islamic and non-Islamic, between those in the region and outside, between maritime and landlocked, between those achieving significant economic growth and otherwise. Even within the Western group, there have always been numerous differences, which have come more to the fore with the abrupt disappearance of East-West tensions.

Given the changing nature of world politics, especially after the Cold War and in the light of an ongoing learning process that can shape views toward state sovereignty and *raisons d'état*, changing alignments and coalitions should be anticipated. Indeed, as world politics change, so does the United Nations. In 1991 the General Assembly, whose majority of developing countries normally reflects concern for traditional notions of state sovereignty, voted by consensus to condemn the military coup in (briefly) democratic Haiti. Subsequently, many of these same countries supported the imposition of economic sanctions—first at the regional level through the Organization of American States (OAS) and afterward through the UN—and eventually military enforcement action authorized by the Security Council to restore the elected government. The nature of government as democratic or authoritarian, a subject that had mostly been considered a domestic affair protected by the principle of state sovereignty, came to be seen by all states as a legitimate subject for diplomatic action through the UN.

In the following pages we inquire more systematically into changing world politics, and what they portend for the United Nations as the world organization gropes with security, human rights, and sustainable human development. These three issues have been selected to provide the focus of this volume. They encompass the central challenges to improving the human condition and hence the central tests for international organization in the present era.

Part 1 of this book introduces the evolving efforts of the United Nations to combat threats to international peace and security. Because it is impossible to understand the nature of international cooperation without a grasp of the Charter's provisions for pacific settlement of disputes, enforcement, and regional arrangements, we first cover the theory of collective security in Chapter 1. Chapter 2 deals with UN security efforts during the Cold War and then turns to economic sanctions and the creation of the peacekeeping function. Although not mentioned in the Charter, peacekeeping is a distinctive contribution of the UN and has been its main activity in the security field for some forty years. In Chapter 3, "UN Security Operations After the Cold War," we explain the renaissance in UN activities, including peacekeeping, enforcement, and a series of other actions in such troubled regions as Cambodia, the former Yugoslavia, Somalia, Rwanda, and Haiti. Chapter 4, "Groping into the Twenty-first Century," contains a discussion of the political dynamics at work and suggestions about changes in the UN to make it better able to address security challenges at the dawn of the twenty-first century.

Part 2 introduces UN efforts to protect human rights and to provide humanitarian relief. Chapter 5 briefly traces the origins of international action on human rights, indicating what the UN contributed to principles on human rights. Chapter 6 focuses on UN activity to help implement the human rights principles that member states have formally accepted. Finally, there is a balance sheet in Chapter 7 on UN developments in the field of human rights, exploring some of the dynamics that drive events and what they portend for the future.

Part 3 introduces efforts by the United Nations to build peace by fostering development and protecting the environment. Chapters 8 and 9 examine the evolution of global responses to underdevelopment and environmental degradation and present some information about how the UN is structured for economic and environmental policymaking. In Chapter 10, we return to the question of the relationship between the UN's social and economic activities and peace and take up in some detail the "functionalist," or indirect, approach to peace through socioeconomic policy. We conclude by exploring the dynamic interrelationships among the UN's mandates and activities in the three areas of peace and security, humanitarian affairs and human rights, and sustainable development in the context of an evolving focus on promoting human security.

Notes

1. Quoted in Robert Gregg, *About Face? The United States and the United Nations* (Boulder: Lynne Rienner, 1993), p. 68.

2. Jarat Chopra, *Peace-Maintenance: The Evolution of International Political Authority* (London: Routledge, 1999).

3. United Nations Development Programme, *Human Development Report 1996* (New York: Oxford Univ. Press, 1996), p. 1.

4. United Nations Development Programme, *Human Development Report 1999* (New York: Oxford Univ. Press, 1999), pp. 38–39.

5. Edward Luck, *Mixed Messages: American Politics and International Organization 1919–1999* (Washington, DC: Brookings Institution, 1999).

6. Lawrence S. Finkelstein, ed., *Politics in the United Nations System* (Durham, NC: Duke Univ. Press, 1988), p. 30.

7. Soo Yeon Kim and Bruce Russett, "The New Politics of Voting Alignments in the United Nations General Assembly," *International Organization* 50, no. 4 (Autumn 1996), pp. 629–652.

Part One

International Peace and Security

1 The Theory of UN Collective Security

The fall of the Berlin Wall in November 1989 and the disappearance of the Soviet Union in late 1991 ushered in a period of rapid change in world politics. These political events outside the United Nations caused fundamental change within the world organization. In the wake of the Cold War, many citizens and diplomats expressed optimism about the role of UN multilateralism in a "new world order." Although the UN has always been dependent for its functioning on the nature of the world political system in which it operates, institutions still matter. How the United Nations organizes itself, what it seeks to do, and how it does it are important. Even if the UN remains largely dependent on the nature and quality of state foreign policy, UN officials have some room to maneuver in carrying out tasks. This is certainly true for security issues, the focus of this first part.

Security, traditionally defined, was supposed to be the primary task of the world organization. With the signing of the UN Charter on June 26, 1945, the world undertook a new experiment in organizing states to control war. Two world wars within two decades, the Holocaust, and the advent of the nuclear age produced the political will to improve on the League of Nations. The international community rejected isolationism and committed itself to trying to safeguard the peace that had been won at great cost. In the inspiring words of the Charter's preamble, the UN's role was to save "succeeding generations from the scourge of war, which twice in our lifetime has brought untold sorrow to mankind."

The League of Nations, although technically not outlawing war, had established a set of procedures constituting a cooling-off period for states contemplating the use of force. This approach to peace was conditioned by the judgment that the advent of World War I had been caused by emotionalism and mistaken perceptions. Time was needed for rationality to prevail. This approach to peace had clearly been inadequate to stop Hitler's premeditated aggressions, which in some ways were not only rational but astute (for example, his anticipation of appeasement on the part of the Western democracies).

Equally deficient was the legalistic approach to peace reflected in the Kellogg-Briand Pact, which outlawed war as an instrument of foreign policy. It did nothing to change the nature of world politics. It did not provide peaceful means of conflict resolution. It just made war illegal.

At the San Francisco conference where the Charter was drafted, diplomats first made the threat or use of force illegal except in self-defense. Then, unlike during the League period, they gave the United Nations the authority to enforce the peace through diplomatic, economic, and even military action in response to "threats to the peace, . . . acts of aggression or . . . breaches of the peace." State power, or perhaps even independent UN power, was to be put at the service of the Security Council to protect the peace.

Even a novice of world politics is aware that the reality of the past half century has diverged dramatically from these ideals. In the 1990s, usually thirty-five "major" wars—that is, with at least 1,000 deaths in a year—were occurring. Yet newspaper headlines and media presentations daily indicate the growing presence of the United Nations in conflicts around the world, symbolized by the first-ever meeting of the Security Council with heads of state in January 1992 and the publication of the then new Secretary-General Boutros Boutros-Ghali's far-reaching report, *An Agenda for Peace*, in June of that year.

Pioneering Cooperation: The Nineteenth Century and the League of Nations

However unrepresentational in terms of population and geography, the "global" system was initially centered upon Europe after the Treaty of Westphalia, which ended the Hundred Years' War in 1648. The equality of states was the purported foundation of the global system, but in practice, inequalities abounded. A variety of institutions gradually grew up in pursuit of order and stability in what remained an "anarchical society."[1] There was no central authority or world government even though there were transnational efforts to manage problems. The four principal institutions were "balance-of-power" diplomacy to prevent the emergence of a hegemon (or dominant power); international law; international diplomatic conferences to settle major problems; and diplomatic practices through which states remained in contact, preferring negotiations to conflict. Individual states were supposedly sovereign, or autonomous. But they recognized that the predictability and stability that resulted from norms and obligations would be in their own self-interest. International organizations, which helped to codify these rules and monitor their implementation, were important elements in what observers now commonly call "international society."[2]

The Congress of Vienna in 1815 represents the first modern attempt at organizing states to preserve the peace. It is the precursor to twentieth-century international organizations. After the defeat of the French emperor Napoleon Bonaparte by Russia, Prussia, Great Britain, and Austria, the victors sponsored a conference to determine the shape of the new Europe. Working with weaker states, they sought to achieve an ongoing distribution of power that would deter future aggression and prevent the rise of another conqueror of Napoleonic magnitude. By raising the stakes of aggression through coordinated foreign policies, the Congress of Vienna wished to ensure against its recurrence. The interests of victorious states became those of the international system.

The sponsors of the conference agreed to meet periodically, but the congress system was too visionary for the realpolitik world in which states sought to maximize their power. It was replaced by the Concert of Europe, a less organized but more durable forum for deliberations by major powers. The Concert limited its attention to problems of international significance as they arose (as opposed to the more prevention-oriented Congress) and met seventeen times from 1830 to 1884. For instance, during an 1884 meeting that continues to have repercussions, the Concert met to divide colonial rights to Africa among vying European imperialist powers after the race to acquire territories threatened to get out of hand. The Congress and Concert opened up diplomatic channels among states and established the beginnings of an executive council somewhat akin to the UN Security Council.

The Hague conferences in 1899 and 1907 sought to regulate the laws of war. Their deliberations were more inclusive than the Concert's and included some states from other continents. Delegates representing twenty-six states, of which five were non-European, attended the first conference. In 1907 this number increased to forty-four states, including twenty-four non-European ones. The Hague conferences represent the first example of gathering diverse countries into an international security system aspiring to universal membership, as the United Nations was to do decades later. The Hague conferences spelled out the framework for the Permanent Court of Arbitration as well as rules governing the conduct of war.[3] They also served as a step to universalize debates on international issues. In so doing, they provided an antecedent for the UN General Assembly.

In addition to these efforts to address security problems directly, several agencies designed to facilitate trade and financial transfers among nations were established in the nineteenth century and became precursors of the types of functional organizations that have grown significantly since World War II.[4] Some see these agencies as contributing to security indirectly by entangling states in a web of social and economic cooperation strong enough to make war irrational. These agencies arose after states recognized the commercial benefits of interstate cooperation. The International Telegraphic Union, which was created in 1865 using the same acronym as the present International Telecommunications Union (ITU), was the first to be established to help provide interstate communication links. Technological advances encouraged the development of new international organizations and led to greater interstate cooperation in such institutions as the Universal Postal Union (UPU), the International Bureau for Weights and Measures, and the International Institute of Agriculture.

But once again, armed conflict on a massive scale led to a significant push to increase the power of the international institutions.[5] In 1919 in the aftermath of the first "war to end all wars," it was apparent that a better means was needed to prevent widespread interstate violence. From the Versailles Peace Conference arose the League of Nations Covenant (or "constitution") on January 20, 1920, but the League ultimately proved unsuccessful in its quest to preserve the peace. However, its experiences provided lessons later about how to structure a collective-security system. Under Article 10 of the League's Covenant, members pledged "to respect and preserve as against external aggression the territorial integrity and existing political independence of all Members of the League." This language was the main target of critics in the U.S. Senate, which ultimately refused to consent to the covenant in spite of the fact that President Woodrow Wilson had championed the League.

Articles 11 through 17 contained the germ of a collective-security system. The two main organs of the League were the Assembly, which contained all member states and met annually, and the less universal Council, which always had the great powers as members, met more frequently, and could be convened in a crisis. The Council normally dealt with matters that threatened the peace, although some of these matters came before the Assembly. The lack of clarity about the roles of the Assembly and the Council was a weakness; all problems regularly came before both bodies.

Voting mechanisms reflected the traditional practices of multilateral diplomacy. Although majority voting existed in principle for some issues, a sovereign state could not be compelled to submit to the will of the majority when, in its own interpretation, its national interests were threatened. Hence, unanimity came to be the standard operating procedure except for inconsequential issues. The League relied on commitments by states not to use force except in self-defense until a process of pacific settlement had been completed. That process was to begin with a complaint by a disputant or by another member of the League. In essence, members undertook a legal obligation to use the organization if they themselves could not end a dispute. At least on paper, the League's Covenant embodied a working system of security.

Several flaws in the League's composition and constitution ultimately contributed to its failure. The Covenant restricted the right to go to war but did not outlaw it, which was the focus of the Kellogg-Briand Pact, also not implemented; recourse to warfare remained an option for states. The assumption of universal membership proved flawed: The United States never joined the League, depriving the collective-security apparatus of a much-needed member; the Soviet Union joined only in 1934; Japan left in 1931, and Italy in 1937; Germany joined in 1926 but left in 1933. Unanimity among all members was required for action, but members could refuse to take part in League-sponsored activities and leave if they chose. Moreover, the provisions for establishing the League were an integral part of the Treaty of Versailles, from which Axis powers were initially excluded, an exclusion leading ultimately to resentment and sabotage.

As time wore on, other problems aggravated these obvious weaknesses. Members reestablished alliance systems and refused to take the necessary institutional actions to check aggression. The League was unable to reverse Japan's takeover of Manchuria; the Italian invasion of Abyssinia; the German remilitarization of the Rhineland and subsequent takeover of the Sudetenland; or the intervention by Italy, Germany, and the Soviet Union in the Spanish civil war. The gradual buildup of war machines proceeded apace, and the collapse of the fledgling collective-security system was complete with the German invasion of Poland in 1939. The League broke down and the international community headed down the road to World War II, although the formal dissolution of the League did not occur until 1946.

Collective Security in General

The idea of collective security can be traced through a long history of proposals to deal with war and peace.[6] The central thread has remained the same: All states would join forces to prevent one of their number from using coercion to gain advantage. Under such a system, no government could conquer another or otherwise disturb the peace for fear of retribution from all other governments. Any attack would be treated as if it were an attack on each of them. The notion of self-defense, universally agreed on as a right of sovereign states, was expanded to include the international community's right to prevent war.

The apparent common sense and appealing simplicity of the logic of collective security can be contrasted with the difficulties of its application. Indeed, some have come to question whether collective security can be relied upon with confidence to protect or restore the peace. Skeptics ask: In a world with a large number of states (almost 190 UN members in 2000), will not states defect from the collective enterprise, in pursuit of their own narrow national interests, and thereby undermine the collective effort? This is the old problem of the hunters and the stag. As the hunters encircle the stag, one defects to chase a rabbit he will not have to share with others. Another does the same. Soon the stag escapes through the gaps in the collective effort.[7]

Experience with collective security indicates considerable "gaps" when this collective effort has been contemplated, whether during the League or the UN era. First, some states have refused to join a collective-sanctioning effort because they have already defined their friends and enemies. It was inconceivable that the United States would have joined in a UN effort at collective security against one of its North Atlantic Treaty Organization (NATO) allies or that the Soviet Union would have done so against its Warsaw Pact allies. Not only is a preestablished alliance system not a form of collective security, but such alliances also are incompatible with global collective security. In an exceptional move, the United States did indeed oppose the British, French, and Israeli invasion of Egypt in 1956 and eventually helped to roll it back by diplomacy. But the United States never seriously considered UN sanctions against its allies in 1956, precisely because it wanted to maintain their cooperation in the Cold War. Under true collective security, all aggressors have to be treated the same. All threats to and breaches of the peace have to be firmly opposed. This requirement seems beyond the realm of most great powers in history, which have always had their cultural and strategic friends.

Second, there is the problem of power. It has been quite clear since 1945 that the international community would have major and probably insurmountable problems in applying collective security against a nuclear state, especially the United States, the USSR, Britain, France, or China. How could one justify the massive destruction that could result from trying to apply forcible collective security against such a state, even if clear-cut aggression had occurred?

But the problem of regulating powerful aggressors goes beyond the nuclear question. Many states control such conventional forces or economic resources that collective security against them would be highly disruptive to international society. For this reason, the international community has had to content itself with diplomatic opposition to such acts as the U.S. invasions of Grenada and Panama in the 1980s, knowing full well that any attempt at military or economic sanctioning would be disruptive and ineffectual. It is not only the great powers that are difficult to manage. South Africa, Saudi Arabia, Israel, Vietnam, and other lesser powers also have considerable economic and military strength that can make them important actors depending upon issues and timing.

Third, collective security can be costly to those supporting it. Sanctions cut both ways, affecting not only the aggressor but the defenders. When it was a member of the League of Nations, Switzerland did not want to put effective economic sanctions on Mussolini's Italy after the invasion of Ethiopia because this would have hurt the part of Switzerland's economy that was interdependent with Italy's. The memory of this situation has helped keep Switzerland from joining the United Nations. Although communist Bulgaria voted in the UN for sanctions against white-ruled South Africa, it then sold arms to South Africa under the table. Bulgaria did not want to miss out on profits from the arms trade despite its formal support for economic collective security against the white-minority government in Pretoria. It was one thing for states to accept that apartheid constituted a threat to the peace. It was another for states to engage collectively against apartheid at a cost to their own narrow national interests.

Fourth, the concept of collective security is based on the assumption that all victims are equally important—that the international community will respond in the same way to an attack on Bosnia or Armenia as to an attack on Kuwait or Germany. Even aside from the issue of standing alliances, this, too, is a very high standard. Historical evidence shows that most states have differentiated between states worth defending and otherwise. In the 1990s the United States was willing to disrupt its home front by putting almost half a million military personnel into the liberation of Kuwait, but it dithered about taking decisive action to liberate Bosnia, which was progressively carved up by ethnic Serbians and Croatians until the Dayton accords of late 1995. The fact that Kuwait possessed much oil sold in the United States and to U.S. allies, and that Bosnia seemed to lack both economic resources and strategic value, was surely not irrelevant to Washington's policy toward the two situations. As a result, decisive and forcible collective security occurred through Desert Storm in 1991. But indecisive and mostly nonforcible collective-security efforts were tried in Bosnia until a Croatian-Bosnian offensive finally goaded the West to act in autumn 1995. Despite increased interconnectedness among states as a general rule, some states still do not matter very much. It is very difficult to apply various forms of collective security on their behalf.

Collective security has been viewed sometimes as a halfway house between world government and the pure state system. It has been seen by some as a process that could make the state system more livable by making it more secure. Forms of collective security have worked at times. Iraqi aggression against Kuwait was supposedly rolled back through collective force authorized by the UN, as was a military coup in Haiti after UN-sponsored economic sanctions fell short. But these tend to be the exceptional examples proving the general rule that collective security, either military or economic, is exceedingly difficult to organize and enforce. After all, despite an overwhelming global consensus that white-minority rule in Africa was wrong, UN economic sanctions against Rhodesia lasted from 1966 until 1979 and probably were not decisive in achieving black self-determination and minority rule in Zimbabwe. States have numerous narrow national interests that they are reluctant to see overridden in the name of peace or justice. They therefore tend to defect from inconvenient collective-security efforts. If the situation were otherwise, one could probably achieve world government, not just collective security.[8]

The United Nations and Security: Some Basics

The foundations of the United Nations were laid in the midst of World War II. In August 1941, four months before the United States entered the war, President Franklin D. Roosevelt agreed on the Atlantic Charter with Britain's prime minister, Winston Churchill. The latter's strong preference for a clear statement about a collective security organization in the postwar world was diluted by Roosevelt, who feared a negative reaction from Congress. Nevertheless, on New Year's Day 1942, less than a month after the American entry into the war, twenty-six governments signed the Declaration of the United Nations, which called for mutual support among the allied signatories and a "more permanent system of general security."

The leaders of the Allied forces (the United States, Russia, Great Britain, France, and China) proceeded over time to negotiate the guidelines for the world organization. At the Teheran, Dumbarton Oaks, and Yalta conferences, these countries mapped out their plans for the postwar era. At the same time, academics and practitioners studied previous experiences in order to guide the international administration of the future.[9]

Later, the Allies invited other countries to join the deliberations that eventually led to the establishment of the United Nations in June 1945 at the San Francisco conference. Tensions began to appear as early as the Dumbarton Oaks conference in August 1944, but a fundamental spirit of cooperation existed among the major powers during the process of designing the world organization. The fifty-one countries invited to San Francisco included all governments that had declared war on the Axis before March 1945 or signed the Declaration of the United Nations. The Allies were fighting a common enemy and supporting one another. The East-West split that came to be the dominant tension in world politics had not yet taken place.

In this environment, Allied leaders drew up plans for an organization based on existing goodwill to prevent the recurrence of another world war. Although the delegates used rhetoric about "the peoples of the United Nations," participants represented governments that in turn represented states that were supposed to be sovereign and independent. The new organization was not intended to be a supranational entity (or world government), and the UN Charter enshrines the doctrine of state sovereignty.

There was only one exception to the rule of seeking a consensus among governments and respecting the narrow calculations of *raisons d'état*, and this exception became the focus of Chapter VII of the UN Charter. Using lessons from the failed League of Nations, the founders designed the United Nations to actively maintain peace around the world, to mobilize military might if necessary to enforce international decisions, and to shift from unanimous to majority voting (exclusive of the veto, to be discussed shortly).

Let us now examine both the institutional and legal bases for action by the United Nations in the security arena.

The Institutional Basics

The two central bodies to directly safeguard the peace are the Security Council and the General Assembly. Chapter V of the UN Charter designates the Security Council as the organ primarily responsible for maintaining international peace and security. It now has fifteen members. It was increased in 1965 from eleven as originally specified in the Charter to reflect the rapid increase in UN membership after decolonization. It may change again to reflect altered power relations (for example, in order to make room for Japan and Germany). In the communications age, both the Secretary-General and other observers have quipped that CNN is already the sixteenth member.

The most powerful states assumed special roles. The lack of participation by several great powers clearly had been a shortcoming at various junctures for the League of Nations. The United States and the Soviet Union insisted on the veto. In the end, these two great powers, along with France, China, and Great Britain, became permanent members, each with a veto over decisions. The remaining ten members are elected to two-year terms by the General Assembly. When

Edward R. Stettinius Jr., chairman of the U.S. delegation, signs the UN Charter in San Francisco on June 26, 1945. President Harry S Truman stands by. (UNCIO Photo 2463)

electing the nonpermanent members, the assembly tries to maintain a geographical balance by including representatives of the four major regions of the world: usually three from Africa, two from Asia, three from Europe, and two from Latin America.

The Security Council, whose permanent members were the most powerful military states in 1945, is vested with the duty of maintaining international peace and security. Unlike in the League of Nations, UN member states are legally required to abide by "decisions." The logic is that since permanent members possess the military capability to act quickly and decisively, no potential aggressor will challenge organizational strictures.

The permanent members are accorded special responsibilities and privileges in the collective-security schema. They pay more of the bills, and no decision can be made on nonprocedural questions unless they agree. The permanent members' veto powers ensure that on important questions they assent, or at least abstain. It was recognized that no enforcement action could take place against one of the great powers of the international system without creating a major war—the very thing that the United Nations had been established to forestall. By preventing action against a permanent member, the veto saved the organization from wrecking itself in destructive operations against its most powerful members. Enforcement actions can be undertaken only with great-power cooperation.

After expanding from eleven to fifteen members in 1965, the Security Council altered its decisionmaking process. Enlargement of the council has reduced the mathematical weight that the permanent members hold in the voting. Nine affirmative votes are now needed to pass a resolution. Barring permanent member vetoes, all permanent members and one nonpermanent member could theoretically abstain from a vote without jeopardizing the passage of a resolution, although some unity among the five permanent members is practically indispensable. Also, the unity of the Non-Aligned Movement on most issues has essentially introduced a type of "sixth veto" when developing countries coalesce against a particular action.

Since the enlargement of the Security Council, disagreement during the formal voting process has been reduced by efforts to gain a consensus during informal consultations before any vote. Two hundred seventy-nine vetoes were cast during the Cold War, but not one was cast from May 1990 until May 1993, and only a few have been used since. With or without vetoes, the need for more flexibility for multilateral diplomacy remained. So instead of the formal sessions riddled with vetoes that characterized the early years, crucial discussions now occur informally under the aegis of the president until the Security Council is ready either to make a decision or to vote formally. The presidency of the council revolves monthly and plays a critical role in this process of smoothing the way to a vote. The president meets with the Secretary-General to identify the parties to a dispute, negotiates with the permanent members to ensure that the veto will not be used, and consults with the nonaligned members of the Security Council and other relevant groups or actors. Accordingly, unified decisionmaking is facilitated and disunity in the council can be reduced.[10]

The General Assembly, where every member state is represented, serves as a more open forum for discussion. Duties include election of heads of other UN organs, budgetary and administrative decisions, and joint control of decisions on Charter amendments and admission of new members to the organization.

The General Assembly's role in relation to international peace and security increased for a time with the passage of the Uniting for Peace Resolution in 1950. In circumstances where the Security Council is unable to act, the General Assembly, acting in accordance with the provisions of the Uniting for Peace Resolution, can take measures in accordance with the purpose and spirit of the world organization. When used, this resolution obscured the distinctions between the Security Council and the General Assembly. There is disagreement whether this procedure is illegal, represents a de facto alteration of the Charter, or constitutes a new legal rule in spite of provisions for formal amendment in Articles 108 and 109. Supporters of the resolution argued that the Security Council's formal responsibility for maintaining peace was "primary" but not "exclusive." In any case, the importance of the resolution was political, symbolic, and psychological, if not legal.

This resolution was enacted to allow the General Assembly to address North Korean aggression in South Korea amidst Security Council inaction after the council's initial condemnation of aggression and approval of assistance to South Korea. The absence of the Soviet Union (protesting Taiwan's occupation of the "Chinese seat" on the council in spite of the victory by the Chinese communists under Mao Zedong) had permitted the council's initial call for assistance and the subsequent military action against North Korea and its allies. But once Moscow ended its boycott and entered the fray, the Security Council was paralyzed by the Soviet veto.

The Uniting for Peace Resolution was not used again until 1956, when permanent members were involved in two crises. The General Assembly approved actions in the Suez crisis because effective action in the Security Council had been blocked by France and Britain; earlier it had censured the use of armed force by Moscow in Hungary. The last use to date was in 1960, after the Security Council became deadlocked over the Congo operation because the Soviet Union and the United States supported different sides in the conflict. These situations are discussed in greater detail in Chapter 2.

The Charter spells out other important actors in this domain: the executive head of the organization (the Secretary-General); the professional staff (the secretariat); and the UN's judicial organ (the International Court of Justice, or ICJ). Selected by the General Assembly upon the recommendation of the Security Council, the Secretary-General is the chief executive officer. The secretariat of the United Nations consists of some 8,700 regular civilian staff members in New York and around the world working directly for the Secretary-General. Their number rises to about 50,000 if the specialized agencies and the Washington-based financial institutions are included. In matters of peace and security, several departments are involved. At the outset of the term of the sixth Secretary-General, Boutros Boutros-Ghali, the central work of the organization in matters of peace and security became the focus of an administrative reform of the inner cabinet under the direction of Under-Secretaries-General for political affairs, humanitarian affairs, and peacekeeping operations. Depending on the number of security operations at any moment in the past ten years, somewhere between 10,000 and 80,000 UN soldiers, police, and other special personnel also have served under the Secretary-General.

Beyond organizing and directing staff, the Secretary-General plays an instrumental role in the mediation of disputes, negotiations between or among warring parties, and deployment of UN-sponsored forces. This role reaches beyond that assigned to any other international official. An important mechanism in this regard is the appointment of special and personal representatives or envoys of the Secretary-General, who undertake missions in conflict areas. As of January 2000, there were no fewer than fifty such special envoys.

Although Article 99 of the UN Charter has not been used much, it makes it possible for the Secretary-General to "bring to the attention of the Security Council any matter which in his opinion may threaten the maintenance of international peace and security." Without formally invoking Article 99, the Secretary-General can still press his views behind the scenes with the great powers. His personal judgment and readiness to run risks and take initiatives is crucial to the accomplishment of his duties.

Article 99 was used only by Secretaries-General Dag Hammarskjöld in the Congo and, arguably, Trygve Lie in Korea and Kurt Waldheim in Iran. But the role of the Secretary-General and the possible resort to Article 99 provide the basis for less dramatic but potentially very useful activities. "Quiet diplomacy" was Hammarskjöld's description, although sometimes the displeasure of governments with "quiet diplomacy" has become noisy.

Whether Article 99 is invoked or not, the Secretary-General's actions are closely scrutinized by governments. Depending upon the political climate, criticism can be scathing, and it certainly affects the UN secretariat. Secretary-General U Thant was stridently criticized by the West for pulling UN troops too quickly from the Sinai in 1967, just as Lie and Hammarskjöld had been criticized by the Soviet bloc for their respective actions in Korea and the Congo. More recently, Secretaries-General Pérez de Cuéllar, Boutros-Ghali, and Kofi Annan have been criticized for their actions in the Persian Gulf, Bosnia, Somalia, and Iraq. As with all visible policy positions, criticism goes with this job. However, since the time of Trygve Lie and the Korean War, the Secretary-General has rarely issued a harsh public judgment concerning armed conflict for the very good reason that he is not effective if he loses the confidence of important states.

The International Court of Justice can have an impact on conflict. Modeled upon the Permanent Court of Justice, which was also based in the Hague, the ICJ is a main organ of the United Nations, whereas its predecessor had functioned outside the League of Nations. Hence, all members of the UN are automatically parties to the ICJ's statute, although they are not bound by its jurisdiction without a voluntary acceptance. Composed of fifteen independent justices serving staggered nine-year terms and elected by a majority of both the General Assembly and the Security Council, the ICJ's jurisdiction covers all matters referred to it. Its decisions on enforcement are binding.

States refer cases to the Court either through general (for example, in a treaty) or ad hoc agreements. As specified in Article 36 of its statute, the ICJ has jurisdiction between or among states that have accepted the same obligation. The Court may also provide nonbinding but useful explanations through advisory opinions when requested to do so by a UN organ or specialized body. The Court's potential for helping to prevent breaches of the peace results from its objective judgments about treaty interpretations, questions of international law, the existence of facts, or the nature of reparations in situations that might otherwise result in the resort to armed force. In reality, the ICJ has had little effect on international peace and security. It generally hands down only a few decisions per year, and rarely have they concerned an international conflict involving serious violence. *Nicaragua vs. the U.S.* (1986) is an exception that proves the generalization.

The Legal Basics

The core of the UN Charter concerning security questions is Article 2, paragraph 4: All states shall refrain from the threat or use of force in their international relations. On the one hand, Article 2(4) is visionary, even idealistic. States have engaged in the threat or use of force repeatedly in the history of world politics. How could it be otherwise when there are few procedures to guarantee peaceful change? That being so, it is quite remarkable that Article 2(4) has not completely withered away under the pressures of a violent world.

On the other hand, a world without the threat or use of force continues to be the primary objective of the United Nations, and of its member states. When Iraq invades Kuwait, the international community starts its response by labeling such action impermissible under the UN Charter. The same process has occurred in numerous other situations, although the language and form of international responses vary. The UN General Assembly opposed not only Iraq's invasion of Kuwait but also the U.S. invasions of Grenada and Panama, Vietnam's invasion of Cambodia, the Soviet Union's invasion of Afghanistan, India's invasion of East Pakistan, and so on.

In fact, Article 2(4) is not a dead letter. After the Cold War, a state contemplating the use of force to resolve a dispute, especially if not a great power, cannot be sure that its action will not result in some type of condemnation and punishment. To be sure, the process is not automatic; UN resolutions may be worded in a soft way, and actual sanctions can vary. As we noted earlier, the functioning of collective security frequently shows one political bias or another. Nevertheless, Article 2(4) is alive and reasonably well as a general standard of achievement.

According to the General Assembly in the 1970s, if a state engages in the first use of force, it has probably committed aggression. That is, the first use of force will normally be regarded as aggressive and nondefensive unless the Security Council holds otherwise. Individual or collective self-defense under Article 51 remains the only legal use of force. Anticipatory self-defense, in which the defender state uses force first, is not completely ruled out, but it is not explicitly endorsed either. The presumption is that the state using force first is the guilty party.

Inherent in this concept is that force means military action. A number of developing countries wanted force to include economic coercion, but this view has not prevailed in General Assembly debates. Analytical clarity requires keeping in mind the continuum from outside military intervention through the everyday exercise of political influence through the unconscious impact of such "soft power" as culture and language.[11] International relations frequently involve states affecting the internal affairs of other countries, although most diplomats prefer to avoid "intervention," which implies the forceful intrusion by outsiders, in favor of "involvement" or "intrusion" or "interference."[12]

In addition to dealing with aggression entailing first use of force, Article 42 states that there can be threats to and breaches of the peace. Neither the Security Council nor the World Court has ever clarified the difference between "aggression" and a "breach of the peace." But it is clear that a situation can create a threat to the peace without necessarily consisting of armed attack by one state on another. In the spring of 1991, for example, the Security Council declared that the human rights situation in Iraq constituted a threat to the peace. At that time the government of Saddam Hussein was engaged in such repression that hundreds of thousands of persons were being displaced within Iraq or were fleeing into Turkey or Iran.

Thus not only interstate force but also other actions constituting a threat to the peace can violate the UN law of peaceful international relations. In the mid-1960s the UN authorized economic sanctions on Rhodesia. That territory was characterized by a unilateral declaration of independence from the United Kingdom, denial of many internationally recognized human rights, and growing violence between the white-minority government and the Patriotic Front. The Organization of African Unity (OAU) and eventually the UN General Assembly called the Patriotic Front a national liberation movement. There was no armed attack by one state on another, yet the Security Council said that there was no peace and that binding economic sanctions were in order.

This brings us to the crucial point that when the Security Council finds a situation of aggression, or threat to or breach of the peace, it can impose binding sanctions. In effect, the council can make international law. Chapter VII of the Charter, containing Articles 39 to 51, gives the council far more legal authority than the Council of the League of Nations ever had. During the Cold War, the Security Council imposed binding sanctions on only two targets: the Ian Smith government in Rhodesia and the makers of apartheid in South Africa. Since the end of the Cold War, the council has levied mandatory economic sanctions on a variety of parties in Iraq, Haiti, Yugoslavia, and elsewhere. It imposed a binding arms embargo on all parties fighting in the Balkans. It did not impose but did authorize military action for the liberation of Kuwait. Likewise, it did not require but did authorize all necessary means for the delivery of humanitarian assistance in both Somalia and Bosnia. All this occurred under Chapter VII of the Charter, leading to legally binding decisions by the Security Council. These decisions were not recommendations; they were mandatory from the viewpoint of international law.

It is still true that most Security Council resolutions, and all General Assembly resolutions except for those setting the budget, constitute recommendations, legally speaking. When dealing with peace and security issues, the council usually acts under Chapter VI, not Chapter VII. Chapter VI deals with the pacific settlement of disputes. Under this part of the Charter the council suggests to parties how they might resolve their disputes. Traditional peacekeeping, even though UN personnel may be lightly armed, takes place under Chapter VI. UN peacekeepers do not shoot their way into situations; they proceed with the consent of the parties, usually to supervise some cease-fire or other agreement by the parties. But the theory of the Charter's operation always entailed the notion that the persuasive role of Chapter VI should be seen against the more forceful role of Chapter VII. If the parties cannot agree, upon pacific urging of the Security Council under the purview of Chapter VI, they might face sanctions under Chapter VII.

One of the great complexities facing the world organization in the twenty-first century is that although the Charter was written for states, much political instability and violence arise today either from violence within states or from violence across state boundaries by nonstate parties. The problems in Somalia and Liberia, to name just two, arose from the absence of a functioning state and a government capable of speaking in the name of the state. In the legal vacuum, various armed factions exercise as much power as they can. In Bosnia, the problems stemmed not just from Yugoslavian and Croatian foreign policies but from the actions of Bosnian Serbs and Bosnian Croats who were, in effect, unrecognized or quasi-recognized rebels in an internationalized internal armed conflict. In Cambodia, four groups vied for power. In Sri Lanka, armed Tamils have long sought to violently carve a new state out of that island.

In these and other situations it is not clear what Article 2(7) means, namely, whether the UN, and presumably also a member state, can intervene in matters of domestic jurisdiction. If repression by the Iraqi government of Iraqis, including those who remain physically within Iraq, constitutes a threat to international peace and security—as the council said in 1991—then what is left to constitute domestic jurisdiction? If the UN and its member states are entitled to use all necessary means to provide a secure environment for humanitarian assistance inside Somalia—as the council stated in 1992—in a situation in which the external material consequences for any other state were extremely slight, then domestic jurisdiction means very little. If the restoration of a deposed but duly elected government is the basis for a Chapter VII intervention in Haiti—as the council stated in 1994—then what is the difference between domestic and international affairs? If the bombing of Belgrade over its repressive actions in its former province of Kosovo is condoned, what actions can be considered purely domestic?

The Permanent Court of International Justice was surely correct when it said in the 1920s that the dividing line between domestic and international jurisdictions was a changing one, depending on the nature of international relations. It is surely true that the realm of international action has been expanding. The political fact is that the Security Council, driven by the foreign policies of its members, is attempting to deal more with the causes of violence even if they arise from conditions within states than just with conditions between states. Legal notions follow from these political facts.

As usual, power matters. If the United Kingdom says that the situation in Northern Ireland is a domestic matter, this view may carry the day because of the power of the UK and its friends. Surely some matters clearly remain a part of domestic jurisdiction. Elections to the legislature in Nebraska, Rhode Island, and South Carolina, said to be internal or domestic by the powerful United States, are not going to be supervised by the United Nations—although national elections in El Salvador, Nicaragua, Haiti, Angola, and Cambodia have been.

Increasingly the United Nations, especially through Security Council action, has undertaken all sorts of deeply intrusive actions pertaining to human rights and economic affairs inside states in an effort to resolve security problems. Security issues do not separate so easily from these other concerns in places like El Salvador. In Cambodia, in theory if not fully in practice, UN personnel were in charge of governmental ministries. In theory at least, the UN governed Cambodia on an interim basis. The limits to UN action, respecting Article 2(7) and domestic jurisdiction, are first and foremost political. If the international community wants to act in Somalia or Cambodia or Iraq, via the UN, Article 2(7) will be redefined to fit the situation. States have ratified the UN Charter, which conveys powers of autointerpretation on the Security Council. What the international political traffic will bear determines the content of this article.

The precise boundaries of state sovereignty are elusive. If sovereignty means that a national government sets policy in its domestic jurisdiction, evolving international standards suggest that this remains true only as long as a national government adheres to international law. Saddam Hussein's government sets policy in Iraq only as long as it does not engage in aggression and does not engage in gross violations of internationally recognized human rights. When it engages in aggression, as against Kuwait, the United Nations puts it into a type of "receivership" in which it forfeits many attributes of a sovereign state—for example, it is no longer free to fashion its national security policy as it thinks best, and it must forgo using certain weapons. When it engages in gross human rights violations, it must tolerate UN protection of some threatened groups on Iraqi soil—for example, the Iraqi Kurds.

The UN Secretary-General was referring to such trends when he wrote in 1992 that the time of absolute sovereignty had passed. Boutros-Ghali wrote in *Foreign Affairs*, "The centuries-old doctrine of absolute and exclusive sovereignty no longer stands, and was in fact never so absolute as it was conceived to be in theory. A major intellectual requirement of our time is to rethink the question of sovereignty." But some have suggested that the former Secretary-General might want to rethink some of his other statements on this subject. At a NAM summit in Jakarta in 1992 he stated, "Under Article 2, Paragraph 7 of the Charter, the United Nations shall never intervene in the domestic affairs of a member state, either in the guise of preventive diplomacy or for humanitarian aims."[13]

His successor, Kofi Annan, has been even more outspoken on the subject:

> State sovereignty, in its most basic sense, is being redefined—not least by the forces of globalisation and international cooperation. States are now widely understood to be instruments at the service of their peoples, and not vice versa. At the same time individual sovereignty—by which I mean the fundamental freedom of each individual, enshrined in the charter of the UN and subsequent international treaties—has been enhanced by a renewed and spreading consciousness of individual rights. . . . This developing international norm in favour of intervention to protect civilians from wholesale slaughter will no doubt continue to pose profound challenges to the international community. In some quarters it will arouse distrust, scepticism, even hostility. But I believe on balance we should welcome it.[14]

Much remains to be done concerning the United Nations and security issues. Under Article 43 of the Charter, all states are obligated to conclude an agreement with the Military Staff Committee, a subsidiary of the Security Council, whereby military forces are made available to the UN for use by the council. No state has ever concluded such an agreement, leaving the council and Secretary-General with the task of constructing military forces mostly de novo for each security crisis in which UN force is contemplated.

In the past the great powers could not agree among themselves about how to construct Article 43 agreements—for example, covering large as opposed to small forces. Some observers thought that during the Cold War neither Washington nor Moscow was seriously interested in these agreements. And in the United States, the question of Article 43 agreements got entangled in the controversy over "war powers," and whether the president alone was entitled to use various types of force pursuant to a Security Council resolution under Chapter VII. So this important matter remains unfinished over half a century after the Charter was signed.[15]

Partly because of this situation, the UN has resorted to the "sheriff's posse"[16] approach to a number of security crises—as in Korea, Iraq, Somalia, Haiti, and East Timor. In effect, the UN enters into a "contract" with the United States or other major powers to enforce UN policy in countering either aggression or threats to the peace. In the former Yugoslavia following the Dayton accords, NATO became the UN's agent. This is not so different from the Rhodesian situation in the 1960s and 1970s, when the Security Council authorized the British navy to enforce the mandatory embargo in Mozambique territory. This approach has the advantage of efficiency, which is no small matter when lives are on the line. But it has the drawback of the loss of UN control over its own policies, entailing loss of accountability for precisely what is done in the name of the UN.

Chapter VIII of the Charter lays out a theory for UN linkage with regional organizations. This subject is important enough for extended analysis, particularly in light of calls to expand regional organizations' roles in the international security arena.

Thus not only interstate force but also other actions constituting a threat to the peace can violate the UN law of peaceful international relations. In the mid-1960s the UN authorized economic sanctions on Rhodesia. That territory was influenced by regional arrangements.

Regional Arrangements

One question is whether it is more appropriate to deal with local conflict through multilateral organizations whose scope is regional (for instance, the European Union or NATO) or universal (for instance, the United Nations).[17] The preference for regional management of regional conflict was enshrined in Chapter VIII of the UN Charter at the urging of Washington, based on the insistence of its Latin American allies. The Persian Gulf War produced a strong sense that the original security provisions of the Charter, including a renewed interest in regional organizations, could sometimes be implemented. Secretary-General Boutros-Ghali's *An Agenda for Peace* contains a chapter on these organizations. A group of eminent persons called together by the Swedish prime minister in 1991 also called upon world leaders to "act determinedly to build a new system for peace and security, at both a global and regional scale."[18] Virtually all policy analyses of multilateralism in the last decade emphasize a division of labor between the United Nations and regional organizations.

There is some reason to believe that regional organizations are an appropriate locus for action because local instability poses a greater threat to regional actors. At the outset of the present Charter regime, the preference for peaceful settlement was clearly articulated. Even Article 21 of the Covenant of the League of Nations noted the validity of regional understandings as a basis for maintaining peace. However, many observers tend to overlook that the relative balance between regionalism and universalism was one of the most controversial aspects at the San Francisco conference.[19]

One of the major themes running throughout this text is the network of institutions linked to the work of the United Nations. The field of security is quite distinct from the other issue areas—human rights and sustainable development—that are treated later. In the area of security, nongovernmental organizations have been relatively inconsequential, but regional institutions play a central role. This generalization is almost the opposite for the issues of human rights and development, which are discussed in Parts 2 and 3 of this volume, because nongovernmental actors have come to play a crucial role in these areas.

The creation of the Security Council, with its enforcement power, gave globalism a significant edge over regionalism; Chapter VIII, "Regional Arrangements," was considered essential. The basic idea was that an effort would be made to settle local disputes regionally before referring them to the United Nations and that the

Security Council would remain an option mainly if regional efforts failed. Chapter VIII was designed to limit Security Council deliberations to the most severe and intractable disputes.

Article 52 of Chapter VIII declares, "Nothing in the present Charter precludes the existence of regional arrangements or agencies dealing with matters relating to the maintenance of international peace and security" under the condition that "their activities are consistent with the Purposes and Principles of the United Nations." This article encourages states to use regional organizations before directing their conflicts to the Security Council and also recommends that the council make use of regional arrangements. Articles 53 and 54 define relations between the UN and regional organizations by prohibiting the latter from taking peace and security measures without Security Council authorization and by insisting that regional organizations inform the council.

The active use of the veto throughout the Cold War not only prevented the use of the Security Council but also meant that regional organizations sometimes provided Washington and Moscow with convenient pretexts for containing disputes within organizations that were themselves under superpower control. In what was then Washington's backyard, crises in Guatemala, Cuba, Panama, and the Dominican Republic were relegated to the Organization of American States, dominated by the United States. In what was then Moscow's backyard, Hungary and Czechoslovakia were in the jurisdiction of the "socialist community" of the Warsaw Pact, dominated by the Soviet Union.

The supposed deficiencies of universal international organizations and the resulting apparent strengths of regional ones should be examined in light of the ambiguity of region as a concept, the overstretched capacities of the UN in international peace and security, and the purported better familiarity with local crises by the member states of regional organizations. There is a lack of specificity in Chapter VIII; in the opening paragraph the framers deliberately avoided precision, thereby allowing governments the flexibility to fashion instruments to foster international peace and security. Although the commonsensical notion of region is related to geography, the ambiguity of the Charter means that a region can also be conceived of geopolitically, culturally, ideologically, and economically. Such groups could include treaty-based organizations that pre- or postdate the United Nations or ad hoc mechanisms created to deal with a specific concern.

In addition to including such geographic entities as the OAU or the OAS, the Charter's definition also includes NATO, the Islamic Conference, the Warsaw Treaty Organization, the OECD, and the Contadora Group. Recent research points to the emergence of such "subregional" units as the Gulf Cooperation Council (GCC) and the Southern African Development Coordination Conference (SADCC) as potentially significant.[20] The concept of regionalism remains a conundrum.

A second issue concerns institutional resources. The United Nations continues to experience grave financial difficulties and sorely lacks sufficient and qualified staff. The steady, skyrocketing growth of its peacekeeping budget until 1996 to meet needs in the former Yugoslavia, Cambodia, and Somalia—while payments remained unacceptably slow and arrears approached $3.5 billion in the mid-1990s—meant the organization was seriously overstretched and groping for help from regional institutions.[21]

The great powers appear reluctant to pay for any substantial expansion of UN conflict management. The end of East-West tensions diminishes the perceived Western interests in many regional conflicts. Great-power resources seem limited, among other things, by the nature of a globalized economy. In the post–Cold War context, governing elites and publics sought to divert expenditure from foreign policy to postponed domestic economic and social needs. Smaller powers traditionally active in peacekeeping are unlikely to continue to pick up more of the tab. They share the economic problems of the larger states.

In this context, regional approaches to crisis management and conflict resolution may seem attractive. States near to a country in conflict suffer most from the destabilizing consequences of war in their area. They receive the refugees and bear the political, social, and economic consequences, willingly or unwillingly, of combatants from neighboring countries seeking sanctuary. They face the choice of pacifying and repatriating combatant and noncombatant aliens on their territory or of resisting hot pursuit by those from whom these refugees have fled. Local conflict and the consequent perceptions of regional instability dampen investment flows and retard growth. They divert public resources into defense expenditures.

States from a region at war appear to be well suited to mediating local conflicts. They understand the dynamics of the strife and of the cultures involved more intimately than outsiders do. Leaders are far more likely to have personal connections to protagonists, and these connections may be used as a basis for mediation. Involvement by other regional powers or organizations is less likely to be perceived as illegitimate interference than would involvement by extraregional organizations. Finally, issues of local conflict are far more likely to be given full and urgent consideration in regional gatherings than in global ones; the latter have much broader agendas and many more distractions.

The apparent advantages of regional institutions exist more in theory than in practice. In reality, these organizations are far less capable than the United Nations. The concept of regionalism is inchoate and not useful as a policy tool to guide decisions under Chapter VIII of the UN Charter. The institutional capacities of non-Western regional organizations are so feeble that they have not been able to carry out mandates in peace and security. The so-called comparative superiority of organizations in the actual region in conflict—familiarity with the issues, insulation from outside powers, and the need to deal with acute crises—is more than offset by such practical disadvantages as partisanship, resource shortages, and local rivalries. Apart from very unusual circumstances (the exception being NATO forces, and NATO has been careful not to call itself regional in order to avoid implying any subservience to the Security Council), regional organizations have neither sufficient military capacity nor diplomatic leverage.

Many of the factors ostensibly favoring regional organizations are questionable. Regional actors do tend to suffer most from the destructive consequences of conflict among their neighbors. At the same time, they frequently have stakes in these conflicts, are committed to one side or another, and stand to benefit by influencing the outcome. Sometimes they even are active participants. In this sense, their structure of interests is more complex than many proponents of regional organizations suggest. Their shared interest in the public good of regional stability is often accompanied by unilateral interest in obtaining specific favorable outcomes.

Since a favorable result for one regional power is likely to enhance its regional position at the expense of others, those others are likely to oppose such initiatives. In the terminology of international relations theory, we have simultaneous considerations of absolute gain (stability) and relative gain (power). There is no certainty that stability will predominate. Indeed, the recent literature provides compelling arguments to the effect that cooperation and regime maintenance are particularly difficult where questions of relative gain (power) are prominent, as in national security.[22] Such issues are far more likely to be prominent in regional international relations than they are at the global level, where they tend to be submerged in the post–Cold War era.

Situating crises in their regional historical and political contexts enhances the overall argument considerably. In Africa, the paralysis and bankruptcy of the OAU in curbing intervention and in managing the civil war in Angola reflected deep disagreement among its own members about the desirable outcome of the process of liberation. With its headquarters in Addis Ababa, the OAU appeared particularly inept in helping to end the Ethiopian civil war. The lack of any substantial OAU initiative also arose from the fact that other African states were deeply implicated in the conflict in pursuit of diverging national interests. Similar difficulties were evident in OAU efforts to cope with crises in Chad and the Western Sahara. In Somalia, OAU efforts were critically handicapped by the initial reluctance of members to sanction outside involvement in an internal conflict. In Liberia, OAU inaction led to Nigeria's use of the Economic Community of West African States (ECOWAS) to contain the violence of a civil war.

In South Asia, it is hard to see how any regionally based initiative to settle the Afghan civil war might have succeeded, not only because of the presence of Soviet forces but also because India had no interest in seeing a pro-Pakistani or Islamic fundamentalist regime in Kabul. To take a more extreme case, the capacity of the South Asian Association for Regional Cooperation (SAARC) to act as a neutral mediator of conflict between India and Pakistan over Kashmir is extremely problematic; the two principal members of the organization are the very states involved. Elsewhere on the continent, efforts by the Association of Southeast Asian Nations (ASEAN) to resolve the Cambodian conflict were handicapped by differing conceptions of Chinese and Vietnamese threats to the region. More recently, the UN Security Council authorized an Australian-led multinational force (IN-TERFET) to restore peace and security in East Timor. This action was successful, but it should be noted that it was taken with the acquiescence of the Indonesian government.

In Central America, the ability of the OAS to deal effectively with civil wars in Nicaragua and El Salvador was inhibited greatly by the U.S. failure to abide by the essential norm of nonintervention in its pursuit of a unilateral agenda to prevent revolution in El Salvador and reverse it in Nicaragua. The capacity of the European Community to come up with an effective response to the civil war in Croatia was significantly constrained by deep differences of opinion between France and Germany, and a number of disagreements among NATO members hampered military humanitarianism in Bosnia and Herzegovina without a UN cover.

Regional organizations replicate regional power imbalances. They may be used by the more powerful to expand their influence at the expense of the weak. Nigeria's manipulation of ECOWAS in Liberia is perhaps the most obvious case. Another is the Arab League's efforts to establish order in the Lebanese civil conflict, largely a fig leaf for one member's pursuing a long-standing desire to form a "greater Syria." Efforts to seek a UN blessing for Russian arbitration of disputes in the former Soviet Union amount to dressing up traditional Russian hegemony in the cloak of Commonwealth of Independent States (CIS) peacekeeping. This problem has appeared, or is likely to appear, in regions where power imbalances are so substantial that it is not possible for weaker states in coalition to balance against the strong. Cases in point include South Africa in southern Africa, Nigeria in West Africa, India in South Asia, Indonesia in Southeast Asia, and the United States in the Americas.

A further concrete problem with regional organizations as managers of conflict is that frequently their membership is not inclusive and their coverage is partial. OAU conflict management in southern Africa has been inhibited by the organization's exclusion of the region's major military and economic power. The same might be said of ASEAN's role, given the historical exclusion of Vietnam, Laos, and Cambodia. In light of the vast differences in their levels of economic development, this situation is unlikely to change once these anomalous exclusions are rectified. The Arab League excludes one of the three major regional powers (Iran). The Gulf Cooperation Council excludes two of three (Iraq and Iran). In a number of these instances (the OAU in southern Africa, the GCC in the Gulf, and ASEAN), the consciousness of the organization is defined in large part by its members' opposition to the threat posed by the excluded parties. The premise of these organizations has been partiality, hardly a capacity for neutral intervention and security management.

Moreover, these organizations have traditionally demonstrated their greatest structural weaknesses in dealing with civil war, the main growth industry for international conflict managers. This shortcoming follows in part from the international legal impediments associated with the doctrine of noninterference in internal affairs. These impediments have proven even more acute for many countries in the Third World preoccupied with exerting control over their own tenuous bases of power.[23]

Perhaps most important in many instances, the reluctance to become involved in civil conflict reflects the sensitivity of regional powers to creating precedents that might later be used to justify intervention in their own countries. In Africa, for example, many governments are themselves threatened by the possibility of civil conflict, which leads to caution about fostering norms that would legitimize regional involvement in such conflicts. Curiously, the challenge to the sovereignty of colonial powers facilitated decolonization. But newly independent countries immediately became the staunchest defenders of state sovereignty, a sentiment that is now also prevalent in central Europe and the former Soviet republics. Respect for conventional definitions of sovereignty has verged on slavishness. This weakness was shared during the Cold War by the United Nations; it is likely to play out more strongly at the regional level.

For all of these reasons, the general case for reliance on regional organizations is weak. If they were in theory the appropriate instrument for conflict management, their organizational, financial, and military capacities, as well as their fund of peacekeeping and conflict management experience, are generally vastly inferior to those of the United Nations. For example, it is illustrative to compare the frequency of regional conflict in Africa with the paucity of substantive attempts by the OAU to manage such conflict and the persistent reliance on external assistance for regional security. Although the OAS has a staff and even enjoys the professionalism of officers in the Inter-American Defense Board (IADB), its domination by the United States has largely discredited the institution in the peace and security arena. During the Nicaraguan and El Salvadoran mediation efforts, the OAS had to take a clear secondary position to the United Nations. Other regional organizations that have been active in regional conflicts, including ASEAN and the Organization on Security and Cooperation in Europe (OSCE), exist more on paper and during intergovernmental sessions than in fact; they have little institutional infrastructure. The OSCE's capacities have, however, begun to develop in response to requests for help in the former Soviet Union and especially in the former Yugoslavia to implement the Dayton agreements and follow-up to the war in Kosovo.

At the same time, the United Nations is overstretched with new and very large operations cropping up on every continent. Given the increasing demands that threaten to outstrip its resources, it would appear desirable to shift some of the burden to regional institutions. The question arises whether the international community should determine on a case-by-case basis the comparative advantages of specific regional institutions. How could such institutions, either constituted by treaty or formed on an ad hoc basis to meet a crisis, work best in tandem with the UN?

The pursuit of the Gulf War and the creation of safe havens for Kurds were clear and successful illustrations of what we might call military "subcontracting" to the Allied Coalition, as is NATO's ongoing presence in the former Yugoslavia. A more controversial and less successful example was Somalia, where a U.S.-led effort was mounted to break the back of warlord-induced famine. Moreover, three Security Council decisions between late June and late July 1994 indicated the relevance of military intervention by major powers in regions of their traditional interests: a Russian scheme to deploy its troops in Georgia to end the three-year-old civil war; the French intervention in Rwanda to help stave off genocidal conflict; and the U.S. plan to spearhead a military invasion to reverse the military coup in Haiti. The decision in Budapest in December 1994 by the then Conference (now Organization) on Security and Cooperation in Europe to authorize troops from the Commonwealth of Independent States and other OSCE member states after a definitive agreement in Nagorno-Karabakh is another illustration, as are earlier efforts by Nigeria and other countries of the Economic Community of West African States in Liberia.

The results from these arrangements have not been consistently superior to the UN's record. Yet the evident gap between the UN's capacities and persistent demands for help could be filled by regional powers, or even hegemons, operating under the scrutiny of a wider community of states.[24] The argument has become stronger in light of the experience in Kosovo and more especially the smooth handover in Timor from the Australian-led force to the UN one in February 2000.

In attempting to determine a possible division of labor between global and regional organizations to meet the exigencies of particular regional conflicts, distinctions should be made between Europe and developing countries as well as between the use of outside military forces to keep the peace and diplomatic measures for negotiations. In Europe, UN diplomacy could well be combined with the use of NATO forces under a UN flag in regional disputes, as in the former Yugoslavia. In developing countries, the division of labor could be different. In crises of manageable size (for example, in Guatemala), the UN could deploy its troops and work closely with regional partners in diplomatic arm-twisting. In more dangerous conflicts like the one in Somalia, UN diplomacy could be teamed with the troops of countries willing to run risks (probably the United States, maybe NATO, perhaps some symbolic troops from elsewhere) in a coalition.

In short, there is good reason to doubt not just the will but also the capacity of regional organizations to perform well in the management of conflict within their areas. The end of the Cold War has done little to change this conclusion. Widespread euphoria about the potential of regional organizations needs to be tempered with the results of recent efforts. We revisit these themes in Chapters 3 and 4.

Straying from the Course

Since 1945, untold numbers of wars have broken out and tens of millions of people have perished as a result.[25] According to the logic of the Charter, the leadership for the UN's peace and security duties rests on the shoulders of a small segment of the international community, notably the great powers. Conflict between Washington and Moscow poisoned the atmosphere and prevented their working together on most issues of security during the Cold War. World politics often made it impossible to act collectively, and states often chose to disobey or ignore the prohibitions and restrictions on the use of force to pursue *raisons d'état*.

In place of the ideal collective-security system, the UN developed alternate means to mitigate certain conflicts under the term "peacekeeping." Familiarity with this particular creation of the UN is necessary to understand the Cold War period and beyond. It is to this story that we now turn.

Notes

1. See Hedley Bull, *The Anarchical Society* (New York: Oxford Univ. Press, 1977).

2. See Adam Watson, "European International Society and Its Expansion," in Hedley Bull and Adam Watson, eds., *The Expansion of International Society* (Oxford: Oxford Univ. Press, 1986), pp. 23–25. For a discussion of historical developments since 1880 in relation to building functional international institutions, see Craig N. Murphy, *International Organization and Industrial Change: Global Governance Since 1850* (Cambridge, UK: Polity Press, 1994).

3. The codification of these rules began and has continued under the auspices of the International Committee of the Red Cross. See David P. Forsythe, *Humanitarian Politics: The International Committee of the Red Cross* (Baltimore: Johns Hopkins Univ. Press, 1977); and *The Geneva Conventions of August 12, 1949,* and *Protocols Additional to the Geneva Conventions of 12 August 1949* (Geneva: ICRC, 1989).

4. For a discussion, see Inis L. Claude, Jr., *Swords into Plowshares* (New York: Random House, 1964), pp. 3–34; Harold Jacobson, *Networks of Interdependence* (New York: Knopf, 1984), chap. 2; and Thomas G. Weiss, *International Bureaucracy* (Lexington, MA: D. C. Heath, 1975), pp. 3–47.

5. For a quantification of this dynamic, see Werner J. Feld and Robert S. Jordan, *International Organizations: A Comparative Approach* (New York: Praeger, 1994).

6. For a discussion, see F. H. Hinsley, *Power and the Pursuit of Peace* (Cambridge, U.K.: Cambridge Univ. Press, 1963), pp. 1–238; and S. J. Hambleben, *Plans for World Peace Through Six Centuries* (Chicago: Univ. of Chicago Press, 1943).

7. Lynn H. Miller, *Global Order: Values and Power in International Politics,* 2nd ed. (Boulder: Westview Press, 1990), pp. 46–50.

8. Chapter 12 of Claude, *Swords into Plowshares,* is still the best single treatment of collective security. The interested reader is also referred to Inis L. Claude, Jr., *Power and International Relations* (New York: Random House, 1962); Ernst B. Haas, "Types of Collective Security: An Examination of Operational Concepts," *American Political Science Review* 49, no. 1 (1955), pp. 40–62; Thomas G. Weiss, ed., *Collective Security in a Changing World* (Boulder: Lynne Rienner, 1993); and George W. Downs, ed., *Collective Security Beyond the Cold War* (Ann Arbor: Univ. of Michigan Press, 1994).

9. See, for example, Egon Ranshofen-Wertheimer, *The International Secretariat: A Great Experiment in International Administration* (Washington, DC: Carnegie Endowment, 1945).

10. Johan Kaufmann, *United Nations Decision-Making* (Rockville, MD: Sijthoff and Noordhoff, 1980), pp. 43–52.

11. See Joseph P. Nye, Jr., *Bound to Lead: The Changing Nature of American Power* (New York: Basic Books, 1990).

12. See Stanley Hoffmann, "The Problem of Intervention," in Hedley Bull, ed., *Intervention in World Politics* (New York: Oxford Univ. Press, 1984), pp. 7–28.

13. Boutros Boutros-Ghali, "Empowering the United Nations," *Foreign Affairs* 72, no. 5 (Winter 1992–1993), pp. 98–99.

14. Kofi Annan, "Two Concepts of Sovereignty, *The Economist* (September 18, 1999).

15. See Eric Grove, "UN Armed Forces and the Military Staff Committee: A Look Back," *International Security* 17, no. 4 (Spring 1993), pp. 172–181.

16. See Brian Urquhart, "Beyond the 'Sheriff's Posse,'" *Survival* 32, no. 3 (May-June 1990), pp. 196–205.

17. For a lengthier discussion, see S. Neil MacFarlane and Thomas G. Weiss, "Regional Organizations and Regional Security," *Security Studies* 2, no. 1 (Autumn 1992), pp. 6–37.

18. See *The Stockholm Initiative on Global Security and Governance* (Stockholm: Prime Minister's Office, 1991), p. 5.

19. See Francis O. Wilcox, "Regionalism and the United Nations," *International Organization* 19, no. 3 (Summer 1965), pp. 789–811; and Tom J. Farer, "The Role of Regional Collective Security Arrangements," in Weiss, *Collective Security*, pp. 153–189.

20. See William T. Tow, *Subregional Security Cooperation in the Third World* (Boulder: Lynne Rienner, 1990).

21. For a discussion of the resulting dangers, see Charles W. Maynes, "Containing Ethnic Conflict," *Foreign Policy* no. 90 (Spring 1993), pp. 3–21; and Stephen John Stedman, "The New Interventionists," *Foreign Affairs* 72, no. 1 (1993), pp. 1–16.

22. On this point, see Joseph Grieco, "Anarchy and the Limits of Cooperation: A Realist Critique of the Newest Liberal Institutionalism," *International Organization* 62, no. 3 (Summer 1988), pp. 488–507; and John Mearsheimer, "Instability in Europe After the Cold War," *International Security* 15, no. 1 (Summer 1990), p. 44.

23. See Mohammed Ayoob, "The Third World in the System of States: Acute Schizophrenia or Growing Pains?" *International Studies Quarterly* 33, no. 1 (March 1989), pp. 67–79; "The Security Predicament of the Third World State: Reflections on State-Making in a Comparative Perspective," in Brian Job, ed., *The Insecurity Dilemma: National Security of Third World States* (Boulder: Lynne Rienner, 1992), pp. 63–80; and *The Third World Security Predicament: State Making, Regional Conflict, and the International System* (Boulder: Lynne Rienner, 1995).

24. The discussion about the components of accountability was first made in relationship to Russia by Jarat Chopra and Thomas G. Weiss, "Prospects for Containing Conflict in the Former Second World," *Security Studies* 4, no. 3 (Spring 1995), pp. 552–583; see also Lena Jonson and Clive Archer, eds., *Peacekeeping and the Role of Russia in Eurasia* (Boulder: Westview Press, 1996). For an extended argument about a "partnership" between the UN and regional organizations, see Alan K. Henrikson, "The Growth of Regional Organizations and the Role of the United Nations," in Louise Fawcett and Andrew Hurrell, eds., *Regionalism in World Politics: Regional Organizations and World Order* (Oxford: Oxford University Press, 1995), pp. 122–168.

25. For a discussion of the unsettling numbers, see Ruth Sivard, *World Military and Social Expenditures* (Washington, DC: World Priorities, 1999). This handy compendium is updated annually.

2 The Reality of UN Security Efforts During the Cold War

The Early Years: Palestine, Korea, Suez, the Congo

Even before World War II officially ended, fifty-five countries signed the UN Charter on June 26, 1945. The Charter's requirement for unanimity among the permanent members of the Security Council indicated the realities of power politics at the time. However, the underlying assumption that members could agree—unrealistic with hindsight and even to astute observers then—was not borne out until after the Cold War. But for a brief time after World War II, an improved international order with greater reason, law, assumption of unity, and collective security seemed feasible.

The Soviet Union's establishment of a communist bloc in Eastern Europe quickly ended the big-power cooperation on which the postwar order had been predicated. With its members polarized into two camps, the United Nations was unable to maintain the peace and prevent conflict as was originally intended. Belligerents in conflicts sought partners in the East or the West. Superpower support in any given case meant that UN conflict management was problematic because either Washington or Moscow would block effective UN involvement. Aggressors could rarely be identified without umbrage being taken in the adversarial superpower's capital.

Nonetheless, in the early years the UN became involved in four major security crises that influenced subsequent developments and possibilities: in Palestine, Korea, Suez, and the Congo. Directly after Israel declared its independence in 1948, war broke out between it and its four neighbors—Egypt, Jordan, Lebanon, and Syria. Soon thereafter, the Security Council ordered a cease-fire under Chapter VII and created an observer team under Chapter VI to supervise it. This group grew into the United Nations Truce Supervision Organization (UNTSO) in 1949 and assumed the role of sentry.

Observer groups deployed along the borders of Israel and those of its neighbors were unarmed and operated with the consent of the parties involved. Close to 600 observers were eventually deployed, including army units from Belgium, France, the United States, and Sweden. The presence of soldiers from France and the United States was afterward considered by some to be an aberration. However, the United Kingdom was involved in the UN operation in Cyprus from the very beginning in 1960; and France, in the operation in Lebanon almost from the outset in 1978. Although the United States normally provided logistics to begin operations, participation by permanent members with ground troops in UN forces normally was avoided.

Troops were unarmed and had no enforcement capability, but their presence sometimes deterred truce violations. They represented the international community, which often enabled them to exercise their mandates without relying upon military might. Also, warring parties knew that their truce violations would be objectively reported to UN headquarters in New York for possible further action. Although observers wore the uniforms of their respective national armies, their first allegiance theoretically was to the world organization, symbolized by UN armbands. Later, blue helmets and berets became the trademark of UN peacekeepers. The observers were paid by their national armies and granted a stipend by the organization. UNTSO's activities continue to be financed from the UN's regular operating budget.

UNTSO has performed a variety of important tasks. UNTSO observers set up demilitarized zones along the Israeli-Egyptian and Israeli-Syrian borders, established Mixed Armistice Commissions along each border to investigate complaints and allegations of truce violations, and verified compliance with the General Armistice Agreements. If a truce violation occurred, the chief of staff of UNTSO attempted to deal with the matter locally, negotiating cease-fires when necessary. Finding means of deescalating crises before they blossom into significant threats to the peace has been a chief function of the operation.

UNTSO also became a training ground and resource center for other peacekeeping operations; its observers and administrators were consistently redeployed in other parts of the world. UNTSO's experience over the years has been integrated into other operations to improve their functioning.

The first coercive action taken in the name of the United Nations concerned the Korean peninsula.[1] UN involvement in this crisis merits careful attention because some observers consider the UN to have engaged in a type of collective security there between 1950 and 1953. Others call UN involvement in Korea a police action. Still others consider the UN role in Korea a unique experience defying standard terminology.

Labels aside for the moment, some history bears recalling. World War II left Korea divided, with Soviet forces occupying the North and U.S. forces, the South. A UN call for withdrawal of foreign troops and elections throughout a unified Korea was opposed by communist governments, leading to elections only in the South and the withdrawal of most U.S. troops. In June 1950, forces from North Korea (the Democratic Republic of Korea) attacked South Korea (the Republic of Korea). The Soviet Union, China, and the rest of the communist world supported the North.

Even though U.S. secretary of state Dean Acheson had previously given a speech indicating that South Korea was not within an extensive U.S. defensive perimeter, President Harry S Truman and Acheson agreed immediately that this attack on a noncommunist small state must be resisted. At the time, the USSR was boycotting the Security Council to protest the presence of a representative from the exiled government on Taiwan in the permanent seat reserved for China, thus excluding from the council the communist government on the mainland. Therefore, the United States knew that the Security Council would not be stymied by communist vetoes and would adopt some type of resolution on Korea. So the United States did not hesitate to refer the Korean situation to the council.

Even so, the Truman administration began to order U.S. military forces to Korea even before the Security Council adopted a resolution under Chapter VII declaring that North Korea had committed aggression, and before the council recommended, but did not require, that UN members furnish all appropriate assistance (including military assistance) to South Korea. When Moscow returned to its council seat, the General Assembly improvised, through the Uniting for Peace Resolution, to continue international action.

In essence, Security Council resolutions on Korea provided international legitimacy to U.S. decisions that would have been the same with or without the United Nations. The Truman administration was determined to stop communist expansion in East Asia, and it claimed that it had the legal right to do so under the U.S. Constitution. It proceeded without a congressional declaration of war or any other specific authorizing measure, and it was prepared to proceed without UN authorization—although once this was obtained, the Truman administration emphasized UN approval in its search for support both at home and abroad.

The UN's symbol and reputation were therefore thrust into a security dilemma of major proportions, even though the permanent members of the council, and the communist government of China outside the council, were definitely not in agreement. Once the USSR returned to deliberations in the council, it became impossible for the council to direct military actions being taken in its name. During the Soviet absence, a unified UN command had been established. In reality, this command deputized the United States to lead the defense of South Korea in the name of the United Nations. When the early tide of the contest turned in favor of the South, Truman decided to carry the war all the way to the Chinese border. This was a fateful decision that prolonged the war by bringing Chinese forces into the fight in major proportions—and thus continued the war until 1953, when stalemate restored the status quo ante. All important strategic and tactical decisions pertaining to Korea that carried the UN's name were in fact made in the White House or the Pentagon. A number of other states fought for the defense of South Korea, but that military operation was, in fact, a U.S. operation behind a blue international fig leaf.

The defense of South Korea was not a classic example of collective security. True, a truncated Security Council clearly labeled the situation one of aggression, something that had not frequently occurred during the Cold War. True, the council in effect authorized military support for the South, but it did not mandate it, a

Prisoners guarded by a South Korean soldier wait to be taken to a POW camp near Inchon in October 1950. (UN Photo 32240)

form of council action that was to be repeated in the 1990s concerning Iraq, Somalia, and Bosnia. But neither the council nor its Military Staff Committee really controlled the use of UN symbols. No Article 43 agreements transferring national military units to the UN were concluded. And the Secretary-General, Trygve Lie of Norway, played almost no role in the situation once he came out clearly against the North Korean invasion. The USSR stopped treating him as Secretary-General. Given that power play, he was eventually forced to resign because of his ineffectiveness. He was legally correct to take a public stand against aggression, but such a stand left him without the necessary political support during the Cold War.

The 1956 Suez Canal crisis was quite distinct from the Korean crisis. It resulted in the first use of what later became known as "peacekeepers" to separate warring parties. France, Britain, and Israel had attacked Soviet-backed Egypt against the

Congolese refugees uprooted from their homes by fighting in Katanga Province wait for water at a refugee camp in September 1961. (UN Photo 71906)

wishes of the United States, claiming a right to use force to keep the Suez Canal open after Egyptian president Gamel Abdel Nasser had closed it. Britain and France used their vetoes, and action by the Security Council was blocked. The General Assembly resorted to the Uniting for Peace Resolution—this time for peacekeeping, not enforcement—and directed Secretary-General Dag Hammarskjöld to create a force to supervise the cease-fire between Israel and Egypt once it had been arranged. The first UN Emergency Force (UNEF I) oversaw the disengagement of forces and served as a buffer between Israel and Egypt. In this instance, Washington and Moscow were not so far apart. In fact, President Dwight D. Eisenhower acted in the spirit of collective security by preventing traditional U.S. allies from proceeding with what he regarded as aggression. UN peacekeeping in 1956 and for a decade thereafter was hailed as a great success.

At the same time, the efforts by the world organization to deal with one of the most traumatic decolonizations, in the former Belgian Congo (then Zaire and more recently once again the Congo), illustrated the limits of peacekeeping. (The tradition of acronyms in English was set aside as operations in Spanish- and French-speaking countries became more widespread beginning in the late 1980s.) The ONUC (or United Nations Operation in the Congo) almost bankrupted the world organization and also threatened its political life; and Secretary-General Hammarskjöld lost his own life in a suspicious plane crash in the country.

UN Secretary-General Dag Hammarskjöld visits children of a village composed of Yemeni immigrants in the Jerusalem hills in May 1956. (UN Photo 50052)

   The conflict was both international (caused by the intervention of Belgium in its former colony) and domestic (caused by the secession of a province within the new state). The nearly total absence of a government infrastructure entailed a massive involvement of UN civilian administrators in addition to 20,000 UN soldiers. After having used his Article 99 powers to get the world organization involved, the Secretary-General became embroiled in a situation in which the Soviet Union, its allies, and many nonaligned countries supported the national prime minister, who was subsequently murdered while under arrest; the Western powers and the UN organization supported the president. At one point the president fired the prime minister, and the prime minister fired the president, leaving no clear central authority in place. As in Somalia later, this type of political vacuum created enormous problems for the United Nations as well as the opening for action.

Instead of neutral peacekeepers, UN forces became an enforcement army for the central government, which the UN created with Western support. In this process the world organization could not count on cooperation from the warring parties within the Congo. Some troop contributors resisted UN command and control; others removed their soldiers to register their objections. The Soviet Union, and later France, refused to pay assessments; Moscow went further in trying to destroy Hammarskjöld's independence by suggesting the replacement of the Secretary-General with a troika (or a three-person administrative structure at the top of the organization).

Four years later, the UN departed a unified Congo, and some observers viewed this as an important achievement. Many African states were threatened by secessionist movements (for example, the one in Biafra that erupted into a Nigerian civil war in 1968). The UN thus helped to keep alive the possibility of the policy adopted by the Organization of African Unity (OAU) at its first meeting in Addis Ababa in 1963, namely, that no colonial border could be called into question. Yet the world organization also had acquired an operational black eye in Africa as a result of its clearly partisan stance. No UN troops were sent again until the end of the Cold War (to Namibia). The UN also had a large budgetary deficit and a hesitancy to become involved in internal wars.

At the end of the 1973 Arab-Israeli War, the Second United Nations Emergency Force (UNEF II) provided another and largely successful example of separation of forces. The rules developed to govern its operation as an armed interpositional force became the blueprint for other traditional peacekeeping operations. UNEF II was composed of troops from Austria, Finland, Ireland, Sweden, Canada, Ghana, Indonesia, Nepal, Panama, Peru, Poland, and Senegal—nations representing each of the world's four major regions. The operation consisted of over 7,000 persons at its peak. UNEF II's original mandate was for six months, but the Security Council renewed it continually until 1979, when the U.S.-brokered Israeli-Egyptian peace accord was signed. Essentially, UNEF II functioned as an impartial force designed to establish a demilitarized zone, supervise it, and safeguard other provisions of the truce. The presence of UNEF II had a calming influence on the region through its ensuring that Israel and Egypt were kept apart.

The success of both UNEF I and II, and the problems with the operation in the Congo, catalyzed traditional peacekeeping, the subject to which we now turn.

Understanding Peacekeeping

As mentioned earlier, the effective projection of military power under international control to enforce international decisions against aggressors was supposed to distinguish the United Nations from the League of Nations. The onset of East-

West tensions made this impossible. The United States sought to keep the Soviet Union at arm's length from UN security efforts. A new means of peace maintenance was necessary, one that would permit the world organization to act within carefully defined limits when the major powers agreed or at least acquiesced.

UN peacekeeping proved mostly capable of navigating the turbulent waters of the Cold War through its impartiality and limited range of activities. Again, global politics determined the nature of UN activities. Although peacekeeping is not specifically mentioned in the Charter, it became the organization's primary function in the domain of peace and security. The use of troop contingents for this purpose is widely recognized as having begun during the 1956 crisis in Suez. Contemporary accounts credit Lester B. Pearson, then Canada's secretary of state for external affairs, with proposing to the General Assembly that Secretary-General Hammarskjöld organize an "international police force that would step in until a political settlement could be reached."[2]

Close to 500,000 military, police, and civilian personnel—distinguished from national soldiers by their trademark powder-blue helmets and berets—served in UN peacekeeping forces during the Cold War, and some 700 lost their lives in UN service during this period. Alfred Nobel hardly intended to honor soldiers when he created the peace prize that bears his name, and no military organization had received the prize throughout its eighty-seven-year history until December 1988, when UN peacekeepers received the prestigious award. This date serves as the turning point in the following discussion to distinguish UN security activities during and after the Cold War.

The Cold War and the Birth of Peacekeeping, 1948–1987

The lack of any specific reference to peacekeeping in the Charter led Hammarskjöld to coin the poetic and apt expression "Chapter six-and-a-half," referring to an expansion of Chapter VI. And certainly peacekeeping "can rightly be called the invention of the United Nations," as Secretary-General Boutros Boutros-Ghali claims in *An Agenda for Peace*.[3] The lack of a clear international constitutional basis makes a consensus definition of peacekeeping difficult, particularly because peacekeeping operations have been improvised in response to the specific requirements of individual conflicts. Despite the lack of consensus and the multiplicity of sources,[4] Under-Secretary-General Marrack Goulding provided a sensible definition of peacekeeping: "United Nations field operations in which international personnel, civilian and/or military, are deployed with the consent of the parties and under United Nations command to help control and resolve actual or potential international conflicts or internal conflicts which have a clear international dimension."[5]

The first thirteen UN peacekeeping and military observer operations deployed during the Cold War are listed in Table 2.1.[6] Five are still in the field. From 1948 to 1987, peacekeepers typically served two functions: observing the peace (that is, monitoring and reporting on the maintenance of cease-fires) and keeping the

TABLE 2.1   UN Peacekeeping Operations During the Cold War and
During the Initial Thaw

Years Active	Operation
1948–present	United Nations Truce Supervision Organization (UNTSO, based in Jerusalem)
1949–present	United Nations Military Observer Group in India and Pakistan (UNMOGIP)
1956–1967	United Nations Emergency Force (UNEF I, Suez Canal)
1958	United Nations Observation Group in Lebanon (UNOGIL)
1960–1964	United Nations Operation in the Congo (ONUC)
1962–1963	United Nations Force in New West Guinea (UNSF, in West Iran)
1963–1964	United Nations Yemen Observation Mission (UNYOM)
1964–present	United Nations Peace-keeping Force in Cyprus (UNFICYP)
1965–1966	United Nations India-Pakistan Observation Mission (UNIPOM)
1965-1966	Mission of the Representative of the Secretary-General in the Dominican Republic (DOMREP)
1973-1979	Second United Nations Emergency Force (UNEF II, Suez Canal and later the Sinai Peninsula)
1974-present	United Nations Disengagement Observer Force (UNDOF, Golan Heights)
1978-present	United Nations Interim Force in Lebanon (UNIFL)
1988-1990	United Nations Good Offices Mission in Afghanistan and Pakistan (UNGOMAP)
1988-1991	United Nations Iran-Iraq Military Observer Group (UNIIMOG)
1989-1990	United Nations Transition Assistance Group (UNTAG, in Namibia)
1989-1991	United Nations Angola Verification Mission (UNAVEM I)
1989-1992	United Nations Observer Group in Central America (ONUCA)

peace (that is, providing an interpositional buffer between belligerents and establishing zones of disengagement). The forces were normally composed of troops from small or nonaligned states, with permanent members of the Security Council and other major powers making troop contributions only under exceptional circumstances. Lightly armed, these neutral troops were symbolically deployed between belligerents who had agreed to stop fighting; they rarely used force and then only in self-defense and as a last resort. Rather than being based on any military prowess, the influence of UN peacekeepers in this period resulted from the cooperation of belligerents mixed with the moral weight of the international community.[7]

Peacekeeping operations essentially defended the status quo. They helped suspend a conflict and gain time so that belligerents could be brought closer to the negotiating table. However, these operations do not by themselves guarantee the successful pursuit of negotiations. They are often easier to institute than to dismantle, as the case of thirty years of this activity in Cyprus demonstrates. The termination of peacekeeping operations creates a vacuum and has serious consequences for the stability of a region, as happened in 1967 at the outbreak of the Arab-Israeli War following the withdrawal of UNEF I at Egypt's request.

Detailed histories of the first decades of peacekeeping are readily available. One illustration of the UN's handling of conflict in this period of East-West tensions helps to set the stage for a discussion of general principles that will bring in other UN operations. The UN Disengagement Observer Force (UNDOF) represents a classic example of international compromise during the Cold War. This operation was designed as a microcosm of geopolitics, with a NATO member and a neutral on the pro-Western Israeli side of the line of separation and a member of the Warsaw Pact and a neutral on the pro-Soviet Syrian side. UNDOF was established on May 31, 1974, upon the conclusion of disengagement agreements between Israel and Syria that called for an Israeli withdrawal from all areas it occupied within Syria, the establishment of a buffer zone to separate the Syrian and Israeli armies, and the creation of areas of restricted armaments on either side of the buffer zone. UNDOF was charged with verifying Israel's withdrawal, establishing the buffer zones, and monitoring levels of militarization in the restricted zones.

UNDOF employed 1,250 armed soldiers, including 90 military observers. Troop deployment emphasized equal contributions by countries that were either politically neutral or sympathetic to the West or East. Originally, Peru, Canada, Poland, and Austria provided troops for the operation. (The Peruvian troops were replaced by Iranians in 1975 and by Finns in 1979.) Canadian and Peruvian forces operate along the Israeli side; Polish and Austrian troops operate in Syrian territory.

Despite the declared hostility between Israel and Syria, UNDOF proved instrumental in maintaining peace on the Golan Heights between the two longtime foes. Since 1977, no major incidents have occurred in areas under UNDOF's jurisdiction. Success is attributable to several factors: The details of the operation were thoroughly defined before its implementation, leaving little room for disagreement; Israel and Syria cooperated with UNDOF; and the Security Council supported the operation fully.

Principles of Traditional Peacekeeping

No cohesive community of NGOs can be said to exist yet around the issues of UN military operations, at least to the same extent as they do in the fields of human rights and sustainable development. Yet a veritable cottage industry of peacekeeping publications has emerged since the award of the Nobel Peace Prize to UN peacekeepers. Continuous learning and adjustments are occurring among practitioners and analysts. The man who helped give operational meaning to "peacekeeping," Sir Brian Urquhart, has summarized the characteristics of UN operations—which can be gleaned inductively from the case of UNDOF—during the Cold War as follows: consent of the parties, continuing strong support of the Security Council, a clear and practicable mandate, nonuse of force except in the last resort and in self-defense, the willingness of troop contributors to furnish military forces, and the willingness of member states to make available requisite financing.[8] It is worth developing each of the points as a bridge to our subsequent discussion of future efforts that go beyond traditional limitations.

Consent Is Imperative Before Operations Begin.   In many ways, consent is the keystone of traditional peacekeeping, for two reasons. First, it helps to insulate the UN decisionmaking process against great-power dissent. For example, in Cyprus and Lebanon the Soviet Union's desire to obstruct was overcome because the parties themselves had asked for UN help.

Second, consent greatly reduces the likelihood that peacekeepers will encounter resistance while carrying out their duties. Peacekeepers are physically in no position to challenge the authority of belligerents (either states or opposition groups), and so they assume a nonconfrontational stance toward local authorities. Traditional peacekeepers do not impinge on sovereignty. In fact, it is imperative to achieve consent before operations begin.

The emphasis that traditional missions place on consent does have drawbacks, as two observers have noted: "Peacekeeping forces cannot often create conditions for their own success."[9] For example, belligerents will normally consent to a peacekeeping mission once wartime goals have been achieved or losses have made belligerents war-weary. In instances where neither of these conditions has been met, it becomes necessary to find alternate ways to induce warring parties to achieve and maintain consent. Moreover, major powers need to pressure their clients not only to consent but also to negotiate. When the political will is lacking, wars either continue unaddressed by the organization or UN peacekeepers become inextricably tied down in conflict, neither able to bring peace to the area nor able to withdraw from it. For example, the United Nations Peace-keeping Force in Cyprus (UNFICYP), originally deployed in 1964 to separate warring Turkish and Greek Cypriot communities, remains in the field because consent for deployment has not been matched by a willingness to negotiate the peace. Likewise, the United Nations Military Observer Group in India and Pakistan (UNMOGIP), established in 1949; UNDOF, created in 1974; and the United Nations Interim Force in Lebanon (UNIFIL), deployed in 1978—all continue to operate because of the absence of political conditions allowing for their removal.

Peacekeeping Operations Must Have Full Support from the Security Council. Security Council support is necessary not only in the beginning stages of the mission, when decisions regarding budgets, troop allotments, and other strategic priorities are made, but also in its later stages, when mandates come up for renewal. The host of problems in the Congo illustrates the dangers of proceeding without the support of the major powers in the Security Council. Backing by both the

United States and the Soviet Union of UNEF I in the General Assembly was the only case in which the United States and the USSR abandoned the Security Council and then resorted to the General Assembly to get around a veto in the Security Council. A practice has developed for the Security Council to renew the mandate of missions several times—frequently semiannually for years on end—in order to keep pressure on parties who may be threatened with the possible withdrawal of peacekeepers. Full Security Council support also enhances the symbolic power of an operation.

Participating Nations Must Be Willing to Provide Troops and to Accept Risks. Successful peacekeeping missions require the self-sustained presence of individual peacekeeping battalions, each of which must be independent but also must function under UN command. Frequently they will be deploying in areas of heavy militarization. Mortal danger exists for peacekeepers. Democratic governments in particular that provide troops must be willing to accept the risks inherent in a given mission, and they also must be able to defend such expenditures and losses before their parliaments.

Permanent members do not normally contribute troops except for logistical support, a specialty of the United States, which during the Cold War essentially airlifted most start-up troops and provisions for UN operations. Keeping major powers from an active role in peacekeeping was imperative for the impartiality that successful peacekeeping strives to attain. Washington and Moscow were thought to be especially tainted by the causes that they supported worldwide.

The experience with exceptions to this rule has been mixed. Because of the special circumstances involved in Britain's possession of extraterritorial bases on the island of Cyprus, the United Kingdom was involved in the UN's operations there from the outset; that effort has been worthwhile. The experience of French peacekeepers deployed in UNIFIL has been a source of problems because of France's perceived involvement as an ex-colonial power on the Christian side of the conflict. Consequently, French troops came under attack by local factions and were forced to withdraw from the zone of operations and to remain in the UN compound in Naquora. This experience was a smaller-scale indication of the problems that would be incurred later by both the United States and France in the non-UN operation in Beirut in 1984, when some 300 soldiers were killed.[10]

A Clear and Precise Mandate Is Desirable.   The goals of the mission should be clear, obtainable, and known to all parties involved. Enunciation of the mission's objectives reduces local suspicion. Yet a certain degree of flexibility is desirable so that the peacekeepers may adapt their operating strategies to better fit changing circumstances. The goals of the operation may be expanded or reduced as the situation warrants. In fact, diplomatic vagueness may at times be necessary in Security Council voting to secure support or to keep future options open.

Force Is Used Only in Self-Defense and as a Last Resort. Peacekeepers derive their influence from the diplomatic support of the international community, and therefore they use force only as a last resort and in self-defense. The *Peacekeeper's Handbook* states this wisdom: "The degree of force (used) must only be sufficient to achieve the mission on hand and to prevent, as far as possible, loss of human life and/or serious injury. Force should *not* be initiated, except possibly after continuous harassment when it becomes necessary to restore a situation so that the United Nations can fulfill its responsibilities."[11]

Peacekeeping techniques differ greatly from those taught to most soldiers and officers by their national training authorities. However, in the past only the Scandinavian states and Canada have trained large numbers of their recruits and officers specifically for the peacekeeping method. Soldiers from other countries have often found themselves unprepared for peacekeeping situations where the prohibition against the use of force contradicts their standard military training.

Using minimal force affords several advantages.[12] With limited military capability, peacekeepers are not threatening to belligerents. So belligerents are apt to treat peacekeepers, who are unable to take part in the conflict militarily, with less suspicion than they direct toward regular forces. Peacekeepers are often able to mediate and forestall local flare-ups of violence.

Traditionally, peacekeeping forces have had the luxury of operating without enemies. The need to operate at peak military efficiency has not been as great as it would have been if "enemies," in the normal sense of the term, had existed. As a result, the administrative, technological, and strategic structures that sustain peacekeeping have reflected the need for professional diplomatic and political expertise more than the need for professional soldiers.

"Chapter Six and a Half" on Hold, 1978–1988

As mentioned earlier, from 1948 to 1978 thirteen UN peacekeeping operations took place. In the ten years after 1978, however, no new operations materialized, even as a rash of regional conflicts involving the superpowers or their proxies sprang up around the globe.[13]

The last operation approved before the hiatus of a decade highlights the difficulties encountered by the United Nations during this period. UNIFIL was beset with problems similar to those experienced in the Congo, where domestic conflict and an absence of government structures had given the world organization an operational black eye.[14] UNIFIL's difficulties illustrate the dangers inherent in operations that lack both clear mandates and the effective cooperation of belligerents and that operate amidst political chaos and great-power disagreement.

UNIFIL was established at the Security Council's request on March 19, 1978, following Israel's military incursion into southern Lebanon. Israel claimed that military raids and shellings by members of the Palestine Liberation Organization (PLO), who were based in southern Lebanon, threatened Israeli peace and security. Israel's response embarrassed its primary ally, the United States. Washington used its influence in the Security Council to create UNIFIL as a face-saving means for Israel to withdraw. The operation's duties included confirmation of the Israeli withdrawal; establishment and maintenance of an area of operations; prevention of renewed fighting among the PLO, the Southern Lebanese Army (Christian militia backed by Israel and led by Major Saad Haddad), and Israel; and the restoration of Lebanese sovereignty over southern Lebanon

At UNIFIL's maximum strength, over 7,000 soldiers were deployed, including contingents from Fiji, France, Ghana, Iran, Ireland, Nepal, the Netherlands, Nigeria, Norway, Senegal, and Canada. UNIFIL encountered significant problems due to the conflicting interests of the major parties involved in southern Lebanon. Israel refused to cede control of the South to UNIFIL, choosing instead to rely upon Major Haddad's Southern Lebanese Army, which resisted UNIFIL's efforts to gain control in the area. The PLO demanded that it be allowed to operate freely in the South to continue its resistance against Israel. The Lebanese government insisted that UNIFIL assume control of the entire region, including areas controlled by Haddad. Consequently, UNIFIL found itself sandwiched between the PLO and Haddad's forces; its contingents routinely came under fire. The PLO continued its military maneuverings against Israel, and Haddad's forces continued their attacks on the PLO. In 1982, as Israel reinvaded Lebanon and marched to Beirut, UNIFIL stood by, powerless, in the face of Israel's superior firepower and the unwillingness of troop contributors or the UN membership to resist. UNIFIL's refusal to stand its ground echoed Egypt's 1967 request to withdraw UNEF I; once UN troops walked away, President Nasser ordered the use of force against Israel.

The lack of political will among the regional participants and troop contributors was matched by the incapacity of the Lebanese government's army and police. Yet, UNIFIL has become part of the local infrastructure,[15] and its withdrawal would be very disruptive. It would have resulted in greater instances of fighting between the PLO, Israel, and Haddad's army, and a probable third Israeli intervention would almost certainly have been countered by direct Syrian opposition. Despite its limitations, UNIFIL continues to operate.

Much of the impetus for the increased tension between East and West and for the end of new UN deployments came from Washington after the Reagan administration assumed power in 1981. Elected on a platform of anticommunism, the rebuilding of the national defense system, and fiscal conservatism, the administration was determined to roll back Soviet gains in the Third World. Washington scorned the UN and cast it aside as a bastion of Third World nationalism and procommunism. The UN's peacekeeping operations were tarred with the same brush.

Noncooperation with the UN reached its peak from 1985 to 1987, when Washington also refused to pay all of its assessed dues (including a portion of the assessment for UNIFIL, which the United States had originally insisted upon).[16] The organization was in near bankruptcy at the same time that traditional respect

Brian E. Urquhart, Under-Secretary-General for special political affairs, answers questions in June 1985 about his mission to the Middle East to free soldiers of the UN Interim Force in Lebanon. (UN Photo 165579/Y. Nagata)

for international law seemed to evaporate and unilateral action gained favor.[17] Intervening in Grenada, bombing Libya, and supporting insurgencies in Nicaragua, Angola, Afghanistan, and Cambodia attested to Washington's preferences. The Soviet Union countered these initiatives, and Central America, the Horn of Africa, much of southern Africa, and parts of Asia became battlegrounds for the superpowers or their proxies. This situation changed only with the Gorbachev regime in the Soviet Union and the advent of glasnost and perestroika, which will figure centrally in the next chapter.

Economic Sanctions

Short of sending international forces, a group of states may attempt to isolate an aggressor by cutting off diplomatic or economic relations with a view toward altering offensive behavior. These are coercive, albeit nonforcible, actions. Diplomatic and economic sanctions are significantly more emphatic than the political influence that makes up the everyday stuff of foreign policy, even if less emphatic than the dispatch of troops.

It is useful to imagine a spectrum ranging from political influence to outside military intervention. Economic sanctions are a form of nonforcible enforcement. For the same reasons that military coercion was not possible during the

Cold War, these milder forms of enforcement were also largely underused. The exceptions were the cases of two pariahs, Rhodesia and South Africa, whose domestic racist policies were considered abhorrent. These earlier experiences are worth discussing, however, as a prelude to actions after the end of the Cold War because the Security Council continues to redefine other types of apparently domestic policies of states as threatening enough to international peace and security to justify Chapter VII action.

As a reaction to Rhodesia's Unilateral Declaration of Independence (UDI) from the United Kingdom in 1965, the Security Council in 1966 ordered limited economic sanctions under Chapter VII of the Charter for the first time in UN history.[18] Whether the trigger was more due to the UDI or the human rights situation for Africans is debatable, but the result was that the council characterized the situation as a "threat to the peace." The council toughened the stance against the white-minority government by including all exports and imports (except for some foodstuffs, educational materials, and medicines). These sanctions became "comprehensive" in 1968.

The sanctions initially extracted some costs from the government of Rhodesian prime minister Ian Smith. But, ironically, they eventually helped immunize the country against outside pressure in the form of nonforcible sanctions because they prompted a successful program of import substitution. Although most members of the UN complied, those who counted did not. The United States, for example, openly violated sanctions after the Byrd amendment by Congress allowed trade with Rhodesia. Many private traders as well as some other African countries also traded, including the neighboring countries of Mozambique (controlled as a Portuguese colony) and the Republic of South Africa.

Although the Security Council authorized a forceful blockade to interrupt supplies of oil and the British navy did halt a few tankers, there was insufficient political will to effectively blockade the ports and coastlines of Mozambique and South Africa. Hence, the Security Council can hardly be credited with the establishment of an independent Zimbabwe in 1979. The costs of the protracted guerrilla warfare ultimately led to the decolonization of Rhodesia through the negotiations at Lancaster House in England under the mediation of Lord Carrington, the British foreign minister. At a key point, South Africa indicated its support for a negotiated solution, thus depriving Ian Smith of his most important sanctions-breaker.

UN-imposed sanctions against South Africa reflected the judgment that racial discrimination (apartheid) was considered a threat to the peace. Limited economic sanctions, an embargo on arms sales to South Africa, embargoes against South African athletic teams, and selective divestment were all part of a visible campaign to isolate South Africa. These acts exerted pressure whose impact is difficult to quantify, although observers usually assert that they have played an important role. Initially, South Africa's high-cost industry thrived by trying to replace missing imports (as had Rhodesia's), and it even managed to produce a variety of sophisticated arms that eventually became a major export. The changes that have occurred in South Africa since 1990 have certainly been dramatic, but they probably result more from the dynamics of the internal struggle by the black majority and the end of the Cold War than from nonforcible sanctions. Sanctions no doubt contributed to altering the domestic balance by demonstrating the risks and the costs of being isolated, but measuring their precise impact requires greater empirical work. Private "sanctions" should also be noted, as a number of Western businesses progressively pulled out of this violence-prone area.

Security Council sanctions are enforcement tools to address a breach of the peace or a threat to international peace and security. They should be analyzed as distinct from bilateral economic sanctions (for example, those used by Washington against Moscow during the Cold War) or those imposed by treaty (for example, the Montreal Protocol). The UN Charter never uses the word "sanctions" in Chapter VII, but Article 41 speaks of "what measures not involving the use of armed force are to be employed to give effect to its decisions." The use of partial or comprehensive sanctions, particularly at early stages in armed conflicts, is a subject to which we return at the end of Chapter 3.

Notes

1. See Leon Gordenker, *The UN Secretary-General and the Maintenance of Peace* (New York: Columbia Univ. Press, 1967); and Leland M. Goodrich, *Korea: A Study of U.S. Policy* (New York: Council on Foreign Relations, 1956).

2. Max Harrelson, *Fires All Around the Horizon: The UN's Uphill Battle to Preserve the Peace* (New York: Praeger, 1989), p. 89.

3. Boutros Boutros-Ghali, *An Agenda for Peace: Preventive Diplomacy, Peacemaking and Peace-keeping* (New York: UN, 1992), para. 46.

4. Other definitions can be found in United Nations, *The Blue Helmets: A Review of United Nations Peace-keeping* (New York: UNDPI, 1990), p. 4; Alan James, *Peacekeeping in International Politics* (London: Macmillan, 1990), p. 1; and Boutros-Ghali, *An Agenda for Peace*, para. 20.

5. Marrack Goulding, "The Changing Role of the United Nations in Conflict Resolution and Peace-keeping," speech given at the Singapore Institute of Policy Studies, March 13, 1991, p. 9.

6. For further analyses of peacekeeping during the Cold War, see Thomas G. Weiss and Jarat Chopra, *Peacekeeping: An ACUNS Teaching Text* (Hanover: Academic Council on the United Nations System, 1992), pp. 1–20; and Thomas G. Weiss, "New Challenges for Future UN Military Operations: Implementing an Agenda for Peace," *Washington Quarterly* 15, no. 3 (1993), pp. 51–66. For a discussion of operations during the Cold War but with an emphasis on transferring lessons to the present, see Sally Morphet, "UN Peacekeeping and Election-Monitoring," in Adam Roberts and Benedict Kingsbury, eds., *United Nations, Divided World: The UN's Roles in International Relations* (Oxford: Clarendon Press, 1993), pp. 183–239.

7. For a discussion of UN and non-UN operations in a comparative military perspective in this period, see John Mackinlay, *The Peacekeepers* (London: Unwin Hyman, 1989). See

also Augustus Richard Norton and Thomas G. Weiss, *UN Peacekeepers, Soldiers with a Difference* (New York: Foreign Policy Association, 1990).

8. Brian Urquhart, "Beyond the 'Sheriff's Posse," *Survival* 32, no. 3 (May-June 1990), p. 198; see also his autobiography, *A Life in Peace and War* (New York: Harper and Row, 1987).

9. John Mackinlay and Jarat Chopra, "Second Generation Multinational Operations," *Washington Quarterly* 15, no. 3 (Summer 1992), p. 114.

10. For a discussion of these issues, see Mackinlay, *The Peacekeepers*, and Pierre Le Peillet, *Les berets blues de l'ONU* (Paris: Editions France-Empire, 1988).

11. International Peace Academy, *Peacekeeper's Handbook* (New York: Pergamon, 1984), p. 56.

12. See F. T. Liu, *United Nations Peacekeeping and the Non-Use of Force* (Boulder: Lynne Rienner, 1992).

13. For a discussion of this period, see S. Neil MacFarlane, *Superpower Rivalry and Third World Radicalism* (Baltimore: Johns Hopkins Univ. Press, 1985); Elizabeth Valkenier, *The Soviet Union and the Third World* (New York: Praeger, 1985); and Jerry Hough, *The Struggle for the Third World* (Washington, DC: Brookings Institution, 1986).

14. For a discussion, see Bjorn Skogmo, *UNIFIL: International Peacekeeping in Lebanon* (Boulder: Lynne Rienner, 1989); and E. A. Erskine, *Mission with UNIFIL* (London: Hurst, 1989).

15. See Marianne Heiberg, "Peacekeepers and Local Populations: Some Comments on UNIFIL," in Indar Jit Rikhye and Kjell Skjelsback, eds., *The United Nations and Peacekeeping* (London: Macmillan, 1990), pp. 147–169.

16. See Jeffrey Harrod and Nico Shrijver, eds., *The UN Under Attack* (London: Gower, 1988).

17. See David P. Forsythe, *The Politics of International Law: U.S. Foreign Policy Reconsidered* (Boulder: Lynne Rienner, 1990).

18. See Henry Wiseman and Alistair M. Taylor, *From Rhodesia to Zimbabwe* (New York: Pergamon, 1981); and Stephen John Stedman, *Peacemaking in Civil War: International Mediation in Zimbabwe, 1974–1980* (Boulder: Lynne Rienner, 1991). The League of Nations had previously tried limited sanctions against Franco's Spain.

3   UN Security Operations After the Cold War

A Changing World: New Goals, New Roles

Vowing to reform his country politically and economically, Soviet leader Mikhail Gorbachev prescribed programs aimed at integrating the Soviet economy into the world economy and reducing East-West tensions. In so doing, he helped reinvigorate multilateralism generally and UN peacekeeping more particularly.[1] Signs became clear in 1987; Moscow vowed to pay its debt of over $200 million to the organization shortly after the Soviet leader's September article in *Pravda* that clearly enunciated, at least to UN- and Soviet-watchers, the possibility of a second chance for the United Nations and collective security.

Gorbachev officially redefined the Soviet Union's relationship with the UN in 1988 at the General Assembly, calling for an extension of his domestic "new thinking" to apply to the management of international conflicts. The shift in Soviet policy resulted from that country's need to withdraw support from numerous conflicts and concentrate on economic reform. A decade of military buildup and wars by proxy had drained its treasury, and the USSR had to retract its overstretched foreign policy. Decisions to withdraw from Cam Ranh Bay in Vietnam and from Cuba, Ethiopia, and Yemen indicated how necessary drastic retrenchment had become in Moscow's priorities. UN peacekeeping provided a face-saving means to withdraw from what Gorbachev described as the "bleeding wound" of Afghanistan.

Changes in Moscow's attitudes toward the UN influenced the international climate and more particularly Washington's approach to the world organization. In 1988, President Ronald Reagan abruptly altered his public stance and praised the work of the organization, the Secretary-General, and UN peacekeepers. After helping to spearhead attacks that had led to almost a decade of UN-bashing, he declared at the General Assembly that "the United Nations has the opportunity to live and breathe and work as never before" and vowed to repay U.S. debts to the organization. This position was continued by President George Bush, a former U.S. permanent representative to the UN. Big-power cooperation grew, allowing the Security Council to resume part of its role as a guarantor of international peace and security, including the dramatic efforts to reverse Iraqi aggression against Kuwait. At the same time, permanent Security Council membership was a convenient way for France, Great Britain, Russia,[2] and perhaps China and perhaps even the United States to maintain international preeminence despite their declining economic, political, and military significance. It is to this story that we now turn.

The First UN Military Operations After the End of the Cold War, 1988–1993

In 1988 and 1989, the collegiality and regular collaboration among great powers in the Security Council, which had been foreseen in the Charter, finally seemed possible during the initial thaw in the Cold War. After a ten-year gap in deploying new UN security operations, five post–Cold War operations (listed at the bottom of Table 2.1) were launched—in Afghanistan, astride the Iran-Iraq border, and in Angola, Namibia, and Central America (for Nicaragua).

These operations were finished by 1993 and were similar to those of the past. It is true that they incorporated some new elements in the improvisation that is so characteristic of peacekeeping. For example, there were large numbers of civilians in tandem with soldiers in Namibia and Central America; the first supervision of domestic elections as well as the collection of weapons from insurgents took place in Nicaragua. These precedents illustrated clearly the UN's capacity for evolution and growth in the new era, although improvisation and task expansion had always been present in earlier UN activities. However, these new operations were extensions of the time-tested recipe for UN peacekeeping. In particular, these initial post–Cold War operations all enjoyed the consent of fighting parties and relied upon defensive concepts of force employed by modestly equipped UN soldiers, few of whom came from armies of the major powers. All operations that were ongoing in 1993 are listed in Table 3.1. Two of them also fall into the traditional peacekeeping category—the follow-up operation in Angola and the one in the Western Sahara.

However, this table also contains operations that are so different in scope and mandate that they could be characterized as "peacekeeping" only by stretching analytical categories beyond the breaking point. Three of them (in Cambodia, the former Yugoslavia, and Somalia) indicate the new challenges of UN operations that are providing the basis for the military departures, as suggested in Boutros-Ghali's *An Agenda for Peace*. The evolution of these and two other subsequent operations (Rwanda and Haiti) illustrate the limits of UN military operations, which is where we conclude this chapter. One operation in Table 3.1 (in Iraq-Kuwait) merits discussion because its deployment followed the first controversial enforcement action of the post–Cold War era, Operation Desert Storm, which figures prominently in our discussion of moving toward the future.

These operations are quite distinct from traditional peacekeeping, which is why Table 3.1 is entitled "UN *Security* Operations in Mid-1993." The distinction between the first and latter operations, with Somalia as the turning point, will become clear by the end of this chapter. Before we analyze precisely how they illustrate challenges for the future, it is useful to examine in more detail a few cases of

TABLE 3.1   UN Security Operations in Mid-1993 (annualized cost about $3.5 billion)

1. UN Truce Supervision Organization (UNTSO), Middle East, June 1948–
   Rough annual cost to the UN: $31 million
   Current strength (military personnel): about 250

2. UN Military Observer Group in India and Pakistan (UNMOGIP), January 1949–
   Rough annual cost to the UN: $7 million
   Current strength (military personnel): about 40

3. UN Peace-keeping Force in Cyprus (UNFICYP), March 1964–
   Rough annual cost to the UN: $20 million, and troop-contributing countries absorb an
      additional $60 million
   Current strength (military and police personnel): about 1,000

4. UN Disengagement Observer Force (UNDOF), Golan Heights, June 1974–
   Rough annual cost to the UN: $40 million
   Current strength (military personnel): about 1,200

5. UN Interim Force in Lebanon (UNIFIL), March 1978–
   Rough annual cost to the UN: $150 million
   Current strength (military personnel): about 5,300

6. UN Iraq-Kuwait Observation Mission (UNIKOM), April 1991–
   Rough annual cost to the UN: $65 million
   Current strength (military personnel): about 350

7. UN Angola Verification Mission (UNAVEM II), June 1991–
   Rough annual cost to the UN: $128 million originally, now considerably less
      (about $35 million)
   Current strength (military and police personnel): about 100, originally about 500

8. UN Observer Mission in El Salvador (ONUSAL), July 1991–
   Rough annual cost to the UN: $35 million
   Current strength (military and police personnel): about 350, originally 1,000

9. UN Mission for the Referendum in Western Sahara (MINURSO),[a] September 1991–
   Rough annual cost to the UN: $35 million
   Current strength (military personnel): about 350

10. UN Transitional Authority in Cambodia (UNTAC), March 1992-September 1993–
    Estimated cost to the UN for 15 months: $1.9 billion
    Current strength (military and police personnel): about 19,500

11. UN Protection Force (UNPROFOR) in the former Yugoslavia,[b] March 1992–
    Rough annual cost to the UN: $1 billion
    Projected maximum strength (military and police personnel): about 25,000, of whom 8,000
       are humanitarain soldiers provided by NATO at no cost to UN budget. NATO also
       discussing the deployment of more troops to enforce or supervise next steps.

12. UN Operation in Somalia (UNOSOM), June 1992–
    Original cost estimate to the UN for 12 months: about $100 million, revised upward to
       $1.5 billion to cover the second phase.
    Current strength (military personnel): 50 unarmed observers and 500 infantry were
       initially posted with another 3,000–4,000 after approval by the parties: Unified Task
       Force (UNITAF), or Operation Restore Hope, consisted of some 27,000 U.S. troops and
       10,000 from 22 other countries beginning in December 1992. This was replaced in May
       1993 by what should be 28,000 UN troops for the second phase of activities.

(continues)

TABLE 3.1   *(continued)*

13. UN Operation in Mozambique (ONUMOZ), December 1992–
     Cost estimate for 12 months: $210 million
     Current strength (military): about 6,500

14. UN Observer Mission in Uganda and Rwanda (UNOMUR),[a] July 1993–
     Cost estimate for 12 months: $17 million
     Current strength (military personnel): 30 observers

15. UN Observer Mission in Georgia (UNMIG),[a] August 1993–
     Cost estimate for 12 months: $30 million
     Authorized military personnel: 90 observers

16. UN Observer Mission in Haiti (UNMIH),[a] September 1993–
     Cost estimate for 12 months: $85 million
     Authorized military and police personnel: about 1,650

17. UN Observer Mission in Liberia (UNOMIL),[a] September 1993–
     Cost estimate for 12 months: $75 million
     Authorized personnel: not available

[a]Not fully operational.
[b]Includes three separate forces keeping the peace in Croatia, escorting convoys in Bosnia-Herzegovina, and monitoring Macedonia's borders to detect incursions.
SOURCE: UN Department of Public Information and authors' estimates as of September 30, 1993.

post–Cold War cooperation that cemented big-power collaboration and made possible the movement toward, as a minimum, bolder UN operations. As a maximum, these cases suggest the revival of collective security as a possible policy option for governments in the new era. This table reflects activities in mid-1993— before UN efforts in Bosnia were exposed as fruitless, before the debacle in Somalia, and before the embarrassments of Haiti and Rwanda.

The Rebirth of Peacekeeping

The UN Good Offices Mission in Afghanistan and Pakistan (UNGOMAP), the UN Iran-Iraq Military Observer Group (UNIIMOG), the first UN Angola Verification Mission (UNAVEM I), and the UN Transition Assistance Group in Namibia (UNTAG) were missions that renewed peacekeeping's visibility and perceived workability in the international arena of conflict resolution. UNGOMAP, UNIIMOG, and UNTAG are also significant because they afforded the UN the opportunity to demonstrate its usefulness in war zones, a capacity that had been frozen from 1978 to 1988. Successes built confidence and allowed the UN to move back toward center stage, and the operations provided the space to experiment with innovations beyond the scope of previous deployments.

These operations are examples of "observation," a diverse set of tasks that occupies the least controversial part of peacekeeping activities. The oldest UN operation, the United Nations Truce Supervision Organization (UNTSO), has been observing the Middle East since 1948. Traditionally, observation has meant investigation, armistice supervision, maintenance of a cease-fire, supervision of plebiscites, oversight of the cessation of fighting, and reports to headquarters. It has been expanded to include the verification of troop withdrawal, the organization and observation of elections, the voluntary surrender of weapons, and human rights verification. These operations are distinct from the other traditional task: interposition (for example, on the Golan Heights), which was discussed earlier.

UNGOMAP verified the withdrawal of Soviet troops from Afghanistan after 1988. The USSR had entered the country in 1979 to ensure a friendly Afghan government in Kabul. By the early 1980s Afghanistan had become the Soviet Union's Vietnam. The Soviets had become inextricably tied down in an unwinnable conflict against the Mujahideen, armed local groups backed by Pakistan and the United States. Soviet withdrawal became an economic and political imperative.

The Gorbachev administration sought a face-saving device to extricate itself. The 1988 Geneva Accords provided the means to achieve Soviet withdrawal, mutual noninterference and nonintervention pledges between Pakistan and Afghanistan, the return of refugees, and noninterference pledges from Washington and Moscow. These accords had been brokered by the United Nations and the indefatigable efforts of Under-Secretary-General Diego Cordovez beginning in 1982.

UNGOMAP was supposed to monitor the implementation of the Geneva Accords. The operation encountered few problems with the Soviet withdrawal because the USSR was eager to leave. But the political will needed to implement the remaining provisions concerning peace, elections, and disarmament was absent. The symbolic size of the operation—fifty officers divided between Islamabad and Kabul—attested to its inability to independently perform tasks other than reporting on the Soviet withdrawal after the fact. However, the operation provided an appropriate face-saving device for Moscow, which helped pave the way to a potential peace by reducing the direct East-West character of the conflict. It helped remove one of the principal stumbling blocks to improved relations between Washington and Moscow.

Just south of Afghanistan, the Iran-Iraq War finally drew to a close. Eight years after the war began, one year after the Security Council ordered a cease-fire with the compulsory intent provided for under Chapter VII, and after about 1 million lives had been lost, UNIIMOG was set up by the Security Council in August 1988 to ensure the maintenance of the cease-fire astride the international border. It established cease-fire lines between Iranian and Iraqi troops, observed the maintenance of the cease-fire, and investigated complaints to defuse minor truce violations before they escalated into peace-threatening situations. The cooperation among the permanent members of the Security Council had begun the previous year in order to work out the language of the original cease-fire, and it continued in this area into the 1990s.

Composed of 350 unarmed observers from over twenty-five states, UNIIMOG played a central role in preserving the cease-fire between Iran and Iraq, two nations whose mutual antagonism continued after the cessation of hostilities. In its first five months alone, UNIIMOG investigated some 2,000 complaints of truce infractions. Although UNIIMOG was instrumental in stopping a deterioration, it was more Iraq's diminished position after the Persian Gulf War that kept the peace than any diplomatic effort.

Much farther south in Africa, Angola, Cuba, and South Africa signed a trilateral agreement on December 22, 1988. This provided for the simultaneous withdrawal of Cuban troops from Angola and of South African troops and administrators from Namibia. This diplomatic breakthrough was monitored successfully by the first United Nations Angola Verification Mission, which led the way for the UN-sponsored peace process that brought Namibian independence on March 21, 1990, from South Africa's illegal colonial rule. The second UNAVEM was more problematic because civil war returned in spite of UN-supervised elections at the end of 1992; the difficulties faced by this group are discussed with other more problematic operations later in this chapter.

Also on the African continent, UNTAG was established to facilitate and monitor South Africa's withdrawal from Namibia and to set up free and fair elections to determine the future government and constitution of Namibia. It was the last major decolonization effort under UN auspices. To achieve these ends, UNTAG was tasked with monitoring and facilitating the departure of South Africa's army and the withdrawal and confinement of the South-West Africa People's Organization's (SWAPO) fighters to base camps in Angola, monitor the southwest African police force controlled by South Africa to prevent meddling in elections, oversee the repeal of discriminatory laws that threatened the fairness of the election, help ensure the respect for amnesty to political prisoners, and provide for the return of all Namibian refugees. UNTAG also registered voters and facilitated information about the election process.

At its maximum deployment, nearly 8,000 persons were involved in UNTAG—about 4,500 military personnel, 2,000 civilian personnel, and 1,000 police officers. It was the first sizable operation in Africa since the contested one in the Congo almost three decades earlier. The operation was rushed into the field in order to respect an April deadline. Hundreds of SWAPO fighters crossed the border on the first day after the UN's deployment in violation of the letter of the agreement, although they claimed that they had interpreted the text otherwise. In any event, South Africa–supported defense forces killed several hundred SWAPO guerrillas, the heaviest casualties in two decades of armed conflict.

But the parties to the conflict, in particular South Africa, were committed to making the operation work. UNTAG is generally considered a success. Virtually the entire population was registered to vote. SWAPO won forty-one of seventy-two seats in the Constitutional Constituents Assembly and was duly empowered to lead the formation of the Namibian government. On March 21, 1990—ahead of schedule and under budget—UN Secretary-General Javier Pérez de Cuéllar swore in Sam Nujoma as president of Namibia.

UNTAG provides a helpful analytical hinge between the old and new types of UN security operations. It went smoothly because traditional rules were followed—especially consent and minimal use of force. At the same time, it undertook several new tasks related to civil administration, elections, and police activities. These tasks foreshadowed new UN activities that would intrude more into the affairs of independent states rather than being part of a decolonization effort.

Moving Toward the Next Generation

The work of the United Nations in Central America during the late 1980s and early 1990s provides a transition in our discussion of the progressive movement toward a new generation of peacekeeping and peace-enforcement operations.[3] World politics was changing and so were the possibilities for action by the UN. Governments removed political obstacles that had previously blocked or impeded activities by the world organization. Although not at all comparable in most ways, the UN's efforts in Central America were similar to the Afghanistan operation in one way: The world organization was helping a superpower move beyond an unwinnable confrontation in its own backyard. An analysis of the United Nations Observer Group in Central America (ONUCA), the United Nations Observer Mission to Verify the Electoral Process in Nicaragua (ONUVEN), and the United Nations Observer Mission in El Salvador (ONUSAL) illustrates the complex transition process that the UN's peace and security functions began to undergo. These also set the stage for the following analysis of the UN-sponsored Chapter VII enforcement action against Iraq. ONUSAL in particular shows the independent nature of UN action when states give the world organization some political room to maneuver.

In the late 1980s, the conclusion of the so-called Esquipulas II agreements between the countries of Central America—Nicaragua, Costa Rica, El Salvador, Guatemala, and Honduras—began the peace process that ended a decade of civil war and instability in the region. The cornerstone of the agreements involved setting up free and fair elections in Nicaragua once border raids had stopped and demobilization had begun. Irregular forces had operated along the borders of nearly every country in the region. It was hoped that these measures would bring lasting peace to the region.

In addition to calling for elections in Nicaragua, the Esquipulas II agreements prohibited aid to rebel groups and the use of the territory of one state for guerrilla activity in another. ONUCA (1989–1992) was established to ensure that these provisions were respected. Although ONUCA was officially an "observer" mission, duties were far-reaching. They included verifying that all forms of military assistance to insurgent forces had ceased and preventing states from sponsoring such activity for infiltration into neighboring countries. ONUCA observers made spot checks and random investigations of areas prone to guerrilla activity along the borders of Nicaragua, El Salvador, Guatemala, Honduras, and Costa Rica. Although the signatories to Esquipulas II were expected to cooperate with ONUCA, the participation of the Nicaraguan resistance movement, the contras, was not ensured until after the electoral defeat of the Sandinista government in February 1990. ONUCA military observers operated in a tense, potentially dangerous situation where armed attacks were possible.

ONUCA's mandate expanded after the Nicaraguan election to include demobilizing the contras. Bases were set up inside the borders of Nicaragua, where many rebel soldiers came and handed over some of their weapons and military equipment to ONUCA soldiers, who destroyed them and helped to advance demilitarization. In spite of the continued existence of arms among disgruntled partisans of both the contra and Sandinista causes, this was the first instance of UN involvement in demilitarization through the physical collection and destruction of armaments. This task is important for conflict resolution in areas where heavily armed regular as well as irregular forces need to be drastically reduced before any meaningful consultative process can occur. The collection of arms has been integrated into numerous subsequent UN peacekeeping operations and has been made even more rigorous.[4] The importance of such a task was recognized by the United Kingdom as part of its efforts to end direct rule over Northern Ireland in 1999–2000.

ONUVEN was created to ensure the fairness of elections in Nicaragua. It was the first example of UN observation of elections inside a recognized state, an extraordinary intrusion according to conventional notions of domestic jurisdiction. It operated in tandem with ONUCA's soldiers, but ONUVEN consisted of some 120 civilian observers who monitored the election process, from start to finish, to ensure that it was free and fair. They verified that political parties were equitably represented in the Supreme Electoral Council; that there was political, organizational, and operational freedom for all political parties; that all political parties had equal access to state television and radio broadcasts; and that the electoral rolls were drawn up fairly. It also reported any perceived unfairness to the Supreme Electoral Council, made recommendations about possible remedial action, and reported to the Secretary-General.

One unusual development was the extent to which the UN operations were linked to supporting efforts from regional and nongovernmental organizations. The Organization of American States (OAS)—in particular the secretaries-general of the UN and the OAS—cooperated closely in diplomatic efforts and in civilian observation. During the Nicaraguan elections, a host of such nongovernmental groups as former U.S. president Jimmy Carter's (the Council of Freely Elected Heads of Government) provided additional outside observers as part of a large international network.

The operation began in August 1989 and ended in February 1990 with the surprising defeat of the Sandinista government. ONUVEN's success—which was fortified by its linkages to the OAS and private groups—has enhanced the prospects of UN election-monitoring teams working within the boundaries of states. This practice has gained wider international acceptance even when no armed conflict has taken place. For instance, from June 1990 to January 1991, the United Nations Observer Mission to Verify the Electoral Process in Haiti (ONUVEH) performed tasks similar to the missions in Nicaragua, which set the stage for subsequent UN action when the duly elected government of Jean-Bertrand Aristide was overthrown. ONUVEN's civilian composition has changed the content of peacekeeping's definition by blurring the distinction between civilian and military operations and between security and human rights.

In neighboring El Salvador, ONUSAL was an essential element in helping to move beyond a decade of brutal civil war in which over 75,000 persons had been killed and numerous human rights abuses had taken place. The government and rebel sides, and their foreign backers, came to a stalemate. This created the conditions for successful UN mediation, although much creativity was required to make it work. Negotiations under the good offices of the UN Secretary-General led to a detailed agreement on January 1, 1992, which was actually initialed a few hours after Javier Pérez de Cuéllar had completed his second five-year term.

An essential component of moving beyond the war was the use of UN civilian and military personnel in what, by historical standards, would have been seen as unacceptable outside interference in purely domestic affairs. Ongoing human rights violations were to be prevented through an elaborate observation and monitoring system that began before an official cease-fire. Previous violations by both the army and the government as well as by the armed opposition, the FMLN, were to be investigated by a truth commission. The highly controversial findings—including the documentation of a former president's approval of the assassination of a dissident archbishop and the incrimination of a sitting defense minister in other murders—served to clear the air, although the exact impact of the political processes within the country took time to have effects. There was also a second commission to identify those military personnel who had committed major human rights violations.

In addition, ONUSAL personnel collected and destroyed many insurgents' weapons and helped oversee the creation of a new national army staff college, where students included former members of the armed opposition in addition to new recruits and members of the national army. Some of the early UN involvement on the ground in El Salvador took place even before the cease-fire was signed, thus putting UN observers at some risk.

Whatever the ultimate value of these experiences for making future UN security operations possible, the renaissance in the world organization can certainly be dated from the Persian Gulf War. The consequences not only influenced governments trying to deal with Central America but also continue to be felt in the international arena. It is to the dramatic actions authorized by the United Nations in 1990–1991 that we now turn.

Moving Toward Enforcement

The operations in the Persian Gulf marked an important point in the history of UN responses to aggression. They also suggested the extent to which changing world politics have created new possibilities for collective security. Diplomats and scholars are struggling with the significance of the international enforcement actions that began in 1990. The implications are uncertain for the nature of state sovereignty and for the practical problems within the political, military, and humanitarian structures of the United Nations.

As indicated at the outset, comprehensive visions and long-term plans for international organizations have limited value. What is vastly more important is world politics and creative adaptations by both the UN of governments and the UN of secretariats. Political changes and crises occur, and then governments and the United Nations react. Precedents are created that circumscribe what is possible later. Given the importance of the actions surrounding events in the Persian Gulf beginning in 1990, it is worthwhile to closely discuss the war, subsequent humanitarian actions, and sanctions.

Strengths and Weaknesses of UN Involvement in the Gulf War

On August 2, 1990, Iraqi armed forces swept past the border of neighboring Kuwait and quickly gained control of the tiny, oil-rich country. The invasion met with uniform condemnation in the United Nations, including the Security Council's first unequivocal statement about a breach of the peace since 1950 and the Korean War. From early August until the end of the year, the Security Council passed twelve resolutions directed at securing Iraq's withdrawal from Kuwait. The council invoked Chapter VII, Articles 39 through 41, to lay the guidelines for the first post–Cold War enforcement action. Resolutions 661 of August 6 and 665 of August 25 called upon member states to establish economic sanctions against Iraq and to use force to police them. Resolution 678 of November 29 authorized member states to use "all necessary means" to expel Iraq from Kuwait and thus represented a major shift in strategy. The organization's experience during the Persian Gulf War contains valuable lessons about the needs of a workable collective-security system for the future.

At Washington's insistence, January 15, 1991, was negotiated as the deadline for the use of military force. Iraq remained in Kuwait past this date, and the U.S.-led coalition of twenty-eight states began military operations two days later.[5] A bombing campaign against Iraq and its troops commenced, followed by a ground war one month later in which about half a million U.S. military personnel were involved. The coalition's victory reversed the Iraqi invasion and occupation. It placed the United Nations at the center of the international security stage.

World politics had changed enough to make possible not only the condemnation of a breach of the peace by the international community but also vigorous action to reverse the Iraqi aggression. Members of the allied coalition lost relatively few lives, but tens of thousands of Iraqi civilians and perhaps many more soldiers were killed, so questions were raised about the proportionality of UN-sponsored actions.[6] The Security Council's process of decisionmaking and the conduct of the war have led some critics to be skeptical about the precise value of the Gulf War as a precedent for subsequent Chapter VII enforcement action.[7] Factors include the overwhelming ability of the United States to lead the organization to serve its goals in the Persian Gulf, the decision to replace nonforcible sanctions with force as the dominant means of ensuring Iraq's compliance with the organization's wishes, the extensive use of force that ensued, and the UN's inability to command and control the operation. Each of these criticisms raises important questions about the ability of the UN's collective-security apparatus to function impartially.

The first criticism of the Persian Gulf War—that the United States too easily used the United Nations to rubber-stamp its own agenda—was a more general criticism of geopolitics after the disappearance of the Soviet Union as a country and as a superpower. Washington used its influence to foster perceived national interests, creating and maintaining a diverse coalition against Iraq. In the view of such critics, the process by which the coalition was created illustrated the extent to which the UN had become a blatant setting for U.S. influence. The UN had never been an impartial forum—Western dominance in the early years had been partially replaced beginning in the 1960s by the Third World's "automatic majority" in the General Assembly, but not in the Security Council. This Third World majority had generated the UN-bashing by two Republican administrations. Yet the United States was able to use its considerable political and economic clout in the Security Council to ensure that its Persian Gulf agenda was approved. Political concessions were provided to the USSR to gain its approval for enforcement and to China for its abstentions (instead of vetoes). Washington promised financial aid and debt relief to a number of developing countries for their votes and withdrew aid commitments to Yemen in retribution for opposing the use of force.

Nonforcible sanctions were overtaken by forcible ones after only three months, since nonviolent means of securing an Iraqi withdrawal also troubled many critics. According to Article 42, the Security Council may authorize force after all other means of settlement, and economic sanctions in particular, have proven inadequate. Yet the Security Council chose to use military force before the sanctions leveled against Iraq had had a chance to take full effect. Critics pointed out that in South Africa, by contrast, partial sanctions had not been discarded in favor of military force even though that country's racist policy had been condemned for decades. They also noted that Israel's expansion and continued occupation of territories had not been met with either economic or military sanctions. At the same time, sanc-

tions take a long time to take effect, and in the meantime violence occurs under occupation. When economic sanctions were applied later to Haiti, some observers said
military force should have been used and would have caused less suffering.

The third criticism of the handling of the Persian Gulf War is that no limits on
the use of force were enacted and that the organization exerted no control over
the U.S. military operation. According to the Charter, military enforcement operations are to be directed and controlled by the Military Staff Committee (MSC)
so that the UN can exercise control and military forces can be held accountable to
the international community for their actions. As in Korea forty years earlier,
command and control of the Gulf War was in the hands of the U.S.-led coalition
forces. Only this time, in the Persian Gulf, there was no blue flag and no decision
specifically authorizing the preponderant U.S. role. The Security Council was essentially a spectator, but U.S. control appeared necessary for reasons of efficiency
as well as political support.

Resolution 678 authorized "all necessary means" and made no restrictions on
what kind of, how much, and how long force could be used. According to critics,
Washington was therefore left with a blank check to pursue the expulsion of Iraq.
Some argue that authorizations of this kind run contrary to the spirit of the world
organization, especially in this case because there was extensive civilian injury and
damage inside Iraq.

These doubts and criticisms about the handling of the Persian Gulf War are
pertinent to the UN's future security operations not because they are necessarily
accurate but because they are widespread. The Persian Gulf War provides the first
example of the existing security apparatus in an enforcement action in the
post–Cold War era. Although the organization proved successful in achieving its
stated objective—the expulsion of Iraq from Kuwait—the way that this goal was
achieved continues to be debated by diplomats and scholars. Continuous UN decisionmaking was conducted through the Security Council, but the Article 42 variety of collective security was impossible because the UN troops and command
structures foreseen in Article 43 had not been previously agreed upon. There was
simply no alternative to the "subcontract" given to the twenty-eight members of
the U.S.-led coalition. In view of the UN's limited capacities, such a procedure for
major operations seems almost inevitable for the foreseeable future.

In spite of recommendations, the creation of a UN standing force would be
prohibitively expensive. Moreover, it would remove the need to obtain approval
from potential troop-contributing governments before sending troops into combat as long as the Permanent Five agreed. Even in the unlikely event that soldiers
were made readily available to the UN on a standing basis, the Secretary-General
himself points out that the UN will "perhaps never be sufficiently large or well
enough equipped to deal with a threat from a major army equipped with sophisticated weapons."[8] The organization was ill prepared to handle the test posed by the
Persian Gulf War. Finding ways to provide the organization with the logistic, military, and oversight capacities for future operations remains a high priority for the
international community, but not one that is likely to be met in the near future.

Medical personnel from the multinational forces carry an Iraqi refugee into a camp near Safwan, Iraq, in March 1991. (UN Photo 158302/J. Isaac)

Forceful Action in Northern Iraq on Behalf of Humanitarian Values

On April 5, 1991, the Security Council passed Resolution 688. It declared that Saddam Hussein's repression of Kurdish and Shiite populations constituted a threat to international peace and security. It insisted that Iraq allow access to international relief organizations so that they could care for the beleaguered groups. Elite troops from the United States, the United Kingdom, France, and the Netherlands moved into Iraq—without explicit approval from the Security Council—and carved out a safe haven above the thirty-sixth parallel, which they guarded to ensure the security of UN relief operations. The council had already taken a broad view of its duty to protect human rights in Rhodesia and South Africa, but this resolution was a dramatic and straightforward linkage between human rights and international peace and security. In Iraq, the Hussein government agreed to the presence of UN agencies working with Iraqi Kurds, but obviously under Western military pressure.

Resolution 688 and ensuing relief efforts represent a controversial response to state-sponsored human rights abuse, which is the focus of Part 2 of this book. Many in the West applauded the resolution as a vigorous step toward establishing a way to enforce human rights protection,[9] but others feared the precedent. "Who decides?" became a rallying cry for those, particularly in the global South, who opposed granting the Security Council, dominated by Western foreign policy interests, the authority of Chapter VII to intervene for humanitarian reasons. Later humanitarian responses—in Somalia, Bosnia and Herzegovina, Rwanda, Haiti, Kosovo, and East Timor—have served to keep the debate alive about the weight to be given state sovereignty relative to the international community's duty to protect human rights.

The effort under UN auspices in northern Iraq was "an extraordinary remedy, an exception to the postulates of State sovereignty and territorial inviolability that are fundamental to the traditional theory if not actual practice of international law."[10] These events suggest a double standard. Certain humanitarian crises and widespread media coverage create a domestic and international political climate that fosters action by Washington and the United Nations. Similar if not greater humanitarian emergencies in other parts of the world (for example, in Liberia, Angola, or the Sudan) are ignored for long periods.

Nonforcible Sanctions in the Post–Cold War Era: Humanitarian Dilemmas

Economic sanctions have become a viable policy option to give teeth to certain international decisions. As with many other policy tools available in theory to the international community, their use was impeded in practice during the Cold War. After using nonforcible sanctions only twice during the Cold War, the Security Council resorted to them more than a dozen times during the decade of the 1990s. Partial or comprehensive sanctions were decided on by the Security Council against various countries: Iraq, the states of the former Yugoslavia, Libya, Liberia, Somalia, Haiti, and Rwanda. Moreover, the council also imposed them on several nonstate actors, including the Khmer Rouge in Cambodia (when it was called Kampuchea) and the National Union for the Total Independence of Angola (UNITA), and the Afghan faction known as the Taliban, which also calls itself the Islamic Emirate of Afghanistan. More needs to be known about their precise impact, in particular about their negative and sometimes dire humanitarian consequences.[11]

Recent applied research reveals three pertinent challenges. The first results from the nature of modern warfare as exemplified by the Persian Gulf War.[12] The Gulf crisis dramatizes the extent to which the international community's responses in modern armed conflicts can themselves do serious harm to people. The political strategies adopted, the economic sanctions imposed, and the military force authorized by the Security Council not only created additional hardships but also complicated the ability of the UN's own humanitarian agencies to help civilians caught in the throes of conflict. OAS and UN economic sanctions harmed as many as 100,000 people in Haiti in 1993, most of whom were children.

Since the international community has available only a limited range of sanctions when a state refuses to respect a decision made by the Security Council, the question arises as to what better approach might be employed. Before the Security Council decides on enforcement action with potentially major humanitarian consequences, organizations with humanitarian competence and responsibilities could be consulted. Whether the impact is upon citizens in the pariah country or elsewhere, the staff of the United Nations Children's Fund (UNICEF), the United Nations High Commissioner for Refugees (UNHCR), and the World Food Programme (WFP) are well situated to warn against, anticipate, and monitor such consequences. Or if the Security Council decides to proceed, governments could provide resources to the UN system so that it could respond fully to the immediate and longer-term human consequences of sanctions.[13] These options were not explored during the Persian Gulf crisis.

The second challenge is an eminently practical one. It concerns how to provide humanitarian sustenance after the initial outpouring of international concern has subsided and humanitarian interests are left to vie with other causes for the international spotlight. Resolution 688 insisted that Iraq provide the United Nations with humanitarian access to its people. As indicated earlier and as will be pursued in the next part of this book, this resolution was a watershed,[14] but the exact impact of sanctions on the behavior of the Iraqi government is not well understood. There was an obvious backlash in Baghdad against assertive humanitarianism. It would be easy to dismiss out of hand the government's actions, which created havoc for some months with UN and NGO efforts, because this was a regime whose human rights abuses against its own population and brinkmanship tactics were well documented; but behind Iraq's machinations were understandable reactions against the political nature of the international treatment of Iraq. International assistance flowed more easily to minority populations in revolt against Baghdad than to civilians in equal need in parts of the country under the central government's control. The Hussein government continued to test Western resolve; among other actions, in 1996 it provided military aid to one Kurdish faction in its fight for control over another.

The international community exacerbated the difficulties by allowing its attention to wander and by isolating humanitarian decisions from world politics more generally. Having insisted on access to Iraqi civilians in April 1991, most governments and citizens did not seem to care if they were barred from such populations a scant year later. In retrospect, the humanitarian content of Resolution 688 probably should have been an integral part of the earlier terms of the cease-fire (Resolution 687). The same clear Chapter VII restrictions ensuring Iraqi compliance with financial and arms control measures then would have applied also to the humanitarian arena.

The third challenge relates to timing the deployment of UN military forces in conjunction with economic sanctions. Enshrined in the UN Charter is the assumption that nonforcible sanctions should be tried first; only when they fail should collective military action ensue. The suffering civilian populations of the former Yugoslavia and Haiti provided compelling reasons to rethink the conventional wisdom. In the former Yugoslavia, the case could be made that a vigorous and earlier preventive deployment of UN soldiers to Bosnia and Herzegovina (rather than just to Croatia, with a symbolic administrative presence in Sarajevo) might have obviated the later need for sanctions to pressure Belgrade and Serbian irregulars and might have prevented the grisly war that ensued. In fact, this was part of the justification for the preventive positioning of UN observers as part of the United Nations Protection Force (UNPROFOR) in Macedonia in December 1992. In Haiti, some observers, with considerable reason, queried whether an earlier military enforcement action to restore an elected government would have entailed far less civilian suffering than extended economic sanctions did, particularly because the willingness to use such overwhelming force was visible in September 1994.

Operational Quandaries: Cambodia, the Former Yugoslavia, Somalia, Rwanda, and Haiti

The United Nations encountered conditions in several operations during the 1990s that highlight the inadequacy of the traditional principles of peacekeeping. In order to deal with the kinds of challenges faced by the United Nations in operations such as the UN Transitional Authority in Cambodia (UNTAC), the second and third UN Angola Verification Missions (UNAVEM II and UNAVEM III), the UN Protection Force (UNPROFOR) in the former Yugoslavia, the first and second UN Operations in Somalia (UNOSOM), the UN Assistance Mission in Rwanda (UNAMIR), and the UN Mission in Haiti (UNMIH), the world organi-

Participants in an UNTAC demining course learn to cope with tripwires near Siem Reap Town, Cambodia, 1993. (UNHCR Photo/I. Guest)

zation had to develop new practices that moved beyond the traditional peace-keeping mold.

These operations were qualitatively and quantitatively different from UN operations that were backed by states during the Cold War. They indicated that the consent of the parties cannot be assumed; the military effectiveness required from and the dangers faced by UN military forces go far beyond the parameters of traditional lightly armed peacekeepers. Moreover, these operations suggest the magnitude of the new demands on the UN for services that threatened to overwhelm troop contributors and to break the bank. After stable levels of about 10,000 troops and a budget of a few hundred million dollars in the early post–Cold War period, the numbers jumped rapidly. In the mid-1990s, 70,000 to 80,000 blue-helmeted soldiers were authorized by the UN's annualized peacekeeping budget, which approached $4 billion in 1995. Accumulated total arrears in these years hovered around $3.5 billion—that is, almost equal to this budget and approaching three times the regular UN budget. The roller-coaster ride continued between 1996 and 1998, when both the number of soldiers and the budget dropped precipitously by two-thirds, at least partially reflecting the world organization's overextension and professional indigestion. It changed again in the year 2000 as police efforts in Kosovo and military ones in Timor and the Congo began. Throughout, arrears remained at a critical level, and the world organization's cash reserves often covered barely one month's expenditures. Table 3.3 depicts ongoing UN security operations as of December 1999, and Table 3.2, those previously completed.

As the 1990s came to a close, significant cash-flow problems continued—former Under-Secretary-General for administration Dick Thornburg earlier had referred to the situation as a "financial bungee jump"—even if this sum appeared almost trivial or a "bargain" according to a prominent group of bankers.[15] It should be compared with the U.S. Defense Department budget, which was, for example, some $275 billion in 2000. The UN's annual budget for security operations during that same period would represent only a few days of Operation Desert Storm or about the annual budget of the New York City police and fire departments. The assessed U.S. contribution to these operations, about 30 percent of the total bill, was only about .05 percent of the U.S. defense budget.

What exactly were the operational quandaries? The Cambodian operation amounted to the UN's taking over, at least in theory, all the important civilian administration of the country while simultaneously disarming guerrillas and governmental armed forces. The United Nations registered most of the nation for the first democratic election in the country's history. In size and complexity, UNTAC rivaled the contested operation from 1960 to 1964 in the Congo. The UNTAC deployment was based—as are most UN undertakings—on national budgetary projections out of touch with real military requirements. These estimates were based on best-case scenarios; the situation on the ground was closer to worst-case ones.

TABLE 3.2   UN Peace Operations: Completed as of December 1999

Location	Acronym/Name	Duration
Middle East	UNEF I/First United Nations Emergency Force	November 1956–June 1967
Lebanon	UNOGIL/United Nations Observation Group in Lebanon	June 1958–December 1958
Congo	ONUC/United Nations Operation in the Congo	July 1960–June 1964
West New Guinea	UNSF/United Nations Security Force in West New Guinea (West Irian)	October 1962–April 1963
Yemen	UNYOM/United Nations Yemen Observation Mission	July 1963–September 1964
Dominican Republic	DOMREP/Mission of the Representative of the Secretary-General in the Dominican Republic	May 1965–October 1966
India and Pakistan	UNIPOM/United Nations India-Pakistan Observation Mission	September 1965–March 1966
Middle East	UNEF II/Second United Nations Emergency Force	October 1973–July 1979
Afghanistan and Pakistan	UNGOMAP/United Nations Good Offices Mission in Afghanistan and Pakistan	April 1988–March 1990
Iran and Iraq	UNIIMOG/United Nations Iran-Iraq Military Observer Group	August 1988–February 1991
Angola	UNAVEM I/United Nations Angola Verification Mission I	January 1989–June 1991
Namibia	UNTAG/United Nations Transition Assistance Group	April 1989–March 1990
Central America	ONUCA/United Nations Observer Group in Central America	November 1989–January 1992
Angola	UNAVEM II/United Nations Angola Verification Mission II	June 1991–February 1995
El Salvador	ONUSAL/United Nations Observer Mission in El Salvador	July 1991–April 1995
Cambodia	UNAMIC/United Nations Advance Mission in Cambodia	October 1991–March 1992

(*continues*)

TABLE 3.2   (*continued*)

Location	Acronym/Name	*Duration*
Cambodia	UNTAC/United Nations Transitional Authority in Cambodia	March 1992–September 1993
Former Yugoslavia	UNPROFOR/United Nations Protection Force	March 1992–December 1995
Somalia	UNSOM I/United Nations Operation in Somalia I	April 1992–March 1993
Mozambique	ONUMOZ/United Nations Operation in Mozambique	December 1992–December 1994
Somalia	UNOSOM II/United Nations Operation in Somalia II	March 1993–March 1995
Rwanda and Uganda	UNOMUR/United Nations Observer Mission Uganda-Rwanda	June 1993–September 1994
Haiti	UNMIH/United Nations Mission in Haiti	September 1993–June 1996
Liberia 1997	UNOMIL/United Nations Observer Mission in Liberia	September 1993–September
Rwanda	UNAMIR/United Nations Assistance Mission for Rwanda	October 1993–March 1996
Chad and Libya	UNASOG/United Nations Aouzou Strip Observer Group	May 1994–June 1994
Angola	UNAVEM III/United Nations Angola Verification Mission III	February 1995–June 1997
Croatia	UNCRO/United Nations Confidence Restoration Organization in Croatia	March 1995–15 January 1996
Former Yugoslav Republic of Macedonia	UNPREDEP/United Nations Preventive Deployment Force	March 1995–February 1999
Croatia	UNTAES/United Nations Transitional Administration for Eastern Slavonia, Baranja, and Western Sirmium	January 1996–January 1998
Haiti	UNSMIH/United Nations Support Mission in Haiti	July 1996–July 1997
Guatemala	MINUGUA/United Nations Verification Mission in Guatemala	January 1997–May 1997

(continues)

TABLE 3.2   (*continued*)

Location	Acronym/Name	Duration
Angola	MONUA/United Nations Observer Mission in Angola	July 1997–February 1999
Haiti	UNTMIH/United Nations Transition Mission in Haiti	August 1997–November 1997
Croatia	United Nations Civilian Police Support Group	January 1998–October 1998
Sierra Leone	UNOMSIL/United Nations Mission of Observers in Sierra Leone	July 1988–October 1999

A particularly pertinent microcosm of this problem was provided by Japan's desire—sustained in part by U.S. and other pressures—to make a large contribution to this operation in "its own region." Seeking to interpret the restrictive Japanese Peace Constitution in a way that would permit Japan's military forces to participate in UNTAC, in mid-1992 the Diet passed the Law Concerning Cooperation for United Nations Peacekeeping Operations. Japanese self-defense forces could be deployed only if they acted impartially, if a cease-fire had been agreed upon and remained in effect, and if agreement had been obtained from host countries and other parties to the armed conflict.

The lightly armed Japanese engineers who were sent to Cambodia were supposedly to work under the modus operandi of the old-style interpositional peacekeeping of a United Nations Disengagement Observer Force (UNDOF), when in reality UNTAC faced a far more complex and demanding task. The Japanese assumptions would have been reasonable ten years earlier, but in 1992 they were unrealistic. The Japanese soldiers were asked to become involved in tasks for which they were both militarily and constitutionally unprepared. Despite sometimes fatal attacks on its personnel, Japan stayed the course in Cambodia—in part because it was urged to stay by Japanese national Yasushi Akashi, who was head of the UN operation in that country.

Years of internal conflict had left Cambodia's infrastructure devastated and its population displaced. In response, the United Nations invested over $1.6 billion and over 22,000 military and civilian personnel. Yet UNTAC's success was hardly a foregone conclusion, particularly in light of the Khmer Rouge's unwillingness to respect key elements of agreements and Prince Norodom Sihanouk's stated position that the peace process and elections should continue with or without the Khmer Rouge. Failure here could have seriously undermined the confidence of member states attempting an undertaking of this scale or complexity elsewhere.

TABLE 3.3   UN Peace Operations: Ongoing as of December 1999

Location	Acronym/Name	Date Initiated
Middle East	UNTSO/United Nations Truce Supervision Organization	June 1948
India and Pakistan	UNMOGIP/United Nations Military Observer Group in India and Pakistan	January 1949
Cyprus	UNFICYP/United Nations Peace-keeping Force in Cyprus	March 1964
Golan Heights	UNDOF/United Nations Disengagement Observer Force	June 1974
Lebanon	UNIFIL/United Nations Interim Force in Lebanon	March 1978
Iraq and Kuwait	UNIKOM/United Nations Iraq-Kuwait Observation Mission	April 1991
Western Sahara	MINURSO/United Nations Mission for the Referendum in Western Sahara	September 1991
Georgia	UNOMIG/United Nations Observer Mission in Georgia	August 1993
Tajikistan	UNMOT/United Nations Mission of Observers in Tajikistan	December 1994
Boznia and Herzegovina	UNMIBH/United Nations Mission in Bosnia and Herzegovina	December 1995
Croatia	UNMOP/United Nations Mission of Observers in Prevlaka	January 1996
Haiti	MIPONUH/United Nations Civilian Police Mission in Haiti	December 1997
Central African Republic	MINURCA/United Nations Mission in the Central African Republic	April 1998
Kosovo	UNMIK/United Nations Interim Administration Mission in Kosovo	June 1999
East Timor	UNTAET/United Nations Transitional Administration in East Timor	October 1999
Democratic Republic of the Congo	MONUC/United Nations Organization Mission in the Democratic Republic of the Congo	November 1999

The elections in May 1993 were a turning point. A Khmer Rouge attack on a UN fuel and ammunition dump three weeks before the elections in May 1993 exposed how inadequately prepared UN soldiers were to resist even symbolic military maneuvers, let alone a return to full-scale civil war. However, the elections were held and returned Prince Sihanouk to power as the head of a coalition that included the former government and part of the opposition but excluded the Khmer Rouge. The UN's achievement was that the Khmer people struggled for power for the first time by means of a secret ballot. The relative lack of violence—the Khmer Rouge had demonstrated that it could attack with impunity—happened in spite of UNTAC, not because of it. However, since the United Nations began to pull out its personnel as quickly as possible after the elections, some wondered whether the withdrawal was not premature and what, if anything, the UN would do if civil war erupted. However, the best-case scenario of the Paris Accords appears to have been correct.

In the former Yugoslavia, the UN became involved in a military operation on European soil after many years in which regional conflicts were assumed to be a monopoly of developing countries. Although the prospect of a UN field operation in Europe seemed almost surrealistic before the collapse of the Soviet Union, the Balkans and some republics of the former Soviet Union emerged as the possible scene of growth in future demand for UN security operations.[16]

The dissolution of the former Yugoslavia entailed violence and displacement of a magnitude not seen in Europe since World War II. The UN's initial involvement in Croatia, with close to 14,000 peacekeepers, achieved some objectives, but there was massive disregard for law and human welfare. These troops did not prevent ethnic cleansing, detention camps, refugees, killing, and atrocities, particularly in neighboring Bosnia and Herzegovina. Europeans and the Western alliance were unable to get the parties to halt their internecine fighting during 1992. The UN was sucked into a conflict that it had sought to avoid. It was the last resort in trying to ensure the delivery of humanitarian assistance to Muslims and Croats under siege from Serbia and Serbian irregulars.

The 1,500 UN soldiers initially assigned to the Sarajevo area quickly proved to be inadequate. The Security Council later authorized adding 8,000 more soldiers to protect humanitarian convoys and to escort detainees in Bosnia and Herzegovina. The United Nations also asked NATO to enforce a no-fly zone for Serbian aircraft. In an approach reminiscent of the voluntary financing of the United Nations Peace-keeping Force in Cyprus (UNFICYP), the Secretary-General insisted that these additional humanitarian soldiers be provided at no cost to the world organization, and NATO countries responded. Later, U.S. airdrops of food to isolated and ravaged Muslim communities were seen mostly as a symbolic gesture by the Clinton administration, but they helped save lives. These efforts were insufficient to halt the bloodshed or inhibit the carving up of Bosnia and Herzegovina by the Serbs and Croats.

UNPROFOR soldiers in Stari Vitez, Yugoslavia. (UN Photo 186716/J. Isaac)

After months of efforts by the UN special envoy, former U.S. secretary of state Cyrus Vance, and the European Community's mediator, former British foreign minister David Owen, a tenuous plan to create a "Swiss-like" set of ten semiautonomous ethnic enclaves within Bosnia and Herzegovina was finally agreed upon by the belligerents. NATO was approached to help make sure that the agreement—however unacceptable to critics who argued that the arrangements rewarded Serbian aggression—would stick.

This operation would have been the most costly and dangerous UN undertaking to date. NATO plans at the time included contingencies from 50,000 to 150,000 troops, on top of the NATO enforcement of the no-fly zone over Bosnia. But these plans were overtaken almost immediately by renewed Serbian and Croatian military offensives. When former Norwegian foreign minister Thorvald Stoltenberg took over from Cyrus Vance in May 1993, it was clear that Bosnia would be partitioned. Serbian war efforts had left Serbia freely in control of 70 percent of the territory, and Croatia held another 20 percent. The Bosnian Muslims were left with what were euphemistically called UN safe areas, a series of European Gaza Strips, only worse, since they were subjected to repeated military attacks.

Preventive deployment also was initiated at this time in what everyone except the Greeks wished to call Macedonia. In an effort to forestall the type of carnage that had struck elsewhere in the former Yugoslavia, the UN began to deploy 1,000 observers in December 1992. This group reached its full strength half a year later.

The need to interdict overflights by Serbian aircraft was yet another advance in efforts to expand UN-approved security operations. The initial calls by the Security Council for a halt to overflights began in autumn 1992, but it was not until summer 1993 that the United States began to press its allies and NATO began to bomb Serbian positions. But by that time, Serbia and Croatia were already in control of most of the Bosnian territory that they sought. Finger pointing and rhetorical attacks continued in the West throughout 1993, as did violence against civilians.

The situation in the Balkans demonstrated that the United Nations also can provide the means for governments to pretend to do something without really doing very much. There was a shift from Chapter VI to Chapter VII operations, but without the necessary political will to make the shift work. It can even be argued that, ironically, the half measures in Bosnia were worse than no action at all. Given their traditional operating procedures and constraints, UN soldiers were not strong enough to deter the Serbs. But they deterred the international community from the possibility of more assertive intervention under Chapter VII because the troops, along with humanitarian workers, were vulnerable targets. Although assistance to refugees saved lives, it also helped foster ethnic cleansing by stimulating the movement of unwanted populations. Airdrops of food made it seem as if people salved consciences while massive and unspeakable human rights abuses continued unabated. Thus, inadequate UN military and humanitarian action may have constituted a powerful palliative.[17]

The initial feebleness was followed by a steadily growing number of additional UN troops that, although mainly from NATO countries, were equally feeble. This contingent ultimately reached about 50,000 (including a rapid-reaction force mounted by NATO in summer 1995) but in fact never acted as a war-fighting force until it was goaded into action by a Croatian-Bosnian offensive in August and September that pushed the Serbs out of Krajina. No-fly zones were imposed but not fully enforced; other forms of saber rattling, including low-altitude sorties over Serbian positions and warnings about possible retaliatory air strikes, were tried; and the Security Council passed what the *Economist* called "the confetti of paper resolutions."[18] As Lawrence Freedman observed, the Security Council "experimented with almost every available form of coercion short of war."[19]

But the West's token half measures under UN auspices did little to halt Serbian irredentism and consolidation of territory in either Croatia or Bosnia; nor did these measures prevent the initial expansion of Croatian claims in Bosnia. The arms embargo instituted in September 1991 had benefited primarily the Serbs, who controlled the bulk of the military hardware of the former Yugoslav army. Given their traditional operating procedures and constraints—not to mention their small numbers and inadequate equipment—UN soldiers were powerless to deter the Serbs. As stated above, their presence impeded more assertive intervention because these troops, along with aid workers, were vulnerable targets and potential hostages until August 1995. At that time, blue helmets consolidated themselves in central Bosnia, and the Croatian-Bosnian offensive altered dramatically the local balance of military force. The vulnerability of UN "protectors" was regularly invoked by Europeans as a rationale against more forceful military measures.

The idea of "safe areas" brought derision because the least safe places in the Balkans were under UN control. The ultimate ignominy arrived in summer 1995 when two of these enclaves in eastern Bosnia were overrun by Bosnian Serbs whose tactics included mass executions of Muslims. Shortly before this, Serbs had chained UN blue helmets to strategic targets and thereby prevented NATO air raids.

UN peacekeepers in Croatia were unable to implement their mandate because they received no cooperation from the Croats or Krajina Serbs. In Bosnia, UN forces were under Chapter VII but lacked the capability to apply coercive force across a wide front. Shortly before resigning in January 1994 from a soldier's nightmare as UN commander in Bosnia, Lt. Gen. Francis Briquemont lamented the disparity between rhetoric and reality: "There is a fantastic gap between the resolutions of the Security Council, the will to execute those resolutions, and the means available to commanders in the field."[20]

The international community's unwillingness to react militarily in the former Yugoslavia until August 1995 provides a case study of what not to do. This inaction left many of the inhabitants of the region mistrustful of the United Nations and lent a new and disgraceful connotation to the word "peacekeeping." Bound by the traditional rules of engagement (fire only in self-defense and only after being fired upon), UN troops never fought a single battle with any of the factions in Bosnia that routinely disrupted relief convoys. The rules of engagement led to the appeasement of local forces rather than to the enforcement of UN mandates. The provisions for economic and military sanctions in the UN Charter were designed to back up international decisions to counteract aggression and to halt atrocities in just such situations as the one in Bosnia. Yet with apt gallows humor, many in Zagreb and Sarajevo referred repeatedly to the UN soldiers as "eunuchs at the orgy."

In fact, a much heavier dose of NATO bombing and U.S. arm-twisting proved necessary to compel the belligerents, sequestered at Ohio's Wright-Patterson Air Force Base in November 1995, to attempt to reach a political settlement. The Dayton peace agreements laid the groundwork for military deployment by almost 60,000 NATO soldiers (one-third from the United States). Many observers wondered why UN peacekeepers—poorly equipped and without a mandate—were deployed when there was no peace to keep and why NATO war-fighters appeared when there was. Observers usually point to the "Somalia syndrome" as the turning point in soured public attitudes toward the world organization (a case that we will come to next). But Richard Holbrooke, the former U.S. assistant secretary of state who became UN Ambassador in 1999 and is generally credited with having engineered the Dayton accords, suggests, "The damage that Bosnia did to the U.N. was incalculable."[21]

The Dayton peace agreement called on the Security Council to establish a transitional administration to govern the region of Eastern Slavonia, Baranja, and Western Sirmium and on January 15, 1996, the Security Council responded by creating UNTAES (United Nations Transitional Administration for Eastern Slavonia, Baranja and Western Sirmium), which comprised both military and civilian components. The 5,000 troops were tasked with supervising and facilitating demilitarization of the region, monitoring the return of refugees and displaced persons, and assisting in implementing other aspects of the Dayton agreement. The civilian component, comprising primarily civilian police, focused on restoring law and order, organizing and conducting elections, and assisting in the coordination of plans for the development and economic reconstruction of the region. The UNTAES mandate terminated on January 15, 1998, having accomplished those tasks within the power of its limited mandate, yet without the Dayton agreement being fully implemented. United Nations presence was continued in the area, but only by a small civilian United Nations Police Support Group (UNPSG) of 180 officers charged with monitoring the performance of Croatian police mainly in connection with the return of displaced persons.

The UNTAES and UNPSG operations were not, of course, to be the end of UN involvement in this troubled region. As discussed later in this chapter, the Bosnian affair and especially the fall of the Srebrenica "safe area" in July 1995 not only continued to haunt the United Nations but laid the foundation for continued turmoil in the region.

The situation in the Balkans was terrible; but Somalia provided another ghoulish model for UN involvement in internal wars. The Middle East had previously provided analysts with the specter of Lebanonization, meaning the fragmentation of a country along sectarian lines, as one of the worst epithets in politics. Somalia became another example of violent fragmentation, but one without an ethnic logic. A single ethnic group sharing the same religion, history, and language split into heavily armed clans. Somalia had no government in any meaningful sense, and one-third of the population risked death from starvation because humanitarians could not reach the needy; the Security Council at the end of August 1992 authorized 3,000 to 4,000 UN soldiers to help, applying Chapter VII to yet another situation by authorizing the reinforcement of the United Nations Operation in Somalia (UNOSOM I). These troops were to be deployed after the belligerents agreed to supplement an initial infantry battalion of 500 and some 50 unarmed observers. Their goal was to help protect the delivery of humanitarian succor throughout that hapless country.

The first battalion was of no use, and the parties never agreed to accept the deployment of the additional troops. In December 1992 President George Bush ignored his lame-duck status and moved vigorously to propose a U.S.-led humani-

Somalian children receiving food in 1992. (UN Photo 146504/J. Isaac)

tarian intervention. Within days of the passage of Security Council Resolution 794, the first of what would become over 27,000 U.S. troops arrived to provide a modicum of security to help sustain civilians. They were augmented by 10,000 soldiers from twenty-two other countries. This effort was labeled Operation Restore Hope from the American side, or the Unified Task Force (UNITAF), an acronym that reflected the authorization from the Security Council to use force to ensure the delivery of humanitarian relief. With virtually no casualties, humanitarian space was created and modest disarming of local bandits began.

UNITAF ceased operations in April 1993, when the second phase of the UN Operation in Somalia began as authorized by Security Council Resolution 814. For the first time, the Secretary-General directly commanded a military force deployed under Chapter VII. The Security Council authorized UNOSOM II under Chapter VII to use whatever force was necessary to disarm Somali warlords who might refuse to surrender their arms and to ensure access to suffering civilians. At its maximum strength, some 20,000 soldiers and 8,000 logistical troops from thirty-three countries were deployed.

As in Cambodia, almost 3,000 civilian officials were expected to take over the administration of a country, only this time one that was totally without a functioning government. Significantly, the United States initially remained on the ground with logistics troops for the first time under the command of a UN general—who was an officer from a NATO country, Turkey—as well as with another

1,300 soldiers under U.S. command held in reserve as a "rapid-reaction force" in boats offshore and 400 Army Rangers.

In retaliation against attacks on UN peacekeepers and aid personnel, U.S. Cobra helicopter gunships were called in by the UN command in June and July 1993 against the armed supporters of one of the main belligerents, General Mohammed Aideed. These attacks were followed by the arrival of U.S. Army Rangers later in the summer. These violent flare-ups got the United Nations into the awkward business of retaliation, which elicited more violence and the assassination of foreign journalists and aid workers and further attacks on U.S. soldiers, including the ugly scene in October 1993 when the bodies of dead marines were dragged by crowds through the streets of Mogadishu in front of television cameras.

The clumsy shift from Chapter VI to Chapter VII—and from UN to U.S. and then back to UN control, but with an autonomous American rapid-reaction capability—along with the lack of an overall political strategy constituted one set of problems. The absence of political commitment and staying power was yet another. In Washington, the approval of Presidential Decision Directive 25 (PDD 25) in May 1994 marked the official end to the Clinton administration's promultilateral attitude and foreshadowed a major political defeat for the Democratic Party in the following November elections, in which purported U.S. subservience to the United Nations was an abrasive theme. Given the virtual necessity for Washington's participation in major multilateral military operations, the unseemly images of eighteen dead marines in October 1993 were considerably more costly than the tragic loss of these individuals. Military multilateralism was put in abeyance. The "Somalia syndrome" was linked to its predecessor, the "Vietnam syndrome."

Observers have criticized the military's involvement in the Horn of Africa on numerous grounds. Figuring prominently in such observations have been the obsession with Mogadishu and the "wild west" hunt, complete with a wanted poster, for Aideed and especially the unwillingness to get involved in disarmament and nation-building. In addition, there was a striking disequilibrium between the military and humanitarian components. The costs of Operation Restore Hope alone, at $1 billion, amount to three times Washington's total aid contributions to Somalia since independence. Seven months of UNOSOM II in 1993 were estimated to cost $1.5 billion, of which the lowest estimate for humanitarian aid was 0.7 percent of the total and the highest 10 percent.[22] Also, as UN objectives expanded, resources were actually reduced.[23]

When the last UN soldiers pulled out of Somalia in March 1995, the ultimate result of military and humanitarian help was unclear. Three years and some $4 billion had left the warring parties better armed, rested, and poised to resume civil war. Five years after the UN withdrawal the territory and people of Somalia remained without a viable national government.

Another horror had developed simultaneously in East Africa, where carnage in Rwanda set new records for the size and rapidity of refugee flows and numbers of deaths (genocide of perhaps 800,000 of Rwanda's Tutsi minority by the Hutu). International military forces were integral parts of the international responses to the genocide and the suffering that emanated from it. UNAMIR had been present in Kigali for about eight months when the genocide commenced on April 6, 1994. The Security Council actually reduced these UN military forces a few days later and augmented them only after at least a half million people lost their lives and 4 million others (about half the country's population) were involuntarily displaced; about half of this latter group were officially refugees outside Rwanda's borders, and half were internally displaced persons (IDPs). There were two stand-alone initiatives: a two-month security effort through the French Opération Turquoise from June to August in order to stabilize the southwestern part of the country on the basis of Security Council Resolution 929; and the massive two-month logistics effort through the U.S. Operation Support Hope in July and August to provide relief to the Goma region in Zaire. Numerous national contingents also deployed to this region in support of the assistance efforts by the UNHCR.

Ironically, fostering a secure environment—a task in which the military has the clear, comparative advantage—was the least visible operation. The military's cautious standard operating procedures accompanied by the widespread concerns among governments about a possible quagmire paralyzed international military responses for two months while as many as 10 percent of Rwanda's population were murdered. Arguably, Opération Turquoise prevented another refugee crisis of the record-setting magnitude of the one in May in Goma, Zaire, where almost 1 million Rwandan refugees appeared virtually overnight. The first crisis was accompanied by a cholera epidemic that is variously estimated to have killed between 50,000 and 80,000 people.[24] It was alleged, however, that Opération Turquoise also shielded some of the Hutus who had committed genocide.

The military was more successful in doing what civilians normally do better, namely, providing direct assistance to people in need. Massive amounts of food, clothing, medicine, shelter, and water were delivered. Outside armed forces thus made essential contributions by using their unexcelled logistical and organizational resources, but only *after* the genocide had occurred. Rapid military action in April proved totally unfeasible, but the costs of the genocide, massive displacement, and a ruined economy (including decades of wasted development assistance and outside investment) were borne almost immediately afterward by the same governments that had refused to respond militarily a few weeks earlier.

The role of the media in provoking international responses continues to be controversial and understudied.[25] Rwanda illustrates probably better than the other cases that such coverage may be necessary for humanitarian assistance even if it is insufficient for timely and robust military action. When enough gruesome images appear in the media, the daily legislative preoccupation with cost-cutting is momentarily suspended. There is evidence that many wealthier societies, in particular those of the West, are viscerally and ethically unable to ignore certain massive tragedies even though the initial reaction is to do nothing. Rwanda shows, however, that if governments are determined not to send troops, even media coverage of sudden and massive genocide may not change that governmental view. Reactions in the face of some 150,000 deaths in the three-year period beginning in October 1993 in neighboring Burundi indicate that changes in international practices lag substantially behind changes in international rhetoric. There are fewer political risks in costly humanitarian assistance than in early preventive action with possible casualties—or the potential for protracted involvement in a civil war.

The UN's action and inaction in response to the Rwandan crisis stands as one of its greatest acknowledged failures. Several years later, Secretary-General Kofi Annan, who had been in charge of the UN's peacekeeping unit during the crisis, felt compelled during a visit to Kigali to confess, "We must and we do acknowledge that the world failed Rwanda at that time of evil. The international community and the United Nations could not muster the political will to confront it."[26] In a later statement he continued, "There was a United Nations force in the country at the time, but it was neither mandated nor equipped for the kind of forceful action which would have been needed to prevent or halt the genocide. On behalf of the United Nations, I acknowledge this failure and express my deep remorse."[27]

As discussed earlier, the evolving situation in Angola posed serious problems for UNAVEM II. The results of the UN-supervised election in September 1997 were contested by the National Union for the Total Independence of Angola (UNITA), and renewed fighting ensued. Accordingly, the Security Council revised the UNAVEM II mandate to include a larger peacemaking role. On November 20, 1994, a peace agreement, the Lusaka Protocol, was signed between the government and UNITA, and in February 1995 the Security Council set up a new mission, UNAVEM III, to monitor and verify the protocol. Plagued by criticisms that UNAVEM II had been understaffed and underfinanced, the new mission was mandated a force of up to 7,000 military troops and another 1,000 civilian personnel and military observers. However, the Council kept UNAVEM on a short leash and kept the respective mandates to short time periods. Not surprisingly this strategy led to "donor fatigue" and frustration regarding "staying the course." In June 1997, the Security Council transformed UNAVEM III into the UN Observer Mission in Angola (MONUA), which was to assist the conflicting parties in consolidating peace while slowly withdrawing UN military personnel. A civilian police component would continue to verify the fulfillment of the peace agreement. Like the mandate of UNAVEM, MONUA's mandate was kept short and was renewed several times, but no real peace was won.

During the week of December 27, 1998–January 2, 1999, two UN-chartered planes were shot down over UNITA-held territory. A month later the Secretary-General recommended and the Security Council endorsed the liquidation of all MONUA personnel. The situation continued to deteriorate. Thus ten years and $1.5 billion later the UN had failed to establish enduring peace.

Meanwhile in the Caribbean, nine months after the United Nations had overseen the first democratic elections in Haiti, the populist priest Jean-Bertrand Aristide was overthrown by a military junta led by General Raoul Cédras. The inclusion of Haiti in our discussion is of interest for a number of reasons. Although Haiti had not really endured a civil war, it had all the attributes—in particular, massive migration and human rights abuses—of countries that have suffered from violent armed conflict. It was also the target of international coercive actions—that is, both nonforcible and forcible sanctions under Chapter VII of the UN Charter similar to those in the other war-torn countries analyzed earlier. Moreover, the basis for outside intervention was the restoration of a democratically elected government; this precedent has potential implications because of its widespread relevance for other countries in crisis.

Multilateral military forces were essential to the solution that ultimately resulted in late 1994. First, however, came the embarrassing performance of the UN Mission in Haiti (UNMIH I), including the ignominious retreat by the USS *Harlan County,* which carried unarmed American and Canadian military observers, in September 1993 following a rowdy demonstration on the docks in Port-au-Prince. In September 1994, the first soldiers of the UN-authorized and U.S.-led Multinational Force (MNF) landed in Haiti on the basis of Security Council Resolution 940. What Pentagon wordsmiths labeled Operation Uphold Democracy grew quickly to 21,000 troops—almost all American except for 1,000 police and soldiers from twenty-nine countries, mostly from the eastern Caribbean. This operation ensured the departure of the illegal military regime and the restoration of the elected government.

Most important for this analysis, the MNF used overwhelming military force—although there was only a single military person killed in action and the local population was almost universally supportive—to accomplish two important tasks with clear humanitarian impacts. First and most immediately, the MNF brought an end to the punishing economic sanctions that had crippled the local economy and penalized Haiti's most vulnerable groups because the programs of humanitarian and development agencies were paralyzed. Second, the MNF established a secure and stable environment that stemmed the tide of refugees, facilitated the rather expeditious repatriation of some 370,000 refugees, and immediately stopped human rights abuses.

Washington expended about $1 billion for troops—of which only one-fifth was over and above what normal Department of Defense expenditures would have been had the troops been at their home base in the United States—and another $325 million on assistance in the first half year, only a small part of which was administered by American soldiers directly. Once the MNF achieved its goals, it was entrusted at the end of March 1995 with the next UN Mission in Haiti (UNMIH II). The 6,000 soldiers from over a dozen countries had an annual budget of about $350 million. The continued involvement of a substantial number of U.S. Special Forces (2,500) and an American force commander for the UN follow-on operation demonstrated concretely Washington's commitment through the end of February 1996. UNMIH was extended for four additional months at about half its former size (that is, without American soldiers) before it was replaced by the even smaller UN Support Mission in Haiti (UNSMIH) in July for a period of twelve months. A small UN presence was continued for the remainder of the decade, working with the government of Haiti to professionalize the Haitian National Police. These latter periods of UN involvement were characterized by Canadian financial, political, and military leadership.

Haiti provides a relatively straightforward and positive balance sheet. There were few complications or casualties, although the intervention did too little to improve the police and judiciary and absolutely nothing to alter fundamental economic relations. The disparity in the distribution of wealth and power between a tiny elite and the vast majority of the population made Haiti one of the world's most polarized societies; this inequality had led to the rise and fall of Aristide. Ironically, the most important humanitarian impact of the Chapter VII military intervention was probably the end of the Chapter VII economic sanctions, which had devastated the local economy and the poor.

As in other military interventions, the perception that the interests of key states were threatened spurred leadership and risk-taking. The geography of the crisis brought into prominence not just Washington but also Ottawa and several Caribbean countries. The success of the security functions by the military was dramatic, especially because the Chapter VII military operation was authorized to restore democracy rather than respond to a complex emergency. (It is noteworthy that both the U.S. Congress and the Pentagon were initially lukewarm about what turned out to be a considerably successful operation.) The effective use of military force and the resulting humanitarian benefits have led some observers to question the chronology and logic of the UN Charter's calling for nonforcible economic sanctions before forcible military action.

A swifter military intervention undoubtedly would have proved more humanitarian than a tightening of the screws through economic sanctions. It would have accomplished the major goal of replacing the de facto regime with the constitutional authorities but would have avoided the massive suffering and dislocations from sanctions. "Sanctions, as is generally recognized, are a blunt instrument," wrote Boutros-Ghali. "They raise the ethical question of whether suffering inflicted on vulnerable groups in the target country is a legitimate means of exerting pressure on political leaders whose behaviour is unlikely to be affected by the plight of their subjects."[28]

The most significant feature of the international responses just discussed has been the growing willingness to address, rather than ignore, fundamental problems within the borders of war-torn states. Eighty-two armed conflicts broke out in the first half decade following the collapse of the Berlin Wall, and seventy-nine were intrastate wars; in fact, two of the three remaining ones (Nagorno-Karabakh and Bosnia) also could legitimately be categorized as civil wars.[29]

Having gone from famine to feast in the mid-1990s, the United Nations had a bad case of institutional indigestion. The climate had changed so much that Secretary-General Boutros Boutros-Ghali was obliged to write a follow-up, *Supplement to An Agenda for Peace*, to his earlier document. In this January 1995 report he noted, "This increased volume of activity would have strained the Organization even if the nature of the activity had remained unchanged."[30]

Ever–Evolving Peacekeeping: Kosovo, East Timor, and Sierra Leone

The UN's peacekeeping activities, however, did not remain unchanged. In the face of new challenges the approaches of the past were found lacking if not totally inadequate. Yet the demand for action was as great as ever. The Balkans erupted once again into full-scale war and ethnic turmoil in Kosovo. What was hoped to be the beginning of a UN-supervised peaceful transition to independence from Indonesia for the people in East Timor turned into a bloody campaign of violence. In addition to renewed war in Angola, internal conflicts raged in numerous countries across Africa. Among the most serious of these, were the civil wars in Sierra Leone and in the Democratic Republic of the Congo, where the horrors in Rwanda had spilled over into open civil war involving more than a half dozen external actors. In addition, the Security Council held sessions in 1999 on the situations in Western Sahara, Ethiopia/Eritrea, Somalia, Guinea-Bissau, Burundi, the former Yugoslav Republic of Macedonia, Croatia, Bosnia and Herzegovina, Central African Republic, Georgia, Tajikistan, Afghanistan, Iraq and Kuwait, Haiti, Cyprus, Lebanon, Syria, Israel, and Libya.

In the face of these crises the critical question confronting the UN was how to respond effectively. The answer to this question emerged on a case-by-case basis, yet with each new response seemingly informed by and building on the last. The following discussion illustrates the evolution in "traditional" UN peacekeeping.

The Continuing Crisis in the Balkans

The pursuit of the Gulf War and the creation of safe havens for Kurds are clear illustrations of what we referred to in Chapter 1 as military "subcontracting," as was IFOR (the Implementation Force in the former Yugoslavia); a more controversial example is Somalia. As mentioned earlier, the growing relevance of military intervention by major powers in regions of their traditional interests had become obvious in mid-1994. However controversial the results, the gap between UN capacities and demands for action led almost inevitably to calls for action by regional powers or even hegemons with the blessing of the larger community of states through either the explicit or the implicit approval of the Security Council.[31]

The actions of NATO in Kosovo in spring 1999 is a dramatic case in point. Depending on how one reads the script of diplomatic code embedded in Security Council resolutions, the action by NATO could be argued to represent a breach of international law or to have been launched with the implicit approval of the council. The Secretary-General of NATO, Javier Solana, of course, chose the latter interpretation of Security Council Resolution 1199 (September 23, 1998). On the other hand, both Russia and China condemned the action as illegal.[32] A close look at the record would seem to indicate that the NATO interpretation was probably more accurate despite the lack of any explicit statement of authorization. In any case, Secretary-General Annan drew harsh criticism for his speech at the opening of the General Assembly in September 1999. Although he wished the Security Council had been able to give explicit approval to the bombing, he nonetheless could not condone idleness in the face of Serb atrocities.[33]

Throughout 1998, allegations and evidence of Serbian humanitarian and human rights atrocities mounted. By early June, U.S. officials began to hint of the possibility of a NATO military action and suggested they would support a Security Council resolution authorizing such action. Months of diplomatic maneuvering proved fruitless, and it was not until late September that agreement could be reached in the council on a resolution (1199) requesting Yugoslavia to order the withdrawal of its security forces engaged in civilian repression in Kosovo. This first Security Council resolution on Kosovo, however, was rather mild and called on both Yugoslavia and the Kosovo Liberation Army (KLA) to refrain from terrorist actions and implement a cease-fire. Although no explicit mention was made regarding the use of force nor was the phrase "all necessary means" used, NATO soon claimed that such authorization was implied.

Diplomacy continued but failed to change Serbian policy. Time and again Yugoslav president Slobodan Milosevic demonstrated his blatant disregard for negotiated agreements. In late January 1999, U.S. officials shifted away from a diplomatic approach and threatened military action. The UN Secretary-General had apparently arrived at a similar conclusion. In a statement before NATO leaders in Brussels he indicated that indeed force might be necessary. In doing so, he praised past UN-NATO collaboration in Bosnia and suggested that a NATO-led mission under UN auspices might well be what was needed. He concluded:

> The bloody wars of the last decade have left us with no illusions about the difficulty of halting internal conflicts—by reason or by force—particularly against the wishes of the government of a sovereign state. But nor have they left us with any illusions about the need to use force, when all other means have failed. We may be reaching that limit, once again, in the former Yugoslavia.[34]

But neither NATO nor the UN was willing to give up totally the diplomatic approach. Hosting a peace conference in Rambouillet, France, in February, the United States, France, Germany, Italy, Russia, and the United Kingdom—the so-called contact group—endeavored to broker a solution between Yugoslavia and an Albanian Kosovar delegation. But neither side was willing to yield on key points and the talks floundered. The situation in Kosovo deteriorated even further.

On March 24, NATO began a seventy-seven-day aerial bombardment of Serbian targets. Soon after the bombing began, Serbian security forces launched an all-out campaign to exorcise Kosovo of its predominant ethnic-Albanian population. Within weeks a huge segment of Kosovo's 1.8 million ethnic Albanians had been displaced from their houses and villages. As the NATO intervention progressed, air strikes intensified until finally, in the context of a Russian mediated settlement, Milosevic agreed on June 3 to an immediate and verifiable end to the violence and repression and to the withdrawal of all Serbian security forces.

Other aspects of the agreement included the deployment under UN auspices of an effective international civilian and security presence with substantial NATO participation, the establishment of an interim administration, safe return of all refugees and displaced persons, demilitarization of the KLA, and a substantially self-governing Kosovo.

The NATO intervention had proceeded without explicit Security Council authorization, yet support for the action seems to have been rather broad-based. Two days after the air war was launched, a Belarus-, Russian-, and Indian-cosponsored draft resolution demanding an immediate end to the use of force by NATO was overwhelmingly defeated in the Security Council by a vote of three in favor (China, Namibia, and Russia) to twelve opposed.

On June 10, 1999, the Council, in a 14–0–1 vote (China abstained), adopted a resolution—S/RES/1244(1999)—authorizing an international civil and security presence in Kosovo under UN auspices. NATO's "humanitarian war" had been unusual to say the least.[35] But this new UN peace mission, the UN Interim Administration Mission in Kosovo (UNMIK) was unprecedented in its nature and scope. NATO authorized 49,000 troops to maintain security, but UNMIK was to assume authority over all the territory and people of Kosovo, including judicial, legislative, and executive powers. It was to move the region toward self-governance; perform all normal civilian administrative functions; provide humanitarian relief, including the safe return of refugees and displaced persons; maintain law and order and establish the rule of law; promote human rights; assist in reconstructing basic social and economic infrastructure; and facilitate the development of a democratic political order.

The mission was path breaking in integrating several non-UN international organizations under a unified UN leadership. It was organized around four substantive pillars: civil administration (UN-led); humanitarian affairs (UNHCR-led); reconstruction (European Union-led); and democratic institution building (OSCE-led). The scope was mind boggling. Civil administration, for example, was to be comprehensive, including health, education, energy and public utilities, post and telecommunications, judicial, legal, public finance, trade, science, agriculture, environment, and democratization. Over 800,000 people had to be repatriated. Over 120,000 houses had been damaged or destroyed. Schools needed to be reestablished; food, medical aid, and other humanitarian assistance provided;

Kosovo refugees from Roma are on the move in search of safety in June 1999. (UN/UN-HCR/R. LeMoyne)

electrical power, sanitation, and clean water restored; land mines cleared and security ensured; and so on. Although the initial UNMIK mandate was twelve months, the return of life in Kosovo to any semblance of normality will be a long time in coming. The notion of helping to create a liberal democracy in an area that had never known it seemed particularly optimistic.

Turmoil in East Timor

After over a decade and a half of UN-mediated efforts to resolve the issue of the status of East Timor, an agreement was reached on May 5, 1999, between Indonesia and Portugal regarding a process to determine the future of that long-troubled territory. The two states agreed that the UN Secretary-General would be responsible for organizing and conducting a popular consultation to determine whether the people of East Timor would accept or reject a special autonomous status within the unitary Republic of Indonesia. A rejection of such special status would mean that the UN would be responsible for administering the territory during the transition to independence. Security Council Resolution 1246(1999) on June 11 established the UN Mission in East Timor (UNAMET) with the mandate of conducting such a consultation. After several postponements the popular vote was held on August 30, and the special autonomy status option was overwhelmingly rejected in favor of independence.

News of the outcome stirred prointegration forces backed by armed militias to violent action. Within a matter of weeks nearly a half million East Timorese were displaced from their homes and villages. Indonesian military troops and police

According to government sources, an estimated 230,000 East Timorese had been displaced to West Timor by the end of September 1999. In Wini Camp, many of the displaced have only palm-frond huts for shelter. (UN/UNHCR/F. Pagetti)

were either unwilling or not able to restore order, and the security situation deteriorated. On September 15 the Security Council, in Resolution S/Res/1264(1999), authorized the creation of a multilateral force to restore order and protect and support UNAMET and welcomed member states to lead, organize, and contribute troops to such a force. Sitting in the wings ready to act, an Australian-led force began arriving in East Timor less than a week later. Numerous arms had been twisted in Jakarta so that Indonesia "requested" the coalition force. In less than a month general order was restored, and the Indonesian People's Consultative Assembly voted on October 19 to formally recognize the results of the popular consultation. The following week the Security Council unanimously approved Resolution S/Res/1272(1999), establishing the UN Transitional Administration in East Timor (UNTAET).

As in the case of UNMIK, the nature and scope of the UNTAET mission was exceedingly ambitious and wide-ranging. It was empowered to exercise all legislative and executive powers and judicial authority; establish an effective civil administration; assist in the development of civil and social services; provide security and maintain law and order; ensure the coordination and delivery of humanitarian assistance, rehabilitation, and development assistance; promote sustainable development; and build the foundation for a stable liberal democracy. To carry out this mandate, authorization was given for a military component of 8,950 troops and 200 observers and a civilian police component of up to 1,640 personnel. As 1999 drew to a close, the security situation in East Timor was stable, and by spring 2000 the peacekeeping transition from INTERFET to UNTAET had been completed and the processes of reconstruction and state building were under way. Any evaluation of such an effort at UN "trusteeship" must await the passage of time.

Reestablishing Stability in Sierra Leone

The year 1999 brought both great sorrow and hope to the people of Sierra Leone, who were reeling from over eight years of civil war. The bloody civil conflict that had intensified during 1998 turned even bloodier in January 1999, when rebel forces once again captured the capital, Freetown, and launched on a four-day spree of killing and destruction. Judges, journalists, human rights workers, government officials, civil servants, churches, hospitals, prisons, UN offices, and others were targets of the rebel alliance, comprising forces of the former junta and the Revolutionary United Front (RUF). Over 6,000 were killed and about 20 percent of the total stock of dwellings was destroyed. The UN Observer Mission in Sierra Leone (UNOMSIL), which had been established in June 1998, was evacuated.

Fighting continued throughout the spring and early summer, uprooting more than a million people, about 450,000 of whom fled to neighboring Guinea. The issue remained on the Security Council agenda, and the Council kept extending UNOMSIL's mandate several months at a time. Finally, on July 7, 1999, a peace agreement, called the Lomé Peace Agreement, was negotiated between the government and the RUF. The Security Council responded positively to this move and on August 20 adopted unanimously Resolution S/Res/1260(1999), extending and expanding the UNOMSIL mandate. The UN presence was further expanded in October when the council adopted yet another resolution (S/Res/1270(1999)), creating a new mission, the UN Mission for Sierra Leone (UNAMSIL), which was mandated the tasks of: establishing a presence at key locations throughout the territory of Sierra Leone in order to assist the government of Sierra Leone in implementing the disarmament, demobilization, and reintegration of rebel troops; ensuring the security and freedom of movement of UN personnel; monitoring adherence to the cease-fire agreement of May 18, 1999 (S/1999/585, annex); encouraging the parties to create confidence-building mechanisms and support their functioning; facilitating the delivery of humanitarian assistance; supporting the operations of UN civilian officials, including the special representative of the Secretary-General and his staff, human rights officers, and civil affairs officers; and providing support, as requested, for the elections, which are to be held in accordance with the present constitution of Sierra Leone.

Although not as broad ranging or complex as the new missions in Kosovo and East Timor, a force of 6,000 soldiers (from Nigeria, Kenya, and Guinea) was authorized under Chapter VII with the authority to use force if necessary to protect UN personnel and civilians under imminent threat of physical violence. In early 2000 the situation in Sierra Leone remained generally stable but tense as 45,000 former combatants remained armed and in control of the diamond mines.

Conclusion

What are the lessons for the United Nations that emerge from the security operations after the Cold War?

These three new operations represent a qualitatively different kind of UN peace mission. Although earlier efforts in Cambodia and El Salvador were ambitious, these are of a different magnitude. They are exceedingly complex and multidisciplinary. They represent attempts to create or re-create civil order and respect for the rule of law where governance and stability has either broken down or been nonexistent. They entail reconstructing the social and economic infrastructure, building democratic political institutions, providing humanitarian assistance, and much more. As stated above, "learning by doing" seems the order of the day. Not to act seems to many unthinkable, and how precisely to act remains uncertain. But these kinds of challenges are what lie ahead for UN peacekeepers in the early twenty-first century.

Lawyers are quick to point out that the language of Article 2(7) of the Charter remains intact. But governmental organizations, intergovernmental organizations (IGOs), and nongovernmental organizations (NGOs) have redefined when, in the language of this article, it is possible "to intervene in matters which are essentially within the domestic jurisdiction of any state." Sometimes there is no sovereign (as in failed or collapsed states like Somalia),[36] and sometimes sovereignty is overridden in the name of higher norms (as in the case of the Kurds in northern Iraq).[37]

Observers continue to debate the extent to which the present world disorder is new or old,[38] but the two dominant norms of world politics during the Cold War—namely, that borders were sacrosanct and that secession was unthinkable—no longer generate the enthusiasm that they once did, even among states. At the same time, an almost visceral respect for nonintervention in the internal affairs of states has made way for a more subtle interpretation, according to which on occasion the rights of individuals take precedence over the rights of repressive governments and the sovereign states that they represent.[39]

Until early in 1993, the dominant perception of outside intervention under UN auspices was largely positive. Rolling back Baghdad's aggression against Kuwait along with the dramatic life-saving activities by the U.S.-led coalitions in northern Iraq and initially in Somalia had led to high hopes. In spite of the lack of resolve in Bosnia, it seemed possible that we were entering an era when governments and insurgents would no longer be allowed to abuse their citizens with impunity. Although it seems almost quaint in retrospect, some analysts even worried then about "the new interventionists."[40]

Subsequently, enthusiasm has been tempered by the realities of UN operations. There certainly is no evidence of a diminishing number of complex emergencies within which the military might help quell ethnic violence, create humanitarian space, and protect fundamental human rights. One is not obliged to agree with Robert Kaplan's apocalyptic visions[41] to recognize a distressing fragmentation of societies that may require outside military intervention if minorities are not to be subjugated or annihilated—which of course is also an option, although states are loath to admit as much publicly.

The virulent backlash against multilateral military intervention seems to have been overcome by the efforts in 1999. However, it is essential to keep in mind that coercive military intervention necessitates a revision of conventional wisdom regarding the lack of consent for Chapter VII operations. By definition, intervention does not require "consent" from the warring parties, but it does from the domestic constituencies of troop-contributing countries and from affected local populations.[42]

Thus there is a progression of three steps underlying this lesson. First, intervention must be preceded by establishing and maintaining the consent of the publics that send their sons and daughters into hostile environments. For example, Americans were prepared for possible casualties prior to Washington's involvement on the ground in Kuwait and Iraq, but they were not prepared, nor was their consent sought, in the Somalia case. Second, although consent by definition is not forthcoming from local belligerents for Chapter VII, the consent of local populations must be sought and nurtured. Again, Somalia illustrates the neglect by third-party intervenors of local populations manipulated easily by belligerents into believing that those who come to assist them are contributing to their pain. Third and finally, with legitimacy established for possible deaths in action of soldiers and for the presence of "outsiders," there should be no compromises made in robustly making all requisite military efforts to establish quickly a secure environment.

If there is no commitment to satisfying all three steps, then there should be no intervention. The "messiness" of intervention comes from both lack of legitimacy and lack of efficiency, which the first lesson addresses. A well-planned, systematic response is required, but only after consent has been garnered from local populations in both troop-contributing states and the area of conflict. It is necessary for outsiders to reestablish security quickly and credibly in part of a disputed territory even if subsequently additional reinforcements are sent or another strategy evolves. This is the opposite of a slowly-turning-the-screws approach in the hopes that either political will or a meaningful strategy will appear over time. If there is no clarity about mission and little commitment to equipping the UN to act responsibly, "then the U.N. and the world at large," in John Ruggie's words, "are better off by lowering the organization's military profile and not muddling in the strategic calculus of states."[43]

And what about the UN as something of an independent variable, the semi-independent actor staffed with a semiautonomous civil service? Without putting too fine a point on it, we maintain that the history of security operations after the Cold War indicates that the United Nations is incapable of exercising command and control over combat operations. The capacity to plan, support, and command peacekeeping, let alone peace-enforcement, missions is scarcely greater now than during the Cold War. And this situation will not change in the foreseeable future.

States have made modest improvements to augment the UN secretariat's anemic military expertise and intelligence capacities—for example, a round-the-clock situation room and satellite telephones—and still others are feasible and desirable. The Canadians and Dutch have been joined by twenty-two other countries as "the friends of rapid reaction," and they proposed in 1996 a mobile military headquarters capable of fielding command teams within hours of a Security Council decision. Seven states (Austria, Canada, Denmark, the Netherlands, Norway, Poland, and Sweden) have signed an agreement to set up a 4,000-member UN Standby High Readiness Brigade, which could be used by the Security Council for peacekeeping or preventive operations. Although its existence would perhaps be helpful in exercising a restraining effect on combatants, the real problem is the reluctance of states to move quickly and to authorize forces large enough to do the job. There is no chance that states will empower the world organization with the wherewithal to contradict Michael Mandelbaum's judgment that "the U.N. itself can no more conduct military operations on a large scale on its own than a trade association of hospitals can conduct heart surgery."[44]

There are two reasons for arguing that the United Nations as actor should distance itself from actually exercising coercion. First, states are unwilling to provide the Secretary-General with the necessary tools for Chapter VII. Standby troops and funds, independent intelligence, and appropriate systems for command and control along with professional personnel are simply not forthcoming. There is simply no question of independent action.

Second, and perhaps more important, the strength of the office of the Secretary-General lies in its impartiality, which is derived from the lack of vested interests. Former UN Assistant Secretary-General Giandomenico Picco has argued persuasively that "transforming the institution of the Secretary-General into a pale imitation of a state" in order "to manage the use of force may well be a suicidal embrace."[45] When the security situation has somewhat stabilized, the Secretary-General must be prepared to facilitate the administration of collapsed states, but *after* the warring parties themselves are exhausted or cleansed from a territory or following a humanitarian intervention. Proceeding in these ways requires separating military intervention from civilian administration in order to break a cycle of violence and to create both a respite and the preconditions for a return of an interim government. Moreover, in order to maintain credibility as a third party, the United Nations—insofar as it is separate from states—should refrain from taking sides. Fen Hampson concludes his comprehensive study on the UN's nego-tiating the end to five ethnic conflicts with the suggestion "Enforcement is there-fore best left to others."[46] The UN Security Council should still authorize enforce-ment on selected occasions, but such efforts should be subcontracted to regional arrangements or coalitions of the willing.

The failure to distinguish between the military operations that the United Na-tions secretariat can manage (traditional and even slightly muscular peacekeep-ing) and those that it cannot and should not (enforcement) has led to obfusca-tion. The latter are problematic under any circumstances, but they have given governments that are unable and unwilling to act decisively the opportunity to treat the United Nations as scapegoat. One is reminded of the third UN Secretary-General, U Thant, who commented wryly, "It is not surprising that the organiza-tion should often be blamed for failing to solve problems that have already been found to be insoluble by governments."[47]

Other illustrations occurred as we went to press. With Richard Holbrooke in the Security Council presiding in January 2000, the focus was on Africa's woes. Everyone agreed that a peacekeeping force in the Democratic Republic of the Congo was desirable. Yet, with what is somewhat hyperbolically called "Africa's World War," the force of some 5,000 soldiers was way too small when there was no peace to keep.

At the same time, a positive recent development within the UN has been the ability, on occasion, to call a spade a shovel. The UN Secretary-General's 1999 re-port on Srebrenica and the Ingmar Carlsson report on Rwanda contain plenty of blame to go around and were followed by two other remarkably frank docu-ments—about the failings of sanctions against Angola chaired by Robert Fowler and about the state of UN peacekeeping machinery chaired by Lakhdar Brahimi.[48] To return to a central theme, it is important to hold states accountable for a lack of political will but also to hold senior officials' feet to the fire because they are autonomous actors in crises who are capable of choices, of doing the right or the wrong thing. Political will, or the lack thereof, is important. But peo-ple matter as well.

Notes

1. For a discussion of this historical period, see Thomas G. Weiss and Meryl A. Kessler, "Moscow's U.N. Policy," *Foreign Policy* no. 79 (Summer 1990), pp. 94–112. For a series of essays about the initial impact of these changes, see Thomas G. Weiss and Meryl A. Kessler, eds., *Third World Security in the Post–Cold War Era* (Boulder: Lynne Rienner, 1991); Thomas G. Weiss and James G. Blight, eds., *The Suffering Grass: Superpowers and Regional Conflict in Southern Africa and the Caribbean* (Boulder: Lynne Rienner, 1992); and G. R. Berridge, *Return to the UN* (London: Macmillan, 1991).

2. When the Soviet Union dissolved, Russia was its successor state. As such, it assumed the permanent seat on the Security Council beginning in 1991.

3. In general see Tom J. Farer, ed., *Beyond Sovereignty: Collectively Defending Democracy in the Americas* (Baltimore: Johns Hopkins Univ. Press, 1996).

4. See Mats R. Berdal, *Disarmament and Demobilisation After Civil Wars* (Oxford: Oxford Univ. Press, 1996).

5. Washington's shift to forcible liberation occurred just after U.S. congressional elections. The Senate approved of the new strategy by only five votes, which almost led to a constitutional crisis in the United States over "war powers."

6. For a discussion of the legitimacy of the Persian Gulf War, see Oscar Schachter, "United Nations Law in the Gulf Conflict," and Burns H. Weston, "Security Council Resolution 678 and Persian Gulf Decision Making: Precarious Legitimacy," both in *American Journal of International Law* 85, no. 3 (July 1991).

7. For a series of skeptical views, see essays by Stephen Lewis, Clovis Maksoud, and Robert C. Johansen, "The United Nations After the Gulf War," *World Policy Journal* 8, no. 3 (Summer 1991), pp. 539–574.

8. Boutros Boutros-Ghali, *An Agenda for Peace: Preventive Diplomacy, Peacemaking and Peace-keeping* (New York: UN, 1992), para. 43.

9. This controversial subject was launched by the French government, especially by Mario Bettati and Bernard Kouchner, *Le devoir d'ingérence* (Paris: DeNoël, 1987); Bernard Kouchner, *Le malheur des autres* (Paris: Odile Jacob, 1991); and Mario Bettati, *Le droit d'ingérence* (Paris: Odile Jacob, 1996).

10. Michael Reisman and Myres S. McDougal, "Humanitarian Intervention to Protect the Ibos," in Richard Lillich, ed., *Humanitarian Intervention and the United Nations* (Charlottesville: Univ. of Virginia Press, 1973), p. 168.

11. See further David Cortright and George A. Lopez, eds., *Economic Sanctions: Panacea or Peacebuilding in a Post–Cold War World?* (Boulder: Westview Press, 1995). Previous research had concentrated largely upon the utility of sanctions as a foreign policy tool of the United States. See Gary Clyde Hufbauer, Jeffrey J. Schott, and Kimberly Ann Elliott, *Economic Sanctions Reconsidered: History and Current Policy*, and *Economic Sanctions Reconsidered: Supplemental Case Histories* (Washington, DC: Institute for International Economics, 1990), which updated *Economic Sanctions in Pursuit of Foreign Policy Goals* (Washington, DC: Institute for International Economics, 1983). However, their forthcoming work has important multilateral dimensions: *Economic Sanctions Reconsidered* (Washington, DC: Institute for International Economics, forthcoming). See also David A. Baldwin, *Economic Statecraft* (Princeton: Princeton Univ. Press, 1985); and Theodore Goldi and Robert Shuey, *U.S. Economic Sanctions Imposed Against Specific Countries: 1979 to the Present* (Washington, DC: Congressional Research Service, 1992). The use of multilateral economic sanctions has recently become the subject of analysis. See, for example, Lisa Martin, *Coercive Cooperation: Explaining Multilateral Economic Sanctions* (Princeton: Princeton Univ. Press, 1992); and *Political Symbol or Policy Tool? Making Sanctions Work* (Muscatine, IA: Stanley Foundation, 1993). For a discussion of the humanitarian consequences, see David Cortright, George A. Lopez, Larry Minear, and Thomas G. Weiss, *Political Gain and Civilian Pain: The Humanitarian Impact of Economic Sanctions* (Boulder: Westview Press, 1997).

12. For a discussion of these issues, see Larry Minear and Thomas G. Weiss, "Groping and Coping in the Gulf Crisis: Discerning the Shape of a New Humanitarian Order," *World Policy Journal* 9, no. 4 (Fall-Winter 1992), pp. 755–777. For more details with particular reference to the performance of international institutions, see Larry Minear, O. B. P. Chelliah, Jeff Crisp, John Mackinlay, and Thomas G. Weiss, *United Nations Coordination of the*

International Humanitarian Response to the Gulf Crisis, 1990–1992, Occasional Paper no. 13 (Providence, RI: Watson Institute, 1992).

13. In many ways, the call to make provisions for vulnerable populations in the wake of sanctions is analogous to efforts to mitigate structural adjustment policies. For a discussion, see Richard Jolly and Ralph van der Hoeven, eds., *Adjustment with a Human Face—Record and Relevance, World Development* (special issue) 19, no. 12 (1991). For general discussions of this issue, see Lori Fisler Damrosch, "The Civilian Impact of Economic Sanctions," in Damrosch, ed., *Enforcing Restraint: Collective Intervention in Internal Conflicts* (New York: Council on Foreign Relations, 1993), pp. 274–315; and Patrick Clawson, "Sanctions as Punishment, Enforcement, and Prelude to Further Action," *Ethics and International Affairs* 7 (1993), pp. 17–37. For a controversial look at the human costs in Haiti, see Harvard Center for Population and Development Studies, *Sanctions in Haiti: Crisis in Humanitarian Action* (Cambridge, UK: Program on Human Security, November 1993).

14. See Thomas G. Weiss and Kurt M. Campbell, "Military Humanitarianism," *Survival* 32, no. 5 (September-October 1991), pp. 451–465; Jarat Chopra and Thomas G. Weiss, "Sovereignty Is No Longer Sacrosanct: Codifying Humanitarian Intervention," *Ethics and International Affairs* 6 (1992), pp. 95–117; and David J. Scheffer, "Toward a Modern Doctrine of Humanitarian Intervention," *University of Toledo Law Review* 23, no. 2 (Winter 1992), pp. 253–293.

15. See *Financing an Effective United Nations* (New York: Ford Foundation, 1993), a report of an expert group chaired by Paul Volker and Shijuro Ogata.

16. For a discussion of these possibilities before the UN's involvement in the former Soviet bloc, see Thomas G. Weiss and Kurt M. Campbell, "The United Nations and Eastern Europe," *World Policy Journal* 7, no. 3 (Summer 1990), pp. 575–592. For a more recent treatment, see Jarat Chopra and Thomas G. Weiss, "Prospects for Containing Conflict in the Former Second World," *Security Studies* 4, no. 3 (Spring 1995), pp. 552–583.

17. This argument is made in greater depth in Thomas G. Weiss, "Collective Spinelessness: U.N. Actions in the Former Yugoslavia," in Richard H. Ullman, ed., *The World and Yugoslavia's Wars* (New York: Council on Foreign Relations, 1996), pp. 59–96.

18. "In Bosnia's Fog," *Economist*, April 23, 1994, p. 16.

19. Lawrence Freedman, "Why the West Failed," *Foreign Policy* 97 (Winter 1994–1995), p. 59.

20. "U.N. Bosnia Commander Wants More Troops, Fewer Resolutions," *New York Times*, December 31, 1993.

21. Quoted by Alison Mitchell, "Clinton's About-Face," New York Times, September 24, 1996, p. A8. For a discussion of the impact of Somalia, see Tom J. Farer, "Intervention in Unnatural Humanitarian Emergencies: Lessons of the First Phase," *Human Rights Quarterly* 18, no. 1 (February 1996), pp. 1–22; and Thomas G. Weiss, "Overcoming the Somalia Syndrome—'Operation Rekindle Hope'?" *Global Governance* 1, no. 2 (May-August 1995), pp. 171–187.

22. See Debarati G. Sapir and Hedwig Deconinck, "The Paradox of Humanitarian Assistance and Military Intervention in Somalia," in Thomas G. Weiss, ed., *The United Nations and Civil Wars* (Boulder: Lynne Rienner, 1995), p. 168.

23. Chester Crocker, "The Lessons of Somalia," *Foreign Affairs* 74, no. 3 (May-June 1995), pp. 2–9.

24. See Larry Minear and Philippe Guillot, *Soldiers to the Rescue: Humanitarian Lessons from Rwanda* (Paris: OECD, 1996); Gérard Prunier, *The Rwanda Crisis: History of a Geno-*

cide (New York: Columbia Univ. Press, 1995); Joint Evaluation of Emergency Assistance to Rwanda, *The International Response to Conflict and Genocide: Lessons from the Rwandan Experience*, 5 vols. (Copenhagen: Joint Evaluation of Emergency Assistance to Rwanda, March 1995).

25. For discussions of this phenomenon, see Robert I. Rotberg and Thomas G. Weiss, eds., *From Massacres to Genocide: The Media, Public Policy, and Humanitarian Crises* (Washington, DC: Brookings Institution, 1996); Larry Minear, Colin Scott, and Thomas G. Weiss, *The News Media, Civil War, and Humanitarian Action* (Boulder: Lynne Rienner, 1996); Charles C. Moskos and Thomas E. Ricks, *Reporting War When There Is No War* (Chicago: McCormick Tribune Foundation, 1996); Edward Girardet, ed., *Somalia, Rwanda, and Beyond: The Role of the International Media in Wars and Humanitarian Crises* (Dublin: Crosslines Communications, 1995); Johanna Newman, *Lights, Camera, War* (New York: St. Martin's Press, 1996); and Nik Gowing, *Real-Time Television Coverage of Armed Conflicts and Diplomatic Crises* (Cambridge, UK: Harvard Shorenstein Center, 1994).

26. Kofi Annan, Address to the Parliament of Rwanda, Kigali, May 7, 1998 (SG/SM/6552).

27. Kofi Annan, "Statement on Receiving the Report of the Independent Inquiry into the Actions of the United Nations during the 1994 Genocide in Rwanda," United Nations, New York, December 16, 1999.

28. Boutros Boutros-Ghali, *Supplement to An Agenda for Peace*, document A/50/60-S/1995, January 5, 1995, para. 70, reprinted in *An Agenda for Peace 1995* (New York: United Nations, 1995) along with the 1992 *An Agenda for Peace*. Paragraph numbers are the same in the original.

29. United Nations Development Programme, *Human Development Report 1994* (New York: Oxford Univ. Press, 1994), p. 47.

30. Boutros-Ghali, *Supplement*, para. 77.

31. See Thomas G. Weiss, ed., *Beyond UN Subcontracting: Task-Sharing with Regional Security Arrangements and Service-Providing NGOs* (London: Macmillan, 1998).

32. *Financial Times*, October 8, 1998.

33. Kofi Annan, "Secretary-General's Speech to the 54th Session of the General Assembly," September 20, 1999.

34. UN Press Release SG/SM/6878, January 28, 1999.

35. Adam Roberts, "NATO's 'Humanitarian War' in Kosovo," *Survival* 41, no. 3 (Autumn 1999), pp. 102–123.

36. Gerald B. Helman and Steven R. Ratner, "Saving Failed States," *Foreign Policy* 89 (Winter 1992–1993), pp. 3–20; and I. William Zartman, ed., *Collapsed States: The Disintegration and Restoration of Legitimate Authority* (Boulder: Lynne Rienner, 1995).

37. For a series of essays, see Gene M. Lyons and Michael Mastanduno, eds., *Beyond Westphalia? National Sovereignty and Intervention* (Baltimore: Johns Hopkins Univ. Press, 1995); Paul A. Winters, ed., *Interventionism: Current Controversies* (San Diego: Greenhaven Press, 1995); Marianne Heiberg, ed., *Subduing Sovereignty: Sovereignty and the Right to Intervene* (London: Pinter, 1994); and Laura W. Reed and Carl Kaysen, eds., *Emerging Norms of Justified Intervention* (Cambridge, MA: American Academy of Arts and Sciences, 1993).

38. See Mohammed Ayoob, "The New-Old Disorder in the Third World," in Thomas G. Weiss, ed., *Collective Security in a Changing World* (Boulder: Lynne Rienner, 1993), pp. 13–30.

39. See Nigel Rodney, ed., *To Loose the Bonds of Wickedness: International Intervention in Defence of Human Rights* (London: Brasseys, 1992).

40. Stephen John Stedman, "The New Interventionists," *Foreign Affairs* 72, no. 1 (1993), pp. 1–16. For an exhaustive review of the literature, see Oliver Famsbotham and Tom Woodhouse, *Humanitarian Intervention in Contemporary Conflict* (Oxford: Polity Press, 1996). See also John Harriss, ed., *The Politics of Humanitarian Intervention* (London: Pinter, 1995); James Mayall, ed., *The New Interventionism: United Nations Experience in Cambodia, Former Yugoslavia, and Somalia* (New York: Cambridge Univ. Press, 1996); and Jan Neederveen Pieterse, ed., *World Orders in the Making: Humanitarian Intervention and Beyond* (London: Macmillan, forthcoming).

41. Robert D. Kaplan, "The Coming Anarchy," *Atlantic Monthly* 273, no. 2 (February 1994), pp. 44–76, and *The Ends of the Earth: A Journey at the Dawn of the 21st Century* (New York: Random House, 1996).

42. We are grateful to Cindy Collins for this insight.

43. John Gerard Ruggie, *The United Nations and the Collective Use of Force: Whither? or Whether?* (New York: United Nations Association of the USA, 1996), p. 1.

44. Michael Mandelbaum, "The Reluctance to Intervene," *Foreign Policy* no. 95 (Summer 1994), p. 11.

45. Giandomenico Picco, "The U.N. and the Use of Force," *Foreign Affairs* 73, no. 5 (September-October 1994), p. 15.

46. Fen Osler Hampson, *Nurturing Peace: Why Peace Settlements Succeed or Fail* (Washington, DC: U.S. Institute of Peace Press, 1996), p. 226.

47. U Thant, *View from the U.N.* (Garden City, NY: Doubleday, 1978), p. 32.

48. Kofi Annan, *Report on the Fall of Srebrenica*, document A54/549, 15 November 1999 and *Report of the Independent Inquiry into the Actions of the United Nations During the 1994 Genocide in Rwanda*, document S/1999/1257, 15 December 1999; *Report of the Panel on United Nations Peace Operations*, document A/55/305-S/2000/809, 21 August 2000; and *Report of the Panel of Experts on Violations of Security Council Sanctions Against UNITA*, document S/2000/203, 10 March 2000.

4 Groping into the Twenty–first Century

Political Dynamics at the End of the 1990s

In looking ahead to UN security operations, one can ask about the political dynamics that will propel UN activities. The political landscape, which reappears in the next two parts of this volume, helps us examine how the Secretary-General and the international secretariats can respond to the security challenges of the post–Cold War era.

Throughout the preceding discussion, certain political factors have emerged that drive the UN's new security operations. The end of the East-West struggle has placed the United States and its Western allies in an unusual leadership position; with their consent and political support the United Nations is theoretically able to play a growing role in maintaining international peace and security. Developing countries—still referred to as the "Third World" or the "Global South"—no longer can block effective international efforts simply because the Western industrialized countries are on the other side.

The end of the East-West struggle has also removed the lid and permitted the explosion of violence and civil wars. States continue to be the main forces in international politics, but they are increasingly subject to pressures from nonstate actors. A more comprehensive view of security characterizes international debates. This view of security reflects a complex reality, not just of the military arena but also of human rights and sustainable development, which we analyze later. A vague sense of moral obligation to those outside one's own borders has always spurred philanthropists and humanitarians; technology now makes awareness of the plight of others instantaneous and more poignant. Interdependence, stemming from technological and communications innovations and also from economic linkages and environmental deterioration, has lessened the control that states exercise over their economies, cultures, and political structures.

What does this all mean for the future of the United Nations? After coping with fifty years of limitations on its activity, can it perform a far more ambitious role as orchestrator of the peace, or will it simply face new limitations? The answer is complex. The peace and security mechanisms of the United Nations need reform;

the world organization is woefully overstretched; and the UN can and must adapt to the needs of the next generation of operations.

The complexity of the answer partially reflects the turmoil of our times. Chapter 3 began with a discussion of the rebirth of the United Nations in the late 1980s and early 1990s and ended with hopeful uncertainty tinged with some disillusionment. Today, the hopefulness of that earlier period seems like ancient history. The almost giddy euphoria surrounding the end of the Cold War was remarkably short-lived; policy and scholarly communities have awakened with a hangover and more sober appreciations of the state of international peace and security.

The two key documents written by the sixth UN Secretary-General, Boutros Boutros-Ghali, reflect this whipsaw in changing world politics and provide a useful way to introduce this chapter and the world organization inherited by the seventh UN Secretary-General, Kofi Annan.[1] We should recall that in January 1992, the Security Council requested that the newly elected Secretary-General assess the promise of the United Nations in a changed world. Less than six months later, in June 1992, *An Agenda for Peace* was published. No other recent international public policy document has generated so much discussion by practitioners and scholars. Boutros-Ghali's report framed debate and contained many intriguing suggestions, but it is at its most ambitious in defining the UN's potential for multilateral conflict management.

Barely two and a half years later—and with the problems in Bosnia, Somalia, and Rwanda very much in the news—Boutros-Ghali recognized how much his proposals had exceeded the expectations of governments and the abilities of the United Nations. In a progress report issued in January 1995 to mark the UN's fiftieth anniversary, *Supplement to An Agenda for Peace*, the Secretary-General trimmed his sails. He retreated and recommended caution because of phenomena that had been partially or totally unforeseen in 1992. Among them are two of the developments that were discussed in some depth in Chapter 3—the intensity and ugliness of internal conflicts and the quantitative and qualitative changes in UN efforts to deploy multifaceted operations. The new document was mainly a call for reduced expectations and UN activities. This new reticence vis-à-vis military efforts was reinforced by a bipartisan set of proposals on the eve of the 1996 American presidential elections.[2] Kofi Annan continued the theme of modest expectations beginning with his acceptance speech in mid-December 1996.

It would be useful to examine these two documents in some depth. The subtitle for Secretary-General Boutros Boutros-Ghali's 1992 *An Agenda for Peace* is *Preventive Diplomacy, Peacemaking and Peace-Keeping*. In each of these areas, the Secretary-General makes proposals to enhance traditional activities where the UN has demonstrated its capacities and to launch new and untried activities that require an increased willingness to run risks. These two kinds of activities are distinct. Boutros-Ghali's document provides a structure for our discussion here because of its importance to states in framing the ongoing international debate about security, particularly regarding the deployment of UN troops.[3]

Kofi Annan, seventh Secretary-General of the United Nations and former Under-Secretary-General for Peace-keeping Operations, confers with Lieutenant-General Philippe Morillon, former UNPROFOR commander in Bosnia and Herzegovina. (UN Photo 183500/M. Tzovaras)

The use of military personnel under UN command and control could be expanded to advantage in a number of areas where they have been used in the past: supervising confidence-building measures related to military downsizing, fact-finding in areas of tension, staffing early-warning and crisis-prevention centers with intelligence data supplied by governments to the United Nations, and participating in operations between belligerents (in either interstate or civil conflicts) when they agree.

For such activities, the report made some concrete suggestions about implementation. Improving personnel, logistics, information, and, above all, financing would be desirable and feasible. Although appropriate action is hardly a foregone conclusion, some of the steps for governments are well understood. A number of countries have indicated their willingness to alter behavior on such items as logistic support and payments schedules, and recent sessions of the General Assembly have made strides toward addressing issues of better financing.

Significant dissent surrounds the idea of reinvigorating the Military Staff Committee (MSC) and creating a standing force.[4] The exact role of the five permanent members versus that of other troop contributors looms large in any possible restructuring of the MSC, which was supposed to support the Security Council's enforcement actions but which remains moribund. The negotiation of Article 43 agreements also poses problems, mostly in terms of removing decisionmaking about combat from governments and of raising domestic legal issues in the United States and elsewhere. NATO procedures for operations are characterized by professionalism and trust in NATO headquarters. In contrast, there are notorious problems of command and control within the United Nations, and these are likely to endure in the near term. The fledgling first efforts in Somalia were hardly encouraging in this respect.

There is virtually no UN track record and even less consensus among governments and experts for the several military initiatives outlined by the Secretary-General. World politics is increasingly characterized by levels of violence in micronationalist struggles that were not imagined by the framers of the Charter or even by pundits a few years ago.[5] The search for order may be no simpler in the near future than it was in the recent past as decolonization and self-determination take new forms and as ethnic particularism comes to dominate the local and global agenda. Already the Soviet Union and Yugoslavia have given birth to almost twenty countries; Somalia and Haiti ceased in 1993 to have anything resembling organized governance, earning the appellation of "failed states."

In the face of this new world disorder, the most important uses of UN security forces involve armed conflicts where consent of the parties may be absent or short-lived, and the military need is likely to be well beyond the traditional light arms used by peacekeepers. Obviously, major political and operational dilemmas result.

For example, preventive deployment of UN forces is the centerpiece of preventive diplomacy to forestall strife. If only one country or party to a civil conflict requests troops, the United Nations could become a party to the conflict by taking sides, thereby hindering mediation by the world organization, which needs a sterling reputation for impartiality in order to mediate. Or even if parties to a conflict agree initially to a preventive buffer, one of them could change its position and ask the UN to leave. The disastrous pullout of forces from UNEF I in 1967 based on an Egyptian request led to war. This serves as a pertinent reminder of what happens when states change policy about the desirability of a cease-fire. The departure of UNEF I inevitably contributed to another Mideast conflagration; now pressures can be exerted on the United Nations to remain when parties change their minds and return to armed conflict. But UN forces cannot be easy targets. If they stay, they have to become combat forces with the chance to prevail.

It is even possible that the early presence of UN forces could foster moves toward violent secession. Preventive deployment still may be desirable in these circumstances, as illustrated by the operation in Macedonia that began in December 1992. Yet governments that provide troops on the basis of consent and the likelihood of low or no casualties may not wish to continue under altered conditions. When a preventive force is deployed, the contingencies that could require various types of escalation later must be agreed on in advance. This requirement may discourage responses from traditional troop-contributing countries or potential new ones such as Japan and Germany.

The protection of UN administrative and humanitarian personnel is an obvious and growing challenge stressed in *An Agenda for Peace*. But citing peacekeeping and the UN guards contingent in Iraq is not useful. As described earlier, the strength of peacekeepers arose more from the moral backing of the international community than from any military wherewithal. Furthermore, UN guards were helpful in Iraq for a time not because of their own military capabilities, which consisted mainly of security officers armed with pistols and clad in blue baseball caps. The successful performance of duties was related to three realities: The UN guards were based in a country whose population and military had been bombed into submission by the allied war effort; Iraq initially found them less odious than Western soldiers; and the physical presence and backup firepower of the allied coalition remained in the area as insurance against Iraqi hostility.

The most significant departures in the report are organized, somewhat surprisingly and confusingly, under the rubric of peacemaking. The usual notion concerns such peaceful measures as mediation and good offices, outlined in Chapter VI of the UN Charter and discussed earlier in this volume. In an unusual stylistic presentation, one that confuses readers and decisionmakers, peacemaking in *An Agenda for Peace* includes even such Chapter VII actions as economic and military sanctions. Although it is not well formulated, this is a key idea. The creation of "peace enforcement units" would be a major departure in the sense that ceasefires would be guaranteed by UN soldiers when parties no longer agreed to respect a negotiated halt to carnage. The Secretary-General recognizes that such soldiers would need "to be more heavily armed than peacekeeping forces and would need to undergo extensive preparatory training" and that the tasks envisioned could "exceed the mission of peacekeeping forces and the expectations of peacekeeping force contributors."[6]

Conceptual issues in *An Agenda for Peace* should be clarified because they obscure practical insights. Diplomats, international civil servants, and scholars need to squarely face a series of conceptual issues. Although there is a different Secretary-General, the issues have not been resolved, and Kofi Annan's term has done little to alter the fundamental ambiguities in concepts.

First, what type of prominence should be accorded to state sovereignty? Several times Secretary-General Boutros Boutros-Ghali affirms the importance of conventional notions of sovereignty. These notions are also reiterated in many debates and international forums. At the same time, he presents a host of arguments about the erosion of state sovereignty. Unlike his predecessor, Javier Pérez de Cuéllar (who at the end of his term began to clearly address the limits of sovereignty in the new order[7]) or his successor, Kofi Annan (who as we have seen above sees a distinct limit to claims of sovereignty when gross violations of human rights are concerned) Boutros-Ghali appeared hesitant to emphasize enforcement actions—for example, in humanitarian emergencies or in gross violations of human rights—where sovereignty is being superseded.

Many countries, not just in the West but also in the Third World, are reevaluating their positions.[8] During the 1990s conventional notions of state sovereignty in countries like Somalia and Yugoslavia made little legal or operational sense. In Somalia there was no effective sovereign; in Yugoslavia genocidal actions meant that sovereignty was being exercised irresponsibly or not at all. The Secretary-General treated this shibboleth gingerly, perhaps seeking to satisfy critics in developing countries who continue to treat the term and the notion of "state sovereignty" as something so sacrosanct that it cannot be called into question.

Second, the nature and dynamics of peaceful relationships require that we pay more attention to nonstate actors and to differentiating among them based on their importance to the issue at hand. *An Agenda for Peace* approaches peace almost exclusively as involving relations among constituted political authorities, especially states. This is an inaccurate view of how peace is negotiated and sustained.

Conflicts have deeper roots than governments or armed opposition groups hoping to assume power. The origins of armed conflicts as well as their mitigation and management must be conceived broadly enough to include a host of such nongovernmental actors as clans and the International Committee of the Red Cross (ICRC). People make war and people make peace. Experience in the Sudan,[9] for example, suggests that the UN as an intergovernmental organization is frequently at a disadvantage in dealing with irregular forces and insurgents. Moreover, private relief agencies may be better placed than intergovernmental ones for delivery of goods in war zones. The role of nonstate intermediaries in internal armed conflicts may be heightened in the post–Cold War era. Nongovernmental organizations (NGOs) and other nonstate actors are less important in the security arena than in human rights and sustainable development, as we see later in this book. Nonetheless, the United Nations must take them more adequately into account in a working international security system.

The final conceptual clarification, with the most direct impact on UN military operations, concerns the changing nature of what John Mackinlay and Jarat Chopra have aptly labeled "second generation multinational operations."[10] In its newest and most dangerous operations the United Nations needs in some cases to move beyond the consent of warring parties and to resort to military capabilities that were not available to UN soldiers in the past.

It is more accurate to speak of a departure from peacekeeping rather than a mere extension of the traditional operations, which are at the opposite end of a continuum from Chapter VII enforcement. The most interesting proposals in *An Agenda for Peace* fall between these extremes: preventive deployment, military assistance to civil authorities, protection of humanitarian relief efforts, guaranteed rights of passage, and enforcement of cease-fires.

These proposals constitute at least a "Chapter six-and-three-quarters" because they are even closer to Chapter VII. They require a level of military professionalism and discipline not commonly found in earlier UN operations. They require routine participation from the armies of major powers. Accomplishing the tasks in these operations goes far beyond both the expectations and the capacities of most countries that have contributed troops to UN peacekeeping operations during the Cold War. In the words of Mackinlay and Chopra, "It has become clear that the UN's resourcefulness as a mediator has outstripped its capability as a military organizer and that a more effective military response is now required by the newly defined tasks of the second generation of UN activity. Peacekeeping cannot be adapted any further to perform these tasks. A more practical instrument is needed."[11]

The United Nations has virtually no professional military expertise, and the secretariat in New York is unable to increase its capacities in this area. A temporary increase in military personnel lent by Western governments was ended in the late 1990s when the G-77 countries complained about the imbalance. As new operations were being initiated in Timor, Kosovo, and the Congo, the Department of Peacekeeping Operations could draw upon fewer staff than the Department of Public Information.

Pacifists can bemoan the resort to force by a peace organization, but Secretary-General Boutros-Ghali addresses new and dangerous challenges. And policy changes by governments and secretariats are proposed to take the world organization in the direction of a more professional military.

The literal position of UN troops is dangerous and awkward. Many analysts, diplomats, and UN staff stumble more figuratively when they fail to distinguish clearly old-style "peacekeeping"—the interposition of neutral forces when warring parties have agreed to a cease-fire, or at least to putting one in place. They employ the same term—even if qualified by such adjectives as "wider" peacekeeping by Whitehall or "aggravated" peacekeeping by the Pentagon—for a variety of situations where consent is absent or problematic and where military capacity outranks moral authority. The confusion is even greater when an operation shifts from Chapter VI to VII (Somalia and Rwanda) or combines the two (the former Yugoslavia).

The United Nations has demonstrated for several decades that it can manage Chapter VI military operations. We should recall that peacekeeping is often called "Chapter six-and-a-half," former Secretary-General Dag Hammarskjöld's clever indication that this UN invention was not foreseen by the Charter's framers. But peacekeeping is really an extension of Chapter VI rather than a would-be Chapter VII. If governments so wished, management and financial reforms undoubtedly could improve peacekeeping because each operation is still put together from scratch in an ad hoc manner and based on best-case scenarios with inadequate resources.

At the same time, the United Nations also has demonstrated its inability to handle Chapter VII, which the Secretary-General clearly recognized in his 1995 *Supplement*: "Neither the Security Council nor the Secretary-General at present has the capacity to deploy, direct, command and control operations for this purpose."[12] The inability to manage full-scale or even selective enforcement cannot be wished away; nor can it be overcome by tinkering. The world organization's

Rwandan refugees returning to Gisenyi from Goma, Zaire, in July 1994. (UN Photo 186788/J. Isaac)

diplomatic and bureaucratic structures are inimical to initiating and overseeing military efforts when serious fighting rages, where coercion rather than consent is the norm.

Part of the problem has been that until very recently the United Nations has relied too heavily on the experience of past operations when coping with post–Cold War crises instead of delineating distinct new characteristics. Peacekeeping should be reserved for consensual missions, which is where the UN secretariat has a comparative advantage. Otherwise, peacekeeping becomes an infinitely elastic concept without operational significance. It is not a cure-all for the chaos of ethnonationalism but a discrete tool for conflict management when consent is present and political rather than military expertise is required.

In his first press conference of 1995, as he was about to introduce the new conventional wisdom, Secretary-General Boutros-Ghali straightforwardly recognized "that the United Nations does not have the capacity to carry out huge peace enforcement operations, and that when the Security Council decides on a peace enforcement operation, our advice is that the Security Council mandate a group of

Member States, (those which) have the capability."[13] In the *Supplement* itself, he notes that peacekeeping and enforcement "should be seen as alternative techniques and not as adjacent points on a continuum."[14]

From the contrast between the changing world politics of 1992 and those of the mid-1990s, as well as the UN Secretary-General's depiction of the world organization's problems and prospects, there emerged three conceptual challenges for the United Nations as it moved toward the next generation of activity: the nature of sovereignty, the role of nonstate actors, and the lack of UN operational capacities. Recent and future UN reforms can be categorized into three groupings that complete this chapter: operational, representational, and professional.

Operational Changes: Adapting to New Conflicts

As has been argued throughout preceding sections, the nature of conflict is changing. And the United Nations is being called on to deal with kinds of armed conflict not imagined when the UN Charter was drafted. The world organization and its member states probably will not often face the classic interstate confrontation that precipitated the collective response in the Persian Gulf War. Instances of cross-border attacks from national armies aimed at annexation of another state's territory are becoming rarer. *Intra*state conflict is replacing *inter*state conflict as the dominant menace to international peace and security. Fueled by ethnic, economic, and nationalist desires for autonomy inside the borders of existing geographic states, civil war is becoming the most common form of armed conflict. Insurgent groups fight existing governments or sometimes other insurgents either for control or for secession.

The UN's security mechanism was not designed to deal with violence and wars of this kind, and the blue helmets have encountered their most significant problems in attempting to quell internal wars. More than 1,500 blue-helmeted soldiers have died while serving in the United Nations since 1948, more than half in the last decade. Although the ideal of collective security could be applied to intrastate activity, the UN Charter was designed to prevent recurrences of World War II— characterized by the invasion of one state by another. The world organization is ill equipped to deal with conflicts existing within internationally recognized borders. Improving its capabilities in this area requires changes in the approach to sovereignty and the operational components of international forces in order to safeguard peace and security.

The extent to which the principle of state sovereignty has been the foundation of the international system should be clear to readers by now. Despite the presence of numerous challenges to the supremacy of states, states are unwilling as a matter of principle in most instances to cede sovereignty to improve the functioning of the UN. However, changes in world politics in the past half century have steadily chipped away at the foundation, and changes since the mid-1980s have created a new potential for multilateral action.[15] Sovereignty, of course, has never been a fixed notion. Notwithstanding the observers who see national interests and military power as the only answer to an anarchical international system, recent political changes—the immediate ones after the Cold War and the deeper ones resulting from interdependence—have on occasion and for some countries shifted the balance between the authority of states and the authority of international society.[16]

The United Nations itself reflects an institutional structure created in one historical period that is trying to cope with the challenges of a different era. A conceptual and operational leap must be made, striking a new balance between state sovereignty and the needs for effective UN security operations in the post–Cold War era. A Westphalian vocabulary is of doubtful utility for Somalias, Rwandas, Liberias, Burundis, Timors, and Yugoslavias. A first step would be a straightforward confrontation with the meaning of "consent" when there is no sovereign or when a sovereign acts in an opprobrious way and pursues genocide as a policy. If the international community is willing through the Security Council to apply, instead of to talk about, the use of overwhelming force, then consent is unnecessary. If not, then the consent of powerful local actors remains the sine qua non of successful UN operations.

Conceptual and practical alterations to the UN's military operations need to parallel those made in the domain of sovereignty. How is the United Nations to operate effectively in intrastate conflicts where the consent of warring parties is likely to be less than that found in traditional operations or where consent evaporates after the parties have agreed to stop fighting but find that elections or other events no longer go their way? The world organization requires military teeth when it runs the risk of encountering active and perilous opposition. Future UN security operations need to be better armed and more able to operate like professional armies. But if political will is not present, it is better to negotiate with powerful parties. Otherwise, the Security Council discredits itself.

In particular, two types of military operations merit and have been receiving more routine implementation. First, there is the growing and obvious need for military support for humanitarian activities.[17] In spite of the UN's efforts in Bosnia and Herzegovina, Somalia, and northern Iraq, former Secretary-General Boutros-Ghali's two reports were remarkably reticent about ensuring that truly opprobrious behavior against civilians by governments or insurgents is no longer tolerated. Such actions amount to "intervention," a term that does not figure in the reports. To enforce new standards of behavior, Boutros-Ghali chose to sidestep this issue, mainly, one suspects, to avoid sensitivities in developing countries toward outside interference in what many governments still argue are their legitimate domestic affairs. As discussed earlier, his successor, Kofi Annan, has been less hesitant in this regard.

On the one hand, it is understandable that Boutros-Ghali wished to avoid the controversy and bitterness of the General Assembly's annual discussions of humanitarian matters. On the other hand, his approach was difficult to fathom because his report responded to a request from the January 1992 summit of the Security Council, which cited the need to respond to nonmilitary threats to the peace, including humanitarian crises. Among the major powers in the South, China and India continued to maintain fervent postcolonial interpretations of nonintervention even as they were willing to intervene unilaterally in Tibet or Sri Lanka. The paradox—Article 2(7) was originally overruled to permit decolonization—has not yet dawned on their diplomats. Militaries around the world have assets that could be used effectively in humanitarian crises; recruitment literature has begun to feature soldiers performing humanitarian duties. A further discussion of this capacity occurs in the next part of this book, which is particularly pertinent because the humanitarian imperative is what appears to be driving foreign policy in much of the Western World and support for enhanced activities by the United Nations.

The second type of operation, peace-enforcement units, represent the crossover point after traditional peacekeeping. Unlike many proposals—for example, for fact-finding or preventive diplomacy—this one is controversial and worrisome: The exact nature of the commitment of governments to the next generation of UN forces will quickly become clear when peace enforcement is debated. The fault line will become obvious with answers to such questions as, What happens when there is a dramatic change in the basis on which contributors have originally supplied troops? What kind of reserve firepower will the Security Council make available? How will the Permanent Five and other major powers participate? Who needs to agree to a cease-fire—all warring parties or just some of these parties or the Security Council? When will the Security Council make the decision to "enforce" the peace—before a breakdown occurs or only after a new crisis has arisen?

Several proposals have been put forth by the Secretaries-General and scholars in regard to ways in which the UN can effectively upgrade its military capacity. In addition to supporting the establishment of peace-enforcement units, they have called for the conclusion of some Article 43 agreements with governments concerning their troop contributions; these negotiations have been stalled since the late 1940s. Standing forces would appear prohibitively expensive, but troops on reserve or standby status (that is, on call for UN service but maintained in their country of origin until duty calls and a government agrees) appear more feasible than in the past.

The world organization would then have a reserve body of trained forces immediately deployable. The existence of standby forces could allow for preventive peacekeeping where conflict seems imminent. Preventive deployment could take place when requested by two states seeking to discourage hostilities from taking place between themselves or by a single country threatened by military attack. Peace-enforcement units, which are outside the framework of Article 43 according to the Secretary-General, would probably never deter aggression by a big power but "would be useful . . . in meeting any threat posed by a military force of a lesser order."[18] Moreover, such forces could serve as a tripwire that when crossed or engaged could unleash Chapter VII proceedings and act, in the words of a group of parliamentarians, "as a deterrent to possible aggression by another state and as a signal of the resolve of the international community."[19]

Although the Cold War stopped the MSC from becoming an operational reality for directing enforcement operations, the ongoing collaboration among the permanent members of the Security Council could be exploited further. Enforcement operations under the command of the MSC are quite unlikely, but the body could serve as a useful, informal source of military expertise for the Secretary-General and his staff. The Security Council would continue to decide, on a case-by-case basis, what type of command and central arrangement would be used.

The organization searches for ways and money to upgrade its military capability to meet future needs. The financing for peacekeeping lags far behind demand. Both Boutros Boutros-Ghali and Kofi Annan, like their predecessors, have been categorical in this regard. Boutros-Ghali, for example, lamented, "A chasm has developed between the tasks entrusted to this Organization and the financial means provided to it. The truth of the matter is that our vision cannot really extend to the prospects opening before us as long as our financing remains myopic."[20] In spite of increased demand and praise, peacekeeping arrears have grown steadily since the Nobel Peace Prize was awarded to UN peacekeeping forces.

An absolute priority should be given to placing ongoing and future UN military operations on more solid financial bases. Implementation of some of the Secretary-General's suggestions could bring relief, particularly those for accelerating payments, reducing arrears through more discipline in payments schedules, and levying interest on arrears. One noncontroversial item, the creation of a $50-million revolving fund to help the United Nations move more swiftly, was implemented in 1993; this fund should be enlarged to reflect UN operations. Budgeting UN military operations as a national defense allocation, as is the case in some countries, rather than as an expenditure of the foreign ministries would go a long way toward better fact-finding, preventive diplomacy, and peacekeeping. UN operations should be recognized as a specific contribution to a country's national security.

As mentioned earlier, the amount contributed by member states should be contrasted with the sums spent on defense worldwide. Annual global defense expenditures were over $1 trillion at the moment that the UN's peacekeeping coffers were over $1 billion in arrears. Ten billion dollars would be available if every country devoted 1 percent of its defense budget to UN military efforts. Other measures such as surcharges on the sale of weaponry and on the use of UN-provided services—for example, ensuring the right of passage for ships—could perhaps help provide more income, although these options are politically dubious. There is no real alternative to governments' respecting their international treaty obligations to pay the bills for UN security operations, the solution supported by an independent group of bankers and politicians.[21]

Representational Changes: Adapting the Organization's Structure to the Interstate System

In the aftermath of the Cold War, the Security Council has begun to fulfill its duties as a guarantor of international peace and security. It has begun to act in a more unified manner and to avoid disagreements about procedures and more important matters. Permanent-member goodwill manifested itself in the shelving of the veto for three years beginning in May 1990, and there has been only scarce resort to it since. However, future changes in the international climate could render the Security Council less able to provide for peace and security. A new economic conflict pitting the industrialized North against the unindustrialized South is smoldering in the ashes of the Cold War. Dominated by security initiatives sponsored by the West, the council requires a more widely shared sense of the societal values underpinning security decisions. This requirement emerges in light of the influence of the United States in the Security Council. States must find a way to address this concern. Two possibilities are reform in the council and greater use of regional organizations.

The collapse of the Soviet Union has left the Security Council with a composition that generally is sympathetic to the interests of the West.[22] With the Soviet Union no longer acting as a counterbalance to the United States, states such as India, Brazil, Nigeria, and Egypt believe that they deserve greater say in the council's decisionmaking. The continuing permanent membership of France and Great Britain, whose international influence has declined significantly since 1945, offends Japan and Germany, whose influence in decisionmaking is in no way commensurate with their funding of the organization's activities. Countries like Canada that contribute troops routinely to all UN operations complain of being left out of decisions that affect their soldiers.

Reform of the Security Council's permanent membership has become a subject increasingly discussed in both the corridors and the plenaries of intergovernmental forums. Possibilities for long-term reform involve changes in the Security Council's permanent membership; shorter-term changes involve longer and more frequent terms on the council for influential countries such as Japan, Germany, Nigeria, India, Egypt, and Brazil.

In spite of unequivocal rhetorical support from Washington and the fact that many other governments have declared themselves in favor of changing the composition of the Security Council, each major structural reform opens another Pandora's box: Which developing countries should be added? Why should they be the most powerful or populous? After a civil war, should a splintered state retain its seat? Why should economic powers whose constitutions impede overseas military involvement be given a seat? Should there be three permanent European members? What about the European Union (EU)? Which countries should wield vetoes?

The introduction of changes could create additional decisionmaking problems that could result in stalemates like those faced by the Security Council during the Cold War. Assuming the continuation of at least some North-South ideological, political, and economic tensions that reflect growing disparities in wealth, decisionmaking in the council could become as paralyzed in the future as it was in the past. Instead of an automatic Soviet veto, other effective vetoes from dissenters or foot-draggers could now thwart the Security Council.

To enhance the decisionmaking power of the council under these circumstances, reform of the veto system also has been proposed. This system has always been controversial because the interests or even the whims of a single permanent member can impede effective action when the rest of the international community is prepared to act. Although it is unlikely that the veto could be eliminated altogether, proposals have been made to lessen its impact. These include limiting the range of areas in which the veto can be used, allowing its use only when an item affects a permanent member's "supreme national interests," instituting a system of weighted voting that would allow the council to override a veto, and increasing the total number of negative votes needed to veto a resolution.

The establishment of trigger mechanisms to ensure that the Security Council at least debates the issues also would facilitate international scrutiny during crises even if decisionmaking were not more rapid or effective. Such triggers could consist of numerical thresholds—for example, numbers of refugees or deaths—or a request from an independent and nongovernmental commission set up for the purpose of keeping members of the Security Council on their collective toes. Currently, the council can refuse to consider matters that some members do not believe threaten international peace and security. Items sensitive for permanent members can be tabled, even those that warrant attention. The enactment of trigger mechanisms could depoliticize the process by which the council chooses to address issues and possibly elicit more consistency, particularly if early warning in several functional areas became a legitimate activity for international secretariats. Developing criteria for other threats—as the Charter attempted generally for responses to aggression—would be an arduous undertaking. But it could facilitate more automatic international action based on the nature of the crisis instead of on the subjective will of member states. After the end of the fiftieth anniversary celebrations, however, there was little evidence that either membership or procedure would be altered in the future.[23]

Expanding the present operational definition of security to include environmental and demographic threats to the peace would open up a new range of tasks for the Security Council.[24] The first-ever Security Council summit attended by heads of state, in January 1992, took a step in this direction by referring to non-military threats as an important and growing concern. More recently, on January 6, 2000, council members took this one step further and held an unprecedented high-level open meeting on "the situation in Africa: the impact of AIDS on peace and security."

The subject of human security figures centrally in the second and third parts of this volume. Suffice it to say here that deforestation, overpopulation, global warming, and environmental degradation often are still perceived by many as localized incidents of environmental neglect when, in reality, they have far wider implications. Pollution originating from the U.S. Midwest causes acid rain in Canada and Scandinavia. Such pollution is obviously a matter of international concern having cross-border implications; the international community has a right to address it. The concept of military security could well be expanded in a number of instances to include environmental security. Would a vigorous international response not be in order if a serious disaster (for example, a nuclear power plant's meltdown) met with an inadequate governmental response? Or because overpopulation can lead to migration, and migration can lead to violence, would it not be sensible to use preventive measures to forestall either overpopulation or migration? These are the types of questions to be faced by decisionmakers with a wider definition for international peace and security.

"Comprehensive security" was an expression originally coined by the former Soviet Union. This holistic conceptualization encompasses all relevant factors—poverty, human rights abuse, health pandemics, and environmental degradation. This idea was originally dismissed by the West as a communist polemical ploy; the disappearance of the Soviet Union has perhaps made it possible to evaluate more dispassionately this concept's merits.

As demonstrated in the case of UNMIK, using regional organizations as a means to supplement the UN's collective-security system has now moved beyond the talking stage. Secretary-General Boutros-Ghali proposed that "regional action as matter of decentralization, delegation, and cooperation with UN efforts could not only lighten the burden of the Council but also contribute to a deeper sense of participation, consensus and democratization in international affairs."[25] Yet, as we argued earlier, even the world's most highly developed regional organizations usually lack the capacity to serve as effective alternatives to UN military operations.

These organizations can play a helpful role in diplomatic arm-twisting, as was witnessed by the Association of Southeast Asian Nations (ASEAN) in Cambodia and by the Contadora Group in Central America. With the exception of the North Atlantic Treaty Organization—which possesses the most authoritative joint force in the world and has advanced cooperative procedures used in both northern Iraq and more recently in the Balkans—regional organizations are and will remain poor sources for supplying international military forces to help quell interstate and local conflicts. The rhetoric about regional organizations flourishes in developing countries, but the hopes placed on them for their contribution to international peace and security seem unduly optimistic, if not altogether misplaced.

Regional organizations' military and financial capacities are lacking; and they inevitably contain states that are so embroiled in conflicts as to make community decisions impossible. The European Community's dithering in the former Yugoslavia illustrates the incapacity of even well-endowed organizations to effectively manage conflicts in their locale. The results reflected the lack of political will; nonetheless observers point to the "indispensability" of the United Nations.[26] NATO, the Western European Union (WEU), and the Conference on Security and Cooperation in Europe (CSCE) discussed helping with humanitarian relief in the former Yugoslavia, but political considerations prevented effective action. The NATO troops in Bosnia and Herzegovina were deployed from 1992 until 1995 under a UN flag. The coalitions in the Persian Gulf and Somalia made use of Security Council authorizations.

Although the United Nations is the most logical and important convener for future international military operations, the use of coercion poses almost insuperable problems for the world organization.[27] Thus, if coercion occurs at all, interventions in the near future will have to compensate for the military inadequacies of the United Nations. Experience suggests that UN decisions should trigger interventions to be subcontracted to coalitions of major states that are willing and able to act. Regional powers (for instance, Nigeria within West Africa and Russia within the erstwhile Soviet republics) could take the lead combined with larger regional (that is, the Economic Community of West African States and the Commonwealth of Independent States) or global coalitions. Perhaps only when regional powers cannot or will not take such a lead should more global powers (for example, France in Rwanda or the United States in Somalia) be expected to do so. However, blocking humanitarian intervention, which some powers are willing to conduct when others are reluctant to get involved (for example, the United States vis-à-vis Rwanda between early April and late June 1994), should be ruled out.

The multilateral capacity for coercion will no doubt depend in the future upon ad hoc coalitions, regional powers, and even hegemons. In the words of the Soros Independent Task Force:

> The United States should oppose giving tasks to the United Nations that it does not have the capacity to perform or that member states lack the will to implement; this applies in particular to Chapter VII peace enforcement operations that require a credible threat of combat and that must be conducted by ad hoc coalition with the endorsement of the Security Council.[28]

Bill Maynes dubbed this "benign realpolitik," which amounts to a revival of spheres of influence with UN oversight.[29] The Security Council is experimenting with a type of great-power politics, which the United Nations had originally been

Bosnian Muslims wait at a checkpoint manned by Croatian and Bosnian police officers and monitored by UN soldiers of the British battalion. (UN Photo 186709/J. Isaac)

founded to end but which is increasingly pertinent in light of some of the inherent difficulties of multilateral mobilization and management of military force.

Boutros-Ghali recognized this reality when calling for "a new division of labour between the United Nations and regional organizations, under which the regional organization carries the main burden but a small United Nations operation supports it and verifies that it is functioning in a manner consistent with positions adopted by the Security Council."[30] Elsewhere in justifying UN monitoring of Nigeria and ECOWAS in Liberia as well as Russia and the CIS in Tajikistan and Georgia, he had this to say: "Finding the right division of labour between the United Nations and regional organizations is not easy. But such cooperation brings greater legitimacy and support to international efforts. It eases the material and financial burden of the United Nations. It allows for comparative advantage."[31]

An observer might ask, "What's new about rationalization? Is the Secretary-General not grasping at straws in justifying a gunboat diplomacy for the 1990s? Is this not simply realpolitik?" Boutros-Ghali is aware of the dangers: "Authorization to serve as a surrogate might strengthen a particular power's sphere of influence and damage the United Nations' standing as an organization intended to coordinate security across regional blocs."[32]

The difference could be that major powers or their coalitions act on their own behalf as well as legitimately on behalf of the Security Council—thus they should be held accountable for their actions by the wider community of states authorizing outside interventions.[33] Although major powers inevitably flex their military muscles when it is in their perceived interests to do so, they do not necessarily agree in advance to subject themselves to international law and outside monitoring of their behavior. The political and economic advantages attached to an imprimatur from the Security Council provide some leverage for the community of states to foster accountability in would-be subcontractors. In light of the incapacity of the United Nations, there is no alternative to making better use of regional organizations, without naïveté and with accountability.

Another conceptual movement has been the evolution of the notion "postconflict peacebuilding." During the recent past the UN's experiences in this regard have being growing as evidenced most pronouncedly by the operations in Kosovo and East Timor. In this regard, peacebuilding is a work in progress, and Secretary-General Kofi Annan has been cautious to clarify in his 1997 *Reform Report* that, although peacebuilding must be supported by humanitarian and development activities, it also needs to reorient them in such a way that they become politically relevant in that they can serve to reduce the risk of resumed conflict and promote reconciliation and recovery.[34]

Professional Changes: Strengthening the Secretariat

Paradoxically, the Persian Gulf War represented the first military enforcement action of the post–Cold War era, but the UN Secretary-General and the secretariat remained virtual outsiders to the process by which the war was waged. This pattern has been repeated, most recently in Kosovo. Although the initial Security Council authorizations were politically necessary, the coalition forces were not accountable to the world organization. Increasing the ability of the secretariat and thereby of the Security Council to monitor enforcement operations has become a subject of heated discussions.[35] The enormous difficulties surrounding the deployment of the first UN troops with Chapter VII provisions under the command and control of the Secretary-General in Somalia serve to highlight the critical nature of this issue.

Several proposals have been put forth to increase the Secretary-General's influence over Security Council decisionmaking and subsequent UN military operations. Article 99 of the Charter already empowers the Secretary-General to bring the Security Council's attention to matters that he believes could threaten international peace and security. Greater use of this article could allow the Secretary-General to place issues on the council's agenda that otherwise might be avoided due to their sensitivity. The double standard with which the council has addressed past threats to the peace could be mitigated if the Secretary-General were to use the powers of his office to ensure a more consistent consideration of issues even when powerful states might prefer to ignore them.

Moreover, the Secretary-General has asked for a mandate to gain advisory opinions from the International Court of Justice under Article 96 of the Charter. These could allow the organization's head to help refine the legitimate definitions of those situations that present threats to the peace as well as to provide more concrete policy options that are both politically and legally acceptable. The key to advisory opinions is in the asking of the question to get a specific enough response. Time is also a problem because the ICJ never acts quickly.

Agreement on standards may be increasingly necessary. Resolutions are often kept vague in order to secure intergovernmental assent ("all necessary means" in the war against Iraq created a host of questions about proportionality, and "all measures necessary" was quintessential UN doublespeak that did not permit sufficient action to help Bosnia's Muslims). The language of international decisions is sometimes too elliptical to allow a determination of which concrete actions and procedures would constitute legitimate follow-up. The Secretary-General—and not just the General Assembly, the Security Council, and other UN organs—should be authorized to request advisory opinions from the World Court to help reduce the criticism of selective application by the Security Council of the principles guiding decisionmaking. Although seeking the Court's opinion would be harmful in the midst of a crisis, it could be useful in anticipating future contingencies.

As part of the reform process, steps have been taken to enhance the secretariat's means of fact-finding so that the Secretary-General can improve his access to timely, unbiased, and impartial accounts of dangerous situations. Special units have proliferated that focus exclusively on early warning and prevention. The mandate of these units is to provide greater access to information about potential threats to the peace, thus enhancing the secretariat's ability to launch preventive diplomacy and possibly to recommend preventive deployment. Of course, much more could be done, and the Secretary-General's office could and should be equipped and staffed to act as an effective crisis-monitoring center for events that threaten the peace.

Useful suggestions have been made to establish a "national security council" within the secretariat, complete with independent sources of intelligence and a means for autonomous interpretation of data supplied by governments, in order to provide early warning about crises. A fledgling effort to establish this type of unit, the Office for Research and Collection of Information (ORCI), was dismantled in 1992 as one of the first changes by newly elected Secretary-General Boutros-Ghali. But the need for a policy-planning unit has become more and more obvious; too few persons are looking toward the future.

Finally, the end of the Cold War has permitted the world organization to move toward reviving old-fashioned ideals of an objective and competent international civil service, upon which the organization was supposedly founded.[36] The success of the organization's activities begins and ends with the people in its employ. A long-ignored reality is the need to overhaul the international civil service, for which qualifications have long been secondary to geographic and political considerations.

After 1997, when Kofi Annan unveiled his strategy of a "quiet revolution" to reform the world organization, meaningful steps began to be taken to make the UN a more effective mechanism for administering and managing peacekeeping operations.[37] The creation and effective implementation of a rationalized cabinet system, consisting of the senior management group (SMG) comprising division heads and an executive committee system, introduced a much greater degree of horizontal cooperation than had been the case before. Senior officials throughout the organization (including those based in Geneva and Vienna through teleconferencing) meet weekly with the Secretary-General to review and discuss important issues. In addition, the executive committee on peace and security, which brings together those senior officials whose units deal with peacekeeping, holds biweekly discussions. This process is supplemented with a number of issue-specific task forces, including special task forces for each multidisciplinary peace operation, as well as special meetings involving a much wider set of actors who serve as operational partners in the field, including development and humanitarian agencies and international financial institutions.

In regard to headquarters operations, a division of authority has been worked out between the Department of Political Affairs (DPA) and the Department of Peace-keeping Operations (DPKO). The former has primary responsibility for preventive diplomacy and peacemaking and the latter takes the lead in peacekeeping. Although these changes represent important steps in enhancing interdepartmental cooperation and improving the effectiveness of peace operations, the continued splitting of peacemaking and peacekeeping across separate administrative units serves to limit the overall effectiveness of such activities.

In the field, on the contrary, coordination has been centralized under the special representative of the Secretary-General, who assumes authority over all UN entities in the mission area. In cases where department expertise is especially crucial, such as in the Central African Republic and Liberia, for example, a UNDP resident coordinator (who in peacetime is the UN's point person) may also be appointed to serve as deputy head of mission. Within this structure special emphasis is placed on working in close cooperation with relevant parties, including NGOs.

As mentioned earlier, the scale of the administrative trusteeship operation in Kosovo was in many ways unprecedented. Among its most innovative features was its administrative structure. For the first time non-UN multilateral agencies were integrated directly into the governance structure of a multidimensional peacekeeping operation. Moreover several of the individuals selected for the team have had extensive experience with NGOs and other elements of civil society. The Secretary-General selected Dr. Bernard Kouchner (founder of Médecins sans Frontières and former minister of health of France) to lead the UNMIK operation

Children performing daily chores in a KFOR-guarded camp of about 5,000 Roma civilians in Pristina area, Kosovo. (UN/UNHCR/P. Peloche)

as his special representative. He then supplemented the administrative structure with four deputy special representatives (DSRs). Tom Koenigs, head of the environmental protection department of the City of Frankfurt and deputy-president of the NGO, the Alliance for the Climate, was selected to represent the United Nations as the DSR for interim civil administration. A long-time UNHCR staff member, Dennis McNamara, was selected as DSR for humanitarian affairs. The head of the OSCE mission to Kosovo, Daan Everts, joined the team as DSR for institution building. And Joly Dixon, director of international affairs of the European Commission, was appointed as DSR for economic reconstruction. The representatives of both the OSCE and the EU are working under the direct authority of the SRSG (special representative of the Secretary-General) and ultimately the Secretary-General.

This administrative arrangement reflects a deeper transformation that has been occurring in peace operations over the past decade. Peacekeeping personnel and contributing partners are being drawn from an ever-expanding range of institutions—international, national, and local. In addition to UN departments, programs, funds, and other bodies, peacekeepers are now being tapped from specialized agencies, international financial institutions, national bureaucracies, military and civilian police forces, regional organizations, NGOs, academia, and the private sector. Each peace mission brings with it a new context with a particular set of historical, cultural, social, and economic conditions, political constraints and requirements, and thus the need for a unique blend of partners and cooperative arrangements.

As the pool of potential partners grows, so does the necessity for developing systematic criteria for determining partnership acceptability. Of course, not all NGOs and other entities from civil society are necessarily constructive forces for building and sustaining peace. Neither may be all regional security organizations, as demonstrated by the numerous allegations of serious human rights violations by members of the Military Observer Group of the Economic Community of West African States (ECOMOG) force in Liberia and Sierra Leone. At the same time, however, a broad conception of partnerships is likely to be even more important in the future than it is now. Given the increasing importance placed on creating the requisite social and economic infrastructures for sustaining peace in conflict-torn regions, it seems that new and innovative types of partnerships with the private sector, religious groups, local governmental bodies, labor, and others will most likely be needed.

Determining whether to get involved or not in the political-humanitarian crises of the 1990s required familiarity with a host of actors besides states. Humanitarian action has made possible new coalitions—the media and the public can demand that something be done, the military can respond, and relief agencies can ask for help because on occasion they recognize both the war-fighting and logistic capacities of the armed forces. Commitments by major powers are greatly affected by their leaders' calculations of domestic costs, benefits, and risks. The arithmetic in part reflects the success of domestic and transnational constituencies in mobilizing support for humanitarian action, and in altering conceptions of interests and rewards.

One example is Washington's change of tack on Haiti in 1994 after effective lobbying by Jean-Bertrand Aristide and the Congressional Black Caucus.[38] American leadership in Haiti beginning in September 1994 and in Bosnia after the Dayton accords in November 1995 (a year and two years, respectively, after the October 1993 fiasco in Somalia) suggests that when interests are perceived to be sufficiently involved and foreign policy is framed accordingly, minds can be concentrated and changed. In Kosovo in 1999, humanitarian arguments managed to carry the day even when aerial bombing entailed deterioration in Washington's relations with Moscow and Beijing. As was the case in northern Iraq, and despite the Vietnam and Somalia syndromes, American interests were framed in Haiti, Bosnia, and ultimately Kosovo to merit use of the military with significant humanitarian motivations and certainly significant humanitarian consequences.

The use of force aside, an equally good example of the importance of numerous actors was the "Ottawa process" on antipersonnel land mines. This case is worth examining because of what its dynamics portend for the future, even if the mindset in Washington on this issue remains for the moment impervious to the humanitarian values that have penetrated the foreign policies of other countries. A transnational coalition successfully imbued the domestic politics of a sufficient number of states with enough humanitarian concern to redefine state interests in a way that led to the treaty.[39] Unlike many cases of transnationalism, this one touches directly on the high politics of military security.

This example suggests the importance of substate and transnational actors in influencing, framing, and ultimately redefining state interests.[40] The initial impetus in the anti-land-mines campaign was provided by a formidable coalition of civil society organizations. The International Campaign to Ban Land Mines, founded in 1993, grew out of private advocacy organizations whose main orientation was domestic and public (that is, oriented toward change in *state* behavior). Its success depended on coopting *states* (and notably Canada, the Scandinavian countries, and South Africa), in "determin[ing] what states want."[41] Their support depended not only on the moral appeal of the cause but also on the consideration of domestic and international political interests and risks.

State involvement was necessary to translate social pressure into international law. The key to the outcome was to move states and alter definitions of perceived interests by persuading politicians. A basic aspect of the process was to remove land mines from the rarefied realm of technical military strategy and to place the issue firmly in the political realm of domestic constituencies.

Humanitarian values are in the forefront of concerns motivating many societal forces that may inform leaders' perceptions of interest. In commenting on the intervention in Kosovo, Max Frankel concluded, "It's those pictures of almost unfathomable atrocity that once again drive our politics."[42] This is not the place to discuss in depth the so-called CNN effect, which influences both the perception of tragedy and the pace of decisionmaking.[43] However, the increasing reach and efficiency of international communications, along with the related growing influence of transnational and nongovernmental actors, point toward a changing domestic environment and decisionmaking context. Armed with graphic images of suffering, these nonstate actors help shape definitions of state interest. We are witnessing a phenomenon not of receding state authority, but of its being influenced by coalitions of actors with humanitarian values. Their agendas to some extent and in some circumstances become those of their governments.[44]

The end of the Cold War raised expectations of the United Nations, just as it unleashed the violence and instability with which the UN has been trying to cope. Depending on perspectives, 1999 was the *annus mirabilis* or *horibilis* for humanitarian action. Kosovo constituted a "humanitarian war." Coercion took place against the Milosevic government to stop persecution. In the West, and Washington particularly, intervention for humanitarian purposes was crucial enough to risk worsened relations with both Russia and China. And in some ways, the international reaction to East Timor was even more remarkable because only area specialists and stamp collectors could have located it on a map a few years ago. But in spite of official and initially strong objections from the world's fourth most populous country, enough international pressure was exerted that Jakarta "requested" the deployment of the Australian-led coalition in Timor, which was followed by UN trusteeship and a UN peacekeeping force. Pressured or induced consent given by the targeted government is the "first cousin" to humanitarian intervention. Comparable actions are out of the question in Chechnya, Tibet, or Kashmir; but efforts in Indonesia suggest that humanitarian action is an option in more than powerless or failed states, even without formally overriding sovereignty.[45]

Member states and peoples across the world are looking toward the world organization to muster multilateral responses for international and civil strife. Collective security has yet to be tested, but changing world politics indicate that the United Nations has been given a second chance to implement the peace and security provisions of its Charter. Human rights, humanitarian relief, and sustainable development play a much less significant role in the Charter than military security. But these "softer" sides of the UN moved forward during the Cold War while collective-security mechanisms stalled. The end of the Cold War has had a decided impact on international efforts to constitute working regimes in these areas, too. Moreover the meaning of "security" has come into question as issues of human rights, democratization, and sustainable human development have worked their way into global discourse about security matters. It is to those issues that we now turn.

Notes

1. Boutros Boutros-Ghali, *An Agenda for Peace 1995* (New York: United Nations, 1995), contains both the original 1992 *An Agenda for Peace* and the 1995 *Supplement*. Paragraph numbers remain the same.

2. See George Soros (chairman of an independent task force), *American National Interest and the United Nations* (New York: Council on Foreign Relations, 1996).

3. For more analysis, see Thomas G. Weiss, "New Problems for Future UN Military Operations: Implementing an Agenda for Peace," *Washington Quarterly* 15, no. 1 (Winter 1993), pp. 58–66. For a longer discussion with case studies, see Lori Fisler Damrosch, ed., *Enforcing Restraint: Collective Involvement in Internal Conflicts* (New York: Council on Foreign Relations, 1993).

4. For a discussion, see Benjamin Rivlin, "The Rediscovery of the UN Military Staff Committee," Occasional Papers Series no. 4, Ralph Bunche Institute, City University of New York, May 1991; and Jane Boulden, "Prometheus Unbound: The History of the Military Staff Committee," Aurora Papers 19, Ottawa, Canadian Centre for Global Security, August 1993.

5. There is a growing literature, including James N. Rosenau, *Turbulence in World Politics: A Theory of Change and Continuity* (Princeton: Princeton Univ. Press, 1990); August Richard Norton, "The Security Legacy of the 1980s in the Third World," in Thomas G. Weiss and Meryl A. Kessler, eds., *Third World Security in the Post–Cold War Era* (Boulder: Lynne Rienner, 1991), pp. 19–34; *Ethnic Conflict and International Security, Survival* (special issue) 35, no. 1 (Spring 1993); Lawrence Freedman, "Order and Disorder in the New World," *Foreign Affairs* 71, no. 1 (1991–1992), pp. 20–37; Morton H. Halperin and David J.

Scheffer, *Self-Determination in the New World Order* (Washington, DC: Carnegie Endowment, 1992); Daniel Patrick Moynihan, *Pandemonium: Ethnicity in International Politics* (New York: Oxford Univ. Press, 1993); Joel Kotkin, *Tribes: How Race, Religion, and Identity Determine Success in the New Global Economy* (New York: Random House, 1993); Damrosch, *Enforcing Restraint;* Michael E. Brown, ed., *Ethnic Conflict and International Security* (Princeton: Princeton Univ. Press, 1993), and *The International Dimension of Internal Conflict* (Cambridge, MA: MIT Press, 1996); Ted Robert Gurr and Barbara Harff, *Ethnic Conflict in World Politics* (Boulder: Westview Press, 1994); Gidon Gottlieb, *Nation Against State* (New York: Council on Foreign Relations, 1993), and "Reconstructing Nations and States," special issue of *Dædalus* 122, no. 3 (Summer 1993). For discussions on the difficulties of negotiating the end to such wars, see I. William Zartman, ed., *Elusive Peace: Negotiating an End to Civil Wars* (Washington, DC: Brookings Institution, 1995); and Fen Osler Hampson, *Nurturing Peace: Why Peace Settlements Succeed or Fail* (Washington, DC: U.S. Institute of Peace Press, 1996).

6. Boutros-Ghali, *An Agenda for Peace*, para. 44.

7. See especially his speech at the University of Bordeaux in April 1991 (see UN Press release S6/SM/4560) and his last "Report of the Secretary-General on the Work of the Organization," September 1991, document A/46/1.

8. For a discussion of relevant issues, see "The New South," four essays in *Washington Quarterly* 15, no. 4 (Autumn 1992), pp. 139–184.

9. See Larry Minear et al., *Humanitarianism Under Siege: A Critical Review of Operation Lifeline Sudan* (Trenton, NJ: Red Sea Press, 1991); and Francis M. Deng and Larry Minear, *The Challenge of Famine Relief* (Washington, DC: Brookings Institution, 1993).

10. John Mackinlay and Jarat Chopra, "Second Generation Multinational Operations," *Washington Quarterly* 15, no. 3 (Summer 1992), pp. 113–134, and *A Draft Concept of Second Generation Multinational Operations 1993* (Providence, RI: Watson Institute, 1993). See also John Mackinlay, ed., *A Guide to Peace Support Operations* (Providence, RI: Watson Institute, 1996).

11. Mackinlay and Chopra, "Second Generation Multinational Operations," p. 113.

12. Boutros-Ghali, *Supplement*, para. 77.

13. Boutros Boutros-Ghali, "Transcript of Press Conference," January 5, 1995, press release SG/SM/5518, p. 5.

14. Boutros-Ghali, *Supplement*, para. 20.

15. See James Rosenau, *The United Nations in a Turbulent World* (Boulder: Lynne Rienner, 1992).

16. See the classic treatment by Kenneth Walzer, *Man, the State and War* (New York: Columbia Univ. Press, 1968), in contrast with Philip Allott, *Eunomia: New Order for a New World* (New York: Oxford Univ. Press, 1990).

17. For a discussion of these issues at the outset of the post–Cold War era, see Leon Gordenker and Thomas G. Weiss, eds., *Soldiers, Peacekeepers and Disasters* (London: Macmillan, 1992); and Thomas G. Weiss and Cindy Collins, *Humanitarian Challenges and Intervention: World Politics and the Dilemmas of Help,* 2nd ed. (Boulder: Westview Press, 2000).

18. Boutros-Ghali, *An Agenda for Peace*, para. 43.

19. From the "Ottawa Declaration on UN Collective Security" adopted by the inaugural meeting of Global Action's Parliamentary Commission on Peacekeeping and Collective Security, May 22, 1991.

20. Boutros-Ghali, *An Agenda for Peace,* para. 69.

21. For other ideas about financing, see the thoughts of a group of experts under the chairmanship of Paul Volker and Shijuro Ogata, *Financing an Effective United Nations* (New York: Ford Foundation, 1993).

22. For a quantitative and qualitative discussion, see Ernest B. Haas, "Collective Conflict Management: Evidence for a New World Order?" in Thomas G. Weiss, ed., *Collective Security in a Changing World* (Boulder: Lynne Rienner, 1993), pp. 63–117.

23. See Bruce Russett, Barry O'Neill, and James Sutterlin, "Breaking the Security Council Restructuring Logjam," *Global Governance* 2, no. 1 (January-April 1996), pp. 65–80.

24. See Jessica Tuchman Mathews, "Redefining Security," *Foreign Affairs* 68, no. 2 (Spring 1989), pp. 162–177.

25. Boutros-Ghali, *An Agenda for Peace*, para. 64.

26. John Zametica, *The Yugoslav Conflict, Adelphi Paper 270* (London: International Institute for Strategic Studies, 1992), p. 67.

27. For an outspoken and skeptical realist view, see John J. Mearsheimer, "The False Promise of International Institutions," *International Security* 19, no. 3 (Winter 1994–1995), pp. 5–49.

28. Soros, *American National Interest*, p. 9.

29. Charles William Maynes, "A Workable Clinton Doctrine," *Foreign Policy* 93 (Winter 1993–1994), pp. 3–20.

30. Boutros-Ghali, *Supplement*, para. 86. For a skeptical view, see Benjamin Rivlin, "Prospects for a Division of Labour Between the UN and Regional Bodies in Peace-keeping," in Klaus Hüfner, ed., *Agenda for Change* (Opladen: Leske and Budrich, 1995), pp. 137–149.

31. Press release SG/SM/5804, November 1, 1995, p. 2. For an extended argument about a "partnership" between the UN and regional organizations, see Alan K. Henrikson, "The Growth of Regionalism and the Role of the United Nations," in Louise Fawcett and Andrew Hurrell, eds., *Regionalism in World Politics: Regional Organizations and World Order* (Oxford: Oxford University Press, 1996), pp. 122–168.

32. Boutros Boutros-Ghali, "Global Leadership After the Cold War," *Foreign Affairs* 75, no. 2 (March-April 1996), p. 95.

33. For a discussion of this difference, see Mario Bettati, *Le droit d'ingérence: Mutation de l'ordre international* (Paris: Odile Jacob, 1996), especially pp. 186–203. For a discussion with reference to the former Soviet bloc, see Jarat Chopra and Thomas G. Weiss, "Containing Conflict in the Former Second World," *Security Studies* 4, no. 3 (Spring 1995), pp. 552–583.

34. Kofi Annan, *Renewing the United Nations: A Programme for Reform* (New York: United Nations, 1997).

35. See John Mackinlay, "The Requirement for a Multinational Enforcement Capability," in Weiss, *Collective Security*, pp. 139–152.

36. The classic treatment of this subject is by Dag Hammarskjöld, "The International Civil Servant in Law and in Fact," lecture of May 30, 1961 (Oxford: Clarendon Press, 1961). For further information, see Thomas G. Weiss, *International Bureaucracy* (Lexington, MA: Heath, 1975); and Robert S. Jordan, ed., *International Administration: Its Evolution and Contemporary Applications* (New York: Oxford Univ. Press, 1971).

37. Kofi Annan, "The Quiet Revolution," *Global Governance* 4, no. 2 (April-June 1998), pp. 123–138.

38. David Malone, *Decision-Taking in the UN Security Council: The Case of Haiti, 1990–97* (Oxford: Oxford University Press, 1998).

39. See Stephen Biddle, et al., *The Military Utility of Landmines Implications for Arms Control* (Alexandria, VA: Institute for Defense Analyses, 1994).

40. See Thomas Risse, Stephen C. Ropp, and Kathryn Sikkink, eds., *The Power of Human Rights: International Norms and Domestic Change* (Cambridge, UK: Cambridge University Press, 1999).

41. Richard Price, "Reversing the Gun Sights: Transnational Civil Society Targets Land Mines," *International Organization* LII, no. 3 (Summer 1998), p. 617.

42. Max Frankel, "Our Humanity Vs. Their Sovereignty," *New York Times Magazine*, May 2, 1999, p. 36.

43. See Nik Gowing, *Media Coverage: Help or Hindrance in Conflict Prevention* (New York: Carnegie Commission on Preventing Deadly Conflict, 1997); Warren P. Stroble, *Late-Breaking Foreign Policy: The News Media's Influence on Peace Operations* (Washington, DC: U.S. Institute of Peace Press, 1997); Edward R. Girardet, ed., *Somalia, Rwanda, and Beyond: The Role of the International Media in Wars and Humanitarian Crises* (Dublin: Crosslines Publications, 1995); Johanna Neuman, *Lights, Camera, War: Is Media Technology Driving International Politics?* (New York: St. Martin's Press, 1996); Colin Scott, Larry Minear, and Thomas G. Weiss, *The News Media, Humanitarian Action, and Civil War* (Boulder: Lynne Rienner, 1996); and Robert I. Rotberg and Thomas G. Weiss, eds., *From Massacres to Genocide: The Media, Public Policy, and Humanitarian Crises* (Washington, DC: Brookings Institution, 1996).

44. See S. Neil MacFarlane and Thomas G. Weiss, "Political Interest and Humanitarian Action," *Security Studies* 10, no. 1 (Autumn 2000), pp. 166–198.

45. Donald K. Emmerson, "Moralpolitik: The Timor Test," *National Interest*, no. 58 (Winter 1999–2000), pp. 57–62.

Part Two

Human Rights and Humanitarian Affairs

5 The United Nations, Human Rights, and Humanitarian Affairs

The Theory

The celebration in 1998 of the fiftieth anniversary of the Universal Declaration of Human Rights served to focus world attention on the important role the UN has played in promulgating and promoting international human rights norms and principles. It served to remind that the principles espoused in the declaration, an elaboration of the UN Charter, placed limits on governments' claims to unbridled sovereignty. According to those principles, there exist certain established standards of civilized conduct that apply to all states and that govern the relationship between governments and those over whom they rule.

Since 1945, states have used their sovereignty more and more to create international human rights obligations that in turn have restricted their operational sovereignty. International agreements on human rights norms have been followed at least occasionally by concrete, noteworthy developments showing that international organizations have begun to reach deeply into matters that were once considered the core of national domestic affairs.

Moreover, the process by which the assumed sovereignty of the territorial state has given way to shared authority and power between the state and international organizations is not a recent phenomenon. Although there have been some dramatic recent events, movement toward promoting and protecting human rights across borders has been going on for a century and a half. These changes accelerated with the start of the United Nations in 1945, became remarkable from about 1970, and became spasmodically dramatic from about 1991. The role of the UN in human rights figures to remain one of the more provocative subjects of the twenty-first century.

Noting these historical changes concerning the United Nations and human rights is not the same as being overly optimistic about these developments. Indeed, some UN proceedings on human rights would "depress Dr. Pangloss," a fictional character from Voltaire who believed all was for the best in this ideal world.[1] Although noteworthy in historical perspective, UN activity concerning human rights often displays an enormous gap between the law on the books and the law in action. At any given time or on any given issue, state expediency may supersede the application of UN human rights standards. Revolutionary change in a given context may not be institutionalized; similar situations can give rise to different UN roles and different outcomes for human rights. Any number of states, some of them with democratic governments, have opposed progressive action for human rights at the United Nations. If the international movement for human rights means separating the individual from full state control, then this movement has not always been well received by those who rule in the name of the state and who may be primarily interested in power, wealth, and independence.

The territorial state remains the most important legal-political entity in the modern world despite the obvious importance of ethnic, religious, and cultural identifications and an increasing number of actors in civil society everywhere. Thus many ethnic and religious groups try to capture control of the government so that they can speak officially for the state. The state constitutes the basic building block of the United Nations. State actors primarily shape the UN agenda and action on human rights, although states are pushed and pulled by other actors such as private human rights groups and UN secretariat officials. In sum, although there are striking new developments at the UN concerning human rights, in general state authorities still control the most important final decisions.

Accelerating and decelerating developments concerning the United Nations and human rights were in evidence in 1993 at the World Conference on Human Rights, held in Vienna. Many states reaffirmed universal human rights, but a small minority of delegations, especially from Asia and the Middle East, argued for cultural relativism in an extreme form—namely, that there were few or no universal human rights, only rights specific to various countries, regions, or cultures. Some of the very delegates making arguments in favor of extreme cultural relativism were representing states that were party to numerous human rights treaties, without reservations. A large number of NGOs attended the conference and tried to focus on concrete rights violations in specific countries, but most governments wanted to deal with abstract principles, not specific violations. At the same time that the U.S. delegation took a strong stand in favor of internationally recognized human rights in general, the Clinton administration refused to provide military specialists and protective troops to conduct an investigation into war crimes, that is, into the possible mass murder of hospital patients in Serbian-controlled territory in the Balkans. These examples show that a certain diplomatic progress concerning international human rights was accompanied by much controversy and some reluctance to act decisively.

Some may wish to draw a distinction between human rights and humanitarian affairs, although any difference may exist more in the eye of the beholder than in reality. Perhaps a distinction can sometimes be made between actions supposedly undertaken because persons have a human right to them and actions undertaken because they are humane—whether persons are fundamentally enti-tled to the actions or not. For example, in the CSCE process during the Cold War, some families divided by the Iron Curtain were reunited in the name of humani-tarianism. The objective was to achieve a humane outcome, sidestepping debates about a right to emigrate. Likewise, some foreign assistance is provided for vic-tims of earthquakes and other natural disasters at least in part because of hu-mane considerations, whether or not persons have a legal right to that interna-tional assistance.

The more compelling point, however, is that a great many international actions are undertaken for mixed motives with various justifications. The UN Security Council authorized the use of force, in effect, to curtail starvation in Somalia. To some, this was a response to the codified human rights to life, adequate nutrition, and health care. To others, this was acting humanely to alleviate suffering. To more than one lawyer, this was expanding the concept of international security to in-clude humanitarian threats so that the Security Council could respond with a binding decision. But the reality was that the United Nations was used by the inter-national community to try to improve order and reduce starvation and malnutri-tion. Whether outside troops went into Somalia for reasons of human rights or hu-manitarian affairs was a theoretical distinction without operational significance.

In this section we refer mostly to "human rights." Sometimes we note that UN involvement in a situation is oriented toward humane outcomes, whether or not the language of human rights is employed. Internationally recognized human rights have been defined so broadly that one can rationalize almost any action de-signed to improve the human condition in terms of fundamental rights, if one wishes to do so.

Understanding Rights

Human rights are fundamental entitlements of persons, constituting means to the end of minimal human dignity or social justice. If persons have human rights, they are entitled to a fundamental claim that others must do, or refrain from do-ing, something. Since governments speaking for states are primarily responsible for order and social justice in their jurisdictions, governments are the primary targets of these personal and fundamental claims. If I have a right to freedom from torture, governments are obligated to respond by seeing to it that torture does not occur. If I have a right to adequate health care, governments are obli-gated to respond by seeing to it that such health care is provided, especially to those who cannot afford to purchase it in private markets.

The legal system codifies what are recognized as human rights at any point in time. The legal system, of course, recognizes many legal rights. The ones seen as most fundamental to human dignity—that is, a life worthy of being lived—are called human rights. There is a difference between fundamental human rights and other legal rights that are perhaps important but not, relatively speaking, fun-damental. This theoretical distinction between fundamental and important rights can and does give rise to debate. Is access to minimal health care fundamental, and thus a human right, as the Canadian legal system guarantees? Or is that access only something that people should have if they can afford it, as the U.S. system implies? Why does the U.S. legal system recognize the legal right of a patient to sue a doctor for negligence but not allow that same person access to adequate health care as a human right?

There is even more debate about the origin of human rights outside of codification in the legal system. Positivists are content to accept the identification of human rights as found in the legal system. But others, especially philosophers, wish to know what are the "true" or "moral" human rights that exist independently of legal codification. Natural law theorists, for example, believe that human rights exist in natural law as provided by a supreme being. Analytical theorists believe there are moral rights associated inherently with persons; the legal system only indicates a changing view of what these moral rights are.[2] The point to be stressed here is that despite this long-standing debate about the ultimate origin of human rights, societies do come to some agreement about fundamental rights, writing them into national constitutions and other basic legal instruments. As we shall see, in international society there is formal agreement on what are universal human rights at the dawn of the twenty-first century.

International Origins

When territorial states arose and became consolidated in the middle of the seventeenth century, human rights were treated, if at all, as national rather than international issues. Indeed, the core of the 1648 Peace of Westphalia, designed to end the religious wars of Europe, indicated that the territorial ruler would henceforth determine the religion of the territory. In the modern language of rights, freedom of religion, or its absence, was left to the territorial ruler. The dominant international rule was what today we call state sovereignty. Any question of human rights was subsumed under that ordering principle. It was unfortunate that the ordering principle of state sovereignty led to considerable disorder.

Later, the Americans in 1776–1787 decided to recognize human rights, and the French in 1789 attempted to do so. These revolutions had no immediate legal effect, and sometimes no immediate political effect, on other nations. In fact, many non-Western peoples and their rulers were not immediately affected by these two national revolutions, oriented as they were to definitions of what were then called "the rights of man." Many non-Western societies, such as China, continued to rely primarily on supposedly enlightened leaders for human dignity and social justice. Such leaders might be seen as limited by social or religious principles, but they were not widely seen as limited by personal rights. No such rights could be found in constitutions, which often were nonexistent anyway. In sum, in the state system human rights were mostly seen and practiced as a national, not an international, matter. Some nations recognized the basic idea of human rights and devised laws accordingly; some did not.

During the middle of the nineteenth century, Western nations, which tended to dominate much of the world at that time, were swept by a wave of international sentiment.[3] It may be true that the notion of human rights was not particularly resurrected then.[4] But growing international concern for the plight of persons without regard to nationality laid the moral foundations for a later resurrection and expansion of the notion of personal rights. Moral concern led eventually to an explosion in human rights developments.

Karl Marx was, in fact, a personification of the trend that focused on the plight of persons without regard for nationality. As is well known, Marx devised a theory of human existence and social change that stressed universal or international dynamics such as economic determinism, social classes, revolution, and classless societies. His driving concern was the plight of "industrialized man"—the proletariat subjected to the debasing conditions of early capitalist industrialization, especially in Western Europe. He mistakenly denigrated local factors, such as the appeal of nationalism, that transcended class differences. In important ways Marx was, in the last analysis, not a defender of the idea of human rights, believing that to surround the person with legal rights was to block the solidarity of the proletariat and hence to block progress, since the working class was the social vehicle for progressive change. Property rights were seen as especially counterproductive to progressive change.

But from the 1860s on, Marxism was one manifestation of a growing Western tendency to view the human person as subjected to forces that were international or transnational in nature—for example, capitalist modes of production. Marx's recipe for social justice and human dignity was also international or transnational—for example, social awareness on the part of the working class, revolution, and socialism. National conditions might affect form and timing, and national proletariats might have a duty to confront their own bourgeoisie, but the problems and solutions were essentially international.

This apparent digression about Marx and Marxism actually helps explain two other developments that occurred at about the same time and that are usually cited as the earliest manifestations of internationally recognized human rights. In the 1860s, about the time Marx wrote *Das Kapital*, a Swiss businessman named Henry Dunant started what is now called the International Red Cross and Red Crescent Movement. Dunant was appalled that in the battle of Solferino (1859) in what is now Italy, which was entangled in the war for the Austrian succession, wounded soldiers were simply left on the battlefield. Armies had no adequate medical corps. European armies of that time had more veterinarians to care for horses than doctors to care for soldiers.[5] He therefore foresaw what became national Red Cross societies, and these putatively private agencies not only geared up for practical action in war but also lobbied governments for new treaties to protect sick and wounded soldiers. In 1864 the first Geneva Convention for Victims of War was concluded, providing legal protection and assistance to fighters disabled in international war.

The comparison between Marx and Dunant should not be pushed too far; Dunant was, after all, a capitalist businessman, although not a very successful one. (For those interested in trivia, Friedrich Engels was much more successful.) Yet both Marx and Dunant saw a widespread or international problem, and both devised (in very different ways) an international solution. Dunant and his successors in the Red Cross and Red Crescent Movement did not immediately use the language of human rights. They spoke in terms of governmental obligation to provide protection and assistance to victims of war. They spoke of the neutrality of medical services. Victims came to be defined not only as sick and wounded combatants but also as civilians in a war zone or under military occupation. Eventually about ten legal instruments came to be called Red Cross law, or international humanitarian law, or the law of human rights in armed conflict. Specific treaty language aside, here was another international development from the 1860s being used to enhance human dignity on an international basis.

Still another effort in the nineteenth century to identify and correct a problem of human dignity on an international basis was the antislavery movement. By 1890 in Brussels, all the major Western states had finally signed a multilateral treaty prohibiting the African slave trade. This capped a movement that had started about the turn of the century in Britain. Just as private Red Cross organizations had pushed for protection and assistance for victims of war, so the London-based Anti-Slavery Society and other private groups pushed the British government in particular to stop the slave trade. Britain outlawed it in the first decade of the nineteenth century; obtained a broader, similar international agreement at the Congress of Vienna in 1815; and thereafter used the British navy to try to enforce its ban on the slave trade.

But the early resistance by the United States and other major slave-trading states was overcome only toward the end of the century. Britain was pushed by private groups and had done much. Yet an international agreement on principles and applications, reaching deeply into the European colonies in Africa, was necessary to really reduce this long-accepted and lucrative practice. In the twentieth century freedom from slavery, the slave trade, and slavery-like practices came to be accepted as an internationally recognized human right. Its roots lay in the transnational morality of the nineteenth century.

This trend of focusing on human need across national borders increased during the League of Nations era, although most efforts met with less than full success. How could it be otherwise in an era of fascism, militarism, nationalism, racism, and isolationism? In retrospect it was nothing short of amazing that much was attempted in the name of transnational moralism and international human rights.

Efforts were made at the Versailles Conference in 1919 to write into the League's covenant rights to religious freedom and racial equality. The British even proposed a right of outside intervention into states to protect religious freedom. But these proposals failed largely because of Woodrow Wilson. Despite a Japanese push for the endorsement of racial equality, the U.S. president was so adamantly against any mention of race that U.S. and UK proposals on religious freedom were withdrawn.[6] During the 1930s the League Assembly debated the merits of an international agreement on human rights in general, but French and Polish proposals to this effect failed to be adopted. Some states were opposed in principle, and some did not want to antagonize Nazi Germany, given the prevailing policy of accommodation or appeasement. Nevertheless, the language of universal human rights was appearing more and more in diplomacy. European NGOs were especially active on the subject.

More successful were efforts to codify and institutionalize labor rights. Whether to undercut the appeals of Marxist revolution, to reflect Marxist concern for labor's plight, or for other reasons, the International Labour Organisation (ILO) was created and based in Geneva alongside the League. Its tripartite membership consisted of government, labor, and management delegations, one from each member state. This structure was conducive to the approval of a series of treaties and other agreements recognizing labor rights, as well as to the development of mechanisms to monitor state practice under the treaties. The ILO thus preceded the United Nations but continued after 1945 as technically a UN agency, although one highly independent of the principal UN organs. It was one of the first international organizations to monitor internationally recognized rights within states.[7]

Although the League's covenant failed to deal with human rights in general, its Article 23 did indicate that the League should be concerned with social justice. In addition to calling for international coordination of labor policy, Article 23 called on the League to take action on such matters as "native inhabitants," "traffic in women and children," "opium and other dangerous drugs," "freedom of communications," and "the prevention and control of disease."

The League was connected to the minority treaties designed for about a dozen states after World War I in an effort to curtail the ethnic passions that had contributed to the outbreak of the Great War in the Balkans. Only a few states were legally obligated to give special rights to minorities. The system of minority treaties did not function very well under the acute nationalist pressures of the 1930s. So dismal was the League record on minority rights that global efforts at minority protection per se were not renewed by the UN until the 1980s—a gap of about fifty years. One UN agency carried the name Subcommission on Protection of Minorities, but it did not in fact take up the question of minority protection for some four decades. The minority treaties provided some useful experience. For instance, under certain treaty provisions individuals could directly petition the League Council, the organization's most important body, for redress of alleged treaty violations. Ironically, the Nazis paid some compensation for early anti-Semitism, responding to individual petitions under this system in 1933.[8]

Also, the League mandate system theoretically sought to protect the welfare of dependent peoples. The Mandates Commission was supposed to supervise the European states that controlled certain territories taken from the losing side in World War I. Those European states were theoretically obligated to rule for the welfare of dependent peoples. Peoples in "A" mandates were supposed to be allowed to exercise their collective right to self-determination in the relatively near future. The League Mandates Commission was made up of experts named by the League Council, and it established a reputation for integrity—so much so that the controlling states regarded it as a nuisance. There was some exercise of the right of individual petition, and the Mandates Commission did publicize some of the shortcomings from the policies of mandatory powers.

In other ways, too, the League of Nations tried to promote humane values—a synonym for social justice. In some cases the League sought to improve the situation of persons without actually codifying their rights. In so doing the League laid the foundation for later rights developments. For example, the League of Nations Refugee Office sought to help refugees, which was useful in 1951 when the UN sponsored a treaty on refugee rights.

In retrospect it seems clear enough that increased interaction among peoples, no doubt produced by changes in travel and communications technology, led in time to an increased moral solidarity—or concern for human dignity across borders. War victims increasingly were seen as entitled to certain humane treatment regardless of nationality. Slavery and the slave trade were seen as wrong regardless of what nationalities practiced them. Labor was seen as needing protective regulation regardless of where the factory or shop was located. Minorities in more than one state were seen as being victimized. Developed states accepted a vague obligation to the League to rule at least some dependent territories for the good of the inhabitants. Refugees came to be seen as presenting common needs, wherever they might be found.

As one scholar has noted, these and other developments in the late nineteenth and early twentieth centuries expressed "an epochal shift in moral sentiment."[9] Another scholar wrote of the growing "moral interdependence" that was to undergird the creation of human rights "regimes" in the UN era.[10] True, this moral solidarity was not cohesive enough to eradicate many of the ills addressed. How could it be otherwise in the 1930s, when some major states (Germany, Italy, and Japan) were glorifying brutal power at the service of particular races or nationalities? One major state (the Soviet Union) had an extensive record of brutal repression and exploitation within its borders. And one major state (the United States) refused to put its putative power at the service of systematic international cooperation. Moreover, at home the United States engaged in its own version of apartheid (namely, legally sanctioned racial discrimination) as well as blatantly racist immigration laws.

Legal and organizational developments were more important as historical stepping-stones than as durable solutions in and of themselves. It might be said that international moral solidarity was strong enough to create certain laws, agreements, and organizations. But states lacked sufficient political will to make these legal and organizational arrangements function effectively. Compassion did not always fit well with traditional *raisons d'état*.[11]

Nevertheless, when the United Nations was created in 1945, there was a growing corpus of legal and organizational experience that the international community could draw on in trying to improve international order and justice. By 1948, without doubt, it became conventional wisdom that internationally recognized human rights would have to be reaffirmed and expanded, not erased. There was no turning back. The UN would have to devise better ways of improving human dignity, through both law and organization.

Basic Norms in the UN Era

By the time of the San Francisco Conference in 1945, at which the Charter of the United Nations was drafted and approved, several actors believed that the new world organization would deal with universal human rights. Despite all the difficulties faced by the international community during the League period in trying to deal with the violation of human rights, European fascism and Asian militarism had convinced important actors that renewed attention should be directed to the safeguard of human rights.

This determination to write human rights into the UN Charter, which had not been done in the League covenant, actually preceded widespread knowledge about the extent of the Holocaust in areas under Nazi control.[12] This renewed attention to fundamental individual rights, therefore, was less a reaction to specific knowledge about German (and Japanese) atrocities and more a culmination of changing opinion that had gained momentum in the 1940s. Intellectual opinion in Britain and the United States, as well as activity by nongovernmental organizations in the latter, had been pushing for an endorsement of human rights as a statement about the rationale for World War II. Franklin Roosevelt had stressed the importance of four freedoms, including freedom from "want." A handful of Latin American states joined in this push to emphasize human rights as a statement about civilized nations. Eleanor Roosevelt became an outspoken champion of human rights in general and women's rights in particular.

The Truman administration, under pressure from both NGOs and concerned Latin American states, and unlike the Wilson administration in 1919, agreed to a series of statements on human rights in the Charter and successfully lobbied the other victorious great powers. This was not an easy decision for the Truman administration, particularly given the continuation of legally sanctioned and widely supported racial discrimination within the United States. Whether the Truman administration was genuinely and deeply committed to getting human rights into the Charter[13] or whether it was pushed in that direction by others[14] remains a point of historical debate. There is some evidence that Truman himself genuinely believed that protecting human rights was indeed linked to a more peaceful international order.

Why Stalin accepted these human rights statements is not clear, especially given the widespread political murder and persecution within the Soviet Union in the 1930s and 1940s. Perhaps Moscow saw this human rights language as useful in deflecting criticism of Soviet policies, particularly since the Charter language was vague and not immediately followed by specifics on application. Another view is that Stalin saw the language of rights as useful in his attempt to focus on socialism—that is, one might accept the general wording on rights if one intended to concentrate only on social and economic rights.[15] This would not be the last time the Soviet Union underestimated the influence of language written into international agreements. The 1975 Helsinki Accord, and especially its provisions on human rights and humanitarian affairs, generated pressures that helped weaken European communism. The Soviet Union indeed initially resisted human rights language in the Helsinki Accord, but it eventually accepted that language in the mistaken notion that the codification and dissemination of human rights would not upset totalitarian control.[16]

The 1945 Charter statements on human rights, although more than some had originally wanted, were vague. Nevertheless, they provided the legal cornerstone or foundation for a later legal and diplomatic revolution.

The Charter's preamble states in its second clause that a principal purpose of the UN is "to affirm faith in fundamental human rights." Again, in Article 1, the Charter says that one of the purposes of the organization is to promote and encourage "respect for human rights and for fundamental freedoms for all without distinction as to race, sex, language, or religion." In Article 55, the Charter imposes on states these legal obligations:

> With a view to the creation of conditions of stability and well-being which are necessary for peaceful and friendly relations among nations based on respect for the principle of equal rights and self-determination of peoples, the United Nations shall promote:
>
> A.   higher standards of living, full employment, and conditions of economic and social progress and development;
>
> B.   solutions of international economic, social, health, and related problems; and international cultural and educational cooperation; and
>
> C.   universal respect for, and observance of, human rights and fundamental freedoms for all without distinction as to race, sex, language, or religion.

Vietnamese refugees in a detention area of Phnom Penh, Cambodia, 1992. (UN Photo 125271/J. Robaton)

This was followed by Article 56, under which "all Members pledge themselves to take joint and separate action in cooperation with the Organization for the achievement of the purposes set forth in Article 55."

The language of Article 55 would have one believe that the Charter was endorsing the notion of human rights because they were linked to international peace and security. There was considerable belief in the Western democracies that states respecting human rights in the form of civil and political rights would not make war on others. In this view, brutal authoritarian states, those that denied civil and political rights, were inherently aggressive, whereas democracies were inherently peaceful. At the same time and as previously explained, many people have accepted the notion of human rights by seeing them as a means to human dignity, not necessarily or primarily as a means to social peace.

Which of these two motivations drove the diplomatic process in 1945? The answer undoubtedly is both. Some policymakers may have genuinely seen human rights as linked to peace, and others may have accepted that rationale as a useful justification while believing that one should promote and protect human rights for reasons of human dignity disconnected from questions of peace and war. Motivation and justification are not the same,[17] but in reality it can be difficult to separate the two.

The relationship between human rights and peace merits additional discussion because of its intrinsic importance to world politics. If there is a clear correlation between at least some human rights and peace, then human rights have importance not only for a direct and "micro" contribution to human dignity. Human rights may also contribute to human dignity in a "macro" sense by enhancing international—and perhaps national—security and stability by eliminating major violence.

Much research has been directed to the question of the connection between various human rights and international and national peace—with peace being defined as the absence of widespread violence between or within nations. It would seem that the following five statements accurately summarize some of that voluminous research:

First, liberal democratic governments (those that emerge from, and thereafter respect, widespread civil and political rights) do not engage in international war with one other.[18] It is difficult to document international war between or among democracies, although some scholars believe that the absence of war is not because of democracy. The United Kingdom and the United States fought in 1812, but one scholar holds that because of the severely limited franchise, the United States did not become a democracy until the 1820s and Britain not until the 1830s.[19] There is great debate about threshold conditions for democracy. For instance, one view is that the United States did not become a democracy until women, 50 percent of the population, gained the franchise. In the American Civil War, the Union and the Confederacy both had elected presidents, but the Confederacy was not recognized as a separate state by very many outsiders, and it also severely restricted the franchise. At the start of World War I, Germany manifested a very broad franchise, but its parliament lacked authority and its kaiser went unchecked in making much policy. Even though some scholars think the historical absence of war between democracies is either a statistical accident or explicable by security factors, other scholars continue to strongly insist that liberal democracies do not war on each other.

Second, liberal democratic governments have used covert force against other elected governments that are not perceived to be truly in the liberal democratic community. The United States during the Cold War used force to overthrow some elected governments in developing countries—for example, Iran in 1953 (Mohammed Mossadeq was elected by Iran's parliament), Guatemala in 1954 (Jacobo Arbenz Guzman was genuinely if imperfectly elected in a popular vote), and Nicaragua after 1984 (some international observers regarded Daniel Ortega as genuinely if imperfectly elected).[20] Several democracies used force to remove the Patrice Lumumba government in the Congo in the 1960s; those elections, too, were imperfect but reflected popular sentiment.[21]

Third, some industrialized liberal democratic governments seem to be war-prone and clearly have initiated force against authoritarian governments. Britain, France, and the United States are among the most war-prone states, owing perhaps to their power and geography. Liberal democratic governments initiated hostilities in the Spanish-American War of 1898 and the Suez crisis of 1956, not to mention U.S. use of force in Grenada and Panama in the 1980s.

Fourth, human rights of various types do not correlate clearly and easily with major national violence such as civil wars and rebellions.[22] In some of these situations a particular human rights issue may be important—for example, slavery in the American Civil War, ethnic and religious persecution in the Romanian violence of 1989, and perceived ethnic discrimination in contemporary Sri Lanka. But in other civil wars and similar intranational violence, human rights factors seemed not to be a leading cause—for example, the Russian civil war of 1917 and the Chinese civil war in the 1930s. The Universal Declaration of Human Rights (discussed further on) presents itself, in part, as a barrier to national revolution against repression. This follows the Jeffersonian philosophy that if human rights are not respected, revolution may be justified. But this linkage between human rights violations and national violence is difficult to verify as a prominent and recurring pattern. Any number of repressive and exploitative governing arrangements have lasted for a relatively long time. And various rights-protective governments have yielded under violent pressure to more authoritarian elites. There does not seem to be one generalized reason, such as human rights violations, economic conditions, or other factors, for intranational rebellion and civil war.

Fifth, armed conflict seems clearly to lead to an increase in human rights violations.[23] If some uncertainty remains about whether liberal democracy at home leads to a certain peace abroad, a reverse pattern does not seem open to debate. When states participate in international and internal armed conflict, there is almost always a rise in violations of rights of personal integrity such as forced disappearance, torture, arbitrary arrest, and other violations of important civil rights. Human rights may or may not lead to peace, but peace is conducive to enhanced human rights.

Whether one accepts as valid a linkage between various human rights and peace—and the broad subject is certainly complex—it remains a historical fact that the UN Charter ushered in an era of lofty rhetoric about universal human rights.

Core Norms Beyond the Charter

The UN Charter presented the interesting situation of codifying a commitment to human rights before there was an international definition or list of human rights. To answer the question of what internationally recognized human rights states are obligated to apply, the United Nations in its early years made an effort to specify Charter principles on this point. On December 10, 1948—now recognized as global human rights day—the General Assembly adopted the Universal Declaration of Human Rights without a negative vote (but with eight abstentions: the USSR and its allies, Saudi Arabia, and South Africa). This resolution, not legally binding at the time of adoption, listed thirty human rights principles. They fell into three broad clusters.

First-Generation Negative Rights

First-generation negative rights are the civil and political rights that are well known in the West, called "first-generation" because they were the ones first endorsed in national constitutions and called "negative" because civil rights in particular blocked public authority from interfering with the private person in civil society. These were the rights to freedom of thought, speech, religion, privacy, and assembly. In the view of some observers, these are the only true human rights. In the view of others, these are the most important human rights because if one has civil and political rights one can use them to obtain and apply the others. In the view of still others, these rights are not so important because if one lacks the material basics of life such as food, shelter, and education, civil and political rights become meaningless.

Second-Generation Positive Rights

Second-generation positive rights are the socioeconomic rights emphasized, rhetorically at least, mostly outside the West. They are called "second-generation" because they were associated with various twentieth-century revolutions emphasizing material benefits, and "positive" because they obligated public authority to take positive steps to ensure minimal food, shelter, and health care. As indicated previously, there is considerable debate as to how important they are. The Carter and Clinton administrations accepted them in theory and gave them some rhetorical attention, the Reagan administration rejected them as not being genuine human rights, and the Bush administration was difficult to characterize.

Third-Generation Solidarity Rights

Third-generation solidarity rights are the group of rights emphasized at least rhetorically by some contemporary actors, called "third-generation" because they followed the other two clusters and called "solidarity" because they supposedly pertain to collections of persons rather than to individuals. Later formulations have included claims to a right to peace, development, and a healthy environment as the common heritage of humankind.

This tripartite breakdown, although perhaps useful to summarize developments, can be overdone. And the increasing trend, pushed especially by the former president of Ireland, who is now the High Commissioner for Human Rights (UNHCHR), Mary Robinson, is that first-, second-, and third-generation rights should be viewed as a "package." [24] In order to apply negative rights, positive action must be taken. The U.S. Department of Justice spends billions each year to see that civil and political rights are respected. Second-generation socioeconomic rights were emphasized very early by the Catholic Church and relatively early by the state of Ireland and various Latin American states. Collective rights can also pertain to individuals. Moreover, they are not so new. The right to national self-determination is actually a right of peoples or nations that has been (a vague) part of international law for decades.

In any event, just three years after the UN Charter came into legal effect, the General Assembly agreed on a list of human rights principles as a statement of aspirations. No state voting for the Universal Declaration of Human Rights succeeded in meeting all its terms through national legislation and practice. This vote was the homage that vice paid to virtue. As readers are no doubt aware, this would not be the last time that state diplomacy presented a large measure of hypocrisy.

Since that time, the Universal Declaration of Human Rights has acquired a status beyond the normal or regular General Assembly recommendation. Some national courts have held that parts of the declaration have passed into customary international law and become legally binding. This seems to be the case, for example, with the declaration's Article 5, prohibiting torture. The overall legal status of the declaration is unclear. Some authorities and publicists believe the entire declaration is now legally binding, whereas others say this is true only of parts of it. The International Court of Justice in the Hague has not rendered an opinion on this question.[25]

The broad impact of the declaration has been considerable. Its principles have been endorsed in numerous national constitutions and other legal and quasi-legal documents. All the new or newly independent European states that once had communist governments accepted its principles in theory in the 1990s, which is not necessarily the same as applying those principles in fact. Of the eight states abstaining in 1948, seven had renounced their abstention by 1993. Only Saudi Arabia continued to object openly to the declaration. Even China, despite its repressive policies and government, issued statements accepting the abstract validity of the universal declaration.

Having adopted the declaration, parties in the United Nations then turned to an even more specific elaboration of internationally recognized human rights. The decision was made to negotiate two separate core human rights treaties, one on civil and political rights and one on social, economic, and cultural rights. This was not done only, or even primarily, because of theoretical or ideological differences among states. The different types of rights also were seen as requiring different types of follow-up. A widely held view was that civil-political rights could be implemented immediately, given sufficient political will, and were enforceable by judicial proceedings. By comparison, socioeconomic rights were seen as requiring certain policies over time, as greatly affected by economic and social factors, and hence as not subject to immediate enforcement by court order. As mentioned earlier, the more recent approach within the United Nations is to blur distinctions and consider rights comprehensively.

By 1956 two UN covenants, or multilateral treaties, were essentially complete on the two clusters of rights. By 1966 they were formally approved by states voting in the General Assembly, the time lag indicating that not all states were enthusiastic about the emergence of human rights treaties limiting state sovereignty. By 1976 the sufficient number of state adherences had been obtained to bring the treaties into legal force by parties giving their formal consent. By 2000 more than 140 states were parties to the two covenants: the UN Covenant on Economic, Social, and Cultural Rights and the UN Covenant on Civil and Political Rights. Few followed the example of the United States, of accepting one but rejecting the other (the United States became a party to the civil-political covenant in 1992, with reservations, but not to the socioeconomic covenant). Most states accepted both covenants.

By 2000 more than forty-five states (not including the United States) had agreed that their citizens had the right to petition the UN Human Rights Committee (after recourse to national efforts) alleging a violation of the civil-political covenant by a government. The Human Rights Committee was made up of individual experts, not governmental representatives. It was not a court but a mediation service that could direct negative publicity toward an offending and recalcitrant government. It worked to prod governments toward fulfilling their international commitments. All states that accepted the socioeconomic covenant were automatically supervised by a UN Committee of Experts. After a slow start, it, too, began a systematic effort to persuade states to honor their commitments. The mechanisms of both committees are treated below.

These three documents, the 1948 Universal Declaration of Human Rights and the two 1966 UN covenants, make up the International Bill of Rights, a core list of internationally recognized human rights. Most of the treaty provisions are clarifications of, and elaborations on, the thirty norms found in the declaration. There are a few discrepancies. The declaration notes a right to private property, but this right was not codified in the two covenants. After the fall of European communism, the General Assembly on several occasions returned to a recognition of property rights. As already noted, there was a broad and formal acceptance of this International Bill of Rights. At the same time, a number of governments were tardy in filing reports with both the Human Rights Committee under the civil-

Guatemalan refugees in the Kanasayab camp in Campeche, Mexico, in 1984.
(UNHCR Photo 14152/12.1984/D. Bregnard)

Afghan refugees in an Iranian refugee settlement at Shamsabad, Khorasan Province, in 1993. This settlement receives clean water from a traditional irrigation system *(khanat).* (UNHCR Photo/23034/06.1993/A. Hollmann)

political covenant and the Committee of Experts under the socioeconomic covenant. But from either 1966 or 1976, depending on which date is emphasized, there was a core definition of universal human rights in legally binding form with a monitoring process designed to specify what the treaties meant.

Supplementing the Core

During most of the UN era, states were willing to endorse abstract human rights. But until the 1990s, they were not willing to create specialized human rights courts—or even to make the global treaties enforceable through national courts. In the next chapter we address ad hoc international criminal courts for former Yugoslavia and Rwanda and the movement toward a permanent international criminal court with broad jurisdiction, as well as the Pinochet case involving national action concerning torture and other crimes against humanity. Traditionally, in the absence of dependable adjudication, states tried to reinforce the international bill of rights, while protecting their legal independence, by negotiating more human rights treaties. This is a way to bring diplomatic emphasis to a problem, to raise awareness of a problem, or to further specify state obligation in the hopes that specificity will improve behavior. The process is similar to some aspects of national law. In the United States, if the Congress is dissatisfied with executive performance under a law, rather than seek adjudication in the courts, an action that frequently is unproductive, the Congress will pass a more specific follow-up law.[26]

At the beginning of the twenty-first century, there exist about 100 international human rights instruments. These include conventions, protocols, declarations, codes of conduct, and formal statements of standards and basic principles. Table 5.1 summarizes the situation. Despite overlap, duplication, and sometimes inconsistency with the International Bill of Rights, the United Nations has seen the emergence of treaties on racial discrimination, apartheid, political rights of women, discrimination against women, slavery, the slave trade and slavery-like practices, genocide, hostages, torture, the nationality of married women, stateless persons, refugees, marriage, prostitution, children, and discrimination in education. The ILO has sponsored treaties on forced labor, the right to organize, and rights to collective bargaining, among others.

Some regional human rights treaties fall outside the domain of the UN, as do some treaties on human rights in armed conflict that are sponsored by the International Committee of the Red Cross and Switzerland, which is the official depository for what is called "international humanitarian law." So diplomatic events technically outside the UN ran in the same direction of specifying international standards on human rights.

In 1949 the international community adopted four conventions for victims of war. Initially drafted by the ICRC, the Geneva Conventions of August 1949 sought to codify and improve on the humanitarian practices undertaken during World War II. For the first time in history, a treaty was directed to the rights of civilians in international armed conflict and in occupied territory resulting from armed conflict. Each of the four Geneva Conventions of 1949 contained an article (hence Common Article 3) that extended written humanitarian law into internal armed conflict. The ICRC, although technically a Swiss private association, was given the right in public international law to see detainees resulting from international armed conflict.[27] And for the first time in history, civilians in occupied territory were given a right to humanitarian assistance.

This body of humanitarian law, in reality the international law for human rights in armed conflict, was further developed in 1977 through two protocols (or additional treaties): Protocol I for international conflict and Protocol II for internal, armed conflict. Normative standards continued to evolve. For example, for the first time in the history of warfare, Protocol I prohibited the starvation of civilians as a legal means of warfare. Protocol II represented the first separate treaty on victims in internal war.

There were also notable regional human rights developments. A regional human rights regime was created in Western Europe, and it served as an excellent model for the international protection of human rights. The European Convention on Human Rights and Fundamental Freedoms defined a set of civil and

TABLE 5.1   UN Human Rights Conventions, May 2000

Convention (grouped by subject)	Year Opened for Ratification	Year Entered into Force	Number of Ratifications, Accessions, Acceptances (May 2000)
General human rights			
International Covenant on Civil and Political Rights	1966	1976	144
Optional Protocol to the International Covenant on Civil and Political Rights (private petition)	1966	1976	95
Second Optional Protocol to the International Covenant on Civil and Political Rights (death penalty)	1989	1991	41
International Covenant on Economic, Social, and Cultural Rights (private petition)	1966	1976	142
Racial discrimination			
International Convention on the Elimination of All Forms of Racial Discrimination	1966	1969	155
International Convention on the Supression and Punishment of the Crime of Apartheid	1973	1976	110
International Convention Against Apartheid in Sports	1985	1988	58
Rights of women			
Convention on the Political Rights of Women	1953	1954	114
Convention on the Nationality of Married Women	1957	1958	69
Convention on Consent to Marriage, Minimum Age for Marriage, and Registration of Marriages	1962	1964	49
Convention on the Elimination of All Forms of Discrimination Against Women	1979	1981	165
Slavery and related matters			
Slavery Convention of 1926, as Amended in 1953	1953	1955	92

(*continues*)

TABLE 5.1   (*continued*)

Convention (grouped by subject)	Year Opened for Ratification	Year Entered into Force	Number of Ratifications, Accessions, Acceptances (May 2000)
Protocol Amending the 1926 Slavery Convention	1953	1953	59
Supplementary Convention on the Abolition of Slavery, the Slave Trade, and Institutions and Practices Similar to Slavery	1956	1957	118
Convention for the Suppression of the Traffic in Persons and the Exploitation of the Prostitution of Others	1950	1951	73
Refugees and stateless persons			
Convention Relating to the Status of Refugees	1951	1954	134
Protocol Relating to the Status of Refugees	1967	1967	134
Convention Relating to the Status of Stateless Persons	1954	1960	49
Convention on the Reduction of Statelessness	1961	1975	21
Other			
Convention on the Prevention and Punishment of the Crime of Genocide	1948	1951	130
Convention on the International Right of Correction	1952	1962	15
Convention on the Non-Applicability of Statutory Limitations to War Crimes and Crimes Against Humanity	1968	1970	43
Convention Against Torture and Other Cruel, Inhuman, or Degrading Treatment or Punishment	1984	1987	118
Convention on the Rights of the Child	1989	1990	199

SOURCE: Adapted from Robert E. Riggs and Jack C. Plano, *The United Nations* (Chicago: Dorsey Press, 1988), updated by the authors in May 2000.

political rights. The European Commission on Human Rights served as a collective conciliator, responding to state or private complaints in order to seek an out-of-court settlement. The European Court of Human Rights eventually existed to give binding judgments about the legality of state policies under the European Convention on Human Rights.

All states in the Council of Europe bound themselves to abide by the convention. All governments allowed their citizens to have the right of individual petition to the commission, a body that could then—failing a negotiated agreement—take the petition to the European Court of Human Rights. All states eventually accepted the supranational authority of the court. Its judgments holding state policies illegal were voluntarily complied with by member states. Such was the political consensus in support of human rights within the Council of Europe. This regional international regime for human rights functioned through international agencies made up of uninstructed individuals rather than state officials—although there was also a Committee of Ministers made up of state representatives.

In the mid-1990s Council of Europe members progressively moved toward giving individuals standing to sue in the European Court of Human Rights without having the commission represent them. Thus an individual would have almost the same legal "personality" or status in the court as a state. Persons came to acquire both substantive and procedure rights of note, a distinctive feature, since formerly it was possible to present a case—or have full "personality," in the language of international lawyers—only as a state.

In fact, the European system for the international protection of civil and political rights under the European Human Rights Convention generated such a large number of cases that, to streamline procedure, the commission was done away with. Individuals were allowed to proceed directly to a lower chamber of the International Court for an initial review of the admissibility of their complaint. If the complaint met procedural requirements, the individual could then move on to the substantive phase, basically on an equal footing with state representatives. There were other regional human rights regimes in the Western Hemisphere and Africa, but they did not match the West European record in successfully protecting human rights.

A number of supplemental human rights treaties are in varying stages of negotiation at the United Nations at the time of writing, including those on indigenous peoples and minorities. A collective right to development has been declared by various UN bodies, including the General Assembly, and may become the subject matter of a treaty. The United States has strongly opposed the entire notion in the past, but the Clinton administration appeared more supportive.

There has been an explosion of diplomatic activity concerning setting human rights standards internationally. There is an already sizable, and still expanding, part of international law dealing with human rights. Human rights have been formally accepted as a legitimate part of international relations. Most states do not oppose these normative developments in the abstract—that is, they do not dispute that international law should regulate the rights of persons even when persons are within states in "normal" times. This generalization also pertains to international or internal armed conflict, and to public emergency—although some rights protections can be modified in these exceptional situations. The United Nations clearly is acting within accepted bounds in establishing human rights standards.

As noted in Part 1, the Permanent Court of International Justice, the first embodiment of the World Court, said in the early 1920s that what is international and what is domestic changes with the changing nature of international relations.[28] The UN era has clearly seen the shrinking of the zone of exclusive or essential domestic jurisdiction. Article 2, paragraph 7, mandates that the UN shall not "intervene" in matters "essentially" within the domestic jurisdiction of states. The diplomatic record confirms, however, that most human rights matters are no longer viewed by most states as *essentially* within domestic jurisdiction. Certainly the establishment of international standards on human rights cannot be logically considered an unlawful intrusion into state internal affairs. And as noted in Part 1 and as will be confirmed in the next chapter, if the Security Council decides that international peace and security are threatened, even UN "intervention"—in the sense of forcible or coercive action—can be taken to rectify human rights violations.

As the extensive standard-setting activity of particularly the UN has made clear, at least in legal theory, human rights have been internationalized. An answer is emerging to the ancient question: *Quis custodiet ipsos custodes?* (Who shall guard the guardians?) In the field of human rights, the United Nations will supervise governmental policy against the background of global norms.

Notes

1. Tom J. Farer, "The UN and Human Rights: More than a Whimper, Less than a Roar," in Adam Roberts and Benedict Kingsbury, eds., *United Nations, Divided World* (New York: Oxford Univ. Press, Clarendon Paperback, 1993), p. 129. A second edition is now available.

2. Jack Donnelly, *Universal Human Rights in Theory and Practice* (Ithaca: Cornell Univ. Press, 1989), pp. 9–27.

3. John F. Hutchinson, "Rethinking the Origins of the Red Cross," *Bulletin of Historical Medicine* 63, pp. 557–578. See also his *Champions of Charity: War and the Rise of the Red Cross* (Boulder: Westview Press, 1996).

4. Jan Herman Burgers, "The Road to San Francisco: The Revival of the Human Rights Idea in the Twentieth Century," *Human Rights Quarterly* 14, pp. 447–478.

5. François Bugnion, *Le Comité International de la Croix-Rouge et la protection des victims de la guerre* (Geneva: ICRC, 1994).

6. Paul Gordon Lauren, *Power and Prejudice: The Politics and Diplomacy of Racial Discrimination* (Boulder: Westview Press, 1988), pp. 76–101; Burgers, "Road to San Francisco," p. 449.

7. Ernst Haas, *Human Rights and International Action* (Stanford: Stanford Univ. Press, 1970). See further Hector G. Bartolomei de la Cruz et al., *The International Labor Organization: The International Standards System and Basic Human Rights* (Boulder: Westview Press, 1996).

8. Burgers, "Road to San Francisco," p. 456.

9. Farer, "UN and Human Rights," p. 97.

10. Jack Donnelly, "International Human Rights: A Regime Analysis," *International Organization* 40, pp. 599–642.

11. Farer, "UN and Human Rights," p. 98.

12. See Burgers, "Road to San Francisco."

13. Cathal J. Nolan, *Principled Diplomacy: Security and Rights in U.S. Foreign Policy* (Westport, CT: Greenwood Press, 1993), pp. 181–202.

14. Burgers, "Road to San Francisco," p. 475.

15. See Nolan, *Principled Diplomacy.*

16. William Korey, *The Promises We Keep: Human Rights, the Helsinki Process, and American Foreign Policy* (New York: St. Martin's Press, 1993).

17. Robert W. Tucker and David C. Hendrickson, *The Imperial Temptation: The New World Order and America's Purpose* (New York: Council on Foreign Relations Press, 1992), p. 86.

18. See, among others, Bruce Russett, "Politics and Alternative Security: Toward a More Democratic, Therefore More Peaceful World," in Burns Weston, ed., *Alternative Security: Living Without Nuclear Deterrence* (Boulder: Westview Press, 1990), pp. 107–136.

19. Samuel P. Huntington, *The Third Wave: Democratization in the Late Twentieth Century* (Norman: Univ. of Oklahoma Press, 1991).

20. David P. Forsythe, "Democracy, War, and Covert Action," *Journal of Peace Research* 29, pp. 385–396.

21. David N. Gibbs, *The Political Economy of Third World Intervention: Mines, Money, and US Policy in the Congo Crisis* (Chicago: Univ. of Chicago Press, 1991).

22. David P. Forsythe, *Human Rights and Peace: International and National Dimensions* (Lincoln: Univ. of Nebraska Press, 1993).

23. Steven C. Poe and C. Neal Tate, "Repression of Human Rights to Personal Integrity in the 1980s: A Global Analysis," *American Political Science Review* 88, no. 4 (December 1994), pp. 853–872.

24. This is the theme of UNDP, *Human Development Report 2000* (New York: Oxford Univ. Press, 2000).

25. See Hurst Hannum, "The Status of the Universal Declaration of Human Rights in National and International Law," *Georgia Journal of International and Comparative Law* 25 (1995–1996), pp. 287–397.

26. David P. Forsythe, *Human Rights and U.S. Foreign Policy: Congress Reconsidered* (Gainesville: Univ. Press of Florida, 1988).

27. To better establish its independence, the ICRC and the government of Switzerland signed a headquarters agreement protecting its premises and personnel from review or intrusion by Swiss authorities, as if the ICRC were an intergovernmental organization. The ICRC seems neither fully public nor fully private, legally speaking; rather it is sui generis (or unique or in a category by itself).

28. Nationality Decrees in Tunis and Morocco, Permanent Court of International Justice, Series B, no. 4, *World Court Report*, p. 143.

6 The United Nations and Applying Human Rights Standards

A variety of offices and agencies within the UN system are active in trying to see that internationally recognized human rights are applied by states and other actors.[1] States that are members of the UN, through their governmental authorities, have primary responsibility in this regard. Individuals and private groups may have obligations in the field of human rights, and nongovernmental actors may play a large role at the UN. But under international law governments are legally obligated to make national law and practice consistent with international agreements.

Where application of rights means protection, the function of the UN system is usually indirect. This means that UN organizations normally try to encourage, push, prod, and ultimately embarrass states into taking steps to guarantee the proper practice of rights. UN organizations normally begin to seek protection through positive steps of encouragement and then gradually shift to more critical stances. There also is a small human rights assistance program that takes a cooperative approach to improving rights protection. On occasion the Security Council authorizes outside parties to undertake direct protection, and it is possible for UN officials themselves to engage in direct protection. We return to these points in the conclusion to this section.

The overall UN process of helping to apply international human rights standards is exceedingly broad and complex. The structure of the main organizational components underpinning that process is illustrated in Figure 6.1. The fundamental point is that the United Nations is extensively engaged in supervising state behavior under international standards on human rights. Actors concerned with other aspects of international relations—for example, sustainable development, as we see in the third part of this volume—are still trying to achieve the extent of international supervision (although not necessarily all its manifestations) already achieved in the field of human rights.

FIGURE 6.1 UN Human Rights Organizational Structure

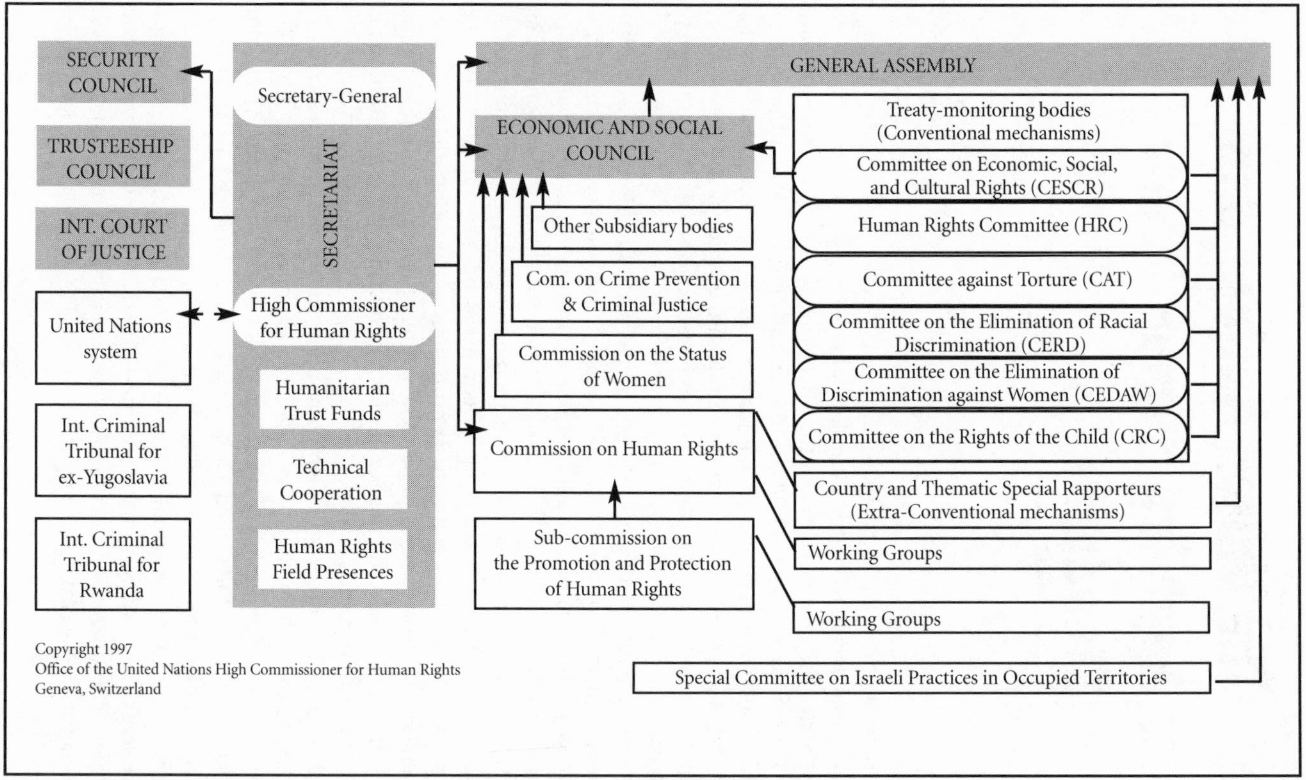

Copyright 1997
Office of the United Nations High Commissioner for Human Rights
Geneva, Switzerland

SOURCE: United Nations High Commissioner on Human Rights, website: http://www.unhchr.ch/hrostr.htm

The Security Council

As explained earlier, the United Nations Security Council has the authority to declare a situation a threat to or breach of the peace. When the council so declares, it can invoke Chapter VII of the Charter and reach a "decision" binding on all states. These decisions can entail economic or military action. On several occasions the Security Council has linked a human rights situation to a threat to or breach of the peace or it has otherwise reached a legally binding decision declaring that economic or military steps are needed to correct a human rights problem. As long as the council links human rights to security issues, it has a broad mandate to act under Chapter VII. Despite the initial concerns of several states, the council in 1993 referred to Chapter VII to create a war-crimes tribunal for the former Yugoslavia. Later it created a similar court for Rwanda. The war-crimes tribunals after World War II, in Germany and Japan, had been created by separate treaty and military executive order, respectively, not by the UN Security Council.

These binding council decisions under Chapter VII are in addition to the more usual suggestive resolutions that, although not directly and legally binding on states, may deal with human rights. For example, the council created in 1989 the UN Transition Assistance Group in Namibia (UNTAG) to oversee the transition to statehood. Among its other duties, UNTAG engaged in the verification of free and fair elections, and thus of the human right to participation in governing arrangements. From a legalistic view, the suggestive council resolutions were not legally binding on states, although they were binding on other UN organs and agencies.

Similarly, the Security Council created a UN commission to collect information about war crimes being committed in the Balkans. Once again, this resolution was not legally binding on states, although it was binding on the rest of the UN system. It has always been true that, in the theory of the Charter, the council would recommend actions, but these recommendations were to be seen against the background of possible further binding action under Chapter VII. The end of the Cold War has allowed this theory to become operational in several situations.

Action by the Security Council under Chapter VII shows the maximum concern for human rights expressed through the United Nations. During the Cold War, only two situations led to the invocation of Chapter VII concerning human rights; both pertained to white-minority rule in southern Africa. We emphasized earlier the coercive aspects of sanctions; here we stress the rationale behind them, namely, the protection of basic human rights.

In 1966, followed by more comprehensive action in 1968, the Security Council voted mandatory economic sanctions on the Ian Smith government of what was then southern Rhodesia. The 1968 resolution mentioned the human rights situation as one justification for the sanctions. Another justification responded to illegal secession from the United Kingdom. These sanctions remained in effect until 1979, when majority rule was obtained in the new state of Zimbabwe. Although the sanctions were too gradual and porous to have been the only cause of the fall of white-minority rule in Rhodesia, they were the first attempt at UN collective economic measures—of a mandatory nature—at least partly in the name of human rights.

In 1977 the Security Council voted a mandatory arms embargo on the Republic of South Africa. Human rights were not explicitly mentioned, only "the situation in South Africa," but the basic issues of concern to the international community were apartheid, the denial of a people's right to self-determination, and majority rule—all defined as human rights issues in international law. The arms embargo, although perhaps manifesting some symbolic value, was too limited and again too porous to end apartheid by itself. It was one element among many that led to progressive change in South Africa by the 1990s.

After the end of the Cold War, the Security Council expanded the use of Chapter VII in relation to human rights. In the spring of 1991, after the Persian Gulf War, known as Operation Desert Storm, the council declared that the human rights situation in Iraq, especially pertaining to the Iraqi Kurds, constituted a threat to international peace and security. Iraqi Kurds were fleeing into both Iran and Turkey to escape repression, although international armed conflict among states was not imminent over this migration. This was the first explicit declaration by the council that violating human rights created a security threat, since the resolutions on both Rhodesia and South Africa had been less specific.

The Security Council did not expressly authorize the use of force to stop Iraqi repression of its citizens, but several states claimed that the council had implicitly authorized force for that purpose. Led by the United States, these states created a protected area for Iraqi Kurds in northern Iraq. Air power was later used in southern Iraq, arguably for the protection of Iraqi Shiites then being repressed by the government, again with the claim that the council had implicitly approved such force. These claims were never authoritatively evaluated.

Three "political" factors were crucial in the evolution of events: the overall weakness of the Iraqi government after its widely condemned and unsuccessful invasion of Kuwait in 1990, continuing U.S. commitment against the various policies of Saddam Hussein, and widespread deference to the United States as the only global military superpower. The United States in the Security Council was widely seen as being tough on Iraq, but not so tough on some other states, such as Israel, concerning implementation of equally demanding council resolutions linked to human rights.

In the Balkans following the breakup of greater Yugoslavia, apart from its other actions, the Security Council authorized the use of "all necessary means" for the delivery of humanitarian assistance in Bosnia. The initial UN peacekeeping forces were deployed under Chapter VI; humanitarian assistance was treated under Chapter VII. Once again, the diplomatic language "all necessary means" was a euphemism for authorizing military force.

In spite of this authorizing language, the lengthy discussion in Chapter 3 made clear that member states of the UN remained more reluctant to use force in Bosnia than in the Persian Gulf without the expressed consent of the various fighting parties. Member states' authorities, including those in the United States, feared a complex and open-ended involvement in the Balkans that might come to resemble the Vietnam War. The cases of Rhodesia, South Africa, and Iraq showed that the council could link human rights violations to international peace and security. Although the Security Council declared the same linkage in Bosnia's case, it was evident that the council might be extremely cautious about implementing what it had declared when the military costs were high. In other words, the costs of enforcement carried weight in considering whether to insist upon respect for agreed-upon standards of human rights.

Likewise, when the council adopted resolutions on the question of Balkan war crimes and related atrocities, the resolutions looked at least for a time more like diplomatic bluff than like strong political will to stop such gross violations of human rights as genocide, political murder, and the use of rape as a political weapon. Information was collected for possible war crimes prosecutions, but initially there was no permanent international criminal court to which that information could be submitted. In early 1993 the Security Council resolved to create such an international court strictly for the armed conflict in the Balkans, but a number of major hurdles remained. The number of suspects was great. The international community did not have physical custody of most of them. A paper trail proving violations of international law was needed that would stand up in court. Moreover, parties seeking a negotiated solution to the political and humanitarian problems of the area needed cooperation from some of the persons identified as potential war criminals.[2]

Political factors had encouraged the Security Council to break new ground concerning human rights in Iraq. But different political factors led to caution by the council in dealing with the Balkans. The council endorsed the Dayton agreements, after which NATO deployed some 60,000 troops, including approximately 20,000 Americans, to constitute IFOR—the Implementation Force. Whereas this military deployment helped end the fighting and secured the disengagement of fighting parties, IFOR was reluctant to use force to try to arrest indicted war criminals or secure the safe return of refugees and displaced persons. Both of these human rights objectives were written into the Dayton accords but were not pursued rigorously.

In 1992, in the context of extensive coverage of the situation by the Western communications media, the council authorized "all necessary means" to create "a secure environment" for the delivery of humanitarian relief in Somalia. In addition, the council declared that in that "unique" situation—referring to the chaos that constituted the absence of sovereignty—civilians had a right to humanitarian assistance. Anyone blocking delivery of that assistance would be committing a war crime for which there was individual responsibility. Under this path-breaking resolution, some 37,000 troops—mostly from the United States—were deployed in Somalia to maintain the order necessary to feed starving civilians. As a result of Security Council Resolution 814, the United Nations took control of this operation with 28,000 of its own blue helmets in May 1993. This was the first Chapter VII military operation under actual command and control of the United Nations.

The primary political factors encouraging these developments in Somalia were not only media coverage and exhortations from the UN Secretary-General but also the absence of a national government, which had disintegrated into a multisided civil war approaching anarchy. Moreover, the costs of the undertaking were judged by military establishments, perhaps mistakenly, to be reasonable. The international community, including developing countries prone to defend the traditional notion of state sovereignty, found it easier to act when there was no national government whose consent was being bypassed. And from the viewpoint of the developed countries, the local armed factions, unlike in the Balkans, were no match for Western military forces.

From these events it was clear that the UN Security Council might authorize direct protection for persons such as the Kurds in Iraq or millions of civilians in southern Somalia, in the name of the international community. International peace and security could mean not just the security of states from foreign attack but also the security of persons inside states. The International Court of Justice (ICJ) would seem to have the right to review such council determinations in the light of the wording of the Charter and other parts of international law.[3] The ICJ had not done so on human rights or humanitarian issues. So the linkage between human rights and a security question was whatever the council said it was. There existed no agreed-upon criteria in the 1990s for coercion to enforce human rights or humanitarian law; such actions reflected what the international political traffic would bear.

In the Somalian case, there was not much risk of international violence, or even much international disruption outside the country. Yet the Security Council still invoked Chapter VII and passed Resolution 794, which ordered fighting parties to resolve their differences and permit humanitarian assistance. In reality, the council was applying Chapter VII to an internal conflict with primary emphasis on humanitarian action. This application has led some observers to conclude that the Security Council was developing, after 1990 and especially in Somalia, a doctrine of truly humanitarian intervention apart from issues of international peace and security.[4] Formally, however, the council asserted not a right of forcible humanitarian intervention per se but a right to respond to situations that it said threatened international peace and security.

Likewise in Haiti in 1994, the council labeled the situation a threat to international peace. The situation clearly did not involve a threat of attack on any other state by the weak authoritarian government. Rather, the most pressing international issue was the flight of asylum seekers to the United States, which stemmed

Haitians take to the streets of Port-au-Prince to celebrate the election of Jean-Bertrand Aristide in 1990. The United Nations Observer Mission to Verify the Electoral Process in Haiti (ONUVEH) and UN security observers assisted with the process of holding the first democratic elections in Haiti's history. (UN Photo 177258/M. Grant)

from an abusive national regime that also failed to promote sustainable development. Once the council authorized the use of all necessary means to restore democracy, the United States was in a strong position to threaten the use of force. The reactionary rulers then agreed to yield peacefully, and migration to the United States ceased. A bevy of UN and other agencies subsequently tried to consolidate the fragile democracy in Haiti. The situation by early 1997 was clearly an improvement over pre-1994, but many problems regarding the situation of human rights remained at the close of the decade.

The actual external agents of outside protection for Iraq, Somalia, the Balkans, and Haiti, for example, were states, through their military establishments. The council played an authorizing role, but a very minor operational role. The delivery of assistance, which was a form of guaranteeing socioeconomic human rights, initially went well in Somalia. But the Balkans showed equally clearly that some situations did not lend themselves easily to outside intervention, even for those with the purest of motives. People had internationally recognized human rights, in both peace and war. But guaranteeing those rights involved complex calculations about feasibility linked to power.

The Security Council can authorize a member state or regional organization to enforce human rights, or the council itself can oversee their direct enforcement.

For the first time, UN personnel in Somalia, beginning in May 1993, directly managed a UN military operation to enforce human rights. What the UN had previously done, in addition to authorizing enforcement by others, was to provide armed observation and reporting elements, usually referred to as peacekeeping forces, in connection with human rights in a number of situations. In places such as Nicaragua, El Salvador, Namibia, and Cambodia, UN forces managed by UN personnel had mainly observed electoral and other agreements. But in these types of operations UN armed personnel had not tried to enforce human rights standards themselves. They had only observed the situation. They had the right—seldom used—to defend themselves with force. And they had reported back to New York on the theory that a UN organ would take steps with national parties to see that rights were protected. The more frequent UN role was not direct protection through enforcement of human rights norms but indirect protection by prodding others to take action.

Increasingly, traditional peacekeeping entailed a human rights element. As Secretary-General Boutros-Ghali wrote in his last annual report in 1996, "The United Nations . . . has moved to integrate, to the extent possible, its human rights and humanitarian efforts with its peace efforts" (para. 1132). The first United Nations Angola Verification Mission (UNAVEM I) verified both troop movements and elections in Angola. The same was true of the United Nations Transition Assistance Group (UNTAG) in Namibia. The United Nations Protection Force (UNPROFOR) in the Balkans was intended to supervise a cease-fire and deliver humanitarian relief. In Cambodia, in an effort to achieve a national peace, the Khmer Rouge—killers of at least a million persons in the 1970s—were persuaded by UN personnel to sign the Geneva Conventions protecting human rights in armed conflict! In fact, all personnel of the United Nations Transitional Authority in Cambodia (UNTAC) were supposed to carry out human rights functions.

Throughout the 1990s it remained controversial whether the UN itself should enforce, rather than observe and mediate, human rights standards. In Somalia during 1993, in an effort to produce national reconciliation and an effective and democratic government, military forces under UN command fired on both civilian demonstrators and combatants and launched military operations against one of the major "warlords" of the country. There were scores of fatalities, and a chain reaction of violence led to declining enthusiasm for international involvement. These events greatly undermined risk-taking in Rwanda during 1994, when perhaps 800,000 persons were killed in ethnic violence. The Security Council did authorize UNAMIR during the later stages of massacres, but the limited military deployment by the French had little effect on political developments and actually led to the sheltering of some Hutus implicated in attacks on other Hutus, as they sought safe haven behind UNAMIR's shield.

Later the Secretary-General contacted a number of states with a view to a military deployment in Burundi, where similar ethnic violence was resulting in the "slow-motion genocide" of perhaps 150,000 persons during a five-year period. Of the fifty states approached, only twenty-one responded. Of these, eleven declined to be of help; of the remaining ten, only three offered ground troops.[5]

The Security Council's response to the evolving humanitarian crisis in Kosovo in 1998–1999 added another twist to the story. Concerned with the increased violence and human rights violations in the territory, the council responded in September 1998 by condemning such acts and calling for an end to all such conflict and terrorism. Yet no concrete preventive or protection action was taken. And when NATO finally acted militarily to deal with the eroding human security situation in March 1999, it did so without explicit UN authorization. As discussed earlier, ironically this NATO action was met at first by a drastic increase in human rights violations against ethnic Albanians in Kosovo by Yugoslav security forces, creating a set of conditions that compelled the majority of the members of the Security Council to act. The UNMIK operation can be viewed in large part as an attempt to design a postconflict peacebuilding model that can bring about a set of conditions necessary to prevent the return of hostilities and provide the self-determination and future human security of the peoples of Kosovo.

The Security Council's complex and multidimensional operational responses to the crises in East Timor, Sierra Leone, and the Republic of the Congo similarly demonstrate a growing willingness to incorporate human rights elements, including special attention to children, directly into peacekeeping operations. They also hint at an increased commitment to the concept of comprehensive human security and peacebuilding.

As discussed in the previous chapter, the operational definition of security employed by the council has been evolving in recent years to include a much broader range of human security concerns, not the least of which are actions to stop genocide and other gross violations of human rights. In an extraordinary move, for example, on August 25, 1999, the Security Council passed Resolution S/Res/1261(1999) focusing on a thematic issue: children in armed conflict. The resolution strongly condemned "the targeting of children in situations of armed conflict, including killing and maiming, sexual violence, abduction and forced displacement, recruitment and use of children in armed conflict in violation of international . . . and calls on all parties concerned to end such practices." How far council members are willing to go in meaningfully addressing such non-country-specific issues is yet to be seen.

The General Assembly

Beyond standard setting, the UN General Assembly practices indirect protection of human rights in two ways. It passes resolutions to condemn or otherwise draw attention to violations of human rights. It also creates various agencies or meetings to deal with human rights and funds them.

About one-third of the General Assembly's resolutions each year deal with human rights. Many of these are adopted by consensus and constitute a rough barometer of which rights policies are judged most acceptable or egregious. For example, the fiftieth General Assembly responded to the execution of a Nigerian human rights and environmental activist, Ken Saro-Wiwa, with a resolution of condemnation of that military government. The vote was 101 to 14, with forty-seven abstentions (mostly by African states). This was one of forty-six human rights resolutions adopted during the 1995 session. The fifty-fourth session of the assembly in 1999 passed well over fifty such resolutions.

When a resolution targets a specific country or violation, it is difficult to evaluate the resolution's effect over time. It might be argued, for example, that the assembly's repeated condemnations of apartheid as practiced in South Africa had some impact on changing attitudes among South Africans. At the same time, many observers are not persuaded that words divorced from coercive power can have much effect.[6] In trying to account for change in South Africa, these observers would emphasize violence against apartheid, formal economic sanctions, and the shrinking of investments by the international business community.

Still, it would seem that General Assembly resolutions on human rights often send important signals, but this observation is difficult if not impossible to measure. The assembly supported the UN Secretary-General, for example, in his mediation of the civil war in El Salvador, which was tied to a human rights accord. Assembly action sent the signal to both the governmental and the rebel sides that the international community supported a negotiated end to that bloody conflict. This signaling role is shared with the Security Council.[7]

There are times when a General Assembly resolution on human rights has worked against the protection of those rights. General Augusto Pinochet in Chile used assembly resolutions to rally nationalistic support for his rule despite the gross violations of basic rights he was overseeing.[8] The assembly's declaration that Zionism was a form of racism not only antagonized Israel but alienated some of Israel's supporters from the assembly. The resolution did nothing for the practice of rights in either Israel proper or the occupied territories that it controls militarily. The resolution was repealed in 1991.

The General Assembly, acting in its second role, has created a segment of the UN secretariat to deal with Palestinian rights and a committee to oversee Israeli practices pertaining to human rights in the territories militarily occupied since 1967. The assembly also voted to hold the World Conference on Human Rights during June 1993 in Vienna. Sometimes the assembly takes a half-step to help with rights. It created the Fund for Victims of Torture, but it refused to make the fund part of the regular UN budget. The fund relies on voluntary donations.

When decisions are not made by consensus, human rights policies reflect the majority controlling the General Assembly. From 1945 until about 1955, the Western majority was not very sensitive to issues of racial discrimination and tended to focus instead on issues like forced labor under communism. There followed a period when the assembly tended to emphasize issues of national self-determination and an end to racial discrimination, reflecting the desires of the developing countries, which had recently become a different "automatic majority" through decolonization. After the end of the Cold War it remained to be seen whether an intensified North-South conflict would completely dominate human rights proceedings in the assembly.

There were certainly manifestations of this North-South conflict, as in the late 1980s and early 1990s when the developing countries successfully reaffirmed the principle of state sovereignty in the face of the industrialized countries' desires to emphasize a right of humanitarian assistance that would supersede state sovereignty. By the late 1990s little had changed in this debate. States from the Global South like Algeria, despite the terrible violence occurring within it, stressed the supremacy of state sovereignty. More stable states from the North, like Sweden, stressed the supremacy of the *droit d'ingérence* or the right of the international community to interfere inside states in the interests of the victims of violence or deprivation. There was simply no consensus in the assembly as to the proper limits of state sovereignty or when the UN was justified in approving action without state consent.

In other manifestations, the General Assembly was also characterized by fragmented views that shifted from issue to issue. On the question of human rights in Iraq, for example, a number of Islamic states thought that the Security Council, as led by the United States, had gone too far in restricting Iraqi sovereignty. On the question of human rights for Muslims in Bosnia, many Islamic states in the assembly wanted the Security Council to go further in challenging Yugoslav and Serbian policies toward Bosnia.

Although the developing countries still controlled the majority of votes in the General Assembly in the 1990s, the Western states had predominant economic and military power. This situation provided the recipe for some accommodation between North and South, especially since the number of developing countries with governments prone to compromise rather than confrontation had grown substantially since the mid-1980s. Hence, in the assembly in the early 1990s, several resolutions endorsed democracy and the integration of civil and political rights into development decisions.[9] These resolutions of the 1990s were not a radical change from some earlier resolutions endorsing the equal value of all human rights, whether civil-political or socioeconomic. They emphasized democracy more than other earlier resolutions. They thus showed a North-South compromise on some human rights language—although this semantic compromise could mask continuing disagreements.

As the decade came to a close, however, two other signs of evolving compromise were in evidence. First, the Fifty-third General Assembly adopted by consensus the "Declaration on the Right and Responsibility of Individuals, Groups and Organs of Society to Promote and Protect Universally Recognized Human Rights and Fundamental Freedoms." This new human rights instrument is aimed at providing a more secure environment within which human rights organizations and advocates can carry out their work.

Second, following a decade of work by the International Law Commission, which the General Assembly had invited in 1989, and the subsequent drafting efforts of the assembly's Preparatory Committee on the Establishment of an International Criminal Court, 160 member states met in Rome in June–July 1998 to attempt to finalize such a convention. Against some difficult odds, this United Nations Conference of Plenipotentiaries on the Establishment of an International Criminal Court was successful in doing just that. The resulting Rome Statute will enter into force upon ratification by 60 states.

However, by early 2000 no major military power had ratified the statute. In fact, only a handful of states had ratified, and the process of securing 60 adherents clearly would prove long. Most disturbingly, the United States not only refused to vote for or sign the statute but also promised to actively oppose ratification by other states. It was hard to see how the projected court could function effectively if the one military superpower in the world, whose support was necessary for all military deployments approved by the United Nations, continued to vigorously oppose the court. Ironically, when the United States undertook the bombing of targets in modern Yugoslavia via NATO in 1999, it placed itself under the jurisdiction of the International Criminal Tribunal for the Former Yugoslavia (ICTFY), which had authority over all possible war crimes in that territory. The United States did not, in fact, contest the jurisdiction of the ICTFY, but the court did not officially pursue reports of possible NATO war crimes, despite some evidence that it could have and/or should have. The Swiss prosecutor shied away from that type of confrontation.

The Office of the Secretary-General

It may sound surprising to some, but prior to the arrival in office of Kofi Annan, UN Secretaries-General did not display a major commitment to human rights per se.[10] The reason may be that all of them have seen their primary role as producing progress on peace and security. This emphasis was understood until the recent past to mean that they could not speak out on specific human rights violations. Had Javier Pérez de Cuéllar, for example, made protection of individual human rights his primary concern, his office probably would have been unacceptable as mediator between Iran and Iraq, or between the Salvadoran armed forces and the FMLN, or in the Afghan situation.

Virtually all Secretaries-General have engaged in good offices or quiet mediation for the advancement of human rights. But only Annan has systematically, though cautiously, thrown the full weight of his office into the quest for human rights protection. Whether one speaks of Dag Hammarskjöld or Kurt Waldheim, two very different Secretaries-General, the point on human rights remains the same. Hammarskjöld, the Swedish economist, was personally not much interested in human rights at the United Nations and concentrated on finding a diplomatic role for the UN in the East-West conflict. Hammarskjöld did find time to take up the case of U.S. airmen detained in China after the Korean War. Waldheim, who served in the German army during World War II, was much less dynamic than Hammarskjöld. Yet he, too, took up human rights or humanitarian questions such as the situation of refugees in Africa, somewhat ironically in light of his own isolation following exposure of his Nazi past. Much the same could be said for U Thant from Burma, who was not as personally committed to individual rights as he was to the collective right of peoples to self-determination. But he, too, engaged in quiet diplomacy on occasion for human rights.

As human rights became more institutionalized in UN proceedings, however, Secretaries-General took a higher profile on rights issues. Pérez de Cuéllar is instructive in this regard. A cautious Peruvian diplomat, he entered office showing great deference to states, especially Latin ones. One of his first acts was to not renew the contract of his chief human rights official, Theo van Boven of Holland. Van Boven had irritated the Argentine junta, then in the process of murdering at least 9,000 Argentines, and its U.S. supporters. By the end of his term, Pérez de Cuéllar had projected the UN, by his own authority, deep into the affairs of both El Salvador and Nicaragua.

In Nicaragua, the UN came to oversee a regional peace accord, to supervise national elections for the first time in a sovereign state, and to collect weapons from a disbanding rebel force. In El Salvador, Pérez de Cuéllar engaged in crucial mediation, following up on a deeply intrusive human rights accord, to help fashion an overall accord for national reconciliation. He also oversaw human rights observers in Haiti in 1991, the first time UN election verification had taken place in a country not wracked at the time by civil conflict.

When human rights were linked to peace, Pérez de Cuéllar and his office came to be bold and innovative. And the two issues were indeed inseparable in places like El Salvador, Nicaragua, Namibia, Angola, Cambodia, Bosnia, East Timor, and Kosovo. The office of the Secretary-General took initiatives, then obtained the backing of both the General Assembly and the Security Council. Increasingly, the Secretary-General was drawn into rights questions that had previously been considered the domestic affairs of states.

Boutros Boutros-Ghali of Egypt followed in his predecessors' footsteps. Upon becoming Secretary-General in 1992, he seemed uninterested in human rights, even appointing an old friend without a human rights record as head of the UN Centre for Human Rights in Geneva. But within the year, Boutros-Ghali was as deeply involved in human rights issues as Pérez de Cuéllar had been. In El Salvador, for example, Boutros-Ghali was active in supporting President Alfredo Cristiani as he tried to purge the army of most of those who had committed gross violations of internationally recognized human rights. Boutros-Ghali was quite outspoken in promoting democratic or participatory values as part of the quest for economic development. This stand may not have been completely desired by some G-77 countries, but his speeches and reports in support of democratic development were supported by many donor countries. In the early 1990s the major donor countries pushed for more grass-roots participation in the search for sustainable development, whether through bilateral programs, the World Bank, or agencies of the UN. The Secretary-General's position fit nicely within this paradigm shift in favor of the human right to participation in public affairs.

Moreover, he appointed the Swedish diplomat who had mediated the Iran-Iraq War, Jan Eliasson, to a new position for humanitarian assistance. This post evolved toward a type of general troubleshooter for humanitarian affairs, which were difficult to insulate from wider human rights issues. By 2000 this position had evolved through several manifestations to become the Office for Coordination of Humanitarian Affairs (OCHA). Its main role is to coordinate rapid and effective relief through the actions of mainly the UNHCR, UNICEF, and the World Food Programme (WFP) and their NGO partners. Ironically, the General Assembly had long been unwilling to formally create the post of a high commissioner for human rights until 1993, largely because of opposition from developing and communist countries. But developing countries tolerated this new post, as well as the new High Commissioner for Human Rights. The Global South saw both as operating on the basis of state consent.

There was a more-or-less straight-line progression: As human rights became more entrenched in UN proceedings, the UN Secretary-General became more openly active on the issue. This was especially true when the human rights issue was integrated with peace and security matters.

Below the highest levels of the office of the Secretary-General, parts of the secretariat have often actively tried to improve behavior under human rights norms. Van Boven, who had annoyed the Argentine junta before his removal by Pérez de Cuéllar, was the clearest example, but other UN officials also were active, frequently behind the scenes. Nevertheless, the Secretary-General sets the tone on human rights for the secretariat, and the fate of van Boven showed that these officials could do only so much without the support of the Secretary-General at the top.[11]

The UN's seventh Secretary-General, Kofi Annan, has been a much more activist human rights leader, including in his priority concerns the encouragement and advocacy of human rights, the rule of law, and the universal values of equality, tolerance, and human dignity as articulated in the UN Charter. One of his most eloquent statements in this regard was his address to the UNESCO (United Nations Educational, Scientific and Cultural Organization) ceremony marking the fiftieth anniversary of the Universal Declaration. In part he said:

> Our belief in the centrality of human rights to the work and life of the United Nations stems from a simple proposition: that States which respect human rights respect the rules of international society. States which respect human rights are more likely to seek cooperation and not confrontation, tolerance and not violence, moderation and not might, peace and not war. States which treat their own people with fundamental respect are more likely to treat their neighbours with the same respect. From this proposition, it is clear that human rights—in practice, as in principle—can have no walls and no boundaries.

Secretary-General Annan also demonstrated the strength of his commitment to the human rights cause in his choice for appointment of a strong-willed High Commissioner for Human Rights: the former president of Ireland, Mary Robinson. She brought more salience to UN diplomacy for human rights than had her predecessor, a former military officer who many thought had perpetuated human rights violations.

The High Commissioner for Human Rights

Debate about the need for a UN high commissioner for human rights had started in the 1940s. The 1993 UN Vienna conference on human rights recommended that the General Assembly create such a post. After a heavy lobbying campaign by a variety of actors, including many NGOs, the Carter Presidential Center, and the U.S. government, the General Assembly finally created the post that autumn. The office had a vague mandate with weak authority. Secretary-General Boutros-Ghali appointed as the first occupant José Ayala-Lasso of Ecuador, who had been foreign minister in a military government. He began his activities in 1994.

The first UN High Commissioner for Human Rights (UNHCHR) practiced quiet diplomacy rather than being a public advocate with an abrasive style. This approach helped alleviate some of the developing countries' fears that the post would be used exclusively to emphasize civil and political rights favored by the Western states, with the developing countries serving as "primary targets." The high commissioner has been received by any number of developing countries with questionable human rights policies; during these visits, those policies have presumably been discussed. Among other activities, the high commissioner has tried to interject more attention to economic and social rights into the work of the UN regional commissions for economic development. This emphasis was continued by Robinson.

Beyond making an annual report on international human rights at the UN, probably the most important work of the high commissioner has been the establishment of human rights field missions inside countries either as part of or as separate from UN peacekeeping operations. The first of these missions was established in Rwanda, where the human rights field staff broke new ground in legal and diplomatic theory but achieved little in practical terms during its early deployment. The high commissioner tried to turn Rwanda into a precedent by then creating field missions in Abkhazia, Georgia, Colombia, and Zaire. By the end of the decade, a UN field presence for human rights had expanded to also include Cambodia, Central African Republic, Democratic Republic of the Congo, El Salvador, Gaza, Guatemala, Indonesia, Liberia, Malawi, Mongolia, Sierra Leone, South Africa, Southern Africa, and South-East Europe. Once more, in the name of universal human rights, the UN was acting on matters that had once been considered fully part of domestic affairs.

The office of the high commissioner also processed requests from states regarding electoral assistance. By the mid-1990s the high commissioner's office was assisting seventeen states in the quest to hold free and fair elections that were internationally supervised. Regional IGOs and NGOs, along with state delegations, were also active in this regard.

The establishment of this post had created some confusion about the overall management and coordination of UN human rights work. Sometimes the high commissioner, the office of the Secretary-General, and the UN Human Rights Commission did not seem to be playing from the same page of music; nor was it always clear who, if anyone, was the conductor. There was some increase in agreements on division of labor as the years progressed. And in 1997 the Center for Human Rights was merged with UNHCHR. But the office of the high commissioner remained chronically short of staff and funds. And questions remained about the organization and effectiveness of the UN's human rights machinery.

The Human Rights Commission

If, when dealing with human rights, the broad and complex UN system is thought of as a wheel, its Human Rights Commission was traditionally the hub.[12] This commission is now made up of fifty-three states elected by the Economic and Social Council (ECOSOC); its history reflects in microcosm the legal and diplomatic revolution on human rights. Despite Western domination of the UN during its early years, the Human Rights Commission was content to promote rights by setting standards rather than by trying to protect them, even indirectly, through various forms of diplomatic pressure. The early commission adopted the position that it lacked the authority to inquire into rights behavior in specific states. When private complaints about rights violations came to the UN, the commission buried them in an elaborate proceeding leading nowhere, one of the most complicated trash baskets ever devised. The early commission, in the words of one careful observer, displayed a "fierce commitment to inoffensiveness."[13]

A North-South compromise, however, opened up new possibilities between 1967 and 1970. As a result, the Human Rights Commission began to deal with specific states and also began to examine private complaints more seriously. Developing states wanted to focus on Israel and South Africa, but developed states broadened the commission's mandate so that states like Greece under military rule (1967–1974) and Haiti under the Duvalier dynasty (1957–1986) also became targets of commission activity. Moreover, states at the commission agreed that private petitions could lead, after screening, to quiet diplomacy and even the publication of a "blacklist" of states with a pattern of gross violations of human rights. These private petitions, however, were treated in a confidential process that minimized the negative publicity that could be directed at an offending government. Ironically, a state could minimize public scrutiny of its rights record by responding somewhat to private petitions in the confidential process.

From the early 1970s to the early 1990s, the Human Rights Commission struggled to find ways of working for human rights in meaningful ways. Through a series of North-South coalitions, propelled partly by the efforts of human rights NGOs, the commission overcame persistent opposition in order to engage in indirect protective activities. It created "thematic procedures" to deal with certain violations. That is, it created either working groups of states or special experts, called rapporteurs, to examine more than two dozen issues such as forced disappearances, arbitrary detention, summary execution, torture, religious discrimination, mercenaries, and deprived or suffering children. Some of these groups not only studied problems with reference to specific states but also sent official telegrams to political authorities and in other ways tried to help persons in the short term. In the mid-1990s the commission's rapporteur on racial discrimination spent considerable time focusing on conditions in the United States. The American media gave almost no coverage to the rapporteur's extended visit in the United States, and the resulting report had virtually no impact on American society.

The Human Rights Commission also dealt in various ways with a series of specific states, both publicly and privately. Over time that list of targeted states became balanced. During the waning days of the Cold War some of these targeted states were aligned with Washington (for example, El Salvador); others were aligned with Moscow (for example, Cuba). Communist China was so targeted after the Tiananmen Square massacre, proving that even permanent members of the Security Council are not immune to pressure. But in 1995 the commission refused, by a one-vote margin, to censure China for its repressive policies. In this same session, however, the commission adopted critical resolutions pertaining to a range of states in the global South such as Zaire, Sudan, and Afghanistan, among others, along with the former Yugoslavia. This pattern continued into the early twenty-first century.

The subject of human rights affects crucial questions of governmental power, and thus an intergovernmental commission was highly politicized. Various double standards and inconsistencies could be documented. Washington at times focused on rights violations in Cuba out of proportion to events there, especially compared to more serious rights violations in allied states like Guatemala and El Salvador.[14] Washington had long used human rights as a political weapon to dislodge the Castro government. Before 1985 Moscow was openly opportunistic, using human rights as a weapon against Washington's allies, such as Pinochet's Chile from 1974 to about 1984, but remaining silent about major violations of human rights in communist states. Again, human rights language was put at the service of ideological and strategic calculations. Most of the developing states paid far more attention to rights violations by South Africa and Israel than to egregious ones in Idi Amin's Uganda or Indira Gandhi's India.

Interestingly, a number of elected governments such as in India and the Philippines opposed certain initiatives designed to help protect human rights.[15] They elevated either solidarity among developing countries or the principle of state sovereignty over rights protection. At times, regional or bloc voting prevailed. A number of Latin American states, including some that were democratic and sensitive to rights at home, tried to shield more repressive Latin American states from the Human Rights Commission's pressure. Again, emphasis on state sovereignty or cultural solidarity superseded UN efforts to protect rights.

For those with a historical perspective, the failure of democratic governments to rally to UN human rights issues should come as no surprise. At the end of World War II, Winston Churchill's government in London wanted to summarily execute high German officials rather than try them at Nuremberg,[16] and London was not enthusiastic about UN Charter language on human rights because it might interfere with the smooth continuation of British colonialism.[17]

Yet the political compromises necessary to secure passage of resolutions operated side by side with the principled work of human rights NGOs that participated heavily in commission proceedings. Overall the Human Rights Commission made fitful progress in monitoring rights over time. NGOs focused on the commission and increased in number over time.[18] By the 1990s large numbers of NGOs were active in all phases of the commission's proceedings.[19] Eventually the East-West conflict dissolved, and a number of former communist states became champions of human rights through the commission. The North-South conflict persisted, especially since more developing states had been twice added to the commission. Although this latter conflict slowed the dynamism of the commission after the Cold War, the commission at the time of writing continued with its thematic procedures and country-specific measures.

Over time the commission dealt mostly with civil rights such as freedom from racial discrimination, torture, forced disappearances, summary execution, and arbitrary detention. This might be seen as a bias stemming from Western states and NGOs, and from developing countries aligned with the West. In defense of this orientation, one could argue that many of these civil rights protected fundamental personal integrity and were necessary to implement a right to life.

The commission did not, in fact, deal very frequently or specifically with socioeconomic rights. Developing states spent time debating a right to development, but most concrete efforts regarding socioeconomic rights in the UN system were handled by agencies like the United Nations Children's Fund (UNICEF) and the World Health Organization (WHO). The WHO, for example, passed resolutions on the human right to health care, then followed up with efforts to get states to adopt health policies consistent with those resolutions. Communist states during the Cold War might have talked about socioeconomic rights, but in their own countries shelter and health care were not treated as equal rights; they were subject to preferential disbursement based on political conformity and status. Apart from the de facto work of the specialized agencies, socioeconomic rights in the UN system had always been, and remain, second-class rights receiving much less specific diplomatic attention than civil rights.[20] By 1996, there was some slightly renewed attention to socioeconomic rights, along with the much-debated right to development. For example, in 1996 the UN held a conference in Istanbul on human settlements. This "Habitat II" conference used the language of a human right to adequate housing. Increased attention has also been focused on the rights of indigenous peoples and other vulnerable groups within society, such as children, women, and ethnic minorities.

The Human Rights Commission also devoted little time and attention to political rights associated with democracy. Most of the states in the world were—and are—authoritarian; even in "democratic times" in history only about one-third of all states have democratic governments. Most of the states represented in the commission were listed by Freedom House, a New York-based NGO, as either partly free or unfree.[21] Thus it was difficult to secure sustained attention to political rights. Additionally, some democratic governments did not want to emphasize democracy in their foreign policy because they had authoritarian allies or, like the Philippines in the 1990s, wanted favors from authoritarian states such as China. Moreover, many of the numerous authoritarian governments were engaged in brutal repression. These conditions caused the commission to focus on fundamental civil rights such as freedom from torture and summary execution. The emphasis was liberalization, not democratization.

It was frequently difficult to prove that the Human Rights Commission had a specific and beneficial impact on a situation. It was one thing to chart changing commission procedures and activity; it was another to demonstrate that these changes inside the commission had led to changed behavior outside that body— namely, within nations. The commission wielded few resources besides diplomatic verbiage. The Security Council could authorize sanctions. The General Assembly commanded more publicity. States and regional organizations like the European Community disposed of economic resources. If a government believed that violation of human rights was necessary for the government's security or the broader national interest, words generated by the commission were unlikely to change the situation in the short term.

Moreover, as demonstrated further on, there were other organizations within the UN system trying to use diplomacy to socialize or shame states into changing their record on human rights. The commission was central, but it was not a "super" agency. It did not supersede or even coordinate most of these other bodies. These latter organizations followed their own agenda and made their own reports without coordination by the UN Human Rights Commission.

Some observers were optimistic about the commission in the 1990s, particularly because its work is seen as most useful when it moves in tandem with efforts by other intergovernmental and nongovernmental organizations working in the same arena. But when they used words like "significant" and "effective," these observers offered little evidence drawn from data or events outside commission meetings.[22] These observers have not always drawn a distinction between efforts to change attitudes over time and efforts to stop violations of rights in the short term. The commission was more likely to help with attitude change over considerable time than it was to turn around a repressive or exploitative situation in the short term. Indeed, several experts and working groups reported back to the commission that many of their protective efforts had gone for naught in the short term. During 1992, the commission held its first emergency session—on the subject of violations of rights in the former Yugoslavia. It appointed as special rapporteur on the subject a former prime minister of Poland (Tadeusz Mazowieki). But when his seventeen reports failed to lead to decisive action to stop atrocities, he resigned in protest in July 1995. A second emergency session was held on the subject of Rwanda, but again no decisive intervention resulted and the genocide there continued until it played itself out.

On a somewhat brighter note, the commission has increasingly come to focus on providing states with advisory services and technical assistance for such activities as reforming national laws to incorporate international human rights norms and promote democratization, training criminal justice personnel, and promoting other related objectives.

Supplemental Human Rights Bodies

The Sub-Commission

The UN Sub-Commission on Prevention of Discrimination and Protection of Minorities is a second all-purpose human rights agency. It is composed of individual experts rather than state or governmental representatives. It screens private petitions before sending them to the Human Rights Commission. Many of these private petitions come from NGOs, not just from victimized individuals. After a dismal start to the petition process, as noted already, the sub-commission finally has begun to display increasing seriousness, but the process has generated only weak pressure. The process is confidential, with a minimum of vague publicity through the parent-commission.

Much of the sub-commission's other work duplicates that of the Human Rights Commission. It has a predictable dynamic on a number of issues, so much so that its recommendations often have been rejected or ignored by government representatives in the commission. At one point during a financial crisis, the sub-commission's sessions were suspended. Many suggested that it be either drastically reformed or dissolved.[23] But at the time of writing it continues—if for no other reason than that its disappearance might send a signal of lessened commitment to human rights.

The Human Rights Committee

Not to be confused with the UN Human Rights Commission, which reports to the General Assembly through the Economic and Social Council, the UN Human Rights Committee was created under the UN Covenant on Civil and Political

Rights. Its membership of individual experts, elected by parties to that convention, functions only in relation to monitoring the implementation of the civil and political rights codified in that treaty. It reports to the General Assembly but is not part of the "regular" UN bureaucracy.

From the late 1970s the Human Rights Committee has processed state reports about implementation of the civil-political covenant and handled individual petitions when state parties have allowed their citizens that procedural right. Despite the Cold War, European communist states became parties to the covenant, and the committee managed to question many states in an objective way about their record on civil and political rights. In a few cases the committee clearly tried to pressure states like Uruguay to improve their records by using negative publicity. In a growing number of countries there is evidence to suggest that because of committee questions and observations a state has been led to change its national legislation to conform to the covenant's requirements. In some court cases judges have made explicit reference to the covenant or committee. One student of the process found matters "quietly encouraging."[24]

But many states are lax about reporting, and some forty-five states that have adhered to the covenant have not consented to the right of individual petition. Some of the changes made by states after legal adherence have been small and technical. By the early 1990s only eight states had reported court cases that applied the covenant directly.[25] The committee seemed most influential when dealing with states committed to human rights but perhaps needing some prodding to conform to all international obligations. The United States, having ratified the covenant with significant and debatable reservations, understandings, and resolutions imposed by the Senate, found itself embroiled in an acrimonious exchange with the committee. The committee, among other things, questioned whether U.S. reservations were compatible with the spirit and purpose of the covenant, and the U.S. Senate, led by Jesse Helms (R-N.C.) as head of its foreign relations committee, questioned the right of the committee to review U.S. actions, then withheld certain appropriations to the UN. But even several U.S. allies questioned whether the United States could become a legal party to the covenant and still reserve the right not to make any changes in its incompatible national laws.[26]

Committee on Economic, Social and Cultural Rights

The UN Covenant on Economic, Social and Cultural Rights authorized the Economic and Social Council (ECOSOC) to supervise the application of the treaty. State parties are obligated to submit a report periodically on state action to implement the covenant. This provision allows some members of ECOSOC to comment on state behavior under the treaty, even though the state making the comments is not a party to the treaty. The United States falls into this category.

In 1979, ECOSOC created a Committee of Governmental Experts to process these state reports. This committee, perhaps because it was drawn from govern-

About 36,000 Cambodians have been disabled by mines as a result of over a decade of bitter civil war. Handicap International runs this workshop for artificial limbs in Siem Reap Town. (UNHCR Photo/I. Guest)

ments, was unable to encourage serious attention to treaty obligations.[27] In 1985 ECOSOC replaced it with a Committee of Individual Experts.

This new socioeconomic committee has proved much more dynamic since 1987, when it first met. Initially taking a cooperative or positive approach toward reporting states, it has tried to get states to establish a national guideline for minimal standards of adequate food, shelter, health care, and the other rights found in the socioeconomic covenant. Thus the supervising committee did not seek at first to establish a global standard, or its standard, for socioeconomic rights. Rather, it prodded states to think seriously about what the covenant meant in their jurisdictions. The focus was on "the extent to which the most disadvantaged individuals in any given society are enjoying a basic minimum level of subsistence rights."[28] The committee sought to establish this not only by examination of legislation but also by socioeconomic statistics.

Alone among the UN monitoring mechanisms, the Committee of Individual Experts accepts written submissions from NGOs as well as from IGOs such as the International Labour Organisation. But most human rights NGOs have not been active regarding these socioeconomic rights.[29] Most NGOs working for adequate food, clothing, shelter, and health care conducted humanitarian rather than human rights programs. This meant that NGOs such as Oxfam have been oriented more toward practical results in a country based on humanitarian concerns and oriented less toward lobbying for socioeconomic rights through the Committee of Individual Experts.

By the early 1990s this monitoring agency was drawing praise from many human rights advocates. According to one observer, by its fifth session the committee showed independence, an effort to maximize its influence, effective procedures, specific and constructive recommendations to countries, and a willingness to say when a country was in violation of its commitments.[30] The Committee of Individual Experts was particularly tough on the Dominican Republic, holding it in violation of the socioeconomic covenant concerning both Haitian workers cutting sugar cane and the right to adequate housing in general.

Several problems have plagued the committee, however. It has functioned in a political vacuum, since few powerful actors have wanted to devote diplomatic efforts to helping implement socioeconomic rights internationally. It has considered only a few state reports each year: in 1990, for example, reports were considered for only six out of a total of ninety-seven state parties. Some reports have been late, and some have been delayed at the request of states. It is clear that this UN effort to monitor and improve state behavior pertaining to socioeconomic rights is to be a long-term project.

Other Supervising Committees

Four other human rights treaties create supervising committees of individual experts. There is the Committee on the Elimination of Racial Discrimination (CERD), the Committee on the Elimination of Discrimination Against Women (CEDAW), the Committee Against Torture (CAT), and the Committee on the Rights of the Child (CRC). They function in similar ways. They may have generated some slight influence on states that are parties to the treaties. None has had such remarkable influence as to merit detailed study.

A few words about CERD and its parent treaty against racial discrimination may help to outline the gap between normative theory and behavioral reality. There are almost 130 parties to this human rights treaty, and much rhetoric has been expended within the UN system about the evils of racial discrimination. Every four years states parties are required to submit comprehensive reports regarding compliance with treaty provisions, with briefer updating reports due every two years in between. Such reports serve as the primary input into the committee's work. Yet many states routinely fail to comply, thus making it difficult for the committee to fulfill its mandate. Also, in the early 1990s only fourteen states had permitted their citizens to bring a private petition to CERD claiming violation of the treaty, as specified under Article 14 of the treaty. Of these fourteen states, only two were African (Algeria and Senegal). No Asian state has agreed to this procedural right of private individuals or groups. In 1991 there was only one such petition; and when a request went out to states to comment on the financing of CERD, only twenty states bothered to reply and only sixteen agreed to contribute more resources. Nothing was done to enhance the functioning of the monitoring committee.[31]

The UN High Commissioner for Refugees

Separate mention should be made of the office of the UN High Commissioner for Refugees (UNHCR). Created by the General Assembly apart from the 1951 Refugee Convention and its 1967 protocol, the UNHCR functions to provide protection and assistance to refugees and people in refugee-like situations. This latter terminology means that the General Assembly has authorized the UNHCR to deal with persons displaced within a state, with those fleeing war or breakdown in public order, and with those identified by the 1951 convention (and hence convention "refugees" who have crossed an international boundary because of a well-founded fear of persecution).

States themselves make the final determination of who is a convention refugee and who is therefore entitled to temporary asylum from persecution. The exact role of the UNHCR in protection can vary according to national law, but in general one primary role of the UNHCR is to help states determine who should not be returned to a situation of possible persecution. The agency calls this "legal" or "diplomatic" protection, and it can involve interviewing those who claim to be refugees, advising executive branches of government, and helping legislators with drafting or submitting legal papers in court cases.

In the late 1990s the number of persons of concern to UNHCR hovered around 22–23 million. In 1998, for example, this target population included about 12 million refugees, 1 million asylum seekers, 3.5 million returnees, and 6 million internally displaced persons (IDPs) and others of concern.

Particularly when faced with an influx of unwanted persons, states may show a racial or ideological or other bias in their procedures that determine who is recognized as a legal refugee—and entitled not to be returned to a situation of danger. At times the UNHCR will publicly protest what a government is doing. For example, even though the United States is the largest contributor to the agency's voluntary budget, the UNHCR officially protested the forced return of Haitians in 1992 without a proper hearing about their refugee status.

The agency also is involved in assistance. Rather than being an operating agency itself, the UNHCR prefers to supervise material and medical assistance to refugees, broadly defined, by contracting with NGOs to provide for the delivery of necessary goods and services to both refugees and internally displaced persons. In 1998 the agency had 244 offices in 118 countries with a staff of 5,528 and a total budget of $1.1 billion. It worked in concert in the field with about 425 NGOs as implementing partners. Most of the amounts raised through voluntary contributions were devoted to assistance, and most of this was spent in Africa and Asia. In the early 1990s the UNHCR was deeply and extensively involved in the Balkans,

The UN High Commissioner for Refugees Sadako Ogata visits Sarajevo in July 1992. (UN-HCR Photo/E. Dagnino, A. G. L. Ronchi)

devoting about a third of its total resources there. From spring 1994 the agency was responsible for coordinating relief to some 2 million persons who had fled Rwanda. The growing emphasis on assistance has led some observers to criticize the diminishing role of traditional protection in the organization's priorities. The logic of this distribution is that many institutions can provide aid but only the UNHCR can protect refugees.

Convention refugees are the victims of human rights violations; those fleeing war and breakdowns in public authority may also be escaping human rights abuses. In general, however, other actors deal with fundamental human rights violations; the UNHCR is left with the intermediate task of coping with refugee flows.

Within this context, it is worth devoting attention to the evolution of the treatment of internally displaced persons.[32] The presence of these war victims who are in what UNHCR calls "refugee-like situations" within their own war-torn countries is fundamentally a human rights issue. As the new century dawns, IDPs have become more numerous than refugees. At the end of the last century, the number of refugees had shrunk to about 13.5 million from earlier totals almost twice that high, but the number of IDPs had grown considerably larger (at least 17–18 million, and conceivably twice that number). When IDPs were first counted in 1982, there were only a million, at which time there were about 10.5 million refugees.[33]

In historical terms, the rapid evolution of measures on behalf of IDPs in the 1990s and the embrace of their plight by IGOs and NGOs demonstrates the in-

A few among the estimated 230,000 displaced East Timorese sought shelter in Assunta Church in Kupang, West Timor, in September 1999. (UN/UNHCR/F. Pagetti)

creasing weight of human rights in state decisionmaking.[34] Efforts accelerated at the beginning of the 1990s, when, as has so often been the case in the human rights arena, individuals and private institutions pushed governments and inter-governmental organizations to find a new way to deal with the growing problem of internal displacement. Roberta Cohen documents that "as early as 1991, non-governmental organizations (NGOs) began calling for the consolidation into a single document of the different international standards that apply to IDPs."[35] As the numbers of internally displaced victims rose, so did the decibel level within the UN Human Rights Commission of the voices of such NGOs as the Quakers, the Refugee Policy Group, the World Council of Churches, and Caritas.

In 1992, then UN Secretary-General Boutros-Ghali submitted the first analytical report on IDPs to the UN Commission on Human Rights in Geneva.[36] In its Resolution 1992/73, and not without considerable controversy, the commission authorized the Secretary-General to appoint a representative to explore "views and information from all Governments on the human rights issues related to internally displaced persons, including an examination of existing international human rights, humanitarian and refugee law and standards and their applicability to the protection of and relief assistance to internally displaced persons." Proceeding deliberately, the commission also specified the breadth of coverage for the special representatives of the Secretary-General (SRSGs) reporting: existing laws and mechanisms; possible additional measures to strengthen the application of such laws; and new ways to address the protection needs that are not covered by existing instruments.

Shortly thereafter the UN Secretary-General designated Francis M. Deng, a former Sudanese diplomat and a senior fellow at the Foreign Policy Studies Program of the Brookings Institution who also directs its Africa Program, as his representative on internally displaced persons. Deng was asked to pursue his mandate on a voluntary, part-time basis, which is usual for the United Nations in the human rights arena. The SRSG actively solicited cooperation from a wide range of experts and autonomous research institutions to such an extent that governments on the Commission on Human Rights characterized the approach as exceptional. The development of a comprehensive global approach for effective assistance and protection of IDPs has thus been independently formulated and financed. At the outset of the effort, the Brookings Institution worked with the Refugee Policy Group (RPG);[37] and Roberta Cohen—a human rights specialist and former U.S. deputy assistant secretary of state for human rights who was a senior adviser at the RPG—eventually joined Deng as an associate at Brookings and codirector of the analytical efforts on behalf of IDPs.

In a number of publications, the Secretary-General's special representative Francis Deng assumes the continuing centrality of the Westphalian system and seeks pragmatically to reconcile international involvement with the traditional prerogatives of the state through "sovereignty as responsibility."[38] To the three characteristics usually considered attributes of a sovereign (territory, a people, and authority), Deng adds a fourth (respect for a minimal standard of human rights). The Secretary-General himself has not gone as far as French activists Bernard Kouchner (currently heading the UN operation in Kosovo) and Mario Bettati would like because he espouses no duty or obligation to override sovereignty.[39] But in his speech to the Fifty-fourth General Assembly, Kofi Annan approached Deng's notion of sovereignty as responsibility.[40]

The power of this approach resides in underscoring a state's responsibilities and accountabilities to domestic *and* international constituencies. Accordingly, a state is unable to claim the prerogatives of sovereignty unless it meets internationally agreed-on responsibilities, which include respecting human rights and providing life sustenance to its citizens. Failure to meet such obligations legitimizes involvement and even military intervention by the society of responsible states. "In the real world, principles often collide," President Bill Clinton told the same General Assembly, "and tough choices must be made."[41] It should be clear to readers by now that the language of UN resolutions and of such public policy discourse as Clinton's and Annan's speeches is not fluff but the veritable stuff of priority-setting when norms clash.

The UNHCR has always found it difficult to negotiate what it calls durable solutions for refugees and those in refugee-like situations. The preferred durable solution is repatriation, but this usually entails fundamental political change in the country of origin—something the UNHCR obviously cannot produce with the wave of a magic wand. The UNHCR does not deal with Palestinian refugees; they are serviced by the UN Relief and Works Agency (UNRWA). But the fundamental problems remain the same. In the Middle East, at least two generations of refugees have been born in camps; "durable solutions" have proven elusive.

Both the UNHCR and UNRWA share other frustrations. Both are dependent on host-state cooperation for security and other policies in refugee camps. For Rwandan refugees in the Congo (formerly Zaire), as for Palestinian refugees in Lebanon or Syria, the host state makes decisions about what groups are allowed to have arms or engage in political activity. In both examples, refugee groups have been active in preparation for launching armed attacks against the Tutsi government in Rwanda or any government in Israel, respectively. UN refugee agencies are caught in these types of political struggles without either the legal authority or the power to make a difference. Because of such considerations in Zaire, some NGOs such as Doctors Without Borders refused to service refugee needs, believing the NGO was contributing to a resumption of violence. The UNHCR decided to stay. It did not want to abandon genuine civilians who had been displaced and were really being held hostage by armed militias.

In the case of refugees and economic migrants from Vietnam, the UNHCR was involved in a negotiated solution under which those who had left Vietnam for places such as Malaysia and British Hong Kong would return in an orderly fashion. The UNHCR distributed monetary payments to persons, as funded by cooperating states, and supervised the returnees inside Vietnam to verify lack of persecution. Thus the plight of "the boat people," who frequently had been subjected to piracy in the South China Sea, was improved, with the UNHCR playing an important intermediary role.

Another durable solution entails resettlement. This option is made difficult because of the very large numbers of people involved in many migrations. In the early 1990s there were about 18 million refugees and persons in refugee-like situations and at least an equal number of internally displaced persons. Permanent resettlement for most refugees was out of the question as far as host states were concerned. For example, almost 5 million persons, or a third of the population, left Afghanistan during the fighting there in the 1980s. Iran and Pakistan hosted many of these persons. Resettlement was not a serious option given not only the numbers but also the lack of economic infrastructure of the two host states. And most refugees do not want to settle in a strange land if there is any hope of a sufficient change to make their home country safe.

Moreover, even smaller numbers of persons may seem too large. The United States tried to exclude as many Haitians as possible from coming to Florida during the 1980s. Many residents of Florida did not want more Haitian resettlement there. In the 1990s the German government decided it had too many foreigners of all nationalities applying for asylum there. The neo-Nazi right wing in Germany carried out a number of violent attacks. Further refugee resettlement, whether

Rwandan children who lost their parents in a massacre rest at Ndosha Camp in Goma, Zaire, July 1994. (UN Photo 186797/J. Isaac)

temporary or permanent, seemed out of the question to a German government struggling to maintain social peace. In fact, all countries of traditional resettlement for refugees, from Canada to Australia, decided to restrict as many refugees as possible during the 1980s and 1990s.

It is relatively easy to restrict numbers when a country is one of second asylum, or resettlement. A state party to the 1951 treaty is not obligated to accept any refugees for resettlement. When dealing with refugees from Vietnam who are in Hong Kong, the United States can select whomever it wishes for entry into the United States.

Only a country of first asylum is legally obligated not to return those with a well-founded fear of persecution. Economic migrants can be returned legally, but for genuine convention refugees, there is no ceiling on the number permitted temporary safe haven in the form of asylum. This can be a problem from the point of view of *raisons d'état.* Thus the UNHCR can find itself trying to protect and assist refugees, but in a context in which the host government may have its own reasons for denying safe haven to as many as possible. The UNHCR does not have the legal authority to make the final determination, much less the power to get states to do what the UNHCR prefers.

For decades the UNHCR tried to protect and assist persons who had fled Cambodia, and sometimes Vietnam, but who became stranded on the Thai-

Cambodian border. The Thai government would not let these persons move to the interior, and the Khmer Rouge in Cambodia would not let them retrace their steps across that country. So the UNHCR and other humanitarian agencies did what they could given the political constraints of the situation. How the UN-HCR could manage the problem without creating a culture of dependency among refugees was not clear. Without the host state's permission to work in the local economy, there was no viable alternative to international welfare.

In trying to manage large and politically sensitive problems, the UNHCR for a time developed a reputation for effectiveness. In 1981 it was awarded the Nobel Peace Prize. Afterward, however, criticisms increased about its internal management and external influence.[42] One high commissioner, Jean-Pierre Hocké of Switzerland, resigned in the midst of controversy. In 1990 Sadako Ogata of Japan became the first woman to head the agency, and the dynamism and reputation of the agency seemed to regain some of the previous high ground. But by the year 2000, questions continued to be raised about what had become a sizable bureaucracy.

It should be emphasized that refugees and those in a refugee-like situation usually are fleeing human rights violations. It is only when the root causes of these human flows are addressed that the preferred durable solution, repatriation, can be achieved. This requires political commitment from the international community. In the meantime, the UNHCR is left to cope as best it can. This has been especially challenging in the context of the deteriorating humanitarian situation throughout much of Africa. Yet the approach to peacekeeping used in Kosovo, East Timor, the Congo, and elsewhere in the late 1990s provided hope for some improved attention to these forcibly displaced.

Supervising Rights and Development

Despite vast amounts of words in the General Assembly and Human Rights Commission about socioeconomic rights and a claimed right of development, the first forty-five years of the United Nations witnessed few concrete efforts to translate this diplomatic rhetoric into policy. For much of the UN's history there was little serious effort among policymakers to devise programs that promoted economic growth in developing countries while integrating internationally recognized human rights. As a former head of the UN Centre for Human Rights documented, rhetoric about human rights and planning for economic growth were kept in separate compartments at the UN.[43] The United Nations Development Programme (UNDP), the World Bank, UNICEF, WHO, the World Food Programme (WFP), and other UN organizations went about their traditional business in developing countries without much regard for the language of rights. There was some programmatic rhetoric about "women in development"; but this was not coordinated with legal instruments oriented to women's rights.

This situation began to change in the late 1980s and early 1990s. Important opinion leaders in developed countries became dissatisfied with the record of attempts to achieve economic growth through authoritarian governments. The record in Africa between 1955 and 1985 was especially poor. Political changes, particularly in Latin America but to a lesser extent elsewhere, gave rise to more democratic governments in developing countries. Seeking macronational economic growth without attention to human rights could lead to marginalization of sectors of society. Even the World Bank, which had long claimed that human rights factors were "political" and therefore not within the bank's mandate, began to reconsider its stance—albeit with considerable confusion. The bank, the largest lender to developing countries, began to emphasize what it called "good governance." This could and sometimes did entail attention to civil and political rights, although competing interpretations abounded. Although the bank still sought to avoid taking a stand about democracy at the national level, it did endorse participatory development. Within the concept of social assessment, it made judgments about the extent of popular participation in development projects.[44]

As part of this broad shift by various actors toward incorporating human rights considerations into "development," the UNDP created indices trying to measure "human freedom" and "human development" in a socioeconomic context, which are suggested in Tables 6.1 and 6.2. Since the effort began in 1990 under the guidance of the late Pakistani economist Mahbub ul-Haq, the annual publication of the *Human Development Report*[45] has provoked a storm of controversy, especially from developing countries.[46] Among other criticisms, publications from the UNDP were said to exceed the responsibilities of an international civil service. Developing countries had long been sensitive to secretariat officials' passing judgment about how states measured up to international standards. Contributing to the controversy was the undeniable fact that the methodology used to rank countries according to various human rights was debatable. UNDP abandoned its freedom index, but like the World Bank, the agency talked more about participatory development. It endorsed an active role for citizens' groups in development projects. This approach entailed defense of civil rights such as freedom of speech and freedom of association.

As noted, from 1987 the expert committee supervising the Covenant on Economic, Social, and Cultural Rights became more assertive than its predecessors. This increased activity, too, fed into the increased efforts at the United Nations conceptually and programmatically to link human rights and development. And the UN Human Rights Commission began to study accurate indicators for social and economic rights. The basic logic of the claimed right to development, which had been accepted in resolution form by the General Assembly but not turned into a treaty right, was that economic development meant more than economic growth. Development meant economic growth with attention to civil-political and socioeconomic rights.

TABLE 6.1 Controversial Human Freedom Index

Countries Scoring High (perfect equals 40)	Countries Scoring Low
Sweden, 38	Iraq, 0
Denmark, 38	Libya, 1
Netherlands, 37	Romania, 1
Finland, 36	Ethiopia, 2
New Zealand, 36	China, 2
Austria, 36	South Africa, 3
Norway, 35	USSR, 3
France, 35	Bulgaria, 4
Germany, 35	Zaire, 5
Belgium, 35	Pakistan, 5
Canada, 34	Vietnam, 5
Switzerland, 34	Indonesia, 5
United States, 33	North Korea, 5
Australia, 33	Syria, 5
Japan, 32	Cuba, 5
United Kingdom, 32	Mozambique, 6
Greece, 31	Saudi Arabia, 6
Costa Rica, 31	Czechoslovakia, 6

SOURCE: UN Development Programme, *Human Development Report 1991* (New York: Oxford Univ. Press, 1991), p. 20. Reprinted by permission of Oxford University Press, Inc.

TABLE 6.2 Human Development Index, 1999

Top Ten	Bottom Ten
Canada	Sierra Leone
Norway	Niger
United States	Ethiopia
Japan	Burkina Faso
Belgium	Burundi
Sweden	Mozambique
Australia	Guinea-Bissau
Netherlands	Eritrea
Iceland	Mali
United Kingdom	Central African Republic

SOURCE: Based on information in UN Development Programme, *Human Development Report 1999* (New York: Oxford Univ. Press, 1999), pp. 134–137. Reprinted by permission of Oxford University Press, Inc.

The logic of the International Bill of Rights is that economic growth is to be pursued primarily according to democratic state capitalism with a welfare state. There is to be political participation, which entails certain civil rights, in making public policy. The state is to exercise broad responsibility for the economy and society; private property is to be respected in principle; and the state is to guarantee minimal standards of material welfare, especially to those unable to purchase it. In hyperbolic synopsis, the International Bill of Rights calls for Sweden writ large.[47] Whether real life could be breathed into the right to development, especially over the opposition of conservatives in the United States, was not clear by the beginning of the new century. Even if the Clinton administration proved more sympathetic than its predecessors to economic and social rights and to the right to development, it has been far from clear that the U.S. Senate would consent to treaties on these subjects or that Congress would provide much foreign assistance to fund projects abroad that were directed to minimum standards of food, clothing, shelter, and health care. The United States ranked last among all OECD states in percentage of its GNP directed to official development assistance. For the United States, as for most other states, rhetoric in favor of human rights exceeded the reality of support for concrete UN human rights action.[48]

Emergency Assistance

But what happens when economic development (meaning economic growth accompanied by internationally recognized human rights) breaks down because of war, public emergency, or natural disaster (sometimes combined with corruption or incompetence)? The UN system has long been involved in trying to cope with natural disasters, whether those that evolve slowly (for example, drought) or suddenly (for example, earthquakes or volcanic eruption). The UN has increasingly become involved in responding to socioeconomic needs resulting from war and public emergencies. In 1998, for example, over $2 billion of humanitarian assistance was requested to aid nearly 13 million people suffering from humanitarian emergencies.

In situations said to be peaceful or in the absence of acknowledged armed conflict, various UN organizations exist either to prepare for these disasters or to respond to them.[49] As mentioned earlier, in 1992 the Department of Humanitarian Affairs, incorporating the UN Disaster Relief Office (UNDRO), was created to coordinate international humanitarian relief. As discussed earlier, as part of the Secretary-General's reform initiative, the department was restructured in January 1998 and renamed the Office for the Coordination of Humanitarian Affairs. OCHA is headed by an Under-Secretary-General who serves as emergency relief coordinator (ERC) responsible for coordinating disaster relief both within and outside the UN system. UNHCR and UNICEF usually play active, and sometimes lead, roles in coordinating international relief. The WFP is usually involved in logistics. WHO and the Food and Agriculture Organization (FAO) usually are not far behind. And the UNDP, which is supposed to coordinate all UN activities within a country, is also involved. The ERC has been mandated the responsibility of overseeing the rapid deployment of staff during crisis situations and ensuring that appropriate coordination mechanisms are set up.

Moreover, a galaxy of private relief organizations also is active. The International Federation of Red Cross and Red Crescent Societies, which loosely coordinates more than 150 national units, sees natural disaster work as one of its primary reasons for being. Hundreds of other private agencies such as Oxfam, Caritas, and Feed the Children try to respond to natural disasters with emergency assistance.

A major problem with all of this international assistance, broadly conceived, is that no one really has been in charge. "Coordination" is an oft-used word to describe a loosely knit network of intergovernmental and nongovernmental organizations as well as state agencies active in humanitarian relief. Every agency is in favor of coordination in principle, but few wish to be coordinated in practice. As has been accurately written, "There is no guarantee that emerging or existing situations of significant human suffering will be brought before the United Nations."[50]

There exists no system for triggering and delivering international disaster assistance; there is rather a hodgepodge of public and private agencies. And the independent role of the communications media in covering or ignoring a story is often important. Whether these actors are motivated to act because of a concern for the human rights to food, clothing, shelter, and health care (which has been rare) or because of humanitarian compassion (more prevalent), all of these actors have proceeded without central coordination—and thus with resulting overlap and confusion.

Various UN organizations have been protective of their decentralized independence. The private agencies have resisted coming under the full control of public authorities. Various agencies have competed among themselves for a slice of the action in a given situation and for credit for whatever accomplishments were achieved—said to be important for fund-raising.

To be sure, emergency assistance has been delivered and lives have been saved in a vast number of situations. Host governments have frequently welcomed international help for natural disasters, although some of the less savory governments have diverted sizable chunks of this aid to the pockets of the elite—for example, in Somoza's Nicaragua after a severe earthquake. The UN General Assembly, mostly reflecting the view of developing countries, has endorsed the idea of international assistance as long as state consent is obtained. Actors like the United States and the European Community have coordinated some of the assistance by providing public money to NGOs (sometimes called PVOs, private voluntary organizations, or VOLAGS, volunteer agencies). At times all of this activity is put under a UN umbrella, as in northern Iraq and the former Yugoslavia. But by and large, coordination in the form of an institutionalized response has been lacking. Coordinated effectiveness has to be constructed almost from scratch for each assistance operation.

Because of this long-recognized situation, the General Assembly in 1991 authorized in Resolution 46/182 a new position of Under-Secretary-General for emergency relief. But this official, however well intentioned and adept, still operates in a milieu in which public and private agencies resist central control over their independence of action and fund-raising. Donor states have expressed growing concern about this "nonsystem" and issued a statement saying, "We commit ourselves to making the United Nations stronger, more efficient and more effective in order to protect human rights." At that time they also called for an "improvement in the UN system . . . to meet urgent humanitarian needs in time of crisis."[51] But decisive change for the better has not really materialized; in fact, the changes have been mainly cosmetic.[52]

With the creation of OCHA and the ERC a step was taken toward rationalizing a more coherent coordination approach. The ERC chairs an interagency standing committee (IASC), which includes major UN and non-UN humanitarian actors. This body strives to facilitate interagency analysis and decisionmaking in response to humanitarian emergencies. Also, in his role as Under-Secretary-General, the head of OCHA serves as convenor of the Executive Committee for Humanitarian Affairs (ECHA), which is a cabinet-level forum for coordinating humanitarian policies within the UN. Only time will tell how effective such coordination will be.

In armed conflicts and public emergencies stemming from so-called human-made disasters, the provision of emergency relief to civilians is only slightly more institutionalized. At least legal rights and duties have been clarified in international wars, and emergency relief in those situations has occurred—although not without problems.[53] In relative terms, emergency assistance has usually fared worse in most internal wars—except for delayed assistance in Somalia.

By law and by tradition, the International Committee of the Red Cross (ICRC) coordinates international relief in international wars. The 1949 Geneva Conventions for victims of war, and the supplemental 1977 Protocol I, give the ICRC a preferred position for this task, especially since protecting powers (neutral states appointed by the fighting parties for humanitarian tasks) are rarely named anymore. As noted, the UN Security Council has affirmed the rights of civilians to international assistance in such wars, and belligerents have a legal duty to cooperate with neutral relief efforts. Protocol I from 1977 states clearly that starvation of civilians is not legally permitted in warfare and that belligerents are not legally permitted to attack objects vital to the survival of the civilian population.

The ICRC is a small private agency whose sources of funds are summarized in Table 6.3. It is specifically recognized in public international law and also by the General Assembly, which has accorded the ICRC observer status. (The Federation of Red Cross and Red Crescent Societies was also given observer status.) For large-scale relief the assembly prefers that UN organizations, along with NGOs,

TABLE 6.3 Top Financial Contributors to the International Committee of the Red Cross, 1995 (excluding services and in-kind donations)

Governments	National Red Cross/ Crescent Societies
USA	German
Switzerland	Swedish
(European Union)	British
Netherlands	Japanese
Sweden	French
Norway	Norwegian
Japan	Austrian
Canada	Dutch
Denmark	Danish
Germany	Finnish
France	

SOURCE: ICRC Secretariat, *Annual Report 1995* (Geneva: ICRC, 1996), pp. 326–327.

be the primary operational agents of humanitarian assistance and that the ICRC adopt a monitoring role.[54] In Somalia in the early 1990s, the ICRC remained to play a central role in relief, even after the Security Council authorized the use of force to deliver that relief. In other violent situations, as on the Indian subcontinent in 1971, the ICRC worked closely with the UN system in monitoring the delivery of food and other socioeconomic relief to East Pakistan/Bangladesh.

But here again the disorganization of the UN system regarding assistance comes into play. There is no institutionalized lead agency for the UN in armed conflict, as is equally true in peace. In the past, head agencies have been selected on an ad hoc basis by the UN Secretary-General. There is now the Under-Secretary-General for humanitarian affairs, who must still negotiate operational details from a welter of options. What is now called the Red Cross and Red Crescent Movement is either disorganized or decentralized; the ICRC does not fully control national Red Cross-Red Crescent units and certainly not their international federation. There have been a number of suggestions concerning how to improve the broad international response to civilian need in violent situations.[55]

The situation is even more complicated in internal armed conflict where one or more fighting parties does not represent a widely recognized state and where most of the fighting occurs primarily on the territory of one state. The laws of war (which also are called humanitarian law, the law of armed conflict, or the law for human rights in war) do not create a clear obligation to cooperate with the purveyors of humanitarian assistance. The ICRC is not given legal rights of leadership in internal war that are quite the same as in international war. Moreover, states and other fighting parties frequently disagree on whether an internal armed conflict exists as compared to a rebellion or insurrection falling under national rather than international law. The number of interstate wars has declined since 1945, but the number of violent situations seen by some as "internal wars" has risen, accompanied by great civilian loss of life and other suffering. A series of events since the end of the Cold War—within the former Yugoslavia and Soviet Union and within Somalia, Angola, Afghanistan, Burundi, Rwanda, Liberia, Mozambique, and Cambodia—suggests that atrocities and brutality seem a prevalent feature of what journalists call civil wars. In December 1996 in Chechnya, six Red Cross workers were murdered in their beds.

Neither the UN organization nor NGOs nor the ICRC has had consistent success in getting humanitarian assistance into places like the southern Sudan or, before that, parts of greater Ethiopia. The government of Indonesia may have been responsible for the deaths of 200,000 persons, mostly civilians, in fighting over East Timor in the 1970s, without any outside involvement to assist or protect civilians. The Khmer Rouge was unobstructed by anyone in the political murder of perhaps a million civilians in Cambodia in the 1970s. The Geneva Conventions and Protocols, supplemented by supportive UN Security Council resolutions, have not made much of an impact on Balkan parties motivated by expansion or revenge. Humanitarian assistance has no meaning to parties engaged in "ethnic cleansing," genocide, deliberate attacks on civilians and supposedly neutral personnel, and widespread rape and starvation as political weapons. Child soldiers and ragtag local militia make inculcation of humanitarian values difficult.

Given the difficulties encountered by both the United Nations and the ICRC in obtaining the consent of fighting parties in internal wars and public emergencies, some NGOs, like Médecins sans Frontières (Doctors Without Borders), have engaged in "cross-border" operations without consent. It has been said that in the war in Afghanistan, fifty private agencies acted on Afghan territory without the consent of Kabul.[56] Organizations like UNICEF and the WFP are reluctant to proceed, although they have occasionally done so. Their policy guidance and funding come from states. Although they have relatively independent secretariats, they are part of an intergovernmental system whose officials must deal with governments in governing councils as well as in field programs. Executive heads of various UN organizations, and the office of the UN Secretary-General, have been creative in trying to cope with famine and disease in places like the southern Sudan and Somalia. But as a practical matter, trying to proceed without the consent of the warring parties can lead—and has led—to attacks on international and local relief personnel. Beyond legal niceties centering on sovereignty, there are practical concerns related to the safety of staff members. In the 1990s, more journalists and aid workers died than peacekeepers.

In general, there is growing international pressure on warring parties in violent situations to permit access to civilians by humanitarian agencies. But UN organizations and the ICRC still have major difficulties in providing relief on neutral or balanced terms. Governmental consent was effectively bypassed by the international community in Somalia because there was no central government. Consent was bypassed to provide socioeconomic relief to Iraqi Kurds because the government in Baghdad was an international pariah after its invasion of Kuwait. Situations in Bosnia and the Balkans, the Sudan, and old Ethiopia presented a different and more typical picture. The fighting parties regarded food relief as a political factor, and outside states saw very high costs in trying to coerce fighting parties into respecting the rights of civilians to adequate food, clothing, shelter, and health care. Many parties recoil at the paradox of "humanitarian war." NATO's bombing of Kosovo and Serbia in 1999 brought this paradox into bold relief.

Addressing the nationalistic, ethnic, and communal wars and tensions of the 1990s was not only dramatic for states; it was traumatic as well for aid agencies. Until recently, the two most essential humanitarian principles (neutrality and impartiality) had been relatively uncontroversial along with the key operating procedure of seeking consent from belligerents. These principles, too, have become casualties in the 1990s.[57] A host of factors have challenged the classical posture: the complete disregard for international humanitarian law by war criminals and even by child soldiers; the direct targeting of civilians and relief personnel; the use of foreign aid to fuel conflicts and war economies; and the protracted nature of many so-called emergencies.[58] War has returned to Europe. In spite of the indictment of a sitting head of state (Slobodan Milosevic), whose head appeared on a "wanted" poster with a $5-million reward offered by Washington, genocide is alive and well. In many ways, international humanitarian law seems to have been formulated to deal with a different world—one populated by governments and regular armies whose interests were often served by respecting the laws of war.[59] In writing of old-fashioned humanitarianism, David Rieff has gone so far as to suggest "the death of a good idea."[60]

In spite of these problems, and "identity crisis" is not too strong a term to describe the individual and collective soul-searching by civilian personnel, the preceding pages should have made clear that humanitarian values and expenditures on emergency assistance have expanded. "In the 1990s," summarizes Adam Roberts, "humanitarian issues have played a historically unprecedented role in international politics."[61] In the dramatic example of the military campaign in Kosovo, Michael Ignatieff notes that "its legitimacy [depends] on what fifty years of human rights has done to our moral instincts, weakening the presumption in favor of state sovereignty, strengthening the presumption in favor of intervention when massacre and deportation become state policy."[62]

Notes

1. In general, see Philip Alston, ed., *The United Nations and Human Rights* (Oxford: Clarendon Press, 1995); and David P. Forsythe, "The UN and Human Rights at Fifty," *Global Governance*, vol. 1 (1995), pp. 297–318.

2. Roger S. Clark and Madeleine Sann, eds., *The Prosecution of International Crimes: A Critical Study of the International Tribunal for the Former Yugoslavia* (New Brunswick, NJ: Transaction, 1996).

3. Thomas M. Franck, "The 'Powers of Appreciation': Who Is the Ultimate Guardian of UN Legality?" *American Journal of International Law* 86, pp. 519–523.

4. Fernando R. Teson, "Changing Perceptions of Domestic Jurisdiction and Intervention," in Tom J. Farer, ed., *Beyond Sovereignty: Collectively Defending Democracy in the Americas* (Baltimore: Johns Hopkins Univ. Press, 1996).

5. *New York Times*, August 22, 1996, p. A9.

6. See, e.g., Paul Gordon Lauren, *Power and Prejudice: The Politics and Diplomacy of Racial Discrimination* (Boulder: Westview Press, 1988), epilogue.

7. David P. Forsythe, "The United Nations, Democracy, and the Americas," in Farer, *Beyond Sovereignty;* Washington Office on Latin America, *Reluctant Reforms: The Cristiani Government and the International Community in the Process of Salvadoran Post-War Reconstruction* (Washington, DC: WOLA, 1993).

8. David P. Forsythe, *Human Rights and World Politics,* 2nd rev. ed. (Lincoln: Univ. of Nebraska Press, 1989), chap. 3.

9. John Tessitore and Susan Woolfson, eds., *A Global Agenda: Issues Before the 47th General Assembly of the United Nations* (Lanham, MD: Univ. Press of America, 1992), p. 240.

10. David P. Forsythe, "The UN Secretary-General and Human Rights," in Benjamin Rivlin and Leon Gordenker, eds., *The Challenging Role of the UN Secretary-General* (Westport, CT: Greenwood Press, 1993), pp. 211–232.

11. A joke circulating about the various recent heads of the UN Centre for Human Rights involved these characters: Van Boven was supposedly the most active and committed; his successor, Kurt Herndl, having seen what happened to van Boven, supposedly kept a low profile; his successor, Jan Martenson, was supposedly preoccupied with a public image for himself and his office; his successor, Antoine Blanca, was supposedly an old crony of the Secretary-General who had no interest in human rights. So the joke went like this: Van Boven (in fact) wrote the book *People Matter;* so Herndl supposedly wrote *States Matter;* Martenson, *I Matter;* Blanca, *It Doesn't Matter.*

12. Howard Tolley, Jr., *The UN Commission on Human Rights* (Boulder: Westview Press, 1987).

13. Tom J. Farer, "The UN and Human Rights: More than a Whimper, Less than a Roar," in Adam Roberts and Benedict Kingsbury, eds., *United Nations, Divided World: The UN's Roles in International Relations* (Oxford: Clarendon Press, 1989), p. 123.

14. For an example of this American bias, see Morris B. Abram, "Human Rights and the United Nations: Past as Prologue," *Harvard Human Rights Law Journal* 4 (1991), pp. 69–83.

15. Tessitore and Woolfson, *A Global Agenda*, p. 236.

16. Telford Taylor, *The Anatomy of the Nuremberg Trials* (New York: Knopf, 1992), p. 29.

17. Cathal J. Nolan, *Principled Diplomacy: Security and Rights in U.S. Foreign Policy* (Westport, CT: Greenwood Press, 1993), chap. 7.

18. Tolley, *The U.N. Commission*, p. 179.

19. Joe W. Pitts III and David Weissbrodt, "Major Developments at the UN Commission on Human Rights in 1992," *Human Rights Quarterly* 15, pp. 122–196.

20. Scott Leckie, "An Overview and Appraisal," *Human Rights Quarterly* 13, p. 568.

21. Raymond Gastil, ed., *Freedom in the World, 1992* (New York: Freedom House, 1993).

22. See Pitts and Weissbrodt, "Major Developments," 17.

23. Karen Reierson and David Weissbrodt, "The Forty-third Session of the UN Sub-Commission on Prevention of Discrimination and Protection of Minorities: The Sub-Commission Under Scrutiny," *Human Rights Quarterly* 14, p. 271.

24. Cindy A. Cohn, "The Early Harvest: Domestic Legal Changes Related to the Human Rights Committee and the Covenant on Civil and Political Rights," *Human Rights Quarterly* 13, pp. 320–321.

25. Cohn, "Early Harvest," p. 321.

26. William Schabas, "Spare the RUD or Spoil the Treaty: United States Challenges the Human Rights Committee on Reservations," in David P. Forsythe, ed., *The United States and Human Rights* (Lincoln: University of Nebraska Press, 2000).

27. David Harris, "Commentary by the Rapporteur on the Consideration of States Parties' Reports and International Cooperation" (paper presented at Symposium: The Implementation of the International Covenant on Economic, Social and Cultural Rights), *Human Rights Quarterly* 9, p. 149.

28. Philip Alston and Bruno Simma, "First Session of the UN Committee on Economic, Social and Cultural Rights," *American Journal of International Law* 81, p. 750.

29. Leckie, "Overview and Appraisal," pp. 566–567.

30. Ibid.

31. UN, *UN Yearbook 1991* (New York: UN), p. 534.

32. For details, see Thomas G. Weiss, "Whither International Efforts for Internally Displaced Persons," *Journal of Peace Research* 36, no. 3 (May 1999), pp. 363–373.

33. On the low side of the estimates, see U.S. Committee for Refugees, *World Refugee Survey 1998* (Washington, DC: U.S. Committee for Refugees, 1998), pp. 2–6; and UN High Commissioner for Refugees, *The State of the World's Refugees, 1997–98: A Humanitarian Agenda* (Oxford: Oxford Univ. Press, 1998), pp. 2–3 and 286–289. On the high estimate side, see Jamie Hampton, *Internally Displaced People: A Global Survey* (London: Earthscan, 1998). The inclusion of Kosovo in the statistics would increase each set of numbers by close to a million.

34. See Thomas Risse, Stephen C. Rapp, and Kathryn Sikkink, *The Power of Human Rights: International Norms and Domestic Change* (New York: Cambridge Univ. Press, 1999).

35. Michael Ignatieff, "Human Rights: The Midlife Crisis," *The New York Review of Books* 46, no. 9 (May 20, 1999), p. 58.

36. Commission on Human Rights, *Analytical Report of the Secretary-General on Internally Displaced Persons*, UN document E/CN.4/1992/23.

37. A predecessor study was Refugee Policy Group, *Human Rights Protection for Internally Displaced Persons: An International Conference* (Washington, DC: Refugee Policy Group, 1991). Probably the most important publication was *Norwegian Government Roundtable Discussion on United Nations Human Rights Protection for Internally Displaced Persons, Held in Nyon, Switzerland* (Washington, DC: Norwegian Refugee Council and Refugee Policy Group, 1993). The RPG ceased operations in 1997.

38. Francis M. Deng, *Protecting the Dispossessed: A Challenge for the International Community* (Washington, DC: Brookings Institution, 1993); Francis M. Deng et al., *Sovereignty as Responsibility* (Washington, DC: Brookings Institution, 1995); and Francis M. Deng, "Frontiers of Sovereignty," *Leiden Journal of International Law* 8, no. 2 (1995), pp. 249–286. For more recent analyses and case studies, see Roberta Cohen and Frances M. Deng, *Masses*

in Flight: The Global Crisis in Displacement (Washington, DC: Brookings Institution, 1998); and Roberta Cohen and Frances M. Deng, eds., *The Forsaken People: Case Studies of the Internally Displaced* (Washington, DC: Brookings Institution, 1998).

39. Bernard Kouchner and Mario Bettati, *Le devoir d'ingérence* (Paris: Denoël, 1987); and Mario Bettati, *Le droit d'ingérence: Mutation de l'ordre international* (Paris: Odile Jacob, 1996).

40. Kofi Annan, "Secretary-General's Speech to the 54th Session of the General Assembly," September 20, 1999. Intervention was also a major theme in the annual *Report of the Secretary-General on the Work of the Organization,* Document A/54/1.

41. William Jefferson Clinton, "Remarks to the 54th Session of the United Nations General Assembly," September 21, 1999.

42. Tessitore and Woolfson, *A Global Agenda,* p. 260.

43. Theo van Boven, "Human Rights and Development: The UN Experience," in David P. Forsythe, ed., *Human Rights and Development* (London: Macmillan, 1989), pp. 121–135.

44. Internal World Bank documents increasingly dealt with human rights. See, for example, C. Mark Blackden, "Human Rights, Governance, and Development: Issues, Avenues, and Tasks," October 10, 1991, p. 17 plus attachments. For an overview, see David P. Forsythe, "Human Rights, Development, and the United Nations," *Human Rights Quarterly* (1996, forthcoming).

45. This was published from 1990 to 2000 by Oxford University Press. The first ten (1990–1999) are available on CD-ROM.

46. Tessitore and Woolfson, *A Global Agenda,* p. 245.

47. Forsythe, *World Politics,* n. 5.

48. David P. Forsythe, "Human Rights and U.S. Foreign Policy: Two Levels, Two Worlds," *Political Studies* 43 (1995), pp. 111–130.

49. For a discussion of these organizations and the difficulties encountered in recent crises, see Larry Minear and Thomas G. Weiss, *Humanitarian Action in Times of War: A Handbook for Practitioners* (Boulder: Lynne Rienner, 1993), and *Mercy Under Fire: War and the Global Humanitarian Community* (Boulder: Westview Press, 1995); Thomas G. Weiss and Cindy Collins, *Humanitarian Challenges and Intervention,* 2nd ed. (Boulder: Westview Press, 2000); and Jonathan Moore, *The UN and Complex Emergencies* (Geneva: UN Research Institute for Social Development, 1996).

50. Francis M. Deng and Larry Minear, *The Challenges of Famine Relief: Emergency Operations in the Sudan* (Washington, DC: Brookings Institution, 1992), p. 125.

51. David J. Scheffer, "Challenges Confronting Collective Security: Humanitarian Intervention," in U.S. Institute of Peace, *Three Views on the Issue of Humanitarian Intervention* (Washington, DC: U.S. Institute of Peace, 1992), p. 5.

52. Thomas G. Weiss, "Humanitarian Shell Games: Whither UN Reform?" *Security Dialogue* 29, no. 1 (March 1998), pp. 9–23.

53. See Larry Minear et al., *United Nations Coordination of the International Humanitarian Response to the Gulf Crisis, 1990–1992* (Providence, RI: Watson Institute, 1992); Cristina Equizabal et al., "Humanitarian Challenges in Central America: Learning the Lessons of Recent Armed Conflicts," Occasional Paper No. 14 (Providence, RI: Watson Institute, 1993).

54. David P. Forsythe, "Choices More Ethical than Legal: The International Committee of the Red Cross and Human Rights," *Ethics and International Affairs* 7 (1993), pp. 131–152.

55. For a discussion of future possibilities, see a series of essays from practitioners in Thomas G. Weiss and Larry Minear, eds., *Humanitarianism Across Borders: Sustaining Civilians in Times of War* (Boulder: Lynne Rienner, 1993).

56. Elizabeth Ferris, "Humanitarian Politics: Cross-Border Operations in the Horn of Africa," paper prepared for the International Studies Association annual meeting, Acapulco, Mexico, 1993, p. 3.

57. See Thomas G. Weiss, "Principles, Politics, and Humanitarian Action," *Ethics and International Affairs* 13 (1999), pp. 1–22; as well as "Responses" by Cornelio Sommaruga, Joelle Tanguy and Fiona Terry, and David Rieff on pp. 23–42.

58. For more extensive discussions of this landscape, see Michael Maren, *The Road to Hell: The Ravaging Effects of Foreign Aid and International Charity* (New York: Free Press, 1997); and Alex de Waal, *Famine Crimes: Politics and the Disaster Relief Industry in Africa* (Oxford: James Currey, 1997). This debate was initiated by Alex de Waal and Rakiya Omaar, *Humanitarianism Unbound? Current Dilemmas Facing Multi-Mandate Relief Operations in Political Emergencies* (London: African Rights, 1994), Discussion Paper no. 5. For a discussion of the disarray among humanitarians, see, for example, John Borton, "The State of the International Humanitarian System," *Overseas Development Institute Briefing Paper* no. 1 (March 1998); Myron Wiener, "The Clash of Norms: Dilemmas in Refugee Policies," *Journal of Refugee Studies* 11, no. 4 (1998), pp. 1–21; and Mark Duffield, "NGO Relief in War Zones: Toward an Analysis of the New Aid Paradigm," in Thomas G. Weiss, ed., *Beyond UN Subcontracting: Task-Sharing with Regional Security Arrangements and Service-Providing NGOs* (London: Macmillan, 1998), pp. 139–159. For a look at the political economy of conflict, see, for example, Mark Duffield, "The Political Economy of Internal War: Asset Transfer and the Internationalisation of Public Welfare in the Horn of Africa," in Joanna Macrae and Anthony Zwi, eds., *War and Hunger: Rethinking International Responses to Complex Emergencies* (London: Zed Books, 1994), pp. 5–69; David Keen, *The Economic Functions of Violence in Civil Wars* (Oxford: Oxford Univ. Press, 1998), Adelphi Paper 320; and François Jean and Christophe Rufin, eds., *Economies des guerres civiles* (Paris: Hachette, 1996).

59. See Adam Roberts, "Implementation of the Laws of War in Late 20th Century Conflicts," Parts 1, 2, *Security Dialogue* 29, nos. 2 and 3 (June and September 1998), pp. 137–150 and 265–280; and a special issue on "Humanitarian Debate: Law, Policy, Action," *International Review of the Red Cross* 81, no. 833 (March 1999).

60. David Rieff, "The Death of a Good Idea," *Newsweek*, May 10, 1999, p. 65

61. Adam Roberts, "The Role of Humanitarian Issues in International Politics in the 1990s," *International Review of the Red Cross* 81, no. 833 (March 1999), p. 19.

62. Michael Ignatieff, "Human Rights: The Midlife Crisis," *New York Review of Books* 46, no. 9 (May 20, 1999), p. 58.

7 Change, the United Nations, and Human Rights

The phrase "the United Nations" refers more to a framework, a stage, or an institutional funnel than to an organization with the capacity for independent action. Although it is true that some persons, such as those in the office of the Secretary-General, can take relatively independent action, "the UN" mostly refers to a process in which the most important policy decisions are made by governments representing territorial states. Most fundamentally, "the UN" has become involved in changing policies toward human rights as states have changed their policies. But other actors have been important, too.

Overview of the United Nations and Rights

The promotion and protection of human rights has become one of the UN's more prominent activities. In the annual *United Nations Yearbook,* more pages are usually devoted to human rights, by far, than to any other subject matter. Those printed pages accurately reflect the attention given to UN diplomacy on human rights.

The United Nations has been crucial to the promotion of human rights, largely through the setting of standards through treaties. This role is logical, given that the UN is the only global intergovernmental organization to define universal human rights. Global rights treaties can be developed outside the UN, as shown by the development of humanitarian law—with the ICRC serving as drafting secretariat and the Swiss government serving as convenor of diplomatic conferences. Yet the UN has provided a crucial contribution by specifying standards. The UN's other promotional work, such as its educational and technical assistance activities in the field of rights, has been less prominent. This does not mean that these activities are not important or should not be expanded.

There are now so many treaties on universal human rights that it can be asked whether the proliferation of norms has become counterproductive to advancing human rights. Internationally recognized human rights now include civil, political, social, economic, and cultural rights. There are demands for even more treaties covering solidarity rights, such as rights to development, peace, a healthy environment, and the fruits of the common heritage of humankind (for example, of Antarctica and the seabed). It is hard to choose a focus. In fact, the General Assembly has dictated a lack of focus by voting that all rights are of equal worth and are interdependent. But where does one begin serious work in the name of rights?

The UN's efforts at rights protection clearly have expanded, making a summary difficult to fashion. Once again, it can be asked whether there are too many monitoring mechanisms and too many protective processes within the UN system.

There is growing concern about the cost of operating all the UN bodies working on rights issues. We noted in the previous chapter that questions had been raised about funding for the Committee on the Elimination of Racial Discrimination (CERD). The committee working for women's rights (CEDAW) had no budget in the early 1990s to pay word processors. At the same time the Centre for Human Rights had only six persons to process 300,000 private petitions alleging violations under the International Bill of Rights. Of the total UN regular (meaning assessed) budget, human rights protective activities have recently doubled but still account for less than 2 percent. This means that in the mid-1990s the UN had about $20 million available for its global work in human rights. This is, in fact, a very small sum for the international public sector. The U.S. Department of Justice alone was spending some $70 million abroad each year in the mid-1990s to help reform court systems. And by comparison to things that really matter, the annual athletic budget at the University of Nebraska in 1995 was $25 million.

Moreover, there is an equally valid question about overlapping jurisdictions. On the subject of torture, the world now has the UN Sub-Commission on Human Rights, which takes up torture issues; the UN Human Rights Commission, which does the same; the Economic and Social Council, which sometimes gets involved; the UN General Assembly, which sometimes tries to exert pressure against governments that torture; the UN Committee Against Torture, which functions under the 1986 Torture Convention; the European Committee Against Torture, which functions under a regional treaty; the ICRC, which functions either under the treaties of humanitarian law or according to its own traditions; and other NGOs such as Amnesty International that are active in this arena.

The fundamental problem is that states are willing to approve human rights treaties and to allow diplomatic pressure short of effective enforcement, to preserve the hope of their freedom of action. It was not until December 1993 that states voted in the General Assembly to create a UN High Commissioner for Human Rights post; even then, as noted in Chapter 6, the mandate was vague and the office's authority was weak. Most states permit weak international implementation efforts, but they do not systematically allow effective international enforcement arrangements.

So for those states whose authorities are genuinely interested in protecting human rights, the best course through the UN seems to be to adopt more treaties in order to emphasize the problems and to create more supervisory bodies for specialized diplomacy. But this strategy only compounds the problem of too many standards with too many overlapping bodies with too few resources. It is indeed a vicious circle.

Several ideas have been put forward to improve the situation, at least in relative terms:

- The Secretary-General or his representative should present an annual human rights report, similar to his annual report on the work of the organization, to the General Assembly each September in which he draws attention to the most important rights problems. The UN high commissioner for human rights already makes an annual report, but it does not receive the same attention as reports coming from the Secretary-General.
- Treaty-monitoring bodies should be allowed to participate in the work of other UN bodies—for example, the UN Human Rights Commission.
- The UN programs of technical assistance and education for human rights should be greatly expanded in order to strengthen national institutions for rights protection and thus to head off major rights problems before they become international crises.
- The office of the Secretary-General, in conjunction with the office of the UN High Commissioner for Refugees and the Office for the Coordination of Humanitarian Affairs, should further improve the UN early warning system to predict gross violations of internationally recognized human rights that are likely to lead to mass migration.
- A concerted effort should be made to integrate more extensively human rights considerations into "development" programs through the UNDP, World Bank, International Monetary Fund (IMF), and UN specialized agencies. Just as there is a new UN body on sustainable development, there should be a coordinating body on human rights in development. These efforts have been grouped under the rubric of "mainstreaming human rights," although to date there has been more rhetoric than real change.
- Greater use should be made of preventive diplomacy, such as the systematic dispatch of UN human rights observers in situations of tension, both to deter rights violations and to provide timely reporting to New York.

These are "doable" steps that could be taken in the near future without a wait for a radical alteration in state attitudes. Nevertheless a full revolution in UN action for human rights depends on further change in state foreign policies. But especially younger developing countries are very protective about any codification of norms encroaching on conventional notions of state sovereignty.

More on Raisons d'État

The boundaries of national interests are not fixed.[1] "National interest," like "state sovereignty," is a social construct. Ideas about national interest are devised by humans in a process of change over time. For schools of thought like realism that emphasize the concept of national interest as a core component of international relations, the concept lacks precise and transcendent meaning. Whether human rights should be, or can be, linked to national interests is a matter of debate. Many states increasingly have included human rights within the domain of state interests. They have pursued the subject through their foreign policies. This can be done in several ways.

The delegations of some states have pursued the subject of human rights at the United Nations as a weapon in power struggles. The objective has been to delegitimize a certain government; the means has been to emphasize human rights violations.

Some states have adopted a broad definition of their own self-interests. They seek not just territorial integrity, political independence, and other goals directly related to the good of the state. They also define their interests in terms of an international society in which human dignity is advanced by serious attention to human rights. Just as governments have defined their domestic interests beyond physical security and economic welfare, so have governments used their foreign policy to advance human rights and humanitarian goals. The states making up NATO did this in Kosovo in 1999.

Some states have adopted a variation on this theme by arguing that the practice of human rights not only advances human dignity but also advances security and national peace. They cite, for example, the lack of major international wars between stable democracies. Or they cite the need to deal with human rights violations to bring peace to countries like El Salvador or Bosnia.

Some states may even lend support to international action on human rights not because they believe any of the arguments but simply because they feel pressured to support such action. For example, if Japan or Germany is to obtain a permanent seat in the Security Council, each will be expected by others to increase its attention to human rights in its foreign policies. That pressure may come from NGOs or from other states.

States have brought about a legal and diplomatic revolution with regard to the treatment of human rights at the United Nations. The same process has occurred in other multilateral fora such as the Council of Europe, the European Community, the Conference on Security and Cooperation in Europe, the Organization of American States, and to a lesser extent the Organization of African Unity and the Arab League.

Any one state may pursue international action on human rights for different reasons at different times, or for many reasons at any given time. In the United States, the Franklin D. Roosevelt administration stressed the famous "four freedoms" in order to give meaning to the sacrifices of World War II. The Truman administration accepted human rights language in the UN Charter for the same reason and because it was pressured by NGOs and Latin American states to live up to its national self-image as a champion of human rights. The Eisenhower administration, like other U.S. governments, used human rights in the struggle with the Soviet Union, as when it used the General Assembly to discuss issues like forced labor. The Carter administration used human rights not only to try to rally domestic support but also because it genuinely wanted at least a Western Hemisphere sympathetic to fundamental personal rights. The second Reagan administration used human rights as part of an appeal to American greatness in the world, and as a way to undercut the radical left. The dictatorial Ferdinand Marcos was eased from power in the Philippines to undercut the New People's Army, and General Augusto Pinochet was eased out of the presidential palace in Chile to forestall a resurgence of radical opposition to his brutal rule.

It may be true, although difficult to prove, that the linkage of human rights to *raisons d'état* is at least sometimes a reflection of increasing moral solidarity in international society. That is, governmental authorities may speak in terms of their interests, but the deeper process may involve a moral stance on the dignity of persons without regard to nationality or borders. John Ruggie has shown that a concern to better the world is deeply ingrained in American culture and history and that this concern has often taken a multilateral form, including great attention to the United Nations, in the twentieth century, although Edward Luck has stressed the fundamental ambivalence in American attitudes toward multilateralism.[2] U.S. officials may speak of American strategic interests in a stable, democratic, and prosperous Europe; but the deeper driving force behind Washington's policy may be moral outrage at atrocities in the Balkans. In Bosnia and other parts of the former Yugoslavia, U.S. policy was intertwined with various multilateral efforts, including those of the United Nations.

It may also be true that moral and practical components of state foreign policy are sufficiently entangled as to be inseparable. The United States may be morally outraged at atrocities in the Balkans and at the same time may believe that self-interest dictates opposition to Serbian atrocities of ethnic cleansing. Not to oppose those human rights violations would be to encourage more atrocities.

Whether state foreign policies are driven by practical or moral wellsprings, or whether it is even possible to say what is expedience as compared to morality, the cumulative effect of this shifting and complex redefinition of the national interest has been to internationalize human rights. State authorities in general consider human rights within a state's territorial boundaries to be a proper subject for international discussion. They often are willing to engage in a wide range of diplomatic activity to promote and also indirectly to protect those rights. At times states are even willing to engage in economic coercion in the name of rights, and more rarely they at least agree to some type of military action to guarantee such fundamental rights as the access by suffering civilians to international help.

States have not abandoned the principle of state sovereignty. It is used as a defensive argument against UN action on human rights by different states on different issues at different times. The principle is especially favored by the authorities of weaker and younger developing countries that fear losing status and influence at the hands of more powerful states. Older, more powerful states like the United States are also not hesitant to trot out the tired slogans of state sovereignty when the international community, through some UN agency, questions American execution of minors or the mentally impaired. Yet over time, the appeal to restrictive notions of state sovereignty and their use has been weakened. As a result, UN organizations have expanded their diplomatic activity for human rights across and even within states; they also have occasionally resorted to economic and military sanctions in this area.

Ironically and paradoxically enough, member states have driven events at the United Nations so that state sovereignty has been weakened. States have used their initial sovereignty to create UN standards and UN supervisory procedures that later have restricted their operational sovereignty in the field of human rights. In legal theory states are no longer free to treat even "their own" citizens as they wish. Internationally recognized human rights impose standards that are binding on governments. In political practice, governments may be pressured or coerced because of human rights violations. The process is far from consistent, systematic, reliable, and effective, but it is irreversible.

State Coalitions

In multilateral organizations like the United Nations, many key decisions are taken by voting, so coalitions among states become important. During the early years of the UN, the Western coalition controlled proceedings in the General Assembly and the Human Rights Commission. The International Bill of Rights was effectively negotiated between 1948 and 1956, and this was an important step in the promotion of internationally recognized human rights. Western states pushed for the Universal Declaration of Human Rights and at least the negotiation of the UN Covenant on Civil and Political Rights and the UN Covenant on Economic, Social, and Cultural Rights. The communist coalition played the game of negotiating the treaties and accepting human rights in theory while opposing the implementation of many internationally recognized rights in practice. Yet there were few breakthroughs in diplomatic action for protecting human rights. This was a time when the Human Rights Commission issued a self-denying ordinance about investigations into specific problems and states. This self-denying ordinance referred to the decision by the UN Human Rights Commission to deny itself the authority to investigate specific human rights practices in specific countries.

Perhaps most important, the United States exercised little constructive leadership on human rights at the United Nations for several decades after about 1948. The United States was a dominant power and, to some states, a hegemonic power on security and economic issues. But it was neither dominant nor hegemonic on human rights. Human rights issues were a sensitive topic in the United States both because of legally sanctioned racial discrimination and because some members of Congress feared a more powerful executive through the treaty process. Many in the U.S. Senate in the 1950s feared that the president and his colleagues in the executive branch would expand their authority at the expense of both the

Constitution and the Congress by concluding human rights treaties. The U.S. Supreme Court held, in *Missouri vs. Holland,* that the federal government can acquire authority beyond the Constitution via the treaty-making power as long as a treaty does not contradict the Constitution. So the executive branch, with two-thirds of the Senate giving advice and consent, can expand on the fundamental rights mentioned in the U.S. Bill of Rights through the conclusion of human rights treaties.[3]

Many senators (joined by many representatives) tried to amend the Constitution to make all treaties non-self-executing. That is to say, if this amendment were adopted, no U.S. treaty could take legal effect within the United States without enabling or supplemental legislation by the entire Congress. This amendment would add a legislative step to the treaty process, similar to that in the United Kingdom, making it more difficult for the executive branch to act via treaties.

President Eisenhower, in order to keep the treaty process as simple as possible and to maintain the authority of the executive branch while holding the line on the authority of the legislative branch, agreed not to press for U.S. ratification of human rights treaties if congressional forces would drop their effort to amend the Constitution through the so-called or generic Bricker amendment—named after the member of Congress who had led the fight for the constitutional amendment. There were several such efforts in the Congress, but no amendments were ever adopted. From Eisenhower's time until Jimmy Carter, no president asked the Senate for advice and consent on the two basic UN human rights treaties.

With the admission of newly independent developing countries from 1955 and the acceleration of this pattern from 1960, the dynamics of voting on human rights at the United Nations changed dramatically. As indicated, the dynamics were fueled by a dialectical process resulting in a new synthesis. Developing countries sought to use the language of human rights to pressure Israel and South Africa, and the West countered with efforts to broaden those rights-oriented maneuvers. Human rights NGOs helped fashion this North-South compromise. The result was a new diplomatic dynamism in UN attempts to protect certain human rights in certain countries. The Soviet coalition added its own emphases, particularly focusing on rights violations in Pinochet's Chile after the overthrow of Marxist president Salvador Allende.

This North-South interchange on human rights, with the European communist states usually aligned with the South, accounted for many human rights developments at the United Nations during approximately 1970 to 1985. This coalition of forces also helps to explain why some things did not happen. For instance, the UN was unable to put diplomatic pressure on Idi Amin's brutal government in Uganda because of the shield provided by the solidarity among developing countries and deferred to by communist countries.

After the transition period of 1985–1991, during which European communism collapsed, the coalitions shifted. There were more democratic governments both in the General Assembly and on the Human Rights Commission, and there was more overall collaboration in the Security Council. Yet democratic governments, especially in the developing countries, were not always enthusiastic about UN activities regarding protection. Several sought to block protective attempts by the Human Rights Commission. And cooperation in the Security Council was sometimes hampered by negative votes or abstentions.

Ambivalence on the part of developing countries about international action for human rights and humanitarian affairs was evident. They knew that their sovereignty was at issue. Most developing countries in the General Assembly refused to elevate a right to humanitarian assistance above the rights of state sovereignty. Resolutions on this subject that were adopted in the late 1980s and early 1990s were complex. Although reaffirming the principle of state sovereignty, Resolution 46/182 indicated that parties in a "country," but not necessarily only the government of a state, might request international assistance. It also suggested that the consent of a state to international humanitarian action might be tacit. In practice, developing countries went along with assertiveness by the international community in defeated Iraq and Somalia.

Beyond developing countries, some permanent members of the Security Council were at times either ambivalent or reluctant about international action for human rights and humanitarian affairs. The Yeltsin government of the Russian Federation, successor to the Soviet permanent seat in the council, expressed open reservations about some of the policies being pursued against rights violations by governments in Iraq and Serbia. The Chinese government did not support international action to protect human rights. But it chose to abstain on most council resolutions rather than veto them and thus to stimulate Western circles of opinion pushing for sanctions on China itself after the Tiananmen Square massacre of June 1989.

Observers will have to wait and see whether an intensified North-South conflict will significantly limit UN efforts to protect human rights and whether Russia and China will join developing countries in obstructing protective efforts.[4] Time will also show whether UN protective action for human rights will be expanded because sufficient numbers of governments from the South and the former USSR join the West in pushing for enhanced protection. At the 1993 Vienna World Conference on Human Rights, most developing and formerly communist countries reaffirmed the idea of universal human rights. But since 1948 the central problem has not been the abstract codification of norms; the problem has been in marshaling sufficient political will to deal with concrete violations of internationally recognized human rights.

Nonstate Actors

States may be the official building blocks of the United Nations, but nonstate actors have been active and sometimes influential in human rights and humanitarian matters. Three types of nonstate actors are discussed here: NGOs, individual experts, and secretariat personnel.

Precision is difficult when gauging the influence generated by NGOs on human rights matters. The most general problem is that their impact becomes intertwined with governmental and other influences, often making it impossible to say where NGO influence leaves off and governmental influence begins. If Amnesty International lobbies for new standards and monitoring mechanisms concerning torture, and if states in the Human Rights Commission and General Assembly finally approve these ideas in treaty form, it is difficult to pinpoint what has occurred because of Amnesty International's efforts and what has occurred because of governmental policy. The same problem has been recognized in trying to chart the influence of interest groups in domestic politics by comparison to governmental officials.

Only a few genuine human rights NGOs are active on a transnational or international basis with a mandate linked to the International Bill of Rights: Amnesty International, the International Commission of Jurists, the International League for Human Rights, the various Human Rights Watch groups, Physicians for Human Rights, Doctors Without Borders, and a few others. The ICRC comes close to meeting this definitional test, although its historical mandate is linked more to the treaties on victims of war than to the International Bill of Rights. Also, the top ICRC decisionmaking body is all Swiss rather than international.

Other broadly oriented NGOs are active on human rights from time to time, but they are linked more to religion or some other normative standard than to the International Bill of Rights. An example is the World Council of Churches.

Moreover, some NGOs with narrower mandates take up particular human rights questions. They have more to do with a particular problem or nationality than with internationally recognized rights per se. Cultural Survival, for example, concentrates on indigenous peoples. Anti-Slavery International focuses on slavery, slavelike practices, and the slave trade. All sorts of nationally based or oriented groups take up particular causes while frequently ignoring the human rights situation in other nations.

The point to be stressed here, beyond these descriptive remarks, is that all of these NGOs have been active on human rights issues at the United Nations. And they certainly have generated some influence for the promotion and protection of human rights in the abstract. Their cumulative impact has been such that various states have opposed UN consultative status for some of the more assertive NGOs. In 1991 Cuba and some Arab states prevented Human Rights Watch, based in New York, from obtaining consultative status via ECOSOC. NGOs want to achieve that status because they gain the right to circulate documents and speak in UN meetings. During the Cold War several human rights NGOs were excluded from consultative status by communist and developing governments, a practice that continues. In 1995 Freedom House, based in New York, was temporarily denied consultative status by a coalition of states including democracies such as India and the Philippines. Had NGOs generated no influence, it is unlikely that certain governments would try so hard to keep them out of UN proceedings. At the 1993 Vienna meeting, this tension between governments and human rights

NGOs was much in evidence. Some governments evidently feared the influence that might be generated by NGOs, perhaps by releasing damaging information to the world press. At a UN human rights conference in Teheran in 1968, NGOs participated in the intergovernmental sessions. In Vienna in 1993, governments denied NGO participation in the official meetings but agreed to a separate NGO parallel conference. This formula was followed at the 1995 Beijing conference on women.

As a separate matter, the ICRC is the only nonstate working for human rights and humanitarian affairs that has been granted observer status in the General Assembly. This came about because of its close work with governments, especially in situations of armed conflict, and because of its reputation. But the ICRC follows a general policy of discretion and therefore does not normally reveal the details of what its delegates have observed inside states. Unlike Human Rights Watch and Amnesty International, for example, the ICRC does not normally rely on detailed public pressure to achieve its objectives.

Large numbers of NGOs have consultative status and participate on the Human Rights Commission. They submit private complaints about a pattern of gross violations of human rights to the UN system. Their information is officially used in most of the monitoring agencies of the UN system such as the Human Rights Committee, the Committee on Economic and Social Rights, CERD, CEDAW, CAT, CRC, and others. Some NGOs have played influential roles behind the scenes (that is, with official or unofficial status) in the adoption of General Assembly resolutions concerning human rights.

Just as private human rights groups have had an impact on national policies concerning human rights, so have NGOs had some influence on UN proceedings. A formal UN vote or document, reflecting the policy of a majority of governments, may have started or been advanced by one or more NGOs. Quite clearly the UN Declaration on Minorities and also the Declaration on Indigenous Peoples were advanced by the efforts of NGOs—although it was states that voted for the declarations. Some 1,000 NGOs attended the Vienna World Conference on Human Rights, conducting their own proceedings and engaging in the specific criticisms that state delegations at the conference agreed to avoid.

Just as it is likely that private groups have teamed with the U.S. Congress to improve human rights reporting by the Department of State,[5] so is it likely that NGOs have teamed with interested governments to improve rights activity through the United Nations. If human rights NGOs had been absent at the UN during the world organization's first forty-five years, it is unlikely that the record would be as good as it is. The record is not good enough in the view of these same NGOs, but some positive steps have been taken.

Had those NGOs been absent, something would have been done on human rights nevertheless—not only because of states but because of secretariat personnel. John P. Humphrey of Canada, the first director-general of human rights, appears to have had some influence on the content of the Universal Declaration of

Human Rights. Other secretariat personnel have advanced ideas or proposals that eventually were accepted by governments voting in UN bodies. Executive heads of UN agencies like UNICEF, WHO, and ILO have clearly taken action on their own for children's health care and for labor rights. All of this is apart from the human rights activity of the office of the Secretary-General itself.

Moreover, the individual experts who have sat in the UN Sub-Commission on Protection of Minorities or who have been rapporteurs or other experts for the Human Rights Commission have often nudged the process along. Most of the monitoring agencies created by treaty have been staffed by individuals acting in their personal capacity. Many have been truly independent from their governments as well as serious about and dedicated to human rights.

Theories of Change

The sum total of state and nonstate input has caused the record of the United Nations regarding human rights to be what it is. Is there a summary statement that clarifies the dynamics of activity on human rights at the UN? Can we theorize why this activity has been what it has been, and can we project what directions this activity will take in the future?

Two related views are noteworthy in this regard. The first focuses on the notion of knowledge. Ernst Haas suggests that if private communities of knowledge come to an agreement on human rights, this agreement eventually will produce a policy consensus in the public sector.[6] When this public consensus emerges, the United Nations and other IGOs become empowered to take important action for human rights. There will be a complete change in the UN, not just partial change. For example, if most human rights groups concluded that civil and political rights were necessary for economic growth or that socioeconomic rights were necessary for stable democracy, that private agreement would affect public policy through the United Nations and would lead to dramatic change.

The second and related view emphasizes learning. George Modelski returns to the ideas of Immanuel Kant to suggest that those who speak for states are in the process of learning a commitment to human rights, especially to the civil and political rights making up a democracy.[7] In this view, historical evolution shows expanded learning of the benefits of democracy—whether in terms of human dignity or in terms of international peace.

If Haas's view is correct about the state of knowledge in epistemic communities, several generalizations emerge. First, if all or most private groups active on human rights agreed on particulars, this consensus of knowledge would eventually inform public policy in such a way that the United Nations would be mandated by governments to take more authoritative and effective action for human rights. We may be seeing a paradigm shift. Even the World Bank, which long sought to avoid the political matters of human rights, now says that economic growth should be pursued with attention to participation, as noted in Chapter 6.

The bank and its supporters have concluded—at least for now—that at least some authoritarian models of economic growth do not work very well. In fact, "good governance" has essentially been defined as the opposite of what authoritarian Third World and Soviet bloc countries did for the 1960s, 1970s, and 1980s. Clearly, the new approaches have positive human rights dimensions. Whether this new policy on "social assessment" by the bank stems from private agreement should be researched.

But in its broad form this demand for private agreement may posit an extremely high—indeed impossibly high—standard to reach before change would occur at the United Nations leading to authoritative and effective action. It is important to observe that knowledge about human rights is not so much scientific knowledge as moral knowledge. It is even more difficult to achieve widespread agreement on moral knowledge than on scientific knowledge. Even within one nation with a dominant culture, private groups differ over such human rights issues as abortion, the death penalty, health care, and adequate nutrition.

It is one thing to get private groups to agree that children are better off if vaccinated. It is hard for medical personnel to disagree with a vaccination program or to advocate keeping WHO out of a poor country where it wants to conduct a vaccination program. Private opinion is based on irrefutable scientific knowledge. It is another thing to get private circles of opinion to agree that internationally recognized human rights should be applied in all cultures and situations. Not all medical personnel agree that health care should be treated as a human right. Not all medical personnel agree that abortion should be legal. There may be agreement on the technical process of how to perform an abortion, for that is based on science. But there clearly is not agreement on whether abortion should be legal, for that is based on moral knowledge. Moral knowledge is greatly affected by varieties of opinion because moral argument by definition is difficult to completely prove or disprove.

It cannot be shown scientifically that everyone will be better off if rights are applied. If repressive governments allow the practice of civil and political rights, many, if not most, will lose power. This may usher in a period of disorder and economic decline. The former Soviet Union is a clear example, at least in the short run. In repressive China, many persons have been advancing economically, since macroeconomic growth as stimulated by an expanding private sector was around 10 percent per year in the early 1990s. Many people in private circles of opinion do not believe that rights would do anything but interrupt this beneficial process in China. Spectacular economic growth has been achieved in Singapore since the 1970s, but without full civil and political rights. Important religious circles in Islamic nations believe freedom of religion and gender equality would hurt society. Even actors that generally seek to protect rights do not insist on the application of rights in every situation. Many Western private groups do not press the issue of the practice of human rights in Saudi Arabia. They also defer to a military coup in Algeria that prevented the election of a fundamentalist Islamic party. Some of these groups believe on moral grounds that Western access to oil or blocking fundamentalist Islam justifies repressive governments. We know for sure that democratic rights in places such as Sri Lanka and Georgia and Iran have led to illiberal governments that discriminate against minorities and commit other rights violations. So a commitment to human rights such as democratic political participation is less a matter of proof of inherent progress and more a matter of moral and political choice.

Beyond the important distinction between scientific and moral knowledge in private networks, the public policy consensus across all governments at the United Nations concerning human rights is weak or incomplete. The formal consensus is broad, but the real consensus is weak. In other words, human rights treaties are widely accepted in law and widely violated in practice.

As long as this weak actual consensus exists, human rights activity will not lead to systematic and authoritative protection by the United Nations. New and potentially important steps may happen spasmodically, but these steps will fall short of full change leading to systematic and effective protection. The Security Council may authorize humanitarian intervention in Somalia, but at roughly the same time it will fail to sponsor decisive action in similar situations in Liberia or the Sudan, much less Rwanda and Burundi. The council may set the stage for use of force in Iraq in the name of persecuted civilians, but it will be lethargic about similarly appalling conditions in the Caucasus.

The issue of the UN and international courts provides a good test of the Haas theory of change, linked to knowledge, and the Modelski theory of change, linked to learning.[8] For a long time the UN's International Law Commission, a technical body of individual legal experts not instructed by governments, discussed the creation of a standing international criminal court with jurisdiction over persons who are individually responsible under international law. Such a court would try those charged with genocide, war crimes, and crimes against humanity.

In 1993, the Security Council created a criminal court under Chapter VII of the Charter with jurisdiction over certain international crimes committed in the territory of the former Yugoslavia during the armed conflict there in the early 1990s. Shortly thereafter, the council created a second ad hoc criminal court with jurisdiction over various international crimes committed in Rwanda from early 1994, when that country was the scene of genocide, political murder, war crimes, and other atrocities.

Under the Modelski theory one can raise the question of whether states, acting through the UN, have shown a propensity to learn that international relations must be governed by a humane rule of law. Are states learning that they will be more secure, and their citizens better off, if there is either a permanent UN criminal court or a series of ad hoc criminal courts to deal with particular situations? Under the Haas theory, are states beginning to reach agreement on the demonstrable truth that just as all national societies have institutionalized procedures for criminal cases, so international relations should, too? Or are states just muddling through on this issue with incomplete agreement leading to the piling up of actions at the UN without any clear and firm overall position on criminal courts?

In the mid-1990s the latter scenario seemed closer to the truth when, after years of consideration, the debates on a permanent UN criminal court had not led to broad agreement on many specific points. Yet, as discussed earlier, general consensus was reached in 1998, and the Statute of the International Criminal Court of Justice was adopted by an overwhelming majority of the 148 states who participated in the final vote at Rome. Perhaps Modelski's theory is at least partially correct. Yet the ICC will be only as effective as the acceptance of its jurisdiction, and that will depend on treaty ratification over time.

Such learning—to the extent that it did occur—was of course not universal. Some states, especially those that contemplate use of their militaries in armed conflict, are reluctant to create a judicial organ to which they would have to turn over their military personnel, and perhaps civilian leaders as well, to face charges of, for example, violations of the laws of war. At the turn of the century, given the mood of the U.S. Congress, which tends toward strong nationalism, unilateralism, and some isolationism, it is difficult to foresee Senate advice on and consent to such a judicial statute. Clearly, the Congress has not "learned" the wisdom of such a step; nor is it clear that knowledge compels movement in this direction. Other states, too, would find it difficult to turn over national officials for trial by foreign judges.

But was the phenomenon underlying the creation of the ICC really "learning" in the sense Modelski means? The two ad hoc UN tribunals, while making a number of progressive contributions to clarification of international law, have not worked especially well. They were formed after the late 1940s, when the Nuremberg and Tokyo trials tried and convicted a number of German and Japanese officials for war crimes, crimes against humanity, and crimes against peace. The two ad hoc courts have faced problems that arose after World War II. In the 1990s some states did not want to expend blood and treasure or complicate their foreign policies by apprehending those indicted by the prosecutor attached to the courts. This was particularly true of NATO states that had military personnel in IFOR in the former Yugoslavia. Sometimes evidence of international crimes was not so easy to obtain, since the fighting parties in neither Rwanda nor the former Yugoslavia had kept meticulous records like those of the Germans and Japanese in World War II.

In general, state learning pertaining to international criminal law showed differences and inconsistencies. States tried ad hoc criminal courts now and then, but they were not sure they wanted to be under the jurisdiction of a UN standing court. States might feel the need to show a response to atrocities by creating ad hoc courts, but the same states might still eschew the costs of a decisive involvement that would curtail the atrocities and punish those responsible. States might agree in theory that individual punishment for atrocities is a good idea, but in particular situations they might like the freedom to negotiate and strike deals with war criminals and the like. No one was more responsible for the onset of violence in the former Yugoslavia than the Serbian politician Slobodan Milosevic; yet in 1995 the West found him crucial to the Dayton peace accords, which greatly reduced both the fighting among combatants and the related violations of the human rights of prisoners and civilians.

One can seek peace and justice through both diplomacy and criminal proceedings. In places like Yugoslavia, it was not clear that one could pursue both avenues at once. If various political leaders had not been defeated and had retained power, and if one then had to include them in negotiations aimed at stopping the fighting and curtailing human rights violations, pursuing them as international criminals might not be the wisest course of action. This type of analysis pertained not just to leaders like Milosevic but also to the late Mohammed Farah Aideed in Somalia.

Then there was the equally complicated question of whether criminal proceedings contribute to or impede national reconciliation after armed conflict. The theory behind criminal courts, national or international, is that license to commit atrocities has to end in order to "clear the air," provide catharsis to the victims and their families, and deter future violations of rights. But one could certainly question whether criminal trials of Hutu leaders in Rwanda while a Tutsi-dominated government controlled the country would achieve the desired objectives. And in many places from South Africa to El Salvador, national and international officials concluded that the way to advance national reconciliation after brutal internal war was to avoid criminal proceedings as much as possible. One might utilize truth commissions to establish facts, but only in places such as South Korea and Ethiopia did trials proceed against former repressive rulers.

Thus acquiring human rights knowledge is a complicated affair about which reasonable persons can differ, and the UN's forays into solving human rights problems have been carried out in the context of a lack of clear consensus and firm commitment.[9]

The relation between knowledge and UN human rights activity can be summarized. It is difficult to achieve a broad consensus about human rights among private networks because one is dealing more with morality than with science. Without agreement about benefits from human rights, the consensus among governments on human rights and public policy will remain thin or incomplete. The situation is one of incomplete change. There is more UN action for human rights now than before; but it still falls short of being fully systematic and institutionalized, as well as authoritative and effective.

As for the question of whether states are learning a commitment to liberal democracy (meaning elected governments that are rights-protective), some evidence seems encouraging. Immanuel Kant suggested that over time liberal democracies would become more numerous. A wave of democratization from about the mid-1970s to the early 1990s seemed to verify that Kantian view from the eighteenth century. But within this democratic trend toward elected governments, there are illiberal democracies that are truly elected but are nevertheless not rights-protective. We have already mentioned Iran and Georgia as clear examples. If it holds, this trend toward liberal democracy would suggest a growing acceptance not only of civil and political rights but of economic and social ones as well. Almost all democracies, except the United States, endorse the latter rights as well as the former.

But we should be wary. No more than about one-third of the states in the world have been truly democratic at any given time.[10] This was still true in the 1990s. Moreover, earlier waves of democracy suffered setbacks or reverse waves, and this could happen again in spite of the widespread democratization under way worldwide. Many states with democratic governments in the early 1990s still manifested strong militaries not fully controlled by elected leaders. Democratic government was overthrown in Haiti in 1991, attacked in Venezuela in 1992, and suspended in Peru in 1992. After disappointing economic developments in many parts of the former Soviet Union, communist parties made a comeback through elections. Other democratic governments could easily suffer similar fates.

Over a rather long time, there has been an increase in recognition of the advantages of liberal democratic government. Respect for civil and political rights has grown, albeit in a zigzag rather than a linear progression. This learning had been enhanced, at least temporarily, by the various failures of authoritarian communism in Europe and authoritarian models among developing countries.

But in many countries ruled by newly democratic governments, there were major obstacles to the consolidation—meaning stabilization and maturation—of democracy. Perhaps most important, economic growth was slow or nonexistent, and the benefits of the economic system were widely perceived as inequitable. It was not self-evident that the new democratic governments, confronted with particularly daunting economic problems, could create the socioeconomic context that would sustain a new and fragile democracy. Particularly in Latin America, but elsewhere as well, democracy has been created but not necessarily consolidated. Consequently, authoritarianism has often returned. Were civil and political rights being learned systematically, or was democratic learning frequently followed by a relearning of the advantages of authoritarianism in a vicious circle? Moreover, not all democratic governments at the United Nations have fully supported its human rights program. U.S. authorities have at times tried to suppress diplomatic pressure on U.S. authoritarian friends. British officials have opposed all sorts of human rights initiatives.[11] The Indian government has at times elevated the principle of state sovereignty above UN pressure for human rights concerning itself and other developing countries.

It has often been said that most situations in which human rights are respected are produced by national conditions—with only secondary influence from international factors.[12] This axiom contains considerable truth but can be overstated. The relaxation of the Soviet grip on Eastern Europe in the late 1980s was the key factor in unleashing local human rights forces. By 1996, there were more IGO,

NGO, and state policies in operation in support of international human rights than ever before in world history. In some cases, as in Haiti in 1994, international factors were decisive—at least in the short run. The international context had definitely changed for the better.

Nevertheless, the demand for rights by powerful groups within national society is normally a factor of great importance. International influences, for the most part, cannot create national demand for rights behavior; they can only support, encourage, or unleash that demand if it exists. Human rights have fared better in Hungary since 1989 than in neighboring Romania because domestic demand and leadership for rights is greater in the former. The international context is almost identical.

Sanctions against both Rhodesia and South Africa did not create the resistance to white-minority rule. But these international actions helped to empower local citizens to confront the policies of governments based on racial discrimination. The Guatemalan ambassador to the United States had it exactly right when describing the democratic resistance to an authoritarian coup in 1993: It was the Guatemalan people, local human rights groups, national business elements, and even sectors of the military that demanded a return to democracy as a human right; the role of the international community was important but secondary.[13] The United Nations then accelerated its efforts in Guatemala, negotiating human rights agreements and mediating conflicts. The role of the UN was to facilitate local trends toward liberal democracy, which by definition encompasses the protection of many human rights.

But when international efforts are tried, they must be pursued with determination. Significant innovations to meet the human rights challenges in the former Yugoslavia have received so little financial and political support that they are mere tokens. Innovative steps include the first-ever emergency session, convened by the UN Commission on Human Rights; the first deployment of field monitors by the UN Human Rights Centre (now UNHCHR); the appointment of a special rapporteur to report to the Security Council on human rights abuses and of a Commission of Experts to report on breaches of the Geneva Conventions; the assignment of human rights responsibilities to UNHCR protection officers in the field; and, most significant, the establishment of an international war-crimes tribunal. But the credibility of these initiatives will be undermined unless they are matched by the resources and leadership to make them work. Ineffectiveness is distressing enough for the victims in the former Yugoslavia. But perhaps even more important is the potential negative impact that discrediting such devices will have for future armed conflicts where effective machinery will obviously be necessary.

Finally, a temporal dimension influences human rights and the United Nations. In historical perspective, there has indeed been a diplomatic and legal revolution in human rights. The UN in the 1990s was acting for human rights in ways unthinkable in the 1940s. At the same time, this diplomatic and legal revolution has yet to lead to a complete and consistent behavioral revolution. Many truly appalling human rights situations continue unchecked by systematic, authoritative, and effective UN action. Human rights have been extensively defined. There have been expanding attempts at indirect protection, largely through diplomatic pressure. Only rarely has direct protection been attempted through the United Nations.

Given the widespread and strong support for the principle of state sovereignty, the international community has come a long way in generating respect for the idea of human rights. But it still has a long way to go before achieving the systematic observance of human rights as called for in the Charter "without distinction as to race [or nationality], sex, language or religion."[14]

Notes

1. See further David P. Forsythe, ed., *Human Rights and Comparative Foreign Policy* (Tokyo: United Nations University Press, 2000).

2. John Ruggie, *Winning the Peace: America and World Order in the New Era* (New York: Columbia Univ. Press, 1996). See also Edward C. Luck, *Mixed Messages.*

3. Cathal J. Nolan, *Principled Diplomacy: Security* (Westport, CT: Greenwood Press, 1993).

4. On voting at the UN and the North-South conflict in particular, see Soo Yeon Kim and Bruce Russett, "New UN Voting Alignments," *International Organization* 50, no. 4 (Autumn 1996), pp. 629–652.

5. David P. Forsythe, *Human Rights and U.S. Foreign Policy: Congress Reconsidered* (Gainesville: Univ. Press of Florida, 1988).

6. Ernst B. Haas, *When Knowledge Is Power: Three Models of Change in International Organizations* (Berkeley: Univ. of California Press, 1990).

7. George Modelski, "Is World Politics Evolutionary Learning?" *International Organization* 44, pp. 1–24.

8. In general see Roger S. Clark and Madeleine Sann, eds., *The Prosecution of International Crimes* (New Brunswick, NJ: Transaction, 1996).

9. For a criticism of these developments, see Human Rights Watch, *Human Rights Watch World Report 1997: Events of 1996* (New York: Human Rights Watch, 1996).

10. Samuel P. Huntington, *The Third Wave: Democratization in the Late Twentieth Century* (Norman: Univ. of Oklahoma Press, 1992).

11. Tom J. Farer, "The UN and Human Rights: More than a Whimper, Less than a Roar," in Adam Roberts and Benedict Kingsbury, eds., *United Nations, Divided World: The UN's Roles in International Relations* (Oxford: Clarendon Press, 1989), p. 126.

12. See, e.g., Jack Donnelly, "Human Rights in the New World Order: Implications for Europe," in David P. Forsythe, ed., *Human Rights in the New Europe* (Lincoln: Univ. of Nebraska Press, 1994).

13. Edmond Mulet, "The Palace Coup That Failed," *New York Times*, June 22, 1993, p. A11.

14. David P. Forsythe, *Human Rights in International Relations* (Cambridge, UK: Cambridge Univ. Press, 2000).

Part Three

Building Peace Through Sustainable Development

8 Development and the United Nations

The First Three Development Decades

According to the Charter of the United Nations, the primary purpose of the world organization is to promote and maintain international peace and security. As we saw in Part 1 of this book, for much of the UN's history that mandate was in practice defined rather narrowly in diplomatic and military terms: the resolution of disputes before they become violent, and response to breaches of the peace. But as we saw in Part 2, there also are nonmilitary dimensions to promoting peace. Some believe that working for human rights not only produces greater human dignity but also helps promote human security as well as reduce or eliminate conditions that give rise to violence among and within states.

Before the end of the Cold War, the linkage between the UN's work in economic and social domains and the world organization's peace mandate was usually made by emphasizing the argument that promoting social and economic development and protecting human rights are indirect approaches to "peace." That is to say, some observers believed that economic equity, the pursuit of economic growth, and the satisfaction of basic human needs can do more than just improve the material quality of life. They argued that at least some of the causes of violence between and within states could be decreased by reducing gross social and economic inequalities and deprivations. In *An Agenda for Peace*, for example, Secretary-General Boutros Boutros-Ghali highlighted this linkage between the UN's work in the social and economic realm and the promotion of international security. He placed economic despair, social injustice, and political oppression among the "deepest causes of conflict."[1] Some also believed international economic cooperation could lead to the institutional structures that can help regulate violence.

But as we discuss in the following chapters, in the post–Cold War context, the UN's peace and security mandate is increasingly viewed as involving much more than simply protecting people physically from military conflict. Promoting human security entails reducing perceived and real threats to individual and collective psychological and physical well-being. From this perspective, protecting people against agents and forces that could degrade their lives, values, and property is what the UN's development work is about.

But other observers continue to be divided in their views on the world organization's peace and security mandate and its development work. They suggest that much activity through the United Nations pursues economic growth—and now also environmental protection—that is unrelated to questions of either political violence or human security. For them, the notion of acting through the United Nations for "development" has meant, and still means, primarily the pursuit of national macroeconomic growth. From this perspective, the goal of development is not to reduce violence among or within states. By the mid-1990s, official UN definitions of development were stated in "sustainable-human-development" terms and linked the pursuit of economic growth to the promotion of human security, not just national security. But this linkage was not always reflected in the policies of states—or even of UN agencies. As noted earlier, a serious concern for human rights was not always integrated into UN development activities. Thus, we have to remind ourselves constantly that the notion of development still means different things to different people.

Whatever the relationship between social and economic well-being, human security, and peace, the UN Charter provided for the establishment of a principal organ, ECOSOC, to promote the objectives and carry out the work of the world organization in the economic and social areas. Moreover, the Second Committee of the General Assembly has been devoted exclusively to economic affairs. The UN's role in this area was supposedly limited, with the main work in social and economic fields being carried out by a system of specialized agencies. Some of these agencies, such as the ILO, existed from the League of Nations era and thus preceded creation of the UN. The ECOSOC was made responsible under the general authority of the General Assembly for coordinating the policies and activities of the United Nations with this larger system of international specialized agencies. So there was the narrow United Nations made up of principal organs, including ECOSOC and numerous subsidiary bodies, and the larger UN system or family, which included the specialized agencies.

Over the years, the size and scope of the UN system have drastically expanded. The Cold War rift between the United States and the Soviet Union brought with it a stalemate in much of the security work of the organization. Much activity in the UN shifted to furthering economic cooperation, which also was the priority among the developing countries that swelled the ranks of member states, particularly between the mid-1950s and the mid-1960s. The successes within the United Nations in promoting decolonization and self-determination yielded a profusion of new states. As these newly independent states were embraced as UN members, the political climate in the world organization rapidly shifted. The promotion of national economic development took center stage on the UN agenda and accounted for upward of 90 percent of human and programming resources during the final years of the Cold War.

As the global political climate has changed after the Cold War, opening up new opportunities for action by the United Nations in the security area, has the economic realm of the UN's work been affected? If so, how? Has the concept of development undergone a change? If so, in what direction, and why? To what extent has the growing interest in environmental protection been incorporated into development concerns? Why has the term "sustainable development" come to dominate discourse about development? Can we even make much sense out of these vague terms?

Mustafa Tolba, the former executive director of the United Nations Environment Programme (UNEP), has argued that "there is nothing static about either 'environment' or its relationship to development."[2] Sustainable development represents an approach to economic growth of endeavoring "to ensure that development meets the needs of the present without compromising the abilities of future generations to meet their own needs."[3] It is therefore much broader than other concepts that historically have dominated global development discussions. An examination of how the idea of sustainable development has come into use and has shaped the debate about development tells us a great deal about the United Nations and economic activity.

The Origins of Development Policy in the World Organization

Merging environmental protection and economic growth as presumably compatible concerns is a very recent notion in international political discourse. Prior to the late 1960s, pursuing economic growth and protecting the environment were treated largely as mutually exclusive. The concerns over environmental protection and conservation that were emerging in some policy circles in the industrialized world during the 1960s generally met with suspicion in developing countries. Industrialization, namely pursuit of national economic growth via manufacturing enterprises, was seen in many quarters of the Third World as the most viable and direct path to a greater gross national product.

The imposition of standards to lower environmental pollution in countries in the early stages of industrial development was greeted as a badly disguised way of preserving huge global economic inequalities. Pollution was seen as a natural by-product of early industrialization. Accordingly, the environment was frequently treated as something to be used and mastered, not protected. Growth was to be promoted, not limited. Natural resources were to be exploited toward such ends, not preserved. Besides, the main consumers of both renewable and nonrenewable natural resources were overwhelmingly in industrialized countries. And if the North had achieved its "developed" status via industrialization, with pollution, why should something different be expected from the South? Was this not a new form of colonialism or imperialism?

In the North, too, misgivings about environmental policy abounded. Environmentalists were frequently accused of wanting to retreat from progress. Progrowth ideology was still pervasive with strong support for the view that environmentalism was a threat to the base for national well-being, which was an expanding economy.

Yet beginning in the early 1970s and especially since the middle of the 1980s, governments from both North and South have become more or less actively engaged in both the debate and practice surrounding sustainable development. The story of how and why this has been the case tells us much about the evolution of the United Nations in the economic domain. The story, however, must begin long before these most recent decades. For ease of reference, Table 8.1 contains a chronology of selected development conferences and activities during the first three UN Development Decades, 1960–1989.

Global intergovernmental organization is very much the product of the industrial age and needs to be placed in that context in order to be understood. Global IGOs got their start through the creation of public international unions—such as the International Telegraphic Union and the Universal Postal Union—during the last half of the nineteenth century. Specialized international organizations—such as the FAO, World Bank, IMF, and General Agreement on Tariffs and Trade (GATT)—that were created during the first half of the twentieth century can be viewed, in large part, as efforts to establish the infrastructure needed to promote the objectives of a liberal economic world order. This system of organizations represented an attempt to create the global economic conditions necessary for the operation of private markets, even if they might be subject to public regulation.

In the context of the early post–World War II years, a primary concern of the Western great powers was the restoration of a viable global economic order based on liberal economic principles. As Murphy has suggested,

Postwar world organizations also took on major new functions, most of them concerned with satisfying interests that would not necessarily benefit from a new wave of industrial change. The GATT allowed industrialized states to maintain systems aiding their own farmers, systems that . . . FAO also supported. The . . . IMF worked to ease specific financial "debt crises" that had undermined inter-war attempts to establish welfare states. The . . . ILO encouraged the collective bargaining systems that secured the OECD countries' "Fordist" compromise between industrial labor and capital in which the discipline of mass production was exchanged for the economic benefits of mass consumption. Most significantly, the UN system created political space for less-industrialized nations to push for decolonization and development assistance, issues that, for most states and peoples, seemed to emerge in lieu of incorporation into the system of privileged economic development that allowed the OECD countries twenty-five years of postwar growth, which even surpassed Europe's growth in the twenty years of the Second Industrial Revolution prior to World War I.[4]

TABLE 8.1 Chronology of Selected Development-Related Conferences and Activities During the First Three UN Development Decades, 1960–1989

1943	United Nations Relief and Rehabilitation Administration (UNRRA)[a]
1947	Economic Commisson for Asia and the Far East (ECAFE) [a]
1948	Economic Commission for Latin America (ECLA) [a]
1950	Expanded Program of Technical Assistance[a]
1955	Afro-Asian Conference in Bandung/Nonaligned Movement[a]
1956	International Finance Corporation[a]
1958	UN Special Fund[a]
	Economic Commission for Africa (ECA)[a]
1960	First UN Development Decade[a]
	Declaration on the Granting of Independence to Colonial Countries and Peoples
	International Development Association[a]
1964	United Nations Conference on Trade and Development (UNCTAD I)[a]
	Group of 77[a]
1965	United Nations Development Programme (UNDP)[a]
	United Nations Industrial Development Organization (UNIDO)[a]
1973	OPEC price increase
1974	Sixth Special Session of UN General Assembly
	Declaration and Programme of Action on the Establishment of a New International Economic Order (NIEO)
	World Population Conference
	World Food Conference
	Economic and Social Commisson for Western Asia (ESCWA)[a]
1975	Seventh Special Session of UN General Assembly
	UN World Conference of the International Women's Year
	UN Development Fund for Women (UNIFEM)[a]
1975-1977	Conference on International Economic Cooperation
1976	UNCTAD IV
	UN Conference on Human Settlements (HABITAT)
	UN Decade for Women[a]
1979	OPEC price increase
	UN Conference on Science and Technology for Development
1980	Independent Commission on International Development Issues (Brandt Commission) Report
	UN World Conference of the Mid-Decade for Women
1984	Second World Population Conference
1985	Third World Conference on Women
1987	UN General Assembly Special Session on Africa
	World Commission on the Environment and Development (Brundtland Commission) Report
	Global Programme on AIDS (GPA)[a]
1988	Multilateral Investment Guarantee Agency (MIGA)[a]

[a]Denotes the establishment of the body or commencement of the activity.

Creation of the liberal economic order that was to be embodied in this new system of organizations proved to be quite elusive. The evolving East-West conflict, the perpetuation of colonial rule over vast areas of the world, and widespread poverty and the lack of industrial capacity within preindustrial societies stood as significant impediments to the liberal vision. A very large part of the problem was control by communist parties over European and other states. Moreover, between 1945 and about 1985 many non-communist developing states did not have the same optimistic view of laissez-faire economics, private markets, and liberal trade as did most of the West, especially the United States.

It was therefore not surprising that in the UN's principal organs, where these socialist and economic nationalist states had voting rights, endorsement of liberal economics was neither quick nor enthusiastic. After the idea of regional commissions was raised and originally rejected at San Francisco, the regional Economic Commission for Europe (ECE) and the Economic Commission for Asia and the Far East (ECAFE) were established within ECOSOC in 1947 to assist in the postwar recovery activities in those two areas. But it took concerted effort by Latin American member states to secure the creation of a similar body, the Economic Commission for Latin America (ECLA), a year later for their region. It was not until a decade later that a regional commission was established for Africa.

The lag in creating the Economic Commission for Africa (ECA), however, was not surprising given the colonial domination of the continent at the time. Indeed, in keeping with the political liberalism written into the Charter, a main thrust within the United Nations during these early years was the self-determination of colonial peoples and the associated development of viable national economies. But blending political and economic liberalism was not easy. Once some peoples had attained self-determination in the form of a legally independent state, they were suspicious of domination by large Western market economies and their transnational corporate enterprises.

It was widely recognized that international assistance would be needed to facilitate national economic growth and perhaps to create stable polities. It was toward these ends that much of the early development-related debate in the United Nations was directed. Providing technical assistance for a variety of social and economic programs was not a completely novel concern for member states. One of the earliest nonmilitary undertakings of the UN alliance during the war had been the creation in 1943 of the UN Relief and Rehabilitation Administration (UNRRA), which provided relief refugee assistance and repatriation to peoples in liberated territories. This same concern was expanded beyond the European and Japanese postwar contexts during the early years of the United Nations when the General Assembly launched the Expanded Program of Technical Assistance (EPTA) in 1950. The aim of EPTA was to promote economic growth through the coordinated transfer of technology from industrial to preindustrial societies via international agencies.

An outgrowth for the most part of President Truman's Point IV initiative and spurred initially by the U.S. government through the 1949 Act for International Development, EPTA provided three main types of assistance: equipment, training, and expertise. The United Nations and its five specialized agencies were the program's original participating parties. Over the next decade and a half, this group was joined by another half-dozen agencies. To coordinate the activities of this diverse set of actors, machinery was established on three levels: the Technical Assistance Board (intersecretariat among the UN and the specialized agencies); the Technical Assistance Administration (within the UN secretariat); and the Technical Assistance Committee (TAC) of ECOSOC (governmental representatives).

This was not the first or the last time that UN coordination, however, worked better on paper than in practice. The autonomously governed and financed specialized agencies were reluctant to submit to centralized coordination from the United Nations. Yet because of these mechanisms that were created to engender greater coordination of this UN systemwide effort, economic development began to evolve as a distinctive focus in its own right. From the perspectives of most UN diplomats, this movement apparently had little to do with international peace, at least according to texts of the various UN documents and programs.

Promoting economic growth required resources other than technical assistance. Finance capital and infrastructure development were other important pillars necessary for starting and sustaining economic growth. Ensuring adequate finance capital, however, was complicated in the context of EPTA because of Washington's insistence that the program be truly multinational in character and not dominated completely by U.S. funding. Although EPTA was symbolically important for establishing a role for the UN in the development area, its expenditures were nominal. Beginning with an initial operating fund of $20 million in 1951, the program grew only moderately over the next decade. The United States reduced its relative contribution from 60 percent to 40 percent of the total.

In the early 1950s, developing countries applied strong pressures to create a Special United Nations Fund for Economic Development (SUNFED). SUNFED was to augment technical assistance activities with long-term low-interest loans aimed at building infrastructure. The move to create such a fund was opposed by major donors, especially the United States. Although at first refusing the idea on the grounds that the American people could not support such a capital fund while underwriting a war in Korea, the United States continued its opposition after that conflict had subsided. Reluctant to commit financial support to a multilateral development assistance fund over which U.S. officials could not guarantee control of disbursements, Washington refused to go along with the majority in the United Nations. Developing countries demonstrated that they had majority votes, but in the final analysis the SUNFED idea was killed for lack of resources. To deflect criticism of the U.S. position in this regard, President Eisenhower insisted that creation of the fund be linked to savings to be realized from multilateral disarmament.

Housewives cut and sew traditional farmers' cotton shirts to
be sold in local markets and the women's cooperative shop in
Mung Mo, Thailand. The Voluntary Fund for the United Nations Decade for Women supports projects such as this in
developing countries. (UN Photo 150947/C. Redenius)

After the SUNFED issue died, the matter of increased financial assistance to the
developing countries stayed alive. In keeping with liberal economic preferences
for promoting growth through private investments while resisting pressures for
the creation of a large-scale public capital grants fund, the members of the General Assembly agreed in 1958 to create a special fund. The purpose of the United
Nations Special Fund was to provide "preinvestment" capital to be used to stimulate private as well as public investment to complement technical assistance and
facilitate economic development projects. These early skirmishes over technical
assistance financing prefaced the much larger battle to come over development financing. At this point in time, however, the United States and other donors were
able to dictate the terms under which the funding they supplied would be given
and used.

Contributions to the Special Fund grew relatively more rapidly than did EPTA contributions, which in theory should not have been a problem given that both funds were to be closely coordinated. In practice, however, the new fund operated quite independently of EPTA. Moreover, the FAO, the UN Educational, Scientific and Cultural Organization (UNESCO), and other specialized agencies that participated in EPTA were reluctant to restrict their autonomy by accepting more centralized coordination directed from the United Nations.

With the goal of engendering greater coordination and more effective performance, the General Assembly moved in 1965 to merge the Special Fund and EPTA into one entity. Thus, the United Nations Development Programme came into being. Although problems of coordination among participating parties did not end, somewhat greater integration of UN-supported development projects in the context of national development began. In an effort to increase the effective use of funds made available through the program, UNDP initiated a study in 1969 directed by Sir Robert Jackson.

The "Jackson report" made a number of recommendations for enhancing coordination.[5] One of the most important recommendations adopted later was the specification of UNDP resident representatives (since 1977 called resident coordinators) in each recipient country. These resident coordinators were to serve as intermediaries, linking national ministries with international agencies and with chief representatives of the UN system in each country. This system may sound impressive on paper, but it has tended to operate very unevenly in the field. The Jackson report tried to establish UNDP as a central coordinating body for development activities in the UN system. The specialized agencies, however, were reluctant to accept the implied subordination of their autonomy and the actual reduction of their fiscal autonomy.

In arguing against the creation of SUNFED, U.S. officials had suggested that the World Bank, not the United Nations, was the appropriate institution through which to channel such multilateral public loans. Other major donors shared this preference for using the Washington-based financial institutions, also known as the Bretton Woods institutions, as the primary multilateral mechanisms for financial assistance. This Western position was understandable because a relatively small number of Western member states controlled the World Bank and the International Monetary Fund through both personnel and finances, as well as finance-related weighted voting. Thus it was no surprise that in the early postwar years nearly all World Bank lending was committed to the task of reconstructing European national economies that had been destroyed by the war. Relatively few loans were granted to developing countries.

After the first wave of decolonization, member states of the World Bank agreed in 1956 to create an affiliate, the International Finance Corporation (IFC), to stimulate private investment for industrial development. The IFC represented a compromise device to avert demands for taking more extreme measures, and it was followed later by the creation of the International Development Association (IDA)—a kind of SUNFED that was under donor control. The role of the IFC is to serve as a catalyst for stimulating private investment capital within developing economies for financing large-scale investments. The IFC may provide up to 25 percent of the capital needed for an individual enterprise, and it encourages additional investments from the world's capital markets.

The nature of IFC lending is restrictive, with investments targeted to industries that are believed to have the potential for making significant contributions to overall national economic development. Thus, these loans leave out small and medium-sized enterprises. Also, the bank's principal loans go primarily where there is a good prospect for a safe return on the loan. So it soon became apparent that capital availability would remain a major problem in the developing countries unless further multilateral action was taken.

Responding to demands from the growing number of developing countries, the World Bank established another affiliate in 1960 to address this concern. The International Development Association was created to provide "soft loans" to developing countries. Typically, soft loans are made on a no-interest basis with a three-fourths of 1 percent annual administrative service charge. Recipients have fifty years to repay on a graduated payment schedule; no payment is required for the first ten years; 1 percent of the principal is payable each year for the second ten years; and 3 percent is payable annually for the last thirty years. The terms are in fact so soft that these investments really are grants in everything except name. They are available only to states whose GNP per capita falls below some specified level, and they must be repaid in hard (that is, convertible) currencies.

Unlike the World Bank and the IFC, the IDA relies largely on contributions pledged by member states to replenish or expand its capital fund. Major donors have, of course, been reluctant to provide the scale of funding demanded by potential recipients among developing countries. To supplement the multilateral lending activities of these universal organizations, a series of regional development banks began to spring up, beginning in Latin America in 1959 with the creation of the Inter-American Development Bank (IDB). This was followed shortly thereafter by the African, Asian, and East African development banks in 1964, 1966, and 1967. These regional banks often work in tandem with the Bretton Woods institutions to widen the scale of capital available. Nonetheless, demand for development financing continued to exceed supply, and this situation intensified as the international political economy underwent significant change.

Winds of Change

Decolonization efforts by the United Nations bore surprisingly rapid fruit during these decades. Brian Urquhart has often noted that in 1945 most observers predicted that 75 to 100 years would be required for decolonization, but the demographics of membership within the UN system shifted significantly from the mid-1950s onward. The logic of the world organization with its foundations in collective security is based on universality of membership. From the original 51 members in 1945, membership in the United Nations more than doubled to 104 in 1961. In 1960 alone, 17 new member states joined, with 10 more following between 1961 and 1962.[6] As mentioned at the outset, there were 189 members in 2000.

With this evolving shift in the demographic composition of the organization came greater pressure to focus the UN's work more on the task of enhancing national economic growth. One of the most visible manifestations of the UN's shifting demographics was Resolution 1710 (XVI), passed by the General Assembly in December 1961 to proclaim the 1960s the United Nations Development Decade. The goal of this campaign was "to mobilize and to sustain support for the measures required on the part of both developed and developing countries to accelerate progress toward self-sustaining growth of the economy of the individual nations and their social advancement." Although this first development decade fell far short of its established targets, the symbolism nonetheless was important in solidifying a prominent place for development on the world organization's agenda. It was also clear that at this stage the concept of development was equated with national economic growth.

The numerical majority of what was then called the Third World in the UN's governing bodies created opportunities for rapidly expanding the arrangements for the organization to work in this area. Whether the United Nations would have the capacity, particularly as measured in terms of economic resources, to make a difference for national economic growth was another matter, as the SUNFED debacle had already demonstrated. Accordingly, during the 1960s a variety of development-related conferences was held and new international development bodies were created. In early 1963, a United Nations Conference on Applications of Science and Technology for the Benefit of Less Developed Areas (UNCAST) was convened to discuss strategies for creating technologies that were appropriate to underdeveloped areas. Later that year, the General Assembly created the United Nations Institute for Training and Research (UNITAR) to train Third World personnel for jobs in international civil service and to enhance development expertise at home.

The year 1964, however, stands as a benchmark in the evolution of political dynamics within the world organization. Although economic growth in the Third World advanced at a relatively rapid pace during the 1950s and early 1960s, frustration grew over the restrained response by multilateral institutions to development needs. The emerging tensions inherent in the gap between affluent and poor societies took shape as members of the world organization, following two years of preparatory work, met in Geneva in 1964 at the United Nations Conference on Trade and Development (UNCTAD).[7] At this conference representatives of developing countries formally joined to form a caucusing group, the Group of 77 (G-77), that would shape the global value dialectic for the next decade and a half. Rallying behind the ideas of Raúl Prebisch, a Latin American economist and international public figure, and other development economists, the Group of 77 moved to institutionalize both the conference and itself by creating an international secretariat for both.

Prebisch characterized the global capitalist economy as an uneven playing field, asymmetrically structured against most nonindustrial countries, which mostly were producers of primary commodities. He argued that an unequal system of trade exists between the North and South, which resulted in chronic and increasing trade imbalances in favor of the rich North. From this perspective the GATT (General Agreement on Tariffs and Trade) international trade regime—most specifically its most favored nation (MFN) principle, which required all parties to conduct trade on a nondiscriminatory basis, and its principle of reciprocity (that is, the requirement to grant reciprocal concessions)—was viewed as a manifestly discriminatory, not a nondiscriminatory, order. Thus, it was hoped that UNCTAD would serve as a mechanism for changing the GATT regime to make it relatively more favorable to the South.

At UNCTAD, the Group of 77 forced the conference, over the opposition of most major donor states, to adopt a set of demands for promoting national economic development that framed intergovernmental debate for the next two decades. The North-South split that was manifest in the voting over the twenty-seven principles passed by the conference would serve as the starting point from which a concerted program of action would be developed by the G-77. The U.S. delegation led the opposition to this new agenda championed by the developing countries, as if foreshadowing the evolving political tensions that would become so divisive later and lead to the UN-bashing of the Reagan years.

The UNCTAD secretariat was created from the conference staff and was based at the UN facility in Geneva at the old League of Nations complex. It operated semiautonomously in regard to the UN's main secretariat in New York. Accordingly, the organ was to have its own Secretary-General. Raúl Prebisch was appointed as the first executive in that position. The intergovernmental body itself was to meet only periodically (every three or four years). The interim governance was delegated to the Trade and Development Board, an intergovernmental committee of the whole that was to meet annually. In short, UNCTAD became a continual and permanent, rather than a single and ad hoc, conference.

The intent was to create a relatively autonomous body, even though it would operate under the authority of the General Assembly, that could circumvent the normal administrative and political constraints of established UN organs. Support from the overall UN budget meant that the UNCTAD secretariat would be partially shielded from the pressure of major contributors. The new body had no real authority to commit the larger world organization to action. Yet it was hoped by its Third World sponsors that the unit would serve as an intellectual and moral force that the larger enterprise would find difficult to ignore.

To complement this trade- and development-oriented body, the Group of 77 was also successful in creating a new organ to deal specifically with industrial development concerns. The United Nations Industrial Development Organization

(UNIDO) was created by the General Assembly in 1965. Like UNCTAD, and for the same initial reasons, UNIDO operated as a semiautonomous unit within the UN until it became a full-fledged and independent specialized agency in 1986. The main focus of the unit has been on increasing manufacturing capacities within developing societies by providing training, technical assistance, information, and research. Like its UNCTAD counterpart, from its inception it has tended to act quite independently of other social and economic organs of the UN, including ECOSOC, which is supposed to coordinate social and economic activities within the world organization.

These institutional foundations represented only the beginning of a more massive, ambitious, and ultimately unsuccessful attempt to change the shape of international economic relations. Over the following decade, the Group of 77 launched a broad-based initiative to create the New International Economic Order (NIEO), which aimed to change the rules of the international economic game and channel greater benefits to developing countries. The force of this movement and its subsequent collapse tell much about the nature of world politics—with the United Nations as a subset or dependent variable.

The Call for the New International Economic Order

During a series of conferences in the mid-1970s, the Group of 77 formulated its ultimate agenda for restructuring the global political economy. The main thrust of the call for the New International Economic Order came during the Sixth Special Session of the UN General Assembly in late spring 1974, where members adopted the Declaration and Program of Action on the Establishment of a New International Economic Order. This action came on the heels of the U.S. government's unilateral actions in late 1971, which effectively destroyed the Bretton Woods fixed-exchange-rate system, and the 1973–1974 oil embargo sponsored by the Organization of Petroleum Exporting Countries (OPEC) with its resulting price increases. The OPEC show of power was viewed by U.S. and many other officials from Western industrialized countries as a direct challenge to the crumbling liberal economic order that they were trying to revive. Furthermore, the oil embargo and the response to it signaled a newfound leverage on the part of OPEC states. For the first time, their demands had to be taken seriously.

The NIEO demands were wide-ranging but can be classified into four broad themes: economic sovereignty, trade, aid, and participation.[8] A substantial amount of concern was expressed over the lack of real sovereignty, that is, over the lack of freedom from outside control and influence in national economic and political affairs and decisionmaking processes. The developing countries had the legal right to make policy affecting society within their borders, but they did not have as much actual power to do so as they wished. This concern led to calls for greater national control over natural resources, freedom from outside intervention, regulation over the activities of transnational corporations, and a reaffirmation of the right to nationalize foreign holdings. A primary target was transnational corporations and their relationships to host governments.

In the area of trade, the major concern was market structures. On one hand, developing countries sought a means by which to stabilize commodity markets and their export earnings. They wanted to create international regulatory machinery and other institutional arrangements. On the other hand, these states desired preferential access on a nonreciprocal basis to the economies of the industrialized market countries. The first Lomé Convention, signed between the governments of the European Economic Community (EEC) and more than forty-six African, Caribbean, and Pacific (ACP) states in early 1975, attempted to institutionalize these ideas on a less than global basis. Under the terms of that convention, ACP member states are exempt from all customs duties on nearly all of their exports to the European Community. Also, a compensatory finance scheme (STABEX, or Stabilization of Export Earnings) was built into the agreement in an attempt to stabilize the export earnings for twelve commodities that were economically important for the ACP countries.

In addition, the EEC members agreed in the convention to increase their official development assistance, which ran over into the third main NIEO category: aid. The Group of 77 called for significant increases in financial assistance in line with specific targets. Aid was also requested in the form of debt rescheduling and the transfer of technology. This latter concern also focused more generally on the improvement of scientific and technological capabilities in the Third World and on the halt in the "brain-drain," or the departure of trained and badly needed personnel to greener economic pastures in the West.

Finally, the matter of participation struck at the core of the Group of 77's frustrations with the Bretton Woods institutions and their official rules and procedures. This concern about participation focused on the issue of equality, both with respect to decisionmaking and with respect to outcomes. The Charter of Economic Rights and Duties of States (UN Resolution 3281 [XXIX]) underscores this concern when it states that "all states are juridicially equal and . . . have the right to participate fully and effectively in the international decisionmaking process . . . and to share equitably in the benefits resulting therefrom." Thus, broadly defined, participation loomed large in the G-77's program of action for restructuring the global economic order.

These issues were raised time and again in various ways and in various settings during the remainder of the decade. The North-South battle lines quickly became unambiguously drawn and a very different version of "cold war" appeared imminent. U.S. president Gerald Ford railed against the "tyranny of the majority" in his speech before the General Assembly in fall 1974, and U.S. ambassador to the UN John Scali echoed the sentiment after the Group of 77 successfully forced the Charter of Economic Rights and Duties of States through the assembly on a 120–6–10 vote, with the United States and most other Western industrial states either voting in opposition or abstaining.

A slum in the city of São Paulo, Brazil, illustrates the shortage of adequate housing as rural settlements are being abandoned by people moving to the cities. (UN Photo 155212/C. Edinger)

In addition to this Sixth Special Session, the General Assembly held other special sessions in 1975 and 1980 that provided the opportunity to press for NIEO demands. Also, a number of "global ad hoc conferences"[9] focusing on specific issues, such as population and food, and the more broad-based Conference on International Economic Cooperation, which met in December 1975 and June 1977, provided additional forums for expanding at the global level what some called dialogue and others invective.

This ongoing process of conference diplomacy helped to build a certain degree of mutual understanding and a common, or at least compatible, orientation toward North-South issues within the Group of 77. At the same time, it also tended to foster disenchantment in some major Western governments and led to a heightened degree of mutual mistrust and a deterioration of relations between the North and South. As governments from the industrialized West stood firm in their resolve not to give in to the South's pressures, the political climate began to shift. Most important, the unanimity required within OPEC to continue to press its demands through oil production and pricing controls proved to be impossible to sustain with consistency, particularly after the world economy slumped. The South was able to retain a remarkably high degree of solidarity through the Seventh Special Session of the General Assembly in September 1975. But cracks began to appear between radical and moderate Southern states, and the United

States stood unbending in its rejection of the NIEO package. These cracks were deepened by tensions in OPEC, especially between the Saudis and Algerians. By the end of the decade in OPEC, rigor mortis had begun to set in. World market conditions, internal OPEC squabbles, and the unwillingness of members to sacrifice individual short-term gain for collective good served to further weaken the cartel during the early 1980s.

The 1980s have frequently been referred to as the "lost decade" for the South. The members of the United Nations moved ahead—at least rhetorically—into the Third Development Decade, but Northern donor states seemed fatigued by the entire process. With a new administration in Washington bent on reassessing all U.S. multilateral commitments and a like-minded conservative prime minister in charge in Britain, the stage was set for a general lull, followed by hostility, in the global development debate.

As seen in the peace, security, human rights, and humanitarian assistance arenas discussed earlier, the end of the Cold War brought about important changes in world politics. For most developing countries, however, the situation has not changed at all for the better. For many of their citizens, the quality of life has steadily worsened in recent years. Indeed for many developing countries, the situation has never been worse. The UNDP *Human Development Report 1996* depicts the situation in stark terms:

> Growth has been failing over much of the past 15 years in about 100 countries, with almost a third of the world's people. And the links between [economic] growth and human development are failing for people in many countries with lopsided development—with either good growth but little human development or good human development but little or no growth. . . . Over much of this period . . . economic decline or stagnation has affected 100 countries, reducing the incomes of 1.6 billion people. . . . In 70 of these countries average incomes are less than they were in 1980—and in 43 countries less than they were in 1970. . . . The world has become more polarized, and the gulf between the poor and the rich of the world has widened even further.[10]

The Cold War at least brought some attention to regions such as the Horn of Africa that were perceived by the superpowers as strategically important. This is not to suggest that the Cold War was a positive force for economic growth in developing countries. But undoubtedly it triggered some form of spending—even though much of that spending can be fairly criticized as unrelated to sustained national growth and insensitive to questions of intranational equity. But as East-West tensions have relaxed, major Western powers have not always seen the problems of developing countries as pressing.

The NIEO movement ran out of steam as the world economy proved not to be amenable to structural reform along the trajectory demanded by the G-77. Or more to the point, developing countries lacked the power to compel developed countries to respond positively to their policy demands. Developing countries had the votes inside the United Nations, but they lacked economic and military power outside the world organization that could be converted to bargaining success. The forum created by the Third World to host debates on international economic issues, UNCTAD, displayed this sense of fatigue and despair. The conferences held in the 1980s (Belgrade in 1983 and Geneva in 1987) accomplished very little.

At the same time, resolutions growing out of the sometimes endless squabble and cacophony of statements in the General Assembly were quickly made obsolete by a decline in the world economic situation. This situation was exacerbated by a new, essentially antimultilateral ideology introduced by the Reagan and Thatcher administrations and by other conservative decisionmakers in the industrialized North. A more pragmatic, less accusatory approach by Third World diplomats was clearly noticeable at the General Assembly Special Session on Africa in 1987. Attacking the West had gotten them little. Fast-breaking changes in world politics further undermined their calls for an NIEO.

The opening of the former Soviet empire revealed an economic and environmental fiasco. One result was to undercut statist demands by developing countries and to reinforce preferences for market solutions. Another result was to provide yet another rationale for declining interest by the North in the South. It would be incorrect to argue that the United States and West European governments were preoccupied in the 1990s with investment and other concerns in areas formerly controlled by European communism. The Bush administration tended to ignore developments in this area until it was goaded into a more active orientation because of public criticism by former president Nixon. Moreover, during the 1992 presidential campaign in the United States, the winning candidate definitely focused on what were supposedly domestic issues; foreign policy issues received scant attention in that campaign. And the West Europeans tended to view Eastern Europe, especially its southern areas, as quite distinct from the rest of Europe.

But it is still true to say that the industrialized democracies were more interested in Eastern Europe and the former Soviet Union, at least its more western regions, than they were in much of the Southern Hemisphere. UN Secretary-General Boutros-Ghali repeatedly pointed out this bias as he pressed the members of the Security Council to show the same interest in Somalia during 1992 that they were showing for the former Yugoslavia, "a rich man's war." By the end of the 1980s, pessimism concerning economic cooperation seemed to dominate the world organization. The United Nations Development Programme's April 1989 draft, "UNDP and World Development by the Year 2000," summarized the state of affairs during this lost decade:

> There is growing uneasiness about the unevenness of . . . progress and the evident deterioration in the human condition in many parts of the world. . . . The 1980s will be remembered as a decade of crisis, depression and lost opportunities for many developing countries.

Progress has become increasingly uneven both among regions and among various classes of individual countries. The reduction of government expenditure and the diminishing ability of the State to support social development programmes has resulted in increases in poverty levels. These problems are compounded by rapid population growth in most developing countries. . . . With the exception of China and South and East Asia, economic growth has slowed in all regions of the developing world since the second half of the 1970s. Average incomes have fallen in much of Africa, the Middle East and Latin America.[11]

Some observers, however, found reasons for modest optimism. The climate of UN debates over development during the 1980s had changed. The dominant orientation was pragmatism. The political-ideological clashes that had characterized the previous decade of relations between the industrialized and the developing countries in the United Nations were all but absent, as was the fiery exchange of accusatory rhetoric. Divisive activities, such as the successful Arab-led movement to have Zionism declared a form of racism, seemed out of place in the late 1980s. (The infamous resolution was rescinded in 1991.) The railings of U.S. ambassadors against what they perceived to be the unruly actions of the Third World majority had subsided. A new pragmatism had taken its place, which reflected changing world economic circumstances.

Economic conditions affecting the poorest countries had changed dramatically for the worse. The abstract issues of global equity and social and economic justice that had sustained the North-South acrimony during the NIEO years had lost their immediacy. As one Latin American ambassador commented to the authors, "What's the use of talking about charters, rights and duties when people are literally dying in large numbers?" In the context of the early 1980s the full attention of many Third World countries had to be focused on their debts and the deteriorating social conditions that debt-inflicted austerity was causing. Others, particularly the governments and peoples of Africa, had to deal with the combined effects of civil war, economic collapse, and ecological disaster. Some states, especially in Asia, showed dramatic economic improvements. But many developing countries did not.

In all of this, the United Nations came to be looked upon more as a conduit for immediate aid and less as a legitimizer of new principles of global order. The organization became, as one Third World representative expressed in an interview, "no longer a forum for defining together what is wrong, [because] the only thing people are interested in is how to get assistance in the midst of a deteriorating situation." Yet even if the furor waned regarding the norms of the NIEO, new debates erupted about rules to govern North-South relations. For example, as noted already in Parts 1 and 2 of this book, the General Assembly in the late 1980s and early 1990s debated how humanitarian assistance was to be provided and whether the international community could engage in "humanitarian intervention" without the consent of sovereign states.

Despite this continuing but different normative debate, most Third World governments began approaching development issues in more businesslike ways, largely by accepting the idea that exposing past injustices would not solve current problems. Moreover, even states like communist China and socialist Zimbabwe accepted the reality of markets as the primary engine for economic growth. They looked to strike bargains via compromises and saw global consensus, not majoritarianism, as the most promising path to international action in areas of major concern. The frequency of consensual decisions on development issues increased in the General Assembly and in the deliberative bodies of the specialized agencies. Slogans and tactics for pursuing the New International Economic Order became obsolete.

By virtue of their situation, developing countries still made familiar demands for debt relief, development capital, technical assistance, access to markets, stabilized commodity prices, food aid, and the wherewithal to satisfy other basic human needs. A good deal of development activity has continued in the UN system. But much of this activity has been in the form of relief measures, emergency relief, or other stopgap moves designed to stem deterioration rather than to promote development. By the early 1990s the social and economic side of the world organization had resigned itself to being more of an "aid" organization providing technical assistance and facilitating technical cooperation, and less of a "development" organization. The increasing directives from governing bodies to devote more resources to the poorest countries ensured that "Bandaids," rather than development of sophisticated economies, were the overriding orientation of the UN system. The eruption and continuation of civil wars in such places as Somalia meant that dwindling resources were devoted to stopgap military and humanitarian operations rather than to investment or aid to development.

For some time now, the United Nations has not been responsive enough to meet the basic needs of those in the South who want immediate assistance, or to satisfy the aspirations of those in both the South and the North who want the world organization to promote social and economic development. Maurice Williams, Secretary-General of the Society for International Development at the time of this quote, presciently summarized the relationship between the UN and world development problems as follows:

> In the face of . . . problems which are beyond the reach of any of the national governments and which threaten our collective survival, we have seen in this decade a retreat from multilateral cooperation at the global level. There have been persistent efforts by major industrial countries to marginalize international organizations in terms of the central problems affecting development and the world economy. For example, the United Nations is looked upon by the major countries mainly for necessary but limited tasks in areas such as human rights, environmental concerns, refugees and famine relief. The focus of the Bretton Woods Institutions, the World Bank and the IMF, has been directed to enhancing the capacity of developing countries to adjust to the fundamentals of lower growth and pay their debts.[12]

Beyond its modest budgets, another indicator of the UN's limitations in the development arena has been the absence of any *operative* global development strategy. The organization's difficulty in formulating a programmatic, cohesive vision has produced in the UN system a prevailing "ad hocism." Throughout the 1990s there was very little real agreement among member states about what the developing countries actually need. Moreover, there has existed no political environment within the UN conducive to reaching such an agreement.

Shifting Ground

As the nature of the development agenda in the United Nations shifted over the first five decades of the organization's existence, a number of important trends could be noted. First, there was a decline in the proposals for development that center on statist solutions and policies. There has been increased recognition that private rather than public actors have important roles to play. Again, this thematic shift has been stronger in theory than in practice, and considerable suspicion remains in certain parts of the Southern Hemisphere about the power of Western-controlled markets and private corporations. Nevertheless, as discussed in Chapter 10, private entities are far more acceptable, in relative terms, in 2000 than they were in the 1960s, the 1970s, and even the 1980s—whether these entities operate for human-rights, ecological, or economic reasons.

This is not to say that with the decline of statism has come a clear decline in devotion to state sovereignty. On many issues developing countries still champion the cause of state sovereignty as traditionally conceived. In principle, they still insist on state consent in order for UN programs to go forward in their countries, whether these programs are concerned with emergency assistance or economic growth. Although state sovereignty is still central to developing countries' view of international relations, they are less insistent that socialism has provided clear solutions to their dilemmas. And they are more open to the possibility that a new developmental approach might actually be in their interests—one encompassing such notions as ecological protection, basic human needs, and increased political participation.

Second, as discussed more fully in Chapters 9 and 10, "development," broadly defined, has come to be treated by most actors as being simultaneously global and local in scope. Thus it requires holistic or comprehensive thinking. This realization was also made clear in the approach taken by both governmental and nongovernmental actors before and during the 1992 United Nations Conference on Environment and Development (the Rio conference). At the same time, ecodevelopment issues require decentralized cooperation and localized action. They require responses that are both governmental and nongovernmental, centralized and decentralized, cooperative and competitive. They require policies and programs that simultaneously use local, national, and international resources and in-

Guatemalan refugees in class at Los Lirios camp in Quintana Roo, Mexico, 1984. (UNHCR 14149/10.1984/D. Bregnard)

stitutions. Furthermore, their long-term governance requires community-based responses to be sustained.

The resort to macrostrategies for collective action that characterized debates about the New International Economic Order and much of the North-South confrontation of the 1970s seemed curiously out of place in the global policy debates of the 1990s. The global strategies that characterized earlier discourse and practice in the social and economic realm in the United Nations have all but evaporated.

Recent global debate has tended to focus on two alternatives for the United Nations: Should the United Nations be an aid institution that focuses its efforts primarily on furnishing various types of assistance to provide basic human needs? Or should the UN be a more ambitious and overarching development institution that acts programmatically around the globe to implement such principles as equity, social justice, economic security, ecological balance, and the general enhancement of the quality of life?

In the early years of his administration, former Secretary-General Boutros Boutros-Ghali and his top staff tended to come down on the side of the former argument. They argued that the UN should concentrate on issues in which it had the comparative advantage (relative to other institutions). That is, the United Nations should focus on providing assistance in situations where conditions are critical or deteriorating. From this perspective, development assistance, which is much broader than critical-aid programs and which substitutes environmentally degrading practices for sustainable ones, should be left to the multilateral development banks and other funding institutions that are presumably far better endowed and equipped for such activities.

In May 1994, however, Boutros-Ghali presented the General Assembly with his widely cited *An Agenda for Development.*[13] Declaring development to be a fundamental human right, he presented a general framework within which he highlighted the interdependent nature of peace, economy, civil society, democracy, social justice, and environment as indispensable components of the development process. In this regard, he pointed to the special position, role, and responsibility of the United Nations in promoting development in all its aspects but with specific regard to setting priorities and facilitating cooperation and coordination. Although it is not clear exactly what the ramifications of this "agenda" have been or might yet be, the long and detailed statement did place the chief executive of the world organization on record as being seriously concerned about the improvement of human security and well-being.

Finally, and perhaps most important, there has been agreement, at least at the level of principle, that "development" means something much broader than simply economic growth. As explored in Chapters 9 and 10, development is increasingly coming to be viewed in human, as opposed to exclusively national economic, terms. Whether this principle is followed in practice or not, UN documents indicate that "development" signifies not only improved material welfare but also improved human rights and social justice. The goal has been to achieve not just economic growth but an improvement in the quality of life as defined beyond the limits of economic indicators.

The term "good governance" came into common use within UN developmental circles in the 1980s and 1990s although the concept is as old as human history. The emergence of the idea of good governance can be traced to international concern with national-level state-dominated models of economic and social development so prevalent throughout the socialist bloc and much of the Third World in the 1950s, 1960s, and 1970s.

From the outset, the United Nations organization was directly concerned with the quality of life and of government services. One of the central ideas motivating the framing of the UN Charter was decolonization, evidenced by creating as one of the six organs the Trusteeship Council; Chapter XIII of the Charter (Articles 86–96) spelled out its mandate. The logic behind self-determination was to provide an appropriate and self-reliant transitional structure so that persons could control their own destinies and that of their countries through independent governments. In ending the structural exploitation of the colonized periphery for the good of the colonial metropole, an important theme—government for the benefit of the population—was born that is directly linked to what would later be labeled "good governance."

After the vast majority of African and Asian countries had become independent by the early 1960s, their governments were defensive about the nature of the newly independent states. They regarded virtually any serious scrutiny within the United Nations as a threat to the fabric of newborn and weak states. By playing off East against West during the Cold War, they were able to deflect certain criticisms by donors and investors who hinted at shortcomings in economic and political management. Suggestions about what was wrong with local economic and social organization in developing and socialist bloc countries were viewed as siding with the "enemy" in the East-West struggle. And the "other" side could be persuaded to be less critical, and even financially supportive, as part of a worldwide competition.

The result was an unquestioning, and at times almost obsequious, acceptance of the status quo. Francis M. Deng and Terrence Lyons have summarized the situation in Africa, but their comment has greater resonance: "Rather than promote good governance by awarding sovereign rights to those regimes that effectively or responsibly administered a given territory, African diplomatic principles, epitomized by the Organization of African Unity (OAU), accepted whatever regime occupied the presidential palace, regardless of who (or even whether) the regime governed."[14]

Ironically, OPEC's ability to increase oil prices in 1973–1974 and again in 1979 strengthened the collective bargaining of the Group of 77 at the same time that it eventually led to foreign exchange shortages and unsustainable indebtedness that, in turn, forced many non-oil-exporting developing countries to accept intrusive structural adjustment. Direct outside interference in economic policy was the quid pro quo for desperately needed international finance. The World Bank and the IMF had been emphasizing domestic policies for some time. But they assumed more weight with increasingly widespread pertinence especially after the September 1981 report from Elliot Berg.[15] The new orthodoxy of more aid and investment in exchange for economic liberalization replaced the earlier building blocks of nonintrusion in domestic policies and what two analysts termed "the global Keynesian social pact suggested by the Brandt Commission."[16]

Such external economic factors as commodity prices and interest rates remain crucial and cannot be minimized as explanations for poverty and poor economic performance. But it became untenable to attribute all of the woes of developing countries to outside forces beyond their control. This was particularly the case after Mikhail Gorbachev's ascension to power in 1985 and the onset of "new thinking" in Moscow, and eventually the fall of the Berlin Wall in 1989 and the implosion of the Soviet Union in 1991. There was no longer an Eastern geopolitical counterweight to Western demands for economic liberalization and political democratization.

Domestic policies and priorities were central to the dire problems faced by both developing countries and members of the socialist bloc. And it became politically more correct in international forums to say so. Beginning a conversation about how state and society were structured, or how good a country's governance system was, became acceptable within debates about international public policy within the UN system.

Efforts to foster *good* governance focus on two undesirable characteristics that were prevalent earlier: the unrepresentative character of governments and the inefficiency of nonmarket systems. As governance is the sum of the ways that individuals and institutions, in both public and private spheres, manage their affairs, the systems of governance in much of the Third World and Eastern Europe had to change. As Morten Bøås has written, "the World Bank operationalised 'bad governance' as personalisation of power, lack of human rights, endemic corruption and un-elected and unaccountable governments." And so, "good governance must be the natural opposite."[17] The discourse of good governance was linked to new policies in those countries receiving development assistance or investments from international lending agencies. Good governance can be seen as a kind of combined political and economic conditionality that is inseparable from debates about appropriate guidelines for bilateral and multilateral financing for developing and formerly socialist bloc countries.

International efforts, especially since the early 1980s, have thus emphasized—at least sometimes—support for political democratization (including elections, accountability, and human rights) and economic liberalization. Criticisms of recent experience, especially by organizations from the UN system, have essentially sought to balance assessments about costs and benefits as well as to confront the political and economic conditionality viewed by many recipient countries as unwelcome intrusions in their domestic affairs.

The lead role in helping to define the characteristics of a population that lives within a society in which governance is good has been the preoccupation of the United Nations Development Programme's annual *Human Development Report*. Following ten years of experience with structural adjustment, the controversial UNDP effort began in 1990 under the leadership of the noted Pakistani development economist Mahbub ul-Haq and continued after 1996 under Richard Jolly. The reports sought to shed light systematically on the actual lives of people, especially those on the bottom of the income scale.[18] In many ways, the decade's collection of the annual *Human Development Reports*—which now are available on a single compact disk—was a prelude to and a prolongation of the 1995 Social Summit in Copenhagen.

Without denying the benefits of growth, the reports and the Copenhagen conference insist on cataloging the aggravation of poverty and the growing divides between rich and poor, within societies and among them; increasing unemployment; a disintegrating social fabric and exclusion; and environmental damage. In addition to an overall analysis, each of the successive reports has emphasized a specific theme: funding priorities (1991); global markets (1992); democracy (1993); environment (1994); gender (1995); growth (1996); poverty (1997); consumption patterns (1998); globalization (1999); and human rights (2000).

The value of the human development index (HDI), which was refined over the decade, is the modification of what constitutes an acceptable way to measure a society with good governance. Economic well-being and human progress are not synonymous. Countries with the same per capita income can have quite different HDIs, and countries with the same levels of income can also have similar HDIs. The clear message is that the content of domestic policies and priorities is crucial.

In attempting to correct the euphoria that had surrounded the so-called Washington consensus of the early 1990s, arguments within the UN have counterbalanced the stereotypical conservative approaches in vogue since the Reagan and Thatcher administrations—namely, that anything the government can do, the private sector can do better; and that more open markets, free trade, and capital flows are necessarily beneficial. In many ways, an attentive reader of UN documents of the 1990s would not have been surprised by the disruptions in Seattle of the World Trade Organization's Third Ministerial Summit in December 1999.

To some extent, an artificial dichotomy had been created between "state" and "market," with an unquestioned faith in the latter throughout most policy circles in the Western world. The intellectual climate had changed so much that for the decade between the mid-1980s and mid-1990s, it was almost heretical to argue that an efficient, thriving market economy and a civil society require an effective and strong government. Perhaps some of the best examples of UN heresy were analyses of the former Soviet bloc, where "shrinking" but not eliminating the state was recommended.

In a departure from its previous orthodoxy and as a sign of the pendulum's swing, the World Bank's *World Development Report 1997* emphasized that the state is capable of, and should perform the role of, producing welfare-enhancing outcomes.[19] The report's subtitle, *The State in a Changing World*, was indicative of a reversal led by Joseph Stiglitz, the controversial chief economist and senior vice-president of the Bank.[20] Essentially, in contrast to the wave of economic liberalization programs of the 1980s, the political liberalization programs of the 1990s placed a greater emphasis on substantive democracy, human rights, the role of law and individual access to justice, and basic freedoms.

Thus, the UN's contribution has been to alter the emphasis in the good governance debate that originally had been cast as the mirror image of the state-dominated model of economic and social development of previous decades. Today's debate about good governance stresses improving the leadership and management of democracies (including the "deepening" of democracy and more active roles for nonstate actors). In contrast to the narrower economic liberalization programs in vogue earlier, the political liberalization programs of the late 1990s (with greater emphasis on leadership and management as well as democracy, human rights, rule of law, access to justice, and basic freedoms) weakened the arguments by proponents of a "minimalist state." Leaders are being held to higher standards of accountability, and they have to contend with the forces of globalization.

Over the decades, "development" thus has taken on various meanings as the global political context has shifted. As we have seen, in the early years, development was defined largely in terms[21] of national economic growth as measured in aggregate and per capita income. Then, it took on the additional meaning of national self-reliance of Third World states. Slowly the added, and somewhat different, value of satisfying the basic needs of people crept onto the scene, but in a much subordinated role. This definition slowly yielded ground to the incorporation of popular participation and local self-reliance in the satisfaction of basic needs. In this way, development discourse has come to embrace simultaneously four widely shared global values: peace (that is, nonviolence), human security (including human rights), sustainable human development, and ecological balance. It is the last of these four to which we now turn our attention.

Notes

1. Boutros Boutros-Ghali, *An Agenda for Peace: Preventive Diplomacy, Peacemaking and Peace-keeping* (New York: UN, 1992), para. 15.

2. Mustafa K. Tolba, *A Commitment to the Future: Sustainable Development and Environmental Protection* (Nairobi: UNEP, 1992), p. 9.

3. World Commission on Environment and Development, *Our Common Future* (New York: Oxford Univ. Press, 1987), p. 8.

4. Craig N. Murphy, "The United Nations' Capacity to Promote Sustainable Development: The Lessons of a Year That 'Eludes All Facile Judgment,'" in Gene M. Lyons, ed., *The State of the United Nations: 1992* (Providence, RI: ACUNS, 1993), p. 51.

5. *A Study of the Capacity of the United Nations Development System* (Geneva: UN, 1969), document DP/5.

6. This subject was analyzed in the midst of this growth by Harold K. Jacobson, "The Changing United Nations," in Roger Hilsman and Robert C. Good, eds., *Foreign Policies in the Sixties: The Issues and the Investments* (Baltimore: Johns Hopkins Univ. Press, 1965), pp. 67–89.

7. For a discussion of the dynamics of its founding and subsequent group processes, see Thomas G. Weiss, *Multilateral Development Diplomacy in UNCTAD: The Lessons of Group Negotiations, 1964–84* (London: Macmillan, 1986).

8. See Robert S. Jordan, "Why an NIEO? The View from the Third World," in Harold K. Jacobson and Dusam Aidjanski, eds., *The Emerging International Economic Order: Dynamic Processes, Constraints and Opportunities* (Beverly Hills, CA: Sage, 1982).

9. See Thomas G. Weiss and Robert S. Jordan, *The World Food Conference and Global Problem Solving* (New York: Praeger, 1976).

10. UN Development Programme, *Human Development Report 1996* (New York: Oxford Univ. Press, 1996), p. 1.

11. UNDP, "UNDP and World Development by the Year 2000," draft of April 17, 1989, pp. 1, 3.

12. Maurice Williams, "New Visions for the 1990s—The Third Barbara Ward Memorial Lecture," *Development* nos. 2–3 (1988), p. 10.

13. Boutros Boutros-Ghali, *An Agenda for Development 1995* (New York: UN, 1995).

14. Francis M. Deng and Terrence Lyons, "Promoting Responsible Sovereignty in Africa," in Francis M. Deng and Terrence Lyons, eds., *African Reckoning: A Quest for Good Governance* (Washington, DC: Brookings Institution, 1998), p. 1.

15. World Bank, *Accelerated Development in Sub-Saharan Africa: An Agenda for Action* (Washington, DC: World Bank, 1981).

16. Enrico Augelli and Craig Murphy, *America's Quest for Supremacy and the Third World* (London: Pinter, 1988), p. 184.

17. Morten Bøås, "Governance as Multilateral Bank Policy: The Cases of the African Development Bank and the Asian Development Bank," *European Journal of Development Research* 10, no. 2 (1998), p. 119.

18. United Nations Development Programme, *Human Development Report 1990* (New York: Oxford Univ. Press, 1990), and the subsequent yearly reports. Mahbub ul-Haq's own account of this effort is found in *Reflections on Human Development* (New York: Oxford Univ. Press, 1995).

19. World Bank, *World Development Report 1997: The State in a Changing World* (New York: Oxford Univ. Press, 1997).

20. See, for example, Joseph Stiglitz, "Redefining the Role of the State: What Should It Do? How Should It Do It? And How Should These Decisions Be Made?" <http://www.worldbank.org>

21. For a discussion, see Louis Emmerij, Richard Jolly, and Thomas G. Weiss, *Ahead of the Curve? UN Ideas and Global Challenges* (Bloomington: Indiana Univ. Press, 2001, forthcoming).

9 Ecodevelopment and the United Nations

Despite the growing attention in the United Nations during the late 1980s and early 1990s to issues of emergency assistance rather than to long-term economic growth and development, the UN system could not escape the avalanche of attention to the environment. Table 9.1 provides a snapshot of the changing political climate within which global environmental discussions and events have taken place in the past half-century.

There were increasing concerns about the implications of uncontrolled economic growth on the ecosystem. Rachel Carson's *Silent Spring*, published in 1962, is an example of the growing popularity of environmental literature that focused attention on human-induced environmental health hazards. At first concern centered largely on issues of resource conservation, nature preservation, and pollution of common resources such as air and water; later in the North concern grew over general environmental deterioration. The publication in *Science* of Garrett Hardin's classic essay, "The Tragedy of the Commons," in 1968 and of the Club of Rome's *Limits to Growth* study in 1972 strongly reinforced these concerns.[1] Once again, private networks of specialists fueled debate over public policy. In the global political context, however, the issue of environmental protection broke onto the global agenda largely as a scientific matter associated with the concept of the biosphere.

The notion that all life on the planet exists within a terrestrial envelope, the biosphere, of which humankind is an inseparable part and an agent of change, was popularized in scientific circles during the 1920s and 1930s. A number of leading scientists of this period, including V. I. Vernadsky and Pierre Teilhard de Chardin, laid the foundations for a more general acceptance of the biosphere concept. All elements of this organic system, it was argued, exist in dynamic interrelationship with one other and make life possible. Humans possess the capacity to damage this life system, and they do, both consciously and unconsciously. These scientists argued that it was important to better understand the nature of interdependence, including the limits of acceptable alteration and the regenerative capacities of the life-supporting system. This image of the earth as an organic, self-sustaining ecosystem was brought to a wider public by the photographs taken by *Apollo 2* astronauts following their 1969 voyage. Growing public concern over oil spills and marine pollution, which gained notoriety following the rupture of the supertanker *Torrey Canyon* in 1967, made the international political climate even more ripe to consider environmental menaces.

It was the emerging scientific concern, however, that first found its way onto the global agenda. This occurred in the UN agency designed to facilitate international scientific cooperation, the UNESCO. After consideration of the issue at its 1966 session, the UNESCO General Conference formally noted the possible transformation of the earth's biosphere and called for an international conference to confront the issue. Accordingly, the Intergovernmental Conference of Experts on the Biosphere (Biosphere Conference) was hosted by UNESCO in Paris in September 1968 in association with the FAO, the International Union for the Conservation of Nature and National Resources (IUCN), WHO, and the United Nations. Emerging from this conference was a growing appreciation of the indivisibility of human social order and natural earth systems. Thus the way was opened for people to revise their viewpoints on environment and development into a viewpoint that linked the two, an initial step toward the evolution of sustainable development.

Scientists were not the only actors attempting to stimulate global action. Following an official initiative in ECOSOC by Swedish ambassador to the UN Sverker Åström, the General Assembly approved holding a global conference on the environment (Resolution 2398 [XXIII]). This resolution also called for the UN Secretary-General to prepare a report on environmental problems in consultation with IGOs, member states, and NGOs.[2] In receiving the report the following year, the General Assembly created both a secretariat and a preparatory committee for the conference. After some politicking, an invitation from the Swedish government to host a conference was accepted. The United Nations Conference on the Human Environment (UNCHE) was convened in Stockholm in June 1972.

UNCHE and Ecodevelopment

During preparations for this conference, development and environment became integrated. More specifically, at a UNCHE Preparatory Committee (PrepCom) meeting of experts in Founex, UNCHE Secretary-General Maurice Strong proposed the "ecodevelopment" notion that would serve as a foundation on which the sustainable development dialogue would be built. Of course, the Club of Rome and others put forward similar notions during this period and earlier. Yet these largely intellectual exercises did not carry the same force or impact as the Founex report.[3] Under the leadership of Strong, the participants were able to bridge some important political divides. By arguing that long-term development depended on dealing with shorter-term environmental problems, he was able to appease divergent North-South interests. He also suggested that the governments of industrialized countries help defray the costs of environmental protection that developing countries would be forced to bear. The concept of "additionality,"

TABLE 9.1   Chronology of Selected Environmental Conferences and Activities

1948	International Union for the Conservation of Nature and National Resources (IUCN)[a]
1962	Publicaton of *Silent Spring* by Rachel Carson
1964	International Biological Program (IBP)[a]
1968	Intergovernmental Conference on Biosphere[a]
1970	Scientific Committee on Problems of the Environment (SCOPE)/ICSU[a]
1971	Founex Panel of Experts on Development and Environment
1972	UN Conference on the Human Environment (UNCHE)
	Environmental Forum
	Limits to Growth published by the Club of Rome
	UN Environment Progamme (UNEP)[a]
1973	Convention for the Prevention of Pollution by Ships (MARPOL)
1974–1981	UN Conference on the Law of the Sea (UNCLOS)
1976	UN Conference on Human Settlement (HABITAT)
1979	World Climate Conference
	Convention on Long-Range Transboundary Air Pollution
1980	Committee of Intenational Development Institutions on the Environment (CIDIE)[a]
	World Conservation Strategy (ICSN/UNEP)
	Convention on Conservation of the Arctic Living Resources
1982	Conference on the Law of the Seas
1985	Vienna Convention on Protection of the Ozone Layer
	International Code on the Distribution and Use of Pesticides
1986	International Geosphere-Biosphere Programme (IGBP)[a]
1987	Montreal Protocol to the Vienna Convention
	World Commission on the Environment and Development (Brundtland Commission) Report
1988	Intergovernmental Panel on Climate Change[a]
1989	Convention on Control of Transboundary Movements of Hazardous Wastes and Their Disposal
1990	Second World Climate Conference
	Global Environmental Facility (GEF)[a]
1990–1992	UNCED Preparatory Committee
1992	UN Conference on Environment and Development (UNCED)
	Rio Declaration and Agenda 21
	Global Forum
	Framework Convention on Climate Change (UNFCCC)
	Framework Convention on Biological Diversity
1993	Commission on Sustainable Development (CSD)[a]
	UN Conference on Straddling Fish Stocks and Highly Migratory Fish Stocks

(continues)

TABLE 9.1   *(continued)*

1994	International Conference on Population and Development (ICPD)
	World Conference on Natural Disasters
	Global Conference on the Sustainability of Small Island Developing States
	UN Conference to Combat Desertification
	UN Conference on Straddling Fish Stocks and Highly Migratory Fish Stocks
	World Summit on Social Development
	Fourth World Conference on Women
1996	Second UN Conference on Human Settlements (HABITAT II)
	World Food Summit
1997	Kyoto Protocol to UNFCCC
	UNGA Special Session on Sustainable Development
1998	Convention on Access to Information, Public Participation in Decision-Making and Access to Justice in Environmental Matters (Århus Convention)
1999	Economic Forum in Davos, Switzerland
	UNGA on Population and Development
	UNGA Special Session on Small Island Developing States
2000	World Summit for Social Development
	Global Ministerial Environment Forum/Sixth Special Session of the UNEP Governing

ᵃDenotes the establishment of the body or commencement of the activity.

meaning to increase resources in order to apply them to a new purpose rather than to pull them from another purpose, helped overcome skepticism in the South over global economic inequities.[4]

The UNCHE served as a benchmark solidifying the place of environmental concerns on the global agenda. Participants from 113 states, excluding the Soviet Union and Eastern European states that boycotted the conference, and NGOs met in Stockholm to formalize the work of PrepCom.[5] They adopted the Declaration on the Human Environment, which laid out twenty-six principles for environmental governance and 109 recommendations for action. Also, they proposed the creation of a new UN body to serve as a focal point for stimulating and coordinating environmental activities in the UN system.

The United Nations Environment Programme (UNEP) was created in 1973 through UN General Assembly Resolution 2997 (XXXVII). The Governing Council of UNEP consists of fifty-eight members elected by the General Assembly. It meets biennially and reports to the General Assembly through ECOSOC. Its main mandate is to encourage and coordinate environmental activities within the UN system. The work of the program is carried out through a modest secretariat headed by an executive director. The agency is based in Nairobi, Kenya, and is financed through the UN regular budget.

The UNEP was assigned the function of forging interagency cooperation throughout the UN system for establishing and promoting environmental protection. Since environmental concerns cut across almost every conceivable area of human activity, this was indeed a broad mandate. In order to understand the problems and prospects for fulfilling that mandate, an overall picture of the actors in the system is important.

Institutional Foundations

As an outgrowth of the Biosphere Conference discussed earlier, an interdisciplinary research program, Man and the Biosphere (MAB), was established to study relationships between humans and their environment. UNESCO also became engaged in a wide variety of other environmental concerns that cut across its main areas of competence: science, education, culture, and communications. The agency's programmatic work in the environmental area took shape in the 1960s, with special concern for marine and water pollution. In 1965, a ten-year program, the International Hydrological Decade, was launched to promote the study of hydrological resources, including water pollution. This early environmental focus was strengthened with the hosting of the Biosphere Conference, the 1970 Helsinki Interdisciplinary Symposium on Man's Role in Changing His Environment, and the 1972 Convention for the Protection of the World Cultural and Natural Heritage. UNESCO has been responsible for the creation of a number of affiliated bodies, such as the International Oceanographic Commission (IOC). This particular body, for example, has been important in promoting international marine scientific research with special emphasis on pollution prevention. Since the late 1980s, the UNESCO secretariat has emphasized proper coordination of the environmentally related activities and programs within its various divisions. It has been actively involved in follow-up activities to the 1992 United Nations Conference on Environment and Development (UNCED) and the implementation of a variety of UNCED-related agreements.

For many years, UNESCO has had a special relationship with the International Council of Scientific Unions (ICSU) and with the work of ICSU's member unions in the environmental area. The ICSU is a nongovernmental organization comprising scientific academies, research councils, and scientific unions. It facilitates and coordinates the work of large international research programs, such as the International Biological Programme (IBP) and the International Geosphere-Biosphere Programme (IGBP). In 1969 the Scientific Committee on Problems of the Environment (SCOPE) was established within ICSU. This committee has been responsible for reviewing information on the implications of human-induced environmental change. Two decades later, in 1989, the Advisory Committee on the Environment was created to provide counsel to the ICSU Executive Board on all ICSU activities related to the environment and global change and to provide a link with external bodies in this regard.

In addition to UNESCO, most other agencies within the UN system have operational mandates linked to ecodevelopment. The environmental relationships of some of these bodies are more obvious and more direct than others. Most, if not all, of the work of the World Meteorological Organization (WMO) focuses on ecodevelopment concerns. Its broad, heavily scientific mandate includes atmospheric pollution, meteorological aspects of water pollution, climate change, the effects of pollution on climate change and vegetation, and the relationship between climate, weather, and agricultural practices. Along with the IOC and ICSU, the WMO cosponsors the World Climate Research Programme (WCRP). This joint initiative examines the dynamic aspects of the earth's climate system and stands as a counterpart to the IGBP, which studies biological and chemical aspects of global change.

The work of WHO focuses broadly on the relationship between human beings and their environments. This institution is concerned with controlling environmental pollution in all forms and modes of transmission as well as all other environmental factors that affect health. The agency undertakes pollution surveys and initiates programs for improving methods for measuring pollution and for designing programs for pollution abatement and control.

The FAO has a vast array of activities on ecodevelopment. They include radioactive contamination, contamination of food by pesticides, and marine pollution related to fisheries. The agency works to establish criteria for water quality management, soil and water resource management, pesticide control, fisheries management, and general control of pollution. Several important environmental conventions fall under FAO auspices, including the International Convention for the Conservation of Atlantic Tunas (ICCAT), the FAO International Code of Conduct on the Distribution and Use of Pesticides, and the Code of Conduct for Responsible Fisheries.

Marine pollution is important to the work of the International Maritime Organization (IMO), established in 1948 under its original name, the Intergovernmental Maritime Consultative Organization. At the heart of this agency's work are concerns about legal liability and the rights of parties to seek redress from pollution by ships and equipment operating in marine areas, as well as how to prevent such pollution. Over the years, the agency has promoted more than two dozen international conventions and protocols, ranging from the International Convention for the Prevention of Pollution at Sea by Oil (OILPOL) in 1959 to the International Convention on Oil Pollution Preparedness Response and Cooperation (OPPRC) in 1990. In fulfilling its environment-related mandate, the IMO has maintained close working relations with UNEP, FAO, ILO, the United Nations

Commission on International Trade Law (UNCITRAL), UNCTAD, and WHO, as well as IUCN, the International Chamber of Shipping, and various other nongovernmental organizations.

The ecodevelopment work of UN agencies often is not obvious. The International Civil Aviation Organization (ICAO), for example, deals with aircraft noise pollution. The ILO has an interest in the impact of various forms of pollution on the working environment. Environmental concerns related to the peaceful uses of nuclear energy, such as radioactive waste management, fall within the realm of the International Atomic Energy Agency (IAEA).

In addition to these UN organizations, a relatively large number of other non-UN intergovernmental organizations have engaged in various ecodevelopment activities. The European Community (EC), for example, is involved in harmonizing national environmental policies and programs, initiating environmental studies, and promoting resource-management and pollution-control activities. The Council of Europe also works toward combining national environmental policies and programs. It is involved in drafting common legal principles for pollution control, resource management, and control of pesticides. Perhaps surprising to many, the Committee on the Challenges of Modern Society (CCMS) of NATO has also been an active player in this area, concerned with disaster relief, air pollution, marine pollution, and the sharing of environmental information. The Organization for Economic Cooperation and Development (OECD), whose membership is essentially wealthy industrialized countries, conducts activities related to the management of air, water, and urban environments. Pollution from pesticides, accidental pollution, and blending national environmental policies and programs are areas of special interest to OECD.

One of the most important international environmental organizations is the hybrid International Union for the Conservation of Nature and National Resources (also known as the World Conservation Union). It comprises states, governmental agencies, and international and national NGOs. Although possessing only a small secretariat, it conducts a remarkably wide range of activities through numerous standing commissions and committees. The IUCN helped forge the conceptual link between development and environment. With the World Wide Fund for Nature (WWF) and UNEP, and in association with FAO and UNESCO, the IUCN launched the World Conservation Strategy in 1980. As a precursor to sustainable development, this initiative set forth principles promoting the sustainable use of the earth's living resources.

In addition to being promoted through formal organizations, global environmental norms have spread through international conventions and declarations. An extensive codification of international environmental law dealing with marine pollution, for example, has come about in this way since the late 1960s. As discussed, the IMO has played an instrumental role in developing an international maritime pollution regime, with important contributions also coming from

Sierra Leonean refugees and Liberian displaced persons construct a new well in Liberia during 1993. (UNHCR Photo/23113/11.1993/L. Taylor)

UNEP and the multiyear negotiations of the Third United Nations Conference on the Law of the Sea (UNCLOS III).

Although these activities often are associated with specific UN agencies or UN-sponsored conferences, they normally transcend the formal structures of these organizations. It makes sense to think in terms of broad norms and policymaking processes that regulate an issue, rather than just in terms of international law and organization.

More recently, governments have agreed upon a regime for protecting the ozone layer. In this case, the 1985 Vienna Convention for the Protection of the Ozone Layer established a general framework upon which to build. The Montreal Protocol, concluded in 1987, added more specific targets and provisions. This protocol was, in turn, substantially strengthened in June 1990. In each instance, UNEP played an important role, especially in the collection and dissemination of authoritative scientific information.

The task of coordinating the environmental activities of these diverse institutional arrangements is massive. These bodies are legally and practically autonomous; many of them were actively engaged in environmental work before the formation of UNEP. Once again, the United Nations appears as the logical choice for coordination, but UNEP has neither the authority nor the organizational wherewithal to coordinate the globe's network of institutions. But this is only a small part of the picture. UNEP must carry out its mandate in the dynamic, complex, and chaotic world of a global political economy.

Static Action in a Dynamic Social Environment

During the 1970s the environmental debate and the work of the UNEP got caught up in the NIEO debate. The work of the program continued to center on ecodevelopment, including the interrelationships among environment, development, population, and natural resources. But over the next decade, UNEP's agenda expanded incrementally to include a number of additional concerns, including appropriate technology.[6]

UNEP seemed to be caught between the proverbial rock and a hard place. Its location in Nairobi, although a symbolic victory for the South, served to marginalize access to the organization by most developing countries' governments. The Group of 77 had no permanent presence in Nairobi. Furthermore, few governments of developing countries had any permanent representation in UNEP. Northern governments preferred that the organization deal primarily with monitoring, assessment, and other technical and scientific endeavors; they were able to ensure the implementation of this preference.

Donor governments and the international agencies through which they preferred to operate began to include environmental considerations in decisionmaking, yet they tended to operate quite independently of UNEP. Meeting in Paris in September 1979, representatives of nine multilateral development banks and other IGOs adopted the Declaration of Environmental Policies and Procedures Relating to Economic Development. This declaration was formally issued in New York the following February with the simultaneous announcement of the creation of the Committee of International Development Institutions on the Environment (CIDIE). Membership in CIDIE has now expanded to sixteen IGOs with twenty bilateral donor governments participating as observers.[7] This body was given the tasks of hosting consultations, facilitating joint activities, and promoting the sharing of information among members in order to fully integrate environmental considerations into their development activities. Members also affirmed their commitment to the Stockholm principles and recommendations.

Adoption of the declaration and the creation of CIDIE show the growing marginalization of UNEP, the UN's principal agency charged with global ecodevelopment discourse and practice. Peter Haas sees UNEP's inability to lead as due to both internal and systemic factors:

> While UNEP attempted to ensure that "environment" became a cross-cutting element in the various development-related activities of the UN system, UNEP lacked institutional leverage within the UN system to effectively influence programmatic efforts by other agencies. Moreover, UNEP suffered throughout the 1980s from internal organizational difficulties which inhibited organizational autonomy. It lacked organizational clout and sufficient money to compel other agencies to change their actions, and was well outside the mainstream because of its Nairobi headquarters.[8]

As this marginalization from the overall development picture took effect, UNEP came to concentrate its program increasingly on monitoring and assessment, as some influential Northern governments had long been suggesting. Operating with a total staff of about 1,000 professional and support personnel, UNEP carries out its functions through three main functional divisions: Environmental Assessment, Environmental Management, and Environmental Policy. The assessment division is charged with conducting and reporting assessments, data management, capacity building, and coordination of the Earthwatch program. The management division deals with a wide variety of other UN-system coordination issues, including the development of an integrated environmental program. The policy division is mandated the task of promoting international cooperation by developing cross-sectoral strategies, policies, and programs. In 1995 the agency had 49 such cooperative projects with other international agencies and over 250 other projects.

These institutional changes took place concurrently with other changes discussed earlier. During the 1970s, the controversy over the role of satisfying basic human needs within development projects became an important element of the global debate. Many Southern governments complained that a basic human-needs approach served to distract attention and divert action from redressing global inequalities; some important Northern donors argued that the approach would divert scarce resources from economic growth. There was a need for a new concept that could play the kind of synthesizing role that ecodevelopment had played in the UNCHE process. But clearly "basic human needs" was not that concept, especially since there was no consensus definition of that term.

A catalyzing idea, however, was emerging within the context of the human needs debate. In 1980, the General Assembly approved the World Conservation Strategy, which placed importance on the *sustainability* of natural life-support systems as they relate to satisfying human needs. This strategy, designed by the IUCN in conjunction with UNEP and WWF, facilitated the process of refocusing the global debate on the issue of sustainability in the development process.

The process of building a consensus around this notion of sustainable development was not without obstacles, however. The environmental aspects of this concept were viewed by many in the South as a potential new form of conditionality, or yet another way that Western donors could make new demands on recipient countries. Indeed, the coincidental formation of CIDIE fueled such speculation.

To sort out these considerations, the General Assembly in 1983 created a special commission, the World Commission on Environment and Development (WCED). Headed by Gro Brundtland, a former prime minister of Norway who became director-general of the WHO in 1999, WCED set about the task of devising a concept of sustainable development. This body, like many others composed of eminent persons to study global issues, took on the chairman's name, thus becoming the Brundtland Commission. Its findings and recommendations were published four years later in *Our Common Future*.[9] Environmental protection, economic equity, and economic growth were brought together.

The Brundtland Commission's formula proved to be very politically attractive. Dealing with environmental problems was seen as being ineffectual unless these actions simultaneously addressed poverty and inequities in the world economy. Building on this foundation, the UNEP Governing Council defined sustainable development as "development that meets the needs of the present without compromising the ability of future generations to meet their own needs and does not imply in any way encroachment upon national sovereignty."[10] Totally statist solutions to ecological and economic problems were declining. But as in the security and human rights fields, developing countries were hardly eager to abandon the traditional concept of state sovereignty.

These new developments notwithstanding, UNEP continued being shunted to the side. A UN agency primarily concerned with the environment could not possibly be *the* UN agency for development. This process was facilitated by the very success that UNEP had enjoyed with its Environmental Fund, and by the fund's role as a catalyst. Under the provisions of the fund, UNEP was to provide limited seed money to UN operational agencies to encourage them to incorporate environmental elements into their activities. However, once these projects were begun, these agencies were forced either to integrate them into their regular programs and budgets or to find additional other funds to support them. Not only did this process lead to a significant expansion of other UN agencies' environmental activities but it also resulted in a growing fragmentation of environmental responsibilities within the UN system. UNEP was not in a position to play an authoritative coordinating role anymore.

Although the World Bank operates mostly independently from the rest of the UN system, its changing policies were symptomatic of the enhanced status of ecological issues. At least partly in response to the well-coordinated NGO Multilateral Development Bank Campaign, the World Bank rapidly expanded its environmental profile in the late 1980s.[11] The creation of the Environment Department and the adoption of the Environmental Assessment Operations Directive in 1989 represented major elements in this regard. Environmental assessments were required of all new projects that would have a significant environmental impact. That directive was revised three years later to provide potentially affected people with access to the information contained in those assessments.

Additionally, the Global Environmental Facility (GEF) was established in November 1990 by twenty-five member states and the UNDP and UNEP, and it went into force in July 1994. This World Bank–administered facility provides grants to developing countries for environment-related projects and facilitates networking and cooperation among donors. It operates in four main issue areas—protection of the ozone layer, international waters, biodiversity, and climate change—and is charged with working with other UN agencies, regional development banks, and bilateral donors in integrated technical assistance and investment projects. This limited coordination role has been complemented in recent years by the work of the Joint Consultative Group on Policy (JCGP). This body has organized collaborative efforts among five other UN agencies: UNDP, the United Nations Fund for Population Activities (UNFPA), UNICEF, the World Food Programme (WFP), and the International Fund for Agricultural Development (IFAD). Despite such attempts to engender cooperation and undertake coordination within and among the very diverse field of actors in this issue arena, fragmentation abounds.

UN international civil servants and NGO representatives have sought to bridge the substantial gulf between the formal sovereignty-based order of interstate diplomacy and the multilateral institutions in which global policies to protect the human environment are defined and pursued. The story of these initiatives provides a way to explore the relationship between actors and institutions in the United Nations as they relate to sovereignty-bound (that is, state) and nonstate actors in international cooperation. It is to this subject that we now turn.

The Role of Civil Society

The environmental area has long been distinctive in the extraordinary degree to which "civic-based actors"—another appellation for NGOs—have been actively engaged in global affairs. The number of transnational civic-based groups and organizations in this area has grown dramatically since the early 1980s, leading to calls for more institutionalized ways for linking these civic-based actors to the work of the United Nations and its organizations. Yet, as became apparent from the activities and events surrounding both the 1972 United Nations Conference on the Human Environment (UNCHE, or the Stockholm conference) and the 1992 United Nations Conference on Environment and Development (UNCED, or the Rio conference), the nature and extent of the linkages between UN agencies and NGOs more frequently than not have been marked by ad hocism and informality. This situation contrasts sharply with the more formalized processes of NGOs that relate to the UN's machinery in human rights and humanitarian areas.

NGOs: A Formal Courtship

From the very beginning, civic-based actors played a significant role in preparing for the Stockholm conference. Although estimates vary, Anne Feraru has calculated that some 237 NGOs were involved in some aspect of the UNCHE process from the first PrepCom meeting in March 1970 through the creation of the United Nations Environment Programme in December 1972.[12] Some NGOs, among them the IUCN, actually had representatives in the intergovernmental working groups that had been created by PrepCom to draft documents for the conference. Also, civic-based groups were able to meet directly with secretariat officials at a number of preconference meetings, including an instrumental PrepCom-sponsored gathering in Founex, Switzerland, in June 1971. Convened by UNCHE Secretary-General Maurice Strong, this session was instrumental in arriving at a consensual statement about the definition of the relationship between environment and development.

Interactions between UNCHE and civic-based actors during this period, however, were mainly through linkages with scientific NGOs. Indeed, most significant contributions to the conference process came from scientific and professional experts and groups such as the IUCN, ICSU, and the International Social Science Council (ISSC), all of which served as consultants to Strong and the secretariat. The formal involvement by nonscientific NGOs in the preparatory process was not very significant. In fact, Curtis Roosevelt, who headed the NGO section of the ECOSOC secretariat at that time, has suggested that UNCHE secretariat staff seemed uninterested in working with nonscientific or nonprofessional NGOs. This outcome might well have been associated with Maurice Strong's early orientation toward NGOs, which Feraru suggests was defined largely in terms of the support that NGOs could provide.[13]

At Stockholm, a number of activities helped to facilitate interactions between nongovernmental and governmental delegates. In addition to the 178 NGOs that were represented formally at the UNCHE, nongovernmental participants held three parallel conferences: the Environment Forum, the Peoples Forum, and another gathering of individuals and civic-based groups called Dai Dong. Conference logistics and scheduling, as well as the antiestablishment nature of some of these NGO activities, limited the degree of interaction between government and NGO delegates. However, an informal mechanism for bridging this gap was provided by the *Stockholm Conference ECO*, a conference newspaper produced daily by two NGOs and placed in the mailboxes of all participants.

Perceptions emerged at Stockholm that existing international institutions were not sufficient to deal with issues of environmental governance. New machinery was required to facilitate transnational environmental networking and coordination. The focal point for such activities within the UN system was to be the UNEP, whose difficulties already have been analyzed.

After UNCHE, NGOs took a number of concerted actions to institutionalize relationships with UNEP and other UN agencies active in the environmental field. In meetings hosted by the League of Red Cross and Red Crescent Societies in Geneva and the Community Development Foundation in New York in October 1972, NGO representatives established two ad hoc committees to serve as liaisons between environmental NGOs and the proposed new UN environmental secretariat. Then, after the creation of UNEP, the World Assembly of NGOs Concerned with the Global Environment was convened in Geneva in June 1973 to work out a process of NGO liaison.

The main mechanism through which NGO relations with UNEP have been facilitated has been the Environment Liaison Centre International (ELCI) in Nairobi, founded in December 1975. Having grown since to comprise 535 member organizations (66 of which are international in scope or membership), this body has served over the years as a formal link among over 6,000 civic-based organizations around the world and UNEP and other IGOs. With the financial support of the Ford Foundation, various governmental sources, and membership dues, it seeks to facilitate information flows and support services and linkages among its members. It has founded a number of regional and functionally based action networks.

Many of the most significant programmatic linkages between UNEP and NGOs, however, extend far beyond the formal liaison mechanisms or other consultative relationships. A number of NGOs, including ICSU, IUCN, the World Wide Fund for Nature (WWF), and the World Resources Institute (WRI), are actively engaged in research and other operational programs with UNEP and other UN organizations. The ICSU promotes multidisciplinary research via formal research programs such as the International Geosphere-Biosphere Programme (IGBP). The Scientific Committee on Problems of the Environment (SCOPE) is the main mechanism by which the ICSU undertakes its activities in the environmental area. It has worked, for example, with UNEP on the World Conservation Strategy, which played an important role in the global value dialectic over ecodevelopment, as discussed earlier.

Growing NGO Influence

On the whole, however, UNEP's relationship with NGOs has been rather staid, reflecting UNEP's marginalized position and narrow, rather technical focus. Both UNEP and NGO officials have sought to foster close working relationships with each other. The main form this has taken in Nairobi has been ELCI and numerous regional, national, and functional NGO networks working in consultation with UNEP personnel. In addition, umbrella organizations such as the IUCN and ICSU have played important roles in broadening communication and contacts among interstate and civic-based actors.

It would be misleading to focus this discussion exclusively on UNEP-NGO relations. In 1982, the World Bank established an NGO committee with membership consisting of NGOs and their consortia as well as senior World Bank staff. The focus of much of this early dialogue was on the interrelationship between adjustment policies and poverty, and on increasing NGO access to World Bank documentation. These topics became more and more associated with environmental concerns during the mid- and late 1980s, when the environmentally focused NGO multilateral bank initiative gained momentum.

This NGO bank initiative was multipronged. Participants lobbied donor governments and recipient states alike, campaigning for more environmentally sound lending policies. They also mounted public demonstrations and targeted bank directors with their proposals for change. Additionally, these NGOs allied themselves whenever possible with lower-level bank staffers in advocating preferred policies.

With the election of Barber Conable as World Bank president in 1986 and the application of such concerted NGO pressure, the bank began to show serious signs of becoming environmentally concerned. Before this time, bank staff demonstrated little, if any, willingness to cooperate in any meaningful way with UNEP or nonbusiness civic-based actors. As Lynton Caldwell has suggested, the idea of sustainable development has been the common denominator bridging the turf and ideological divide that otherwise separates the financial and monetary institutions from other members of the UN family.[14]

Although it is not entirely clear to what extent the NGO–World Bank initiative has actually been successful in making the international financial agency "greener," the World Bank, in conjunction with UNEP, UNDP, and other international governmental agencies that deal with environmental concerns, has undertaken initiatives to establish closer and more institutionalized working relationships with civic-based organizations and movements. In 1987, for example, the UNEP Governing Council asked the UNEP executive director to "take steps to ensure that NGOs were involved in all relevant aspects of the environment programme, adequate staff resources were provided for co-operation with NGOs and ways were found to expand the small grants scheme" to NGOs.[15] Concurrently, the secretariat was asked to support the creation and operation of regional networks of NGOs, especially in regions of Africa, Asia, and Latin America. At about this same time, the World Bank established its Environmental Department (mid-1987), and Moeen Qureshi, senior vice president for operations, issued a directive to the bank's regional offices to "identify specific countries, sectors, and operations in which to pursue a major expansion of work with NGOs."[16] Over the next year, over 200 projects were identified, and in August 1989 an official operational manual statement (OMS), "Collaborating with Nongovernmental Organizations," was issued. Through its External Grants Program and other mechanisms, the World Bank undertook to build NGO capacity (especially in developing countries) to contribute to the dialogue about and the implementation of development policies and projects. Yet, as the recent UNCED experience has indicated, the interface between most civic-based organizations and these and other IGOs remains rather distant. Linkages are largely informal and ad hoc.

The Second Wave

The convergence around sustainable development as a theme in international development debate and practice was facilitated by the coincidence of a number of factors over the decade of the 1990s. As discussed in Chapter 8, the demands for the establishment of the NIEO had stalled, and the viability of the Group of 77 as a cohesive mobilizing and caucusing force had become doubtful. Past approaches to development were seen as having done little to reduce the poverty, squalor, and other symptoms of underdevelopment, with a few notable exceptions—for example, Taiwan and Korea.

The ideas associated with sustainable development seemed to fit well with the more pragmatic attitudes prevailing throughout the North and the South from the late 1980s. Furthermore, some Northern donors had grown weary of the constant demands to increase official development assistance. Seeing little evidence that past assistance had made any appreciable difference in alleviating poverty, "donor fatigue" became a prevalent explanation for diminished overseas development assistance (ODA). There was little indication that the quality of life of the average person in assisted developing countries had improved. The message inherent in sustainable development was that development assistance needed to get to the people. This sentiment generally struck a positive chord in the North.

As already analyzed, the end of the Cold War, the collapse of communist control in Central Europe, and the breakup of the former Soviet Union distracted attention in the North from the development concerns of the Third World. This was especially true in Washington, where the South had suddenly become strategically much less important. Those calling for greater attention to development were searching for a way to capture the attention of Northern donors. Sustainable development provided a potential means to recapture some of the lost focus and garner Northern support for Third World development.

In addition, heightened concern in the North during the 1980s over the depletion of the ozone layer, climate change, and the loss of diversity of biological species helped to focus attention on environmental issues and raise their visibility on national and global policy agendas. Growing scientific evidence supported the observation that environmental degradation and poverty were dynamically linked. Projections for undesirable global changes suggested that developing countries would need to understand the wisdom of environmental protection in order to avoid undesirable future degradations in the global physical environment. The more cooperative atmosphere of North-South relations made such a change plausible.

From the mid-1980s onward, ecodevelopment, particularly as translated into sustainable development, provided a focal point for the development dialogue. Riding the tide of the sustainable development credo, this crest of the second major surge of global environmental diplomacy was marked by a series of events, negotiations, and other activities during 1991–1992 in connection with the United Nations Conference on Environment and Development (UNCED) held in Rio de Janeiro in June 1992. These diverse activities have come collectively to be referred to as the Rio process.

The Rio Process

The preparations for and activities surrounding the Rio "Earth Summit" parley in June 1992 far exceeded almost all normal conceptions of a conference, as did the extensive documentation.[17] The Rio process was massive. In addition to the intergovernmental conference, which incorporated a summit meeting of heads of government during its final days, the Rio gathering included a series of related events, unparalleled in scope and sponsored by civic-based entities that together were referred to as the Global Forum. These parallel activities drew tens of thousands of participants and an estimated 200,000 onlookers. A record number of national governmental delegations, along with 1,400 nongovernmental organizations, attended the Earth Summit, with approximately 18,000 participants in the various activities of the Global Forum.

Movement among the respective sites for activities, however, was severely restricted by logistics. The intergovernmental conference (UNCED) was held at the Rio-Centro at the edge of the city; the nongovernmental activities in the Global Forum were held around Rio's Flamingo Park, forty kilometers away. Moreover, the Global Forum was more of a "happening" or cluster of events than a centralized and well-focused conference. Various activities were held at several dozen sites around the city. Their scope at the two conferences was so overwhelming and the general scale of associated activities was so great that participation in both the major intergovernmental and nongovernmental events was very difficult.

Even though the intergovernmental conference produced two environmental conventions, a global action plan now known as Agenda 21, and a general agreement over the text of two declarations, the Rio process itself was perhaps the most significant product. This process, however, began long before the summer of 1992. In response to the Brundtland Commission's report, the UN General Assembly moved in December 1989 (Resolution 44/228) to sponsor a conference for the purpose of developing strategies to "halt and reverse the effects of environmental degradation in the context of increased national and international efforts to promote sustainable and environmentally sound development in all countries."

Over the next eighteen months a concerted effort was launched to produce a package of agreements that could be finalized ceremoniously by heads of government at the Earth Summit. A set of negotiations conducted by the UNCED

UNITED NATIONS CONFERENCE ON
ENVIRONMENT AND DEVELOPMENT
Rio de Janeiro 3-14 June 1992

Brazilian president Collor de Mello acknowledges the applause of world leaders after he formally closes the UN Conference on Environment and Development in June 1992. (UN Photo 180108/T. Prendergast)

Preparatory Committee focused on drafting a comprehensive development and environment agenda for action (Agenda 21), a declaration on environmental principles (the Rio Declaration on Environment and Development, or the Rio Declaration), and a statement on forest principles. The evolving agenda came to center on nine main environmental issues and nearly two dozen related development concerns. The environmental side of the deliberations focused on issues related to the atmosphere, biotechnology, the diversity of biological species (biodiversity), freshwater, hazardous wastes, human health, human habitats, oceans, and land resources. The development-related issues were equally, if not more, wide-ranging, in keeping with the broad concept of sustainable development. The negotiation process was further complicated by the need to hammer out many institutional and financial issues.

The road to Rio, then, was a long and arduous one. Participants were engaged in the preparatory process almost continuously for three years. Maurice Strong, who again was selected to serve as Secretary-General of the conference secretariat, had said in reference to UNCHE nearly twenty years earlier that in many important respects "the process was the policy." The process of building consensus around ecodevelopment was regarded by many participants as being just as important an outcome of UNCED as any set of declarations, treaties, or other specific products. As demonstrated in the PrepCom negotiations, however, that process was not always an easy one, and the end products were not satisfactory to a majority of the participants. After three years of laborious and often tedious negotiations, for example, the specification of timetables, qualitative and quantitative targets, and acceptable limits still eluded negotiators as they rushed to finalize agreement on the conventions, statements of principles, and plan of action.

Basic North-South tensions that underpinned multilateral politics in general surfaced during the political process of negotiating consensus around the massive conference agenda. As at Stockholm, Southern governments were skeptical of the Northern push to impose ecological imperatives on the global development agenda. This reluctance should not imply that the dynamic relationships between poverty and other aspects of underdevelopment and environmental degradation were not perceived or taken seriously in the South. A great many environmental concerns, including depletion of freshwater and other resources, deforestation, and atmospheric pollution, were seen as serious threats to improving the overall quality of life. Yet other issues stressed in the North, such as ozone depletion, hazardous waste pollution, and global warming, were seen by many Southern participants as being historical products of industrialization as well as overconsumption in the North.

If Northern governments now wanted the active partnership of the South in redressing these problems, that participation should not come, the South argued, at the expense of its development. In exchange for Southern participation, Northern donor governments should make available additional financial and technical resources. There was ample incentive for such sacrifice, the South argued, because as deforestation, industrial pollution, desertification, and other environmentally degrading conditions continued to intensify within Southern societies, they loomed as ominous threats to overall global security.

These North-South tensions were brought into particularly sharp focus during the debate over forest principles. Southern negotiators, led by the Brazilians, Indians, and Malaysians—many of the same countries that reacted similarly when sovereignty was under siege in the security and human rights arenas—forcefully resisted any incursion into the principle of sovereignty over natural resources. Similarly, tensions also prevailed in drafting the Rio Declaration. This declaration was constructed to serve as a guide to governments and nongovernmental actors in implementing the many provisions of Agenda 21. With its unmistakable flavor of compromise between negotiators from Northern industrial countries and Southern developing ones, this declaration integrated many of the most important elements of the development and environment perspectives of both sides. Even as the rights to exploit resources within a state's geographical boundaries were reaffirmed, the responsibility of states to exercise control over environmentally damaging activities within their boundaries also was proclaimed. In addition, among the twenty-seven principles embodied in the declaration was one stating that the cost of pollution should be borne at the source and should be reflected in product cost at all stages of production.

In addition to the PrepCom negotiations, two legally binding international conventions—on biodiversity and on climate change—were incorporated as part of the larger Rio process. The Convention on Biodiversity requires signatories to pursue economic development in such a way as to preserve existing species and ecosystems. The Convention on Climate Change embodies a general set of principles and obligations aimed at reducing greenhouse gases. Due largely to the intransigent position of the Bush administration during the negotiation process, formal intergovernmental negotiations over the creation of these two legal conventions proved to be difficult to finalize. The final documents emerging from the Earth Summit represented "framework conventions." Although these conventions designated general principles and obligations, specific timetables and targets were left unspecified and subject to future negotiations over protocols—that is, additional treaties.

At center stage in the Rio process was Agenda 21. In its final form this document comprised over 600 pages of text and covered an enormous array of issues. Although the vast majority of this text was agreed to before UNCED, a number of contentious items were carried over to the Earth Summit. In keeping with the general tenor of debates, problems included issues related to biodiversity, biotechnology, deforestation, and institutional and procedural issues involving financing, technology transfer, and institutional arrangements for carrying out the elements of the action agenda.

A number of these issues, including certain details about institutional arrangements to carry out the action program, proved to be intractable and remained unresolved at the close of UNCED. Foremost among them was how to generate the financial resources needed to implement the program of action and associated activities. Estimates varied; the calculations made by the UNCED secretariat put the price tag at well over $100 billion per year for the first decade alone. These figures were, of course, quite unprecedented. They reflected the massive scope of the components inherent in the marriage between development and environment as they had come together within the Rio process.

Linked to the issue of financing was governance. At the core of governance is the question: Who decides when and how such resources are to be spent? As the negotiations during the Rio process clearly revealed, some minimal basic agreement about governance is a prerequisite for agreement over financing. Again, North-South tensions fueled the debate.

The issue of multilateral development financing was, of course, not specific to this particular social setting. In keeping with past practice, the Northern negotiators, led by the United States, pressed to have all such financing channeled through the World Bank group of financial institutions and instruments. In that setting, the locus of control would be well established, with the Group of Seven (G-7) largest industrial countries possessing effective veto power. The Global Environmental Facility was in place and might be expanded to encompass a broader mandate.

This proposed solution, however, was not acceptable to most Southern participants, who preferred what they called a "more democratic" arrangement. These governments proposed the creation of a new "green fund," which would operate on more egalitarian voting principles. Most major Northern donors found this proposal wholly unacceptable. For them to commit significant levels of funding, some guarantee of control on their part was required. A compromise was achieved to enhance the South's participation while retaining for donor states elements of control. Interim financing for Agenda 21 implementation would be provided under the aegis of the World Bank group. The Global Environmental Facility would be expanded and its decision rules altered to provide for decision-making by consensus among equally represented groupings of donors and recipients. Although the governance issue has, at least temporarily, been put to rest, the matter of securing the requisite financial resources remains problematic, with only a very small fraction of the resources actually committed.

Beyond financial considerations, the UNCED conferees formalized agreement over the creation of the Commission on Sustainable Development (CSD). This body has the same membership as ECOSOC. Dual responsibilities are overseeing the implementation of the provisions of Agenda 21 and coordinating the sustainable development activities of the various organizations within the UN system beyond the boundaries of that system.

Agreement was not readily forthcoming over many important details about how this new commission was to be empowered to fulfill its mandate effectively. Although CSD was assigned the role of being the primary mechanism within the UN system for coordinating sustainable development, its relationship to UNEP, the World Bank, the Committee of International Development Institutions on the Environment, and other intergovernmental entities remained to be defined at a later date. Also left in flux was the nature of the relationship between CSD and the civic-based order within which it and all the other sovereignty-bound actors must operate.

CSD convened its first meeting in February 1993 to organize its work and develop an agenda for the future. This initial agenda emphasized the need to integrate and coordinate the work related to sustainable development by multilateral funding agencies with the work of the commission. Moreover, inherent in the Rio Declaration and Agenda 21, as well as in the Rio process itself, was the overt recognition that implementation of these agreements and of sustainable development programs and policies required close and integrated involvement of all sectors and levels of world society, including industries, scientific communities, local and national governmental bodies, civic groups, social movements, and individuals.

Harking back to the first words of the UN's own Charter, the Rio process stressed the primacy of people in creating sustainable development and in protecting and preserving the environment. Principle 10 of the Rio Declaration made explicit reference to the relationship between governments and civic-based actors:

> Environmental issues are best handled with the participation of all concerned citizens, at the relevant level. At the national level, each individual shall have appropriate access to information concerning the environment that is held by public authorities, including information on hazardous materials and activities in their communities, and the opportunity to participate in decisionmaking processes. States shall facilitate and encourage public awareness and participation by making information widely available. Effective access to judicial and administrative proceedings, including redress and remedy, shall be provided.[18]

Accordingly, an important mandate for the Commission on Sustainable Development was to strengthen the role of major societal groups as effective participants in sustainable development decisionmaking processes at all levels. This "mainstreaming" (that is, integration) of civic-based actors as participants in governance processes at all levels was underscored in the Rio Declaration. Moreover, the text of Agenda 21 specifically addressed the roles of eight major groups: NGOs, indigenous peoples, local governments, workers, businesses, scientific communities, farmers, and women, children, and youth.

Exactly how this mandate for mainstreaming was to be institutionalized in practice, however, had been left ambiguous. Although only eighteen NGOs were represented at the first CSD meeting, ECOSOC had authorized the CSD to consider including in the work of the new body all 1,400 NGOs that had been represented at the Earth Summit. In addition, the UN Secretary-General was to appoint a high-level advisory panel to the CSD, consisting of between fifteen and twenty-five eminent persons.

As recognized in both Agenda 21 and the Rio Declaration, fulfilling this mandate effectively is the fundamental cornerstone for successful implementation of sustainable development programs and practices. Therefore the mandate poses a tremendous challenge for CSD, as well as for the UN system and multilateral organization more generally. Establishing an effective relationship between the sovereignty-based world of interstate multilateral relations and the world civil society within which that interstate order exists was an elusive quest during the first half century of the UN's existence.

As explored in Chapter 10, when added to the myriad other challenges inherent in the post-Rio institution-building process, the work confronting the Commission on Sustainable Development, UNEP, the World Bank, and other major UN system players is awesome. Effective follow-up and effective governance for promoting sustainable development will require coordination and cooperation among a wide diversity of actors and interests.

The Post-Rio Process

In the years immediately following the Earth Summit, two overriding challenges to making the post-Rio process succeed confronted the international community. The first was how to generate and sustain effective cooperation. This problem had both horizontal and vertical dimensions. Effective cooperation would be required horizontally across different autonomous organizational domains, legal jurisdictions, and sectors of society as well as vertically across different levels of social aggregation, from individuals in their roles in groups and communities to representative governance in international forums.

The second challenge was how to reorient UN discourse and practice to overcome the constraints inherent in the organization's legal foundations in state sovereignty. The preceding discussion of the UN's involvement in ecodevelopment and its activities in international peace and security and human rights matters illustrates the limitations of working with a system so circumscribed by the concept of sovereignty. The foundations of the Charter, especially Article 2(7), and the institutional structures and practices of multilateral diplomacy, constrain attempts to incorporate nonstate actors into a full partnership in global policy processes.

These challenges seem forbidding, but as the heads of government at Rio pointed out, the costs of not rising to the challenge could be perilous. As they warned in the preamble of Agenda 21, "Humanity stands at a defining moment in history. We are confronted with a perpetuation of disparities between and within nations, a worsening of poverty, hunger, ill health and illiteracy, and the continuing deterioration of the ecosystems on which we depend for our well-being." The Agenda 21 text argues that only by creating global partnerships and involving all sectors of world society can the world's peoples expect "the fulfillment of basic needs, improved living standards for all, better-protected and better-managed ecosystems and a safer, more prosperous future." Creating the necessary global partnerships on an unprecedented scale will, in turn, require meeting the twin challenges of cooperating effectively and moving beyond the confines of sovereignty. Before exploring the nature and scope of those challenges, however, we need a better understanding of the dynamic interplay of the forces and tensions that have given shape to the contemporary discourse and practice of sustainable development.

The Evolving Development Discourse: Issue Linkage and Convergence

As we saw in regard to the evolution of the involvement of international financial and monetary institutions in development activities in Chapter 8, most major global issues have, to one degree or another, become framed in terms of sustainable development. In such cases as international finance, this convergence occurred earlier than in others; nonetheless, such a synthesis has occurred for many other issues.

Scene at the Non-Governmental Organizations Forum held in Huairou, China, as part of the UN Fourth World Conference on Women held in Beijing, China, September 4–15, 1995. (UN/DPI Photo/M. Grant)

It was in the late 1970s in the context of the new world information and communication order (NWICO) debates in UNESCO that global information and communication issues were seen largely in development terms. This synthesis became manifest in UNESCO's International Programme for the Development of Communication (IPDC). As in UNESCO's other main areas of functional competence—culture, education, and science—nearly every programmatic activity in the communications field became linked in some way to the larger global discourse on development.

This was also the case in respect to issues such as population, human settlements, health, food, and women. This shifting focus was captured in the names of special organizational campaigns, programmatic slogans, and conference titles such as the Health for All by the Year 2000 campaign, the UN Development Fund for Women (UNIFEM), United Nations Conference on Environment and Development, the World Conference on Education for All, the International Conference on Population and Development, and the World Summit on Social Development. This evolving emphasis on development was given enhanced visibility through the reports of a series of special high-level, independent global commissions comprising eminent persons, including the Independent Commission on International Development Issues (the Brandt Commission), the World Commission on the Environment and Development (the Brundtland Commission), the

South Commission, the Commission on Sustainable Development, and the Commission on Global Governance.

The important point here is that there was a growing awareness that dealing with global issues required a perspective and responses that were simultaneously holistic, historical, interdisciplinary, and structural. It was not helpful and actually harmful to view the world as being divided into discrete spheres of reality. Narrowly conceived functionalist thinking and logic slowly gave ground to more dynamic and synthetic approaches.

These changes were accompanied and fostered by large, growing networks of transnational actors, a great many of whom traveled from conference to conference and from organization to organization promoting their special interests, programs, projects, and priorities. Although these transnational actors are in essence interest groups—whether they represent NGOs, transnational corporate enterprises, governmental bureaucracies, or transnational social movements—they were forced to approach their endeavors more holistically. Yet their narrower, interest-specific foundations made cooperation and consensus-building difficult. In this light, we now return to examining the constraints to building and sustaining effective cooperation for promoting sustainable human development in the wake of the Rio conference.

Getting Beyond Rio: Engendering Effective Cooperation

There was much déjà vu surrounding the formation in 1992 of the Commission on Sustainable Development and its new coordination mission. The UNEP had been created two decades earlier to serve as the UN's main mechanism for "policy review and coordination" on environmental issues, including those associated with development. In this regard, sentiments expressed earlier at Stockholm were echoed at Rio: Environmental activities and functions should be carried out by existing organizations (international and national) to the extent possible. Like UNEP, the CSD was to serve as a main coordinating mechanism and as a catalyst for promoting the ecodevelopment activities of existing UN organs. Neither UNEP nor CSD was given primary responsibility to take on operational functions that might interfere with the work of others.

At the same time, however, both UNEP and CSD were superimposed on existing interorganizational systems of action. When UNEP was created, a number of UN agencies—including UNESCO, FAO, WHO, and WMO—were already engaged in environmental work. In addition, several UNESCO-related scientific programs—including the International Oceanographic Commission, the International Hydrological Program, and the intergovernmental Man and the Biosphere project—either were functioning or were in some stage of development. The Commission on Sustainable Development was dropped into an even more complex and somewhat chaotic multiorganizational system. Although CSD possessed the potential to serve as a complement to the coordination work of UNEP, the history of international organizations would seem to suggest that CSD was just as likely to act as a fierce competitor.

These two "lead" agencies in the ecodevelopment field are confronted with dual tasks. One consists of deciphering the complex social and political milieu in which they must operate and coming to some form of agreement about what needs to be done by whom. The second concerns designing compatible coordination strategies with which to undertake their respective yet overlapping mandates and activities. Moreover, they must carry out these tasks in the context of an established set of mechanisms that also have primary interagency coordination responsibilities. Although a discussion of coordination may seem mundane, it is essential for understanding the complexities of policymaking and implementation in the UN system.

The main coordination mechanisms at the headquarters level are the Administrative Committee on Coordination (ACC) and its subsidiary bodies. These permanent mechanisms, although used occasionally as the need has arisen, have not played an important role in the ecodevelopment area. When it occurs at all, coordination more often than not takes place in the field, where multiagency projects or program actions are implemented. As discussed in Chapter 8 and by agreement among agencies, the UNDP resident coordinator in each country is supposed to serve as the primary intermediary and coordinating agent. As with the ACC, however, this system of coordination has tended to be somewhat ad hoc. Unlike in more hierarchical institutions like the military or transnational banks, effectiveness of coordination is often linked to such idiosyncratic factors as the chemistry among UN officials in a country or working in a particular substantive area. Effectiveness has been further complicated by the persistent reluctance of the World Bank group to participate in coordination activities of the UN system. Although bank officials have pledged more cooperation, the Washington-based financial institutions are likely to remain distant and autonomous.

To facilitate the coordination mandate of UNEP, in 1972 General Assembly Resolution 2997 (XXXVI) created the Environment Coordination Board in the context of the ACC. This body, which was chaired by the executive director of UNEP, failed, primarily for the reasons discussed earlier. As a result, the functions of this board were reintegrated within the ACC coordination machinery in 1978, and a new senior-level working committee, the Designated Officials for Environmental Matters (DOEM), was set up within the ACC to deal with interagency planning and coordination at the operational level.

The work of DOEM has been complemented since 1980 by CIDIE, which reviews member agencies' progress toward implementing the provisions of the Declaration of Environmental Policies and Procedures Related to Economic Development. The creation of this new body represented an important step in enhancing systemwide coordination, given the traditionally reserved posture taken by the Bretton Woods institutions in the ACC. The UNEP secretariat serves as the secretariat for CIDIE and thus provides an important link between these two entities.

The process of systemwide interagency coordination in ecodevelopment evolved slowly over time through much trial and error. In UNEP's early years, a comprehensive procedure for systemwide review, called joint programming, was adopted. Interagency discussions focused on selected environmental topics. The objective of these discussions was to identify gaps in existing knowledge and practices and to design strategies to fill them. Over the years, these exercises expanded from bilateral to multilateral thematic programming.

If we are to place these coordination activities in clearer perspective, the precise nature of UNEP's mandate as it relates to other UN agencies needs to be understood. One of the most important roles of UNEP is generating international norms and setting standards to protect the human environment. The agency has played an instrumental role in the negotiations and adoption of a number of major international environmental conventions, including the Vienna Convention for the Protection of the Ozone Layer, the Convention on Climate Change, and the Convention on Biodiversity. Although UNEP does administer certain environmental projects, it is not primarily a project-executing agency in the sense that most specialized agencies are. Also, UNEP is not primarily a source of financing, unlike UNDP, the World Bank group, and other multilateral funding agencies. It does, however, disperse funds through its Environment Fund. The result has been a somewhat confused mandate, which has been muddied further by the creation of the Commission on Sustainable Development with its overlapping functions.

Effective project implementation most often requires coordination at the operational level in the field. Although UNEP is not primarily involved in executing program actions at the country level, it is involved with scores of other organizations in overseeing the implementation of projects that are supported through resources from the UNEP Environment Fund. A great many of these projects are executed by "cooperating agencies" (that is, UN system agencies and bodies), primarily FAO, UNESCO, WHO, WMO, and UNCHS (UN Center for Human Settlements, or Habitat). Other resources from this fund go to support project implementation by other intergovernmental organizations, NGOs, research institutions, and other civic-based bodies (referred to in UNEP as supporting organizations). When projects also include UNDP sources, the resident coordinator in the country in which the project is located serves as the primary point person for coordination activities in the field.

This overlapping jurisdiction on coordination adds a significant degree of complexity and ambiguity to UNEP's function, as have certain of the major changes within the UN system over the past decade. There has been a definite trend toward greater decentralization, regionalism, and involvement of civic-based entities in global governance, which has greatly complicated the overwhelming task of making the UN system hang together and function coherently. The United Nations' continuing financial predicament, of course, has exacerbated the problem.

In order to understand the impact that these changes may have on post-Rio ecodevelopment activities and the work of CSD, the intergovernmental side of the coordination issue needs to be brought into focus. An important reason for UNEP's failure to serve as an effective systemwide coordinating mechanism was that a number of major donor governments, most notably the United States, preferred to bypass UNEP regarding all financial matters. In such a position, UNEP should be a technical agency concentrating largely on environmental monitoring and assessment.

Money was seen, by many donor governments as well as social scientists, as being directly related to power (that is, the ability to influence outcomes). Since control over financial decisionmaking could be controlled best in the context of the multilateral development institutions, that is where the action on important decisions should be taken. Given that the governance procedures in CSD are based on the ECOSOC model, there is little reason to assume that these large donors will be willing to permit CSD to carry out its coordination mandate any more effectively than UNEP has. The relatively autonomous functions of CIDIE in the area of multilateral ecodevelopment financing are not likely to be diminished by the presence of this new commission.

Agenda 21 anticipated, and at least gave lip service to, addressing this concern. It called for strengthening UNEP and its Governing Council, although the means of doing so were left rather ambiguous. It stressed the role of UNDP as the lead agency in organizing UN system activities for building the capacity for sustainable development. Again, however, the method went unspecified. The intergovernmental components of UNEP, UNDP, and the CSD are to march side by side in this new post-Rio order to bring sustainable development to fruition, but little in the way of effective cooperation has materialized so far. The challenge is clear, but in order to meet that challenge, serious coordination deficiencies will need to be addressed on a very different plane.

The UN Secretary-General attempted to increase interagency cooperation by establishing the High-Level Advisory Board on Sustainable Development. That board is composed of twenty-one eminent persons in the ecodevelopment area. It advises the Secretary-General and the CSD on policy formulation and interagency cooperation and coordination issues. But again, the results to date are not clear.

Beyond Sovereignty

The politics of sustainable development and the challenges for effective coordination within the UN system cannot be adequately understood unless we remove the blinders of sovereignty-based thinking and revise our ideas about the linkages between intergovernmental organizations and nongovernmental actors. The foundation of the UNCED conference, for example, was deeply ingrained in and dependent upon the work of scientific NGOs, not because of their consultative status but because they were fully engaged participants that brought with them the weight of their scientific findings and global scientific action. As mentioned earlier, the importance of the scientific NGOs in the UNCED process was underscored by the fact that UNCHE Secretary-General Maurice Strong invited ICSU to become the principal scientific adviser to the UNCED secretariat. Furthermore, as implied by the outcomes of the International Conference on an Agenda of Science for Environment and Development into the Twenty-first Century (ASCEND 21), the work of global scientific communities played an important role in elevating sustainable development to the status of an acceptable topic of global policy discourse. Also, over fifty NGOs made contributions to the preparation of UNCED and a number of independent parallel events.

Paradoxically, however, the road to Rio for NGOs was not well paved by either UNEP or UNCED conference planners. From the perspective of the United Nations, NGOs were largely left to their own devices and creativity. In retrospect, they seem to have met the challenge quite effectively. Growing out of two NGO meetings (in Vancouver and Nyon) in June 1990, an International Facilitating Committee (IFC) was created to encourage NGO participation in the UNCED process. This body was composed of twenty-five individuals from various "independent" sectors, including representatives from the Centre for Our Common Future and the Conference on NGOs in Consultative Status with ECOSOC (CONGO) as rotating members. Along with ELCI, IFC played an instrumental role in planning the NGO activities in Rio, and especially the Global Forum, which brought together 18,000 participants from civic-based organizations and movements.

Also in preparation for UNCED, ELCI hosted a meeting in Paris in December 1991 to produce a "Brazil document" to present an NGO perspective on environment and development. Out of this meeting emerged an unprecedented effort by NGOs at treaty writing, which was coordinated by the steering committee for the International Forum of NGOs and Social Movements. Using a computer network, NGO representatives produced over thirty treaties covering five main topics: NGO cooperation and institution building, alternative economics, environment, food production, and cross-sectoral issues.

In spite of appearances of cooperation, civic-based actors are not more likely to coordinate activities than members of the UN system are. In the Rio process, for example, NGOs remained largely fragmented, and much tension existed below the surface. The differences, conflicts, and tensions in the interstate order are relatively well documented and discussed; this is not true of the nonstate "order" (if the term is to be meaningful). The world of civic-based actors in the ecodevelopment area—as it became manifest before, during, and after Rio—is at least as diverse and contentious as interstate relations operating within the conventional structure of international law and diplomacy. The population of civic-based actors at Rio represented every conceivable element of the social spectrum, from businesses to anticorporate activists, neo-Malthusians to cornucopians, lawyers to activists, conservationists to progrowth exploitationists.[19]

Refugees returning to Cambodia in 1992 under the oversight of the UN Transitional Authority in Cambodia were offered different forms of UNHCR assistance, including a house plot and house kit. This man assembles a home in Battambang Province. (UNHCR Photo/K. Gooi)

The challenge for CSD is overwhelming. Agenda 21 has mandated that this relatively small entity with little financial support is to undertake the task of creating support for a new global economic order based on sustainable development principles. Doing so requires creating partnerships with civic organizations on a scale never seen before. This, in turn, requires that ways be found for "mainstreaming" these diverse civic-based actors into the world of interstate relations. Partnerships mean participation. Engendering greater participation by civic-based entities—especially those from the South, where the tradition of popular participation often is not strong and where governments easily feel threatened by such groups—entails relinquishing control over processes that consequently are not likely to be as predictable as Northern states would prefer. As with human rights, dealing in this area, which can be politically sensitive for national governments, would not be risk-free for an international agency that is totally dependent for funding on member states whose control over decisionmaking would be most challenged.

Government delegations at Rio were unable to reach agreement over the relationship between CSD and NGOs, but participants within the civic-based NGOs were not content to adopt a wait-and-see posture. Immediately following UNCED, UNCHE Secretary-General Strong and twenty-eight experts formed a new NGO, the Earth Council. The body has its legal basis in the Costa

Rican–based Earth Council Foundation. The Earth Council's statement of purpose identifies two principles that will guide its activities: It exists to encourage popular participation in development decisionmaking and management, and it will serve an ombudsman role, assessing and reporting responses for implementing Agenda 21 and other major instruments agreed to at the Earth Summit. Also, the Earth Council program endeavors to facilitate the expansion and implementation of the People's Twenty-first Century Agenda, which grew out of the proceedings of the Global Forum. The Earth Council was envisioned by its founders as serving as a mechanism to help link the Commission on Sustainable Development and civic-based organizations. This self-proclaimed role as NGO articulator did not rest well with many other nongovernmental participants who were actively engaged in the Rio process.

Several umbrella NGO mechanisms were already in place for facilitating linkages between international governmental and nongovernmental actors in the environmental arena. In addition to the Nairobi-based ELCI, CONGO and several other umbrella NGOs with long histories in global environment and development were reluctant to acquiesce to some new and rather ad hoc form of representation. Moreover, it was not likely that the Business Council for Sustainable Development and other business-related bodies, such as the International Chamber of Commerce's International Environmental Bureau in Geneva and the World Environment Center in New York, would be willing to subordinate themselves to a broader scheme of NGO cooperation. This was especially true because many civic-based NGOs and social movement actors had targeted corporate actors as a major part of the problem, not the solution.

Although the Rio Declaration and Agenda 21 both argue the need for integrating nongovernmental organizations, citizens' groups, and other civic-based actors into international environment and development decisionmaking, creating the capacity to do so remains elusive. The challenge is not constructing some massive mechanism for the central coordination of NGOs. Such an apparatus would be quite unwelcome to most NGOs and probably would not yield greater cooperation. As in the human rights case, diversity in the NGO community can lead to dynamism, and no monolithic structure would be able to pull together the multiple moving parts. What is needed in the context of the Rio Declaration, Agenda 21, and the post-Rio political process is a nonintrusive mechanism to facilitate NGO participation in multilateral decisionmaking and to enhance cooperation among member states, international agencies, and nongovernmental actors.

As a concept for guiding development thinking, sustainable development may fade. But the social forces and global changes that underlie thinking on sustainability are not likely to go away. Thus it is important for students of international organization to think systematically about why processes and structures in the United Nations have evolved as they have in regard to sustainable development, and about what directions development activities might take in the future. It is in this context that a dispassionate assessment can be made of what the UN can and cannot do to promote sustainable development.

A traditional starting point for such an assessment is to examine these sustainable development activities in the context of functionalism. Functionalists argue that "growth of technology and spread and intensification of the desire for higher standards of material welfare" lead to greater international cooperation in search of expanded political authority.[20] A functionalist perspective suggests that popular interest in sustainable development results from expanded technical cooperation in developmental and environmental concerns. Accordingly, technical cooperation for development has spilled over into the environmental area, and technical cooperation on ecological concerns has come to encompass development issues. The interplay between the two has thus become so pervasive that environment and development are no longer separate concepts.

Proponents of this thesis point to the evolving process, beginning around the time of the Stockholm conference, whereby the concept of ecodevelopment came onto the global agenda. In attempting to lay the foundations of a global plan of action for dealing with environmental issues, Secretary-General Strong and other UNCHE planners quickly came to perceive the inseparability of the two previously separate issues. This orientation evolved over later decades as the environmental science community, development assistance practitioners and scholars, international financiers, government officials, and many others came to see their own work to be achievable only in the context of a more holistic ecodevelopment worldview.

The two explanations examined in Chapter 7 for the spread of cooperation in the human rights area—that is, consensual-knowledge communities and social learning—grow out of this more general functionalist perspective. The first explanation suggests that the convergence of development and environment into sustainable development on the global public policy agenda grows from consensual agreement over ecodevelopment in private communities of knowledge. The second explanation emphasizes the importance of institutional learning and argues that the convergence is a product of a learning process in which state actors have recognized the inherent inseparability of the two issues.

Proponents of the consensual-knowledge approach point to the tremendous growth and involvement, at least of Northern civic actors, in sustainable development politics at the global intergovernmental level. They also point to the evolution of the role of NGOs since Stockholm, to the activities of NGOs in the Rio process, and to the influence of knowledge communities on issues such as protection of the ozone layer as evidence that this approach is valid.[21]

The nature of the evolution of NGO involvement in the sustainable development area, however, casts doubt on the validity of this view. There are hundreds of opinion communities concerned with sustainable development. Yet the diversity and often outright antagonisms among these communities challenge the notion that some dominant consensual body of knowledge underlies events within global sustainable development processes.

This is not to suggest that at a general level there has not been a convergence of interests over sustainability issues. Indeed, the concept has come to dominate much of the debate over both development and environment. For example, there was a substantial increase in the number of articles about sustainable development in scientific journals in the years immediately before the Rio conference. These figures, however, can be misleading.

Although growing consensus can be observed within specific areas of environmental concern, that consensus has yet to be translated into a coherent global scientific consensus about sustainable development. Moreover, a large gulf still separates basic and applied scientists over many ecodevelopment issues.

Similarly, the notion that some coherent and identifiable social learning process underpins global sustainable development activities is suspect. For example, it was not until after the election of Barber Conable as World Bank president in 1986 and the application of concerted pressure by NGOs that the World Bank showed any serious signs of becoming environmentally concerned. Before this time, bank staff demonstrated little, if any, willingness to cooperate with UNEP or nonbusiness civic-based actors. As argued above, the idea of sustainable development has served as a common denominator bridging the turf and ideological divide that otherwise separates the financial and monetary institutions from other members of the UN family.[22]

Furthermore, there is no universal consensus about definitions. In global debates, Northern delegates tend to define sustainability rather narrowly as environmental protection and resource conservation. Southerners normally define the concept with specific reference to meeting basic human needs and reducing poverty. The focus here is on people, on promoting economic growth that produces employment and encourages the wider participation of people in economic processes.[23] Economists have their own definition. They say sustainable development is "an economic process in which the quantity and quality of our stocks of natural resources (like forests) and the integrity of biogeochemical cycles (like climate) are sustained and passed on to the future generations unimpaired."[24]

How then are we to account for the convergence of people and interest around sustainable development in the United Nations? And what are the implications for the future of the UN systems' work in promoting sustainable human development and security. It is to these questions that we turn in Chapter 10.

Notes

1. Garrett Hardin, "The Tragedy of the Commons," *Science* 162 (December 13, 1968), pp. 1243–1248; Donella Meadows et al., *Limits to Growth* (New York: Universe Books,

1972). For an overview of the evolution of ecodevelopment politics, see Lynton K. Caldwell, *International Environmental Policy: Emergence and Dimensions*, 2nd ed. (Durham, NC: Duke Univ. Press, 1991).

2. Sverker Åström, *Ogonblick: Fran ett halvsekel i UD-tjanst* (*Moments: From Half a Century of State Department Service*) (Stockholm: Bonnier Alba), pp. 158–160.

3. UNEP, "Development and Environment: The Founex Report: In Defense of the Earth," *The Basic Texts on Environment*, UNEP Executive Series 1, Nairobi, 1981.

4. Branislav Gosovic, *The Quest for World Environmental Cooperation: The Case of the UN Global Environment Monitoring System* (London: Routledge, 1992).

5. The Soviet Union and its allies officially snubbed the conference in protest of the exclusion of the German Democratic Republic over political issues related to the Cold War.

6. Peter M. Haas, "From Theory to Practice: Ecological Ideas and Development Policy," Working Paper Series, no. 92–2, Center for International Affairs (Cambridge, MA: Harvard Univ. Press, 1992), pp. 31–34.

7. Union of International Associations, *Yearbook of International Organizations 1992/1993* (Brussels: Union of International Associations, 1993), pp. 280–281.

8. Haas, "From Theory to Practice," p. 34.

9. World Commission on Environment and Development, *Our Common Future* (New York: Oxford Univ. Press, 1987).

10. UNEP Governing Council Decision 15, Annex II, May 1989.

11. Robert Wade, "Greening the Bank: The Struggle over the Environment, 1970–1995," in Devesh Kapur, John P. Lewis, and Richard Webb, eds., *The World Bank: Its First Half Century* (Washington, DC: Brookings Institution, 1997), Vol. 2, pp. 611–734; Richard Haeuber, "The World Bank and Environmental Assessment: The Role of Nongovernmental Organizations," *Environmental Impact Assessment Review* 1 (1992), pp. 1–17; World Bank, *Funding Ecological and Social Destruction: The World Bank and the International Monetary Fund* (Washington, DC: Bank Information Center, 1990); and Sierra Club, *Bankrolling Disasters: International Development Banks and the Global Environment* (San Francisco: Sierra Club, 1986).

12. Anne Thompson Feraru, "Transnational Political Interests and the Global Environment," *International Organization* 28, no. 1 (1974), pp. 36–37.

13. Ibid., pp. 43, 46.

14. Caldwell, *International Environmental Policy*, p. 81.

15. United Nations, *Yearbook of the United Nations 1987* (New York: UN, 1988), pp. 684–685.

16. World Bank, *Meeting of the World Bank-NGO Committee and Recent Progress in Bank-NGO Cooperation* (Washington, DC: Bank Information Center, 1989), p. 6.

17. For a review of the documentation see Shanna Halpren, *The United Nations Conference on Environment and Development: Process and Documentation* (Providence, RI: Academic Council on the United Nations System, 1992).

18. UNCED, *The Global Partnership for Environment and Development: A Guide to Agenda 21* (Geneva: UNCED, April 1992).

19. Haas, "From Theory to Practice."

20. Harold Jacobson, *Networks of Interdependence* (New York: Alfred A. Knopf, 1984), pp. 62–63.

21. See, for example, Peter Haas, "Banning Chlorofluorocarbons: Epistemic Community Efforts to Protect Stratospheric Ozone," *International Organization* 46, no. 1 (Winter 1992), pp. 187–224.

22. For an overview of the evolution of ecodevelopment politics, see Lynton K. Caldwell, *International Environmental Policy: Emergence and Dimensions*, 2nd ed. (Durham, NC: Duke Univ. Press, 1991), p. 81.

23. Alvao Soto, "The Global Environment: A Southern Perspective," *International Journal* 15, no. 8 (Autumn 1992), pp. 679–705; and UNDP, *Human Development Report 1993* (New York: Oxford Univ. Press, 1993). This theme reappears in all subsequent annual reports.

24. Anil Agarwal, "What Is Sustainable Development?" *Concordare* no. 4 (Spring 1993), p. 2.

10 Sustainable Development and Human Security

Problems and Prospects for the 2000s

The role that sustainable development has played in traversing the turf and ideological divide that otherwise separates actors in the global arena provides a key for speculating about the future of the UN's development work. In the Rio process and beyond, sustainability has served as an important bridge in institutional bargaining. The associated political process has been characterized more by bargaining among autonomous and self-interested participants striving for consensus and less as a regime-building process dominated by consensual knowledge communities. Operating under a veil of uncertainty about the likely effects of their alternative choices, these participants engage in transnational alliance formation and politics that link issues.[1] Many participants may be associated with specific communities of knowledge, but the political process is a pluralistic one in which groups of participants perceive and act on differing conceptions of problems, values, interests, and stakes.

The convergence around sustainable development as a bridging theme in the international development debate was helped by a number of coincidental factors beginning in the mid-1980s. First, the demands coming from the global South for the establishment of the NIEO had stalled, and the viability of the Group of 77 as a cohesive mobilizing and caucusing force had become questionable. Pragmatism and fragmentation characterized the global South in the 1990s, and the ideas associated with sustainable development seemed to fit well with these attitudes.

Second, the end of the Cold War, the collapse of communist control in central Europe, and the breakup of the former Soviet Union distracted attention in the North away from Third World development concerns. This was especially true in Washington, where the South had suddenly become strategically much less important, but this was true more generally throughout the West. Those calling for greater attention to Southern development were searching for a way to capture the attention of Northern donors as development assistance monies, in real terms and as a percentage of GDP, decreased.[2] Sustainable development provided a potential means to recapture some of the lost focus and garner support for Third World development.

Third, heightened concern in the North since the mid-1980s over the depletion of the ozone layer, climate change, and the loss of diversity of biological species helped to focus attention on environmental issues and to raise their status and visibility on national and global policy agendas. Growing scientific evidence seemed to support the observation and intuition among many citizens that environmental degradation and poverty are dynamically linked. Projections of likely future trends for undesirable global changes suggested that developing countries would need to be brought on board the environmental protection wagon in order to prevent future degradations of the global physical environment.

Fourth, during the 1990s an evolving series of global conferences helped to refocus and redirect the global development agenda. They included the World Summit for Children (1990); World Conference on Education for All (1990); UN Conference on Environment and Development ("Earth Summit," 1992); Eighth, Ninth, and Tenth Sessions of the United Nations Conference on Trade and Development (UNCTAD VIII, 1993; UNCTAD IX, 1996; UNCTAD X, 2000); World Conference on Human Rights (1993); International Conference on Population and Development (1994); World Summit on Social Development (1995); Fourth World Conference on Women (1995); Second UN Conference on Human Settlements (HABITAT II, 1996); World Food Summit (1996); Earth Summit+5 (1997); and General Assembly Special Session on the International Conference on Population and Development (1999).

One of the most striking outcomes to emerge from these conferences was that the development debate took on a new character as the concepts of human development and sustainable development became fused in the concept "sustainable human development." This concept began to take more concrete form in the mid-1990s as the UNDP/UNFPA Executive Board (Decision 94/14) adopted sustainable human development as a new mission for the technical assistance agency. Like other development concepts before it, sustainable human development was viewed as a key requisite for creating and maintaining a secure and peaceful world order. The barrage of political discourse over development in the 1990s led most member states of the world organization to expect the United Nations to play some meaningful role in bringing about such a goal.

Fifth, the series of UNDP *Human Development Reports* issues throughout the 1990s painted a very bleak picture of global development. Although about a dozen-and-a-half countries in the global South have demonstrated remarkable economic growth since 1980, for most residents of the developing world, poverty is increasing, and the gap between the rich and poor is growing. Despite the rhetoric about popular participation, the vast majority of the world's people continue to be excluded from active involvement in economic and political decisions that affect them. The reports suggest that in much of the South, economic expansion has, in fact, been "jobless growth." Employment has lagged behind increases in economic output. Growth has not been translated into empowerment, which lies at the foundation of sustainable development ideas. Moreover, most of the developing world experienced only limited success in sustaining growth at levels needed for poverty reduction. The 1998 UNDP report succinctly summarized the situation as follows:

> Well over a billion people are deprived of basic consumption needs. Of the 4.4 billion people in developing countries, nearly three-fifths lack basic sanitation. Almost a third have no access to clean water. A quarter do not have adequate housing. A fifth have no access to modern health services. A fifth of children do not attend school to grade 5. About a fifth do not have enough dietary energy and protein. Micronutrient deficiencies are even more widespread. Worldwide, 2 billion people are anaemic, including 55 million in industrial countries. In developing countries only a privileged minority has motorized transport, telecommunications and modern energy. . . . In 70 countries with nearly a billion people consumption today is lower than it was 25 years ago.[3]

For many countries conditions got even worse immediately following the global financial and economic crises of late 1997 and 1998.

What began as a currency crisis in Thailand in July 1997 quickly spread to other East Asian economies by the end of the year. Given the interdependence of international financial markets and the global trading order, the contagion spread and contributed to economic decline and disorder elsewhere. As commodity prices fell and short-term investment and private lending declined, the rippling effects made their way around the world.

The developing world and transitional economies were by far the hardest hit. In 1998, the rate of growth of GDP of the developing countries as a whole registered the smallest amount since 1983.[4] In fact, the World Bank's *Global Development Report,* released in April 1999, substantially adjusted downward its forecast for economic growth in the developing world. Instead of the 2.7 percent growth previously predicted for 1999, the new forecast projected only a 1.5 percent growth rate. These revised figures reflect a continuing deterioration of international trade, especially nonpetroleum commodity trade. The World Bank report also indicated that the net flow of financial aid to developing countries had also fallen significantly (by 6 percent in 1997) and had reached its lowest level in real terms since 1981. Net concessional assistance to developing countries has fallen by a third during the last decade, and Japan, the United States, and Germany have all significantly cut aid as a percentage of GDP.[5]

Sixth, there has been a steady decline in the capacity of the state to help fulfill basic human needs, and the report called for the development of new patterns of national and international governance. "The nation-state now is too small for the big things, and too big for the small," the 1993 UNDP report said.[6]

Yet these new patterns of governance are vague and unspecified. Decentralization of power is lauded as one of the best ways to bring about the empowerment of people, but the report recognizes that decentralization at whatever level—local, state, national, global—can result in empowering elites even more, rather than empowering people in the sense of popular participation. This distinction is important because sustainable growth and development require the active participation of people at all levels of governance.

As one observer has argued, "We cannot expect any act of intergovernmental will to transform the global IGO system into a rational, efficient system for assuring that individual basic needs are met—with the Food and Agriculture Organization . . . ensuring we all have enough to eat, the World Health Organization . . . assuring we are all healthy, the International Labour Organization . . . assuring we all have good jobs, etc."[7] As another astute observer noted, engendering effective global cooperation is, at its core, a political and not a functional issue:

> With regard to the United Nations, the most difficult choice may be between the traditional focus on the specialized agencies and the growing need to raise environmental concerns in broader, cross-cutting arenas. In the post-UNCED era, the discourse of environmentalism is clearly moving in the direction of cross-cutting themes. The traditional ecosystemic focus on air, land, water and species is giving way to a social-systems focus on international trade, global finance, sovereignty, development and other key processes and institutions. The old focus was consistent with the functional organization of the United Nations into specialized agencies; the emerging focus demands a new forum.[8]

But no matter what form future international cooperation takes, one thing is clear: For global responses to be effective, people, not states, must occupy center stage.

Although basic human-needs approaches to development attracted little support in intergovernmental diplomatic circles in the 1970s and early 1980s, a new version of human-needs development seemed to find its way into the development debates of the 1990s. Moreover, as we have seen in Parts 1 and 2 of this book, discourses on national security, human rights, humanitarian affairs, and development have spilled over into debates on global security. This has been true even in the disarmament area, as witnessed by the UN conference in August-September 1987, which focused on disarmament and development. Debates over security, like debates over development, have increasingly come to embrace the four shared global values discussed earlier: peace (nonviolence), human security (including democracy and human rights), sustainable human development, and ecological balance. And all of these values deal with human beings and their environments. Viewed in this context, sustainable development can be seen as being aimed at cumulatively improving and sustaining human security and reducing perceived and actual threats to physical and psychological well-being from all manner of agents and forces that could degrade people's lives, values, and property. Both sustainable human security and sustainable human development require democracy and the protection of fundamental human rights. In short, enhancing human security is what both development and democracy are about. Only by involving the affected people in their own governance can such outcomes be attained. But what, then, can we expect from the United Nations and other IGOs in the future as diplomats, government officials, and concerned citizens everywhere set about the task of rethinking the meaning of peace and human security in a post–Cold War world?

The UN and Human Security in the Twenty-first Century

The involvement of the UN in enhancing human security is exactly the question with which the UNDP has been grappling in its *Human Development Report* series. In this regard, the UNDP's *Human Development Report 1993* provides a useful point of departure and insight for identifying requisites of effective global governance and for assessing potential roles for the United Nations and the UN system. The report proposed "five new pillars of a people centered world order: new concepts of human security, new models of sustainable human development, new partnerships between state and markets, new patterns of national and global governance, and new forms of international cooperation."[9]

Human Security

Peacekeeping, peacemaking, and peace enforcement continue to be important UN activities in the post–Cold War world, and these in fact dominate Western and particularly American media coverage of the world organization. However, making human beings secure means more than protecting them from armed violence and alleviating their suffering. If international organizations are to contribute meaningfully to the promotion of *human* security, security needs to be defined in much broader terms than protection from threats to physical well-being from military violence. Moreover, as noted a little further down the same page in the 1993 UNDP report, human security "must stress the security of people, not only of nations. . . . The concept of security must change—from an exclusive stress on national security to a much greater stress on people's security, from security through armaments to security through human development, from territorial security to food, employment, and environmental security."[10] Thus sustainable human development can be viewed as a process of improving and sustaining human security.

Sustainable development, like human security, is a qualitative condition that entails individual and collective perceptions of low threats to physical and psychological well-being from all agents and forces that could degrade lives, values, and property. At a minimum, people may be considered secure if they are protected from the threat of the physical destruction of their lives or property as a result of assault from others. At the opposite extreme, maximum human security can be imagined in a totally threat-free environment where human beings are protected against all threats to their lives, values, and property. Various qualities of

A mother and child seeking security at the Morini border crossing between Kosovo and Albania in April 1999. (UN/UNHCR/R. Chalasani)

human security can be imagined depending on the relative ordering of the priorities that people place on the satisfaction of various needs, values, and interests.

The UNDP assigns to itself and other multilateral development agencies the task of elevating the quality of security in human environments. Although this amounts in many ways to pouring an old conceptual wine called "development" into a new conceptual bottle called "human security," the new conceptualization is useful because it emphasizes the psychological end state of development instead of the more mechanical processes of investment and returns in the form of growth. Enhancing human security—meaning that individuals sense and perceive themselves as increasingly secure—is what development is all about. "Development" involves much more here than altering the economic and social profiles of societies. Perceived results are more important than statistics.

A "booby trap" mine. Returning Kosovars in 1999 had to live in fear of being injured or killed by land mines as they worked in the fields and collected firewood for winter. (UN/UNHCR/R. Chalasani)

As we have discussed, human security also bridges the traditional divisions of international organizational agendas, where questions of "war and peace" have been strictly separated from "economic and social" ones. According to this new conceptualization, peace as the lack of direct violence is only one attribute of a secure environment, and international organizational action is the means of establishing this peace.

Further, the notion of human security focuses the attention of international organizations directly on individuals and their circumstances, thereby constituting a subtle challenge to state sovereignty. Making people psychologically secure may, under some circumstances, be the antithesis of making the governments of states and their territorial boundaries physically secure, especially when states themselves are the perpetrators of individual insecurities. Pressing international organizations into the service of individually focused human security could therefore constitute an incremental step toward circumventing or marginalizing states and legitimizing supranational governance.

Most important, conceptualizing the mission of IGOs as one of comprehensively promoting human security rather than separately promoting economic and social development, sustainable development, military security, or a variety of other goals frees the policy imagination to contemplate holistically the nature and variety of threats to individual environments. It further frees the policy imagination to consider how such threats may be removed and to wonder how international organizations might contribute to removing them. Because the sources of human insecurity vary from region to region, so, too, will the definition of human security and the missions of international organizations. It may be that in many, if not most, cases multilateral agencies are not very appropriate, efficient, or effective mechanisms for transferring material development assistance. They appear to be relatively better suited to promoting and enhancing human security via policies, programs, and activities that focus on nonmaterial resource transfers and exchanges, including training and the exchange of ideas and information. But such a shift of institutional focus requires rethinking the nature and meaning of sustainable human development.

Toward New Models of Sustainable Human Development

Creating the foundation for sustainable human development entails empowering individuals, groups, and communities to become engaged constructively and effectively in satisfying their own needs, values, and interests, thereby providing them with a genuine sense of control over their own futures. Simply stated:

> Human development is development *of* the people *for* the people *by* the people. Development *of* the people means investing in human capabilities, whether in education or health or skills, so that they can work productively and creatively. Development *for* the people means ensuring that the economic growth they generate is distributed widely and fairly. . . . [D]evelopment *by* the people [means] giving everyone a chance to participate.[11]

As the 1993 UNDP report argued, "People's participation is becoming the central issue of our time," and it is inextricably linked with and is an inherent component, if not a requisite, of both sustainable human development and larger notions of sustainable human security. Yet the concept of participation has proven to be woolly and the debate about its meaning, unfocused. In the World Bank, for example, popular participation has at various times and in various contexts been articulated as and associated with the "empowerment" of NGOs and the enhancement of their involvement in making bank policy; increased bank accountability and control of the bank's programs, projects, and activities by "domestic" actors; and the active engagement in project planning of previously excluded individuals and groups with an emphasis on the importance of local knowledge and the satisfaction of local needs. These aspects of participation are important, but this discourse has so far done little to change the course of the bank's policy so as to enhance its role in promoting human security or to construct new models of development focusing on the satisfaction of basic human needs and values. Debate has not even succeeded in integrating in any creative and constructive way various elements of society into the bank's work. Development models and institutional policies that fail to take adequate account of human needs may actually work to erode human security and inhibit sustainable human development.

Participation and empowerment were two of the priority themes stressed by the UN's central development arm, the UNDP, throughout the 1990s in its annual reviews on human development. The associated discourse gave shape and meaning to the concept of participation. The way to eradicate poverty, the UNDP reports argued, is to empower the poor and marginalized elements of society to provide for the satisfaction of their own basic needs and values. The UNDP "promotes the empowerment of people through measures to build their coping and adapting capacities, to increase their productivity and income, and to participate more fully in decision-making."[12]

The UNDP has adopted a multipronged strategy in its war on poverty. One cornerstone of that strategy is good governance. Well-functioning, effective, and accountable public and private institutions that are viewed as legitimate in the eyes of those being governed are required in order to mobilize the social capital required for sustaining development. Thus UNDP programs provide support for holding free and fair elections, respecting fundamental human rights and the rule of law, building strong and vibrant civil societies, enhancing local institutional capacity for supporting decentralized policymaking processes, and increasing the accountability and transparency of government institutions and operations.[13]

Creating sustainable livelihoods is another dimension of the agency's strategy. This entails supporting local cooperatives and micro-enterprises, providing assistance and extending credit to disadvantaged and previously marginalized groups in society, increasing employment opportunities for displaced persons and refugees, and making technology available and spawning local productive enterprises. An important element of this strategy is to redefine economic growth so as to link it to family income, not solely to national account statistics. Closely linked to this strategic dimension is a strong commitment to "gender mainstreaming"— that is, ensuring that men and women are accorded equal opportunities to develop their productive potentials and sustainable livelihoods: "UNDP works both 'upstream' to sensitize policy makers to gender issues and to create national capacity for gender analyses, and 'downstream' to extend women's access to education, training, credit and other assets."[14]

Although sustainable human development has remained a somewhat ambiguous concept in many respects, almost all definitions have at least one common element—concern for environmental regeneration and resource sustainability. The UNDP development strategy is no exception and focuses on helping governments design and implement development programs and projects that aim to protect the human environment and promote sustainable economic growth and the management of natural resources in a way that will benefit and preserve development choices for future generations. The agency's activities, for example, focus on the key role of food security in building human security, on improving aid and debt coordination and management, and the reform and modernization of financial institutions.

No matter what direction new models of development may take, it is clear that even the remotest areas of human settlement have been permeated by the forces of globalization and the capitalist global economy. If human development is to take place at all, it must occur in that context. In this regard, promoting sustainable development and human security requires new forms of cooperation and partnerships among states, markets, the private sector, voluntary and civic organizations, and local communities.

New Partnerships Among State, Markets, and Other Elements of Society

It is stimulating to consider what happens when conceptualizations of governance are delinked from worldviews based on the centrality of the state. Such conceptualizations elevate "politics" as a sphere of reality beyond the process of value allocation by authorities such as church and state. National governments, though important institutional mechanisms affecting patterns and processes of value allocation, are not the only or even the primary controllers of such processes for most of the world's peoples. The identification with state or nation is but one form of identity grouping that provides legitimacy for authoritative governance structures and processes. In many cases, religious identity, ethnic identity, identity with the workplace, and other forms of identity are at least as important, if not more important, in determining the authoritative allocation of values.

Conceiving of social order in this way, however, entails moving beyond state-based conceptions of world order. Promoting human security and sustainable human development for most of the world's peoples requires an adequate mapping of all relevant realms of social space so that creative partnerships may be formed among those diverse, often contradictory, and sometimes conflictual social forces and entities.

In this vein, a central component of Secretary-General Annan's "Quiet Revolution" has been to build and expand constructive UN partnerships with civil society and particularly the private sector. Underpinning this strategy is the belief that "people should guide both the state and the market, which need to work together in tandem, with people sufficiently empowered to exert a more effective influence over both."[15] An important task for the UN's development work is to help create the conditions that are necessary for such people-centered development.

Within the developing world this initiative to forge new partnerships has taken a variety of forms and complexions. In general there has been a move to strengthen the UNDP and other UN agencies' direct involvement with diverse elements of society, including NGOs, the private sector, and what are increasingly called civil society organizations (CSOs). Similar efforts have also been made in the Bretton Woods institutions. Although active engagement with NGOs has been widely recognized for some time, cooperation with private-sector entities at the country level has been less widely publicized. Of course, however, these excursions behind the veil of sovereignty are not without controversy.

Examples of specific private-sector support initiatives should give the reader a chance to reflect on the range of new activities under way. They include MicroStart, a $41-million initiative operating in twenty-five countries and designed to strengthen the capacity of microfinance institutions to provide credit to individuals to assist them in starting or expanding small businesses; the African Project Development Facility, providing entrepreneurs in twenty-nine African countries with investment funds; Money Matters: Private Finance for Development, assisting emerging market economies to mobilize and attract private finance for sustainable human development; the Africa 2000 Network, providing small grants up to $50,000 to villages so that they may engage in community-based sustainable human development activities; and the Sub-Regional South Asia Poverty Alleviation Programme, which has provided assistance to help train community organization leaders and organize villagers into community-based organizations in Bangladesh, India, Nepal, Maldives, and Sri Lanka.

Concerted action has also been taken since the mid-1990s to reform the way UN bodies relate to indigenous institutions as well as to each other at the country level. The UNDP field system has been revitalized, with the resident coordinator serving as the designated representative of the Secretary-General for development operations in the field as well as being the designated leader of the UN country team. The system has been further bolstered by instituting more rigorous selection criteria for resident coordinators, enhanced training, performance evaluations, and increased planning and reporting requirements. Again, much depends on the selection of personnel and the good faith of participants. However, the machinery is now in place.

The country-team notion has been strengthened by a move to establish "UN Houses," shared premises for all UN agencies, funds, and other bodies working at the country level. This action has been coupled by a move to provide common administrative services for those agencies. Beyond the obvious cost-cutting and efficiency-enhancing aspects of these moves, the goal is to create a more effective UN presence for building the necessary linkages and partnerships required for making sustainable human development a reality.

Building a more unified country approach has also been the objective of creating the UN Development Assistance Frameworks (UNDAFs) program. UNDAFs are basically collaborative planning, programming, and resource-coordinating frameworks designed to enhance the overall contribution by UN bodies to national development strategies and policies. They are to be prepared in close consultation with governments and in support of the Country Strategy Notes process. Once the pilot phase, involving systematic experiments in nineteen countries, has been evaluated, uniform UN-system-wide guidelines will be produced, and the system will be implemented and expanded.

Underlying all these initiatives is the assumption that good governance—at all levels—is required in order to achieve sustainable human development goals: "Poverty eradication and good governance are inseparable. Good governance brings about a proper balance among state action, the private sector, civil society, and the communities themselves."[16]

New Forms of Governance

Given the relationships among human security, human rights, and sustainable development and the UN's preeminent role in promoting human security, it is important to clarify exactly what we can expect of the world organization in relation to promoting development. The UN seems to have an important role in alleviating the plight of starving people, sick children, and others who cannot provide for themselves. In this regard, dispensing welfare via transfers of material resources would seem to be an important and relevant function and one that multilateral agencies are equipped to perform—even though material resource transfer is not a substitute for sustainable development and should not be considered such. As was emphasized earlier, the UN's main function in promoting sustainable development involves its role as a forum for exchanging ideas and its associated roles in setting standards and creating and promoting norms. The global debate among culturally diverse peoples on the clarification of values is an essential element of creating new models for sustainable human development that go beyond the sloganizing of the past.

It would seem that the most important element of this global debate over values revolves around the triangular nexus of global governance: democracy and participation, sustainable human development, and human security. None of these concepts should be seen as culturally or ideologically neutral. Nor are they value-free with regard to prioritizing the satisfaction of certain human needs and values or of particular social groups at the expense of others. Thus the role of the UN system in promoting goals related to these concepts is likely to be controversial. Privileged positions and ideologically narrow and culturally specific meanings will be strongly challenged by other preferred meanings and as strongly defended. Indeed, those who claim the "high moral ground" in these ideological debates might well in the end oppose any meaningful role by the United Nations in furthering individual human security, a cause that inherently challenges the shibboleth of state sovereignty.

Promoting human security requires new patterns of national and global governance. The UNDP is committed to doing just that. Accordingly, since 1995 it has identified good governance as one of the five key focus areas of its mission. Good governance projects currently comprise the single largest share—28 percent—of the agency's budget, and a new division has been instituted to focus on these issues. Under the program, priority has been placed on the following capacity-building objectives:

- democratization and political empowerment of the poor through participation and strengthening of civil society organizations;
- strengthening of judicial, electoral, and parliamentary systems;
- human rights and the rule of law, with special emphasis on women's legal rights;
- decentralization and strengthening of local governance;
- policies and frameworks for market-based economic transitions, private sector development, and globalization challenges;
- public administration reforms for accountable governance; and
- crisis management and rebuilding government capacities in postconflict situation, including for reconstruction and rehabilitation.

All of these objectives feed into a commitment to build stable, open, well-functioning, and accountable political institutions that are perceived as legitimate in the eyes of those being governed. "[W]e must learn from past mistakes," former UNDP administrator Gus Speth has argued, "and ensure that development cooperation supports the polity and not just the economy. . . . The challenges of growing poverty and widening inequity will not be met without democratization and good governance."[17]

This focus on promoting good governance represents a not so subtle challenge to the concept of sovereignty that underpins the interstate legal order and the UN system itself. Consider, for example, two newly launched projects in the Philippines. One project is aimed at strengthening the investigative skills of journalists to expose poor performance or unethical behavior of public officials. The other project established an electronic network—the "Good Governance Forum"—among policymakers, NGOs, private enterprises, and civil society organizations for the purpose of promoting policy dialogue on good governance.[18]

Two, and perhaps even one, decades ago such activities would have been deemed outrageous and totally unacceptable intrusions by most UN member states. In the global political climate of the late 1990s, however, that challenge did not seem as troubling. The forces of globalization and interdependence have eroded (from top down, bottom up, and outside in) much of the pretense associated with this legal notion, which as former Secretary-General Boutros-Ghali's quote indicated earlier was never as set in concrete as many international lawyers would argue. Indigenous social, cultural, political, and economic forces have brought complementary pressures from the other direction. The national state has been wedged in between, and in many cases the capacity of states to respond effectively to forces of change has been lacking.

As reflected above, the issues of people's participation and democratization have become central themes in the discourse and practice over development and governance. Neither of these issues is clear-cut or without its problems. Questions and challenges about representation and representativeness surround discussions. Whose voices, claims, and interests are to be heard and acted upon? How do UN agencies decide between and manage competing and conflicting claims? Also, how does one create democratic institutions in the absence of democratic culture? If decentralizing government is one of the best means of promoting participation and increasing local decisionmaking, how do you do so meaningfully in societies where resources, political power, and wealth are highly concentrated at the central government level? And how do UN agencies respond to and resolve issues related to basic contradictions between democratic values and liberal capitalist values and practices?

Of course, there are no straightforward answers to these questions. They represent thorny political issues with which the General Assembly and other multilateral institutional bodies must deal in the years to come. In fact, these issues are one of the primary challenges faced in organizing the Millennium Assembly in September 2000.

Good governance and creating new patterns of governance, of course, do not stop at the water's edge. Two other important dimensions of good governance have taken center stage at the UN. One deals with promoting effective governance within the UN itself and among international agencies. The other dimension focuses on the larger issue of global governance. In recent years, UN officials and member states have acted to deal with both.

At the heart of the Secretary-General's reform program lies the reorientation and reorganization of the UN's administration and management. As we have seen, in his effort to bring unity of purpose to the diverse activities of the world organization and provide clear lines of responsibility, he has created a cabinet structure, the Senior Management Group, comprising the various Under-Secretaries-General, the heads of UN funds and programs, and the Deputy-Secretary-General (a post created in 1998 and held by Louise Frechette, who among other things is responsible for overseeing the reform process and the coordination of development activities). In addition, there are four thematic executive committees (Peace and Security, Humanitarian Affairs, Economic and Social Affairs, and United Nations Development Group) that are charged with overseeing the coordination of policy development, management, and decisionmaking. The convenors of each of these committees sit on the Senior Management Group.

Two of these executive committees are of particular importance for development. The Economic and Social Affairs Executive Committee is convened by the Under-Secretary-General for economic and social affairs and comprises representatives from eighteen UN bodies, including the UNDP, UNCTAD, and other development assistance units. The United Nations Development Group Executive Committee is convened by the administrator of UNDP and includes the United Nations Fund for Population Activities (UNFPA), UNICEF, and WFP. This body also serves as the secretariat for the United Nations Development Group (UNDG), which was created in 1997 to provide better coordination among the numerous UN funds, programs, and other bodies that have proliferated over the years in the development area. Membership of the group includes the UNDP, UNFPA, UNICEF, WFP, UNIFEM, United Nations Office for Project Services (UNOPS), Joint United Nations Programme on HIV/AIDS (UNAIDS), United Nations Centre for Human Settlements (UNCHS), United Nations International Drug Control Programme (UNDCP), United Nations Department for Economic and Social Affairs (DESA), IFAD, UNHCHR, ECOSOC's five regional commissions (ECA, ECE, ESCWA, ESCAP, and ECLAC), and the Special representative of the Secretary-General for Children in Armed Conflict. In addition to its own operational activities, the UNDP administers several special-purpose funds and programs, including the UN Capital Development Fund (UNCDF), UNIFEM, United Nations Volunteers (UNV), and the Special Unit for Technical Cooperation Among Developing Countries (SU/TCDC). And in cooperation with the World Bank and UNEP, the UNDP serves as an implementing agency for GEF, which provides concessional funding and grants for certain environmentally sound development projects.

Beyond the UNDG, the UNDP works in conjunction with units in other thematic areas in a variety of ways. It assists the Department of Economic and Social Affairs to support the UN's standard-setting and normative work in developing countries and to provide integrated follow-up to the UN's global conferences of the 1990s. It works in the security realm to support elections, demobilization and reconciliation initiatives, and human rights, and to promote preventive development. Linkages in the humanitarian field include support for disaster prevention, mitigation, and preparedness; the reintegration into society of refugees, former combatants, and internally displaced people; the implementation of postdisaster national plans for reintegration, reconstruction, and recovery; and similar activities.[19]

Part of Kofi Annan's "Quiet Revolution" has endeavored to address a much more intractable issue: UN-system-wide coordination. Several steps have been taken in this regard in the development area. In an attempt to reinvigorate the ACC and make it more effective, an Assistant Secretary-General for policy coordination and interagency affairs has been appointed and mandated the responsibility of identifying ways to strengthen support for the ECOSOC and its coordinating role and to unify the work of the various autonomous UN-related agencies. For two consecutive years (April 1998 and April 1999), a joint high-level meeting was hosted in New York between ECOSOC and officials of the Bretton Woods institutions. At the behest of the General Assembly (A/Res/53/169) the 1999 meeting focused on the "functioning of international financial markets and stability in financing for development." The president of the World Bank, the managing director of the IMF, the UN Deputy-Secretary-General, the chairman of the IMF's Interim Committee, the chairman of the Development Committee of the World Bank, and finance ministers from the IMF/World Bank's biannual meetings of the Interim and Development Committees were among the participants. These meetings were noteworthy in that they represented a different spirit of cooperation between the UN and the Bretton Woods agencies that in the past has been lacking. As Michel Camdessus, managing director of the IMF, declared during the 1999 meeting, better integration of the UN and Bretton Woods institutions is needed to lay the foundation for a more stable global economic order.[20]

That same spirit of cooperation was demonstrated in August 1998 when the UN Secretary-General and the World Bank President, James Wolfensohn, held a retreat. Also, the UNDP and the World Bank have initiated a pilot program at the country level to explore the interface between UNDAF and the World Bank's Country Assistance Strategy. This spirit of cooperation may strengthen even further in the future as the newly appointed UNDP administrator, Mark Malloch Brown, settles into the job. Before assuming this role in 1999, he had served since 1996 as vice president for external affairs and vice president for UN affairs at the World Bank.

These initiatives came at a time when finance flows—both public and private—to developing countries had significantly declined. Official overseas development assistance (ODA) reached an all-time low (0.22 percent of GDP) in 1997 as the world continued to reel from the effects of a global economic crisis. But the "ODA crunch" began long before the global financial crisis of the late 1990s. ODA and other kinds of development assistance have declined significantly since the early 1990s, with bilateral assistance flows accounting for most of that decline. In contrast to previous dramatic expansion, private finance flows also fell as international bank lending dropped dramatically.[21] Creating stability for development financing is of particular concern for the least-developed countries (LDCs), which rely heavily on ODA as the main source of their external resource flows and which are extremely vulnerable to such shifts.

A final dimension of good governance relates to the global political economy as a whole. In the wake of the Asian financial and global economic crises questions are being raised about the wisdom of "letting the market rule." This was precisely the question that Secretary-General Annan was asking when he called on the Group of 8 (the G-7 plus the Russian Federation) "to adopt policies favouring more balanced patterns and higher levels of output growth, to consider additional steps to protect the international financial system against instability, to take quick action to reduce the debt of the poorest countries and to increase development aid." He challenged this group of influential member states to take the lead in creating a new financial architecture for the global economy, for which the UN would provide the "soft infrastructure."[22] Global governance requires new forms of international cooperation, and in the development field, experiments with cooperation are under way.

New Forms of International Cooperation

The UN has been actively engaged in building partnerships with other international organizations, local governments, NGOs, the private sector, and civil society. Each of the private-sector support initiatives discussed above involves transnational partnerships linked to local sustainable human development projects. UNDP's Money Matters: Private Finance for Development initiative, for example, has six global corporate cosponsors, including Fidelity Investments, Banque Nationale de Paris, and State Street Bank. Similarly, international banks have been instrumental in supporting the agency's MicroStart program. Along with other UN agencies, the UNDP has initiated a partnership—World Alliance of Cities Against Poverty—with civil society, the private sector, and local governments to carry out the goal of the 1995 "Social Summit."

With ODA on the downswing, the UNDP and other UN agencies have stepped up their efforts to find alternative sources of development transfers to LDCs. The "Partners for Development Summit," hosted by UNCTAD in Lyon, France, in November 1998, is illustrative of the kinds of innovative approaches being taken. The summit brought together representatives of governments, the private sector, NGOs, civil society, and international organizations and treated them as equals. It was organized around two tracks, one focusing on "global electronic trade UN partnerships" and the other on "profit and development." In order to broaden the spectrum of the forum, several other events were held in parallel: the annual meeting of the World Association of Investment Promotion Agencies, the fifth World Trade Point Meeting, and the sixth World Summit of Young Entrepreneurs. In essence, the summit represented an attempt to put theoretical ideas about building partnerships to "the test of a real-life meeting in which Governments and non-governmental actors would be given equal treatment."[23]

A slightly different approach has been taken by the UNDP. In March 1999, for example, UNDP officials announced that sixteen major global corporations, headquartered in eight different countries, had joined discussions aimed at establishing a Global Sustainable Development Facility (GSDF). Each of the sixteen companies had contributed $50,000 to cover the initiation phase of the project, which is designed to integrate the UN's goal of promoting UNDP.[24] The UNDP and UNCTAD, for another example, have launched a $4-million program on Globalization, Liberalization, and Sustainable Development, which brings together experts from the international organizations, the private sector, civil society, and academia to explore ways and develop a strategy to help developing countries better manage their integration into the world economy.[25]

These attempts have not generated significant resources, but they have created new forms of international cooperation. At the same time, they have not been without their critics. Many governments, for example, still cling tenaciously to the tenets of sovereignty and resent actions by multilateral agencies that do not respect the sanctity of that legal norm. Various NGOs and civil society groups also have expressed concern about UN agencies becoming too closely involved with the private sector, especially large global corporate enterprises and international banks. The response from UN agencies has been clear. In order to promote sustainable human development effectively, they need to find new mechanisms to generate the needed resources.

In responding to criticism by NGOs about UNDP's private-sector initiative, the agency's administrator put it this way:

> We are exploring with banks ways in which they might make resources available to microfinancing initiatives—initiatives which have proven not only to contribute to poverty eradication but are also financially viable investments. . . . We are convinced that the innovation, technology and resources that corporations are known for can have a positive impact on SHD [sustainable human development], and this is what we are exploring. If we can help bring new processes, products, technologies and partnerships to the poor, we will have contributed something important. The reality is that developing countries are increasingly seeking out investments by the transnational corporations. Similarly, these companies are continuously searching for new production bases and new markets. The question, therefore, is not whether global corporations will increase their investments in developing countries, but how can we, as the United Nations Development Programme and others committed to sustainable human development, seek to ensure that at least some of these investments occur in ways that are pro-poor, pro-environment, pro-jobs, and pro-women?[26]

In conclusion, what these examples illustrate most clearly is that by refocusing and reconceptualizing the UN's overall mission as being one of comprehensively promoting human security and sustainable human development—rather than separately promoting peace and security, economic and social well-being, development, human rights, and other goals—the policy imagination within the world organization has been freed to innovate. The new forms of international cooperation help the UN circumvent on occasion the constraints of sovereignty and get more directly to the mandated tasks.

However, at the same time, we must be realistic about what can be expected from the United Nations. It is time to reconsider the proposition that tinkering, tailoring, and taking a surgical tuck here and there in an attempt to "reform" the UN will, in some meaningful way, enhance the world organization's effectiveness in the operational development sphere. This is not to say that administrative, budgetary, programmatic, and structural reforms are not needed or important. What we are suggesting is that it is naive to assume, no matter how extensive and successful reform efforts might be, that they will transform the UN into an effective development organization. Moreover, the UN's role in the development arena is not likely to be improved significantly by enacting any of the reforms that are on the table—for example, an Economic Security Council and a streamlined ECOSOC. The coordination of development assistance should take place at the lowest, not the highest, organizational level. The UN system is decentralized and likely to remain so in spite of proposals by Erskine Childers and Brian Urquhart to return to a more centralized version.[27] A "shopping-mall" model—stressing competition among suppliers and cooperation driven by functional need, or "coordination without hierarchy"—might be far more appropriate for engendering effective cooperation toward the promotion of human security.

Notes

1. Oran Young, "The Politics of International Regime Formation: Managing Natural Resources and the Environment," *International Organization* 43, no. 3 (Summer 1989), pp. 349–375.

2. See Tony German and Judith Randel, eds., *The Reality of Aid 1999–2000* (London: Earthscan, 1999).

3. UNDP, *Human Development Report 1998.*

4. United Nations, *World Economic Situation and Prospects for 1999*, New York, 1999.

5. World Bank, *Global Development Report 1999* (New York: Oxford Univ. Press, 1999).

6. UNDP, *Human Development Report 1993*, p. 5.

7. Craig Murphy, "Global Institutions and the Pursuit of Human Needs," in Roger A. Coate and Jerel A. Rosati, eds., *The Power of Human Needs in World Society* (Boulder: Lynne Rienner, 1988), p. 217.

8. Ken Conca, "Greening the UN: Environmental Organizations and the UN System," in Thomas G. Weiss and Leon Gordenker, eds., *NGOs, the UN, and Global Governance* (Boulder: Lynne Rienner, 1996), pp. 114–115.

9. UNDP, *Human Development Report 1993* (New York: Oxford Univ. Press, 1993), p. 2.

10. Ibid.

11. UNDP, *Human Development Report 1993.*

12. UNDP, *UNDP Today: Reform in Action,* 1999.

13. Ibid.

14. Ibid.

15. UNDP, *Human Development Report 1993*, p. 4.

16. UNDP, *UNDP Today: Fighting Poverty,* 1999.

17. "Non-Benign Neglect: America and the Developing World in the Era of Globalization," National Press Club, Washington, D.C., October 14, 1998.

18. UNDP, *UNDP Flash,* April 12, 1999.

19. UNDP, *UNDP Today: Introducing the Organization,* 1999.

20. Press Release ECOSOC/5818, April 29, 1999.

21. UN, *Development Update,* no. 27, March 1999.

22. Press Release PI/1142, May 26, 1999.

23. UNCTAD, TD/B/EX(20)/2, January 27, 1999.

24. Press Release, March 12, 1999.

25. UNDP Press Release, February 2, 1999.

26. UNDP Press Release, March 17, 1999.

27. Erskine Childers with Brian Urquhart, *Renewing the United Nations System* (Uppsala, Sweden: Dag Hammarskjöld Foundation, 1994).

Conclusion

Learning from Change

In a time when winds of change are blowing very strong, we must rest content with knowing that foresight is always imperfect and that choices must always be made in ignorance of their full consequences. That is the price we pay for being able to make the world over by changing our own behavior, individually and collectively, in response to cherished hopes and shared purposes, framed in words. Our capacity to err is our capacity to learn and thereby achieve partial and imperfect, but real, improvement in the conditions of human life.
—William H. McNeill, "Winds of Change," *Foreign Affairs* 69, no. 4 (May-June 1995)

From the outset of this book, we have portrayed the United Nations and the broader system of UN-related autonomous organizations as highly interdependent with their political context. We have shown the dynamic interplay of interstate politics as the primary force determining the evolution of the UN system. Conversely, as the blinders of Cold War worldviews are being removed, it is becoming clearer that global organizations have had some influence in determining the course of world politics—especially when viewed from a longer-run perspective. In this context, we need to remind ourselves that for the first time in recorded history, the empires of both victors and losers have been dismantled. Of course, for the United Nations to become the centerpiece of global governance, as envisioned by some of its proponents, states would need to transfer loyalty, power, and authority to the world body so that it could influence its surroundings rather than the reverse. But such a radical change is still distant. Yet world politics continue to evolve and change, and there is a pressing need to manage transnational problems.[1]

It would help us analyze the United Nations and chart its future if we had a sure grasp of the nature of world politics after the Cold War. In William McNeill's words, it would certainly be nice to know in which direction the winds of change are blowing. Alas, this is not easy. The initial euphoria about the end of the Cold War and optimism about possibilities for democratization have given way to a more realistic, and perhaps normal, caution. The winds seem to be swirling in no discernible direction. As we have portrayed in the previous chapters, UN security operations increased rapidly beginning in 1988, then declined, then underwent renewed attention. The notion of security has been broadened incrementally and inconsistently to encompass the idea of human security—a still evolving concept. The requirements for global action in the humanitarian affairs and human rights arenas have been expanding, yet the world organization's capacity to respond has not kept pace with demands; budgetary shortfalls hinder effective responses. Moreover, some challenges to the predominance of liberal democracy seem to be gaining strength. On the human development front, the world is becoming ever more polarized between the rich and poor with the poorest losing absolute as well as relative ground.

James Rosenau tells us that world politics is characterized by "turbulence" in which basic patterns are not clear.[2] In this view, world politics can be conceptualized as having "macro" and "micro" dimensions, with "macro" covering the world of states and IGOs and "micro" covering the world of individuals, local communities, and other elements of civil society. Both are in such turmoil at the beginning of the twenty-first century that one can only project alternative scenarios for the future, not specifically describe the likely structure or basic features of world politics.

Our readers may have noted also that during the world organization's first half-century the density of the microportion of UN politics, covering individuals and NGOs, was quite different in the three parts of the book. In the security arena, where states historically have presumably had a monopoly on force—except over insurgents and terrorists—considerably fewer nongovernmental organizations have dealt with large-scale force than with human rights or sustainable development. In the human rights and sustainable development arenas, NGOs are active in analysis, lobbying, and operations to such a degree that students may be blinded by the number of acronyms that appear in this text. Yet in today's turbulent world political climate and the increasingly nonstate character of threats to global peace, there are mounting pressures to think in terms of human security—as opposed to state security—and a need to integrate elements and dimensions of civil society into the security sphere.

Some scholars attempt to deal with such turbulence by focusing on the importance of competing forces in shaping world politics and international organization. Some frame their analyses in terms of simultaneous forces of integration and disintegration. For example, West European states formed the European Community (now European Union), which transcends the territorial state in some ways, creating a supranational authority for some issues. In some of these very same states, political movements—such as the Basque movement in Spain—are seeking smaller political-legal units. For an example of competing forces within a single country, some circles of opinion in the United States want more multilateral diplomacy; others insist that the United States should withdraw from most IGOs and pursue a unilateral foreign policy that is driven strictly by narrow American interests and that is unaffected by the interests of the international community. In yet another contrast, the United States, Canada, and Mexico negotiate a free trade agreement (the North American Free Trade Agreement, or NAFTA) directed at the larger collective good while former federal Yugoslavia disintegrates into a bloody conflict of smaller nationalisms. Competing centripetal and centrifugal forces are integral to the clash between globalism and localism highlighted in the preceding pages and will remain so in the foreseeable future.

World politics after the Cold War seems to be at a watershed. The United Nations is caught in a political transition. The old patterns of interaction have broken down or changed significantly, but new patterns have not yet crystallized. Many old norms are under challenge, but new ones have not yet emerged. Old ways of doing things may prove insufficient for new problems, yet new ways may be characterized by mistakes. States may be dissatisfied with the record of the old United Nations, but they may not yet have reached the point of providing the political will and material resources necessary for a new UN to manage world politics after the Cold War.

Even in more stable times, it is not easy to agree on the principal lessons to be learned from history. History has been as much misused as well used in guiding foreign policy.[3] Many U.S. policymakers misused the "lesson of Munich" in fashioning policy for Southeast Asia in the 1960s and 1970s. Believing that in 1938 the Western states whetted the aggressive appetite of Hitler by appeasing him through the "giveaway" of Czechoslovakia in negotiations at Munich, these policymakers were determined not to "give away" South Vietnam to the communists. This, it was thought, would only whet the aggressive appetite of other communist leaders in Hanoi, Beijing, and Moscow. Yet the eventual creation of a communist Vietnam in 1975 did not lead to falling dominoes throughout Asia and the world. Indeed, by the 1990s communism itself was retreating virtually everywhere. Even governments that called themselves "communist," as in China and Vietnam, used increasingly capitalist policies in their pursuit of economic growth. The United States lost some 55,000 of its own military personnel in Southeast Asia and killed a much larger number of Asians by using a myth as a guide. The intentions may have been noble to the extent that U.S. policymakers believed that they were fighting for freedom, but the results were disastrous for almost everyone involved.

One can try to be careful and systematic in wrestling with the lessons of history.[4] One can try to separate what is known from what is unknown or just presumed. In using historical analogies, one can try to be precise about the similarities to, or differences from, a current situation. One can delve into the details of history, clarify current options, guard against presumptions, avoid stereotypes. But in the final analysis, there is much room for debate about the pertinence of particular historical lessons.

Nevertheless, when many policymakers look at a contemporary problem, they draw on historical evidence. The ones who do not even try are justly criticized for this deficiency. In the 1990s the UN secretariat was fairly criticized for not having a policy-planning group able to draw historical lessons from past use of UN force. Certain state bureaucracies, and many academics, were prepared to evaluate UN peacekeeping against the historical background of what had gone wrong with ONUC in the Belgian Congo in 1960 to 1964, or what had gone right in Central America regarding ONUSAL and ONUCA.

The next time there is a UN enforcement action inside a country, whether to deliver humanitarian relief or to disarm fighting parties, it will be only natural to try to draw historical lessons from events in northern Iraq, Somalia, Bosnia, Rwanda, Haiti, or Kosovo in the 1990s. The next time the UN Security Council authorizes the use of force in response to aggression, many policymakers will draw comparisons with the historical lessons from events of 1990–1991 in Iraq and Kuwait. The fact that there was a decline in UN peacekeeping operations during the mid-1990s does not lessen the need for organizational learning. Experience in Kosovo and Timor in the last year of the twentieth century indicated that there would be cases in which peacekeeping and enforcement actions would be deemed necessary in the twenty-first century—in the Democratic Republic of the Congo, for example.

One factor that complicates the task of learning is the pace of change in the 1990s; the other is the culture of the UN bureaucracy. An examination of UN military operations is illustrative of a more general problem of learning within the world organization. We noted at the outset of this book the dramatic acceleration in the number and variety of UN military missions—the Security Council approved over twice as many operations from 1989 to 1996 as during the previous forty years. There also has been a proliferation of analyses about multilateral military operations from a variety of perspectives since 1990, mostly in journals rather than books.[5]

A new field meant opportunities for scholars and other interested parties to capture what amounted to an open market for the publication of ideas, analyses, and reflections. Generous government and philanthropic funding provided an additional incentive to quickly establish oneself as an "expert" or perhaps to be "recycled." The increasing demand for analyses of peace operations partially explains the recent supply in the literature. This is not a judgment about the quality of analyses; it is simply an explanation of the quantity produced in a relatively short time.

It has become increasingly arduous for newcomers to discern publications that are grounded equally in logic and hard data and that provide the necessary description, analysis, and assessment to understand past and present peace operations and their potential future role in international conflict management. The literature overflows with claims to knowledge about the nature of changing world politics, theories and recommendations for institutional reform and conflict resolution, and firsthand accounts from the field. The volume and accelerated pace of literature produced have equaled the volume and pace of peace operations in general. As one outspoken UN official wrote, we "too often find ourselves steering a rattling vehicle that is moving at breakneck speed, without an up-to-date roadmap, while trying to fix the engine at the same time."[6]

We are now at the point in the evolution of the literature to take stock of the insights gained by the community of writers, institutions, policymakers, and practitioners as well as to determine what lessons have been learned—keeping in mind, however, a clear distinction between the two activities of gaining insights and actually deriving lessons.[7] If lessons have been learned in policymaking and planning, those who profess such knowledge should address directly who has learned the lessons and which procedural and institutional changes actually have been implemented. Otherwise, one is vaguely speaking only of insights into patterns of behavior that either support or undermine the effectiveness of multilateral security efforts. "The art of learning from experience begins with understanding linkages and the conditions under which events took place" and requires the institutional integrity to expose rather than paper over mistakes.[8]

Learning lessons is different from adapting, because adapting is more reactive and less comprehensive and is represented by incremental and often ambiguous institutional change. As two of the foremost analysts of institutional learning, Peter and Ernst Haas, have written, "Organizations characterized by irreconcilable disagreements over desirable world orders or ineptitude may not even be made capable of learning to manage interdependence rather than merely adapting to it."[9]

The United Nations still has to make a substantial effort to digest the lessons from the recent past in order to formulate a workable strategy for future military operations. The mere establishment of the Lessons-Learned Unit in the Department of Peace-keeping Operations (DPKO), along with similarly labeled units in the Department of Political Affairs (DPA) and Office for the Coordination of Humanitarian Affairs (OCHA), is not necessarily evidence of progress. These units were established in the 1990s but are largely bureaucratic responses by both of the "two United Nations"—the first, where governments meet and make decisions, and the second, comprising the various secretariats, officials, and soldiers who implement these decisions.

The social realities drawn from historical lessons affect not only the policy options considered but also the nature of the information collected and how that information is used. An important element of policymaking in international organizations is establishing mechanisms to build a consensus that transcends secretariat, delegate, body, and member-state boundaries. What is needed is a more-or-less homogeneous worldview on the issue in question.

In drawing historical lessons, it is important to consider closely three fundamental political tasks that are characteristic of policymaking and problem solving: articulating interests and consolidating interest groups, making rules, and applying those rules.[10] We conclude this analysis of the first fifty years of the United Nations with our evaluation of what has been learned along these lines. We chart change at the UN before and after the Cold War, and we suggest what these changes portend for the immediate future.

Articulation of Interests and Aggregation of Interest Groups

It is important, albeit elementary, that governments of states have learned that they need the United Nations. After the Cold War many new states wanted to join the UN; none of the old members wanted to get out. Since 1945 only one state, Indonesia, has withdrawn even temporarily from the world organization, and its quixotic attempt to create a rival organization soon collapsed. The delegation from South Africa was barred for a time from participating in the General Assembly, but the state was still a member of the organization. All states recognize that they need the UN to build diplomatic coalitions, make rules, and monitor adherence to and enforce those rules. The cliché happens to be true: If the UN did not exist, it would have to be invented. This is true in Washington as elsewhere—notwithstanding rambling from Senator Jesse Helms and the Heritage Foundation.

In our preface and introduction we noted the importance of how states defined their *raisons d'état,* and how these definitions affect the UN's evolution. We noted the crucial nature of short-term and narrow interests. As a general rule, "the United Nations is successful over the long haul only if it helps to uncover or develop genuinely shared interests."[11] A dominant state or coalition can control policy for a time, but the United Nations is likely to be more effective if it is used in pursuit of widely shared interests.

After the Cold War, the United States was the most important state in the UN. It was the only state capable of projecting military power everywhere in the world, it had the world's largest economy, and at least since 1941 it had periodically played a leadership role in world politics. In fact, the United States had always been the UN's most important member state. The UN had never undertaken the use of force, for either peacekeeping or enforcement, without genuine U.S. support. The UN had attempted human rights and economic programs in opposition to U.S. policy, but these programs had not achieved much. The rejection of SUNFED is a good example of the futility of attempting a major program without Washington's support. One should also recall the fate of demands for the NIEO, which floundered largely because of adamant U.S. opposition.

To be sure, many UN members were not altogether happy with U.S. domination of the UN in the early 1990s. At one point the General Assembly passed a resolution criticizing the United States for continuing its economic pressures against Cuba. This was a viable manifestation in UN proceedings of resentment against U.S. power. The lack of support from Washington for the Convention on the Rights of the Child, the treaty to ban land mines, and the International Criminal Court was a mixture of diplomacy and distaste.[12] Yet for the most part states restricted their criticisms of the United States to private conversations. They recognized the problems inherent in offending the remaining superpower. And beyond the political fact of widespread deference to Washington's hegemonic position, there were indeed a number of issues at the UN on which there was genuine shared interest among UN members. Most states were opposed to Iraqi aggression. Most states were appalled at human suffering in Somalia. Most states were in favor of at least diplomatic support for human rights. Most states recognized the need to promote sustainable development.

In this regard, however, we must keep a close eye on the shifting winds of change. The UNDP *Human Development Report 1996* argued that if the past quarter century of economic growth rates is any indication of things to come, the next century may be an Asian one, not an American- or Euro-centered one: "The more than 7% average annual per capita income growth rate of East Asia in the 1970s and 1980s is the most sustained and widespread development miracle of the twentieth century, perhaps all history."[13] Then came the Asian financial and economic crisis of the late 1990s. In that context there was much rhetoric about the wonders of the American sustained economic growth during the Clinton administration. Talk about the East Asian or Indonesian or Japanese model of sustainable development gave way to a renewed emphasis on the American model.

To prepare ourselves for dealing with the future, whatever it may hold in store, we need to have a firm grasp on the past. Let us, then, examine our three main themes—security, human rights, and sustainable human development—with respect to what has been learned about the articulation of interests and the aggregation of interest groups.

Security Interests

In the 1990s the United States was a primary player in the UN campaign to repel Iraqi aggression against Kuwait, to pressure Iraq to comply with various UN resolutions after Desert Storm, to deliver humanitarian relief in Somalia, and to make other UN security operations succeed. In a continuation of past patterns, no UN security operation was undertaken against the wishes of Washington. When the UN was less than fully effective in some security matters, as early on in Bosnia or Haiti, it was largely a reflection of the unwillingness of the United States to engage fully. The United States, standing alone, was able to block a second term for Boutros Boutros-Ghali as Secretary-General.

This is not to say that other states were unimportant after the Cold War in UN security affairs. Japan played a very large role in UNTAC's efforts to stabilize and democratize Cambodia. The British and French deployed relatively large numbers of peacekeeping troops in the Balkans. Canada and Norway and some other states continued to be stalwart supporters of UN peacekeeping. The French mounted an operation in Rwanda, the Russians in Georgia, and the Nigerians in Liberia. And indeed, it should be recalled that all the permanent members of the Security Council have to at least avoid using the veto for UN decisions in peace and security matters to be made. Apart from Security Council members, numerous states have supported UN peace and security efforts. For example, Costa Rica and other Spanish-speaking states played important roles in supporting mediation by the UN Secretary-General in Central America.

Nevertheless, both the Bush and Clinton administrations were and have been far more supportive of the United Nations in the security domain than the Reagan administration was, and the results are obvious. The UN was able to be involved in places like the Persian Gulf and the Horn of Africa primarily because the United States wanted at least the UN's collective approval, and sometimes the UN's more direct help, in managing security. The one remaining superpower learned that the UN could be useful in addressing a variety of security issues.

Despite U.S. unilateral use of force in places such as Grenada and Panama and its almost total exclusion of the UN from the negotiations leading to the Dayton peace accords for the former Yugoslavia, the dominant trend among all states, including the United States, is to involve the UN in managing military security problems. Even in finessing the Security Council for the actual bombing in Kosovo, the United Nations was the scene of much debate preceding the actual bombing and in the postwar politics. There is a desire to share responsibility and costs, especially where so-called national vital interests are not obvious. As explained in Part 1, one of the reasons for relying on the UN for the collective management of security issues is that most other collective options, aside from NATO, offer so little prospect of success; at a minimum, the world organization is required to be associated with security efforts to make subcontracted states and coalitions of the willing more accountable for actions undertaken in the name of the larger community of states. For instance, when Nigeria became bogged down in trying to pacify Liberia and Sierra Leone through the use of ECOWAS, this had the effect of increasing, not lessening, demands that the UN become more involved, which in fact actually transpired.

Overall, both great and small powers have sought to confer on the UN an enhanced security role after the Cold War. The articulation of interests and aggregation of interest groups have varied from issue to issue. And states have not always provided sufficient political and material support to enable UN forces and representatives to succeed. Nevertheless, most states seem to have learned that major problems can be entailed in pursuing unilateral action. Apart from direct threats to a state's existence, multilateral security diplomacy has been the preferable option. For example, no state wanted to intervene unilaterally in what was then eastern Zaire in 1996 to guarantee refugee security; Canada was willing to lead a multilateral effort via the UN but was slower than the rebels, who took matters into their own hands and liberated Hutus held hostage in camps.

Human Rights Interests

As explained elsewhere, the United States has been much less of a dominant or hegemonic leader in human rights than in security and economic affairs.[14] The articulation of human rights interests and the aggregation of human rights interest groups, principally through the UN Human Rights Commission, has come about less because of the United States and more because of a series of compromises among a large number of states. Nevertheless, at the 1993 Vienna World

Conference on Human Rights, U.S. delegates played the leading role in pushing for reaffirmation of universal human rights. At one point they circulated an informal list of the states that were dragging their diplomatic feet. And when it came to the matter of delivering humanitarian assistance in situations of armed conflict, the UN took the most decisive steps in northern Iraq and Somalia, precisely where the United States displayed the most energy.

Whatever the U.S. role, just as most states sought to involve the UN in the management of security issues, so most states sought to use the United Nations to promote human rights through international standards and to give at least some attention to their implementation by diplomacy. Particularly after the Cold War, human rights were vigorously articulated by many democratic governments that had succeeded authoritarian ones—whether communist or otherwise. The Czech Republic and Uruguay are just two examples of governments that sought extensive UN action on human rights as a result of their own previous and traumatic experience with the denial of most internationally recognized rights.

Certainly there were states—for example, China, Iraq, Syria, Vietnam, and Malaysia—that resisted this dominant trend. Others, such as Saudi Arabia, Algeria, and various states throughout the Middle East, also opposed UN action on human rights, but they found it politically prudent to keep a low profile.

But it remains true that most governmental officials have articulated either a moral or an expediential interest in internationally recognized human rights. They have learned that the advancement of such rights is conducive to human dignity or that such rights have politically desirable consequences—for example, international peace, domestic tranquillity, and uninterrupted foreign assistance. There has been little alternative for states but to use the United Nations for the articulation and aggregation of universal human rights interests. One can in theory develop universal human rights standards outside the UN. International humanitarian law was developed in this way for human rights in armed conflicts, but this is the major exception that proves the general rule that international society needs the United Nations for the articulation and aggregation of global human rights rules. The UN has been the scene of debates about the wisdom of various types of international criminal courts.

Sustainable Development

The UN system, broadly defined, has been used for the articulation and aggregation of interests related to economic growth and environmental protection. But especially regarding economic growth, many of the actual resources made available to developing countries have been provided through channels outside the United Nations. The World Bank, the International Monetary Fund, bilateral transfers, and private foreign investment have accounted for far more resources than has the UN Development Programme or the nonfinancial specialized agencies put together.

The UN network has been used mostly by developing countries to articulate, as an aggregate, their view of what should be done. Some of their demands, such as for SUNFED and the NIEO, have not led to "planetary bargains" between North and South, but some compromises have been struck through the United Nations. Perhaps an even more important outcome has been the rising debate over worldviews that challenge Northern liberal economic explanations of the international political economy. Although Northern liberal perspectives have predominated in the long run, the political debate resulting from challenges to Northern worldviews has served the important function of grouping interests. At a minimum, the debate in global forums like the General Assembly has raised interest aggregation to a level above caucusing and other ways of consolidating interest groups.

Concerning ecology, states have used the United Nations to articulate how environmental protection should be combined with economic growth. This was most evident at the 1992 UN conference in Rio, where the lengthy Agenda 21 was hammered out and articulated as a policy guideline for the twenty-first century and where treaties on biodiversity and rain forests were negotiated. The processes of negotiation represent important steps in interest-group aggregation and articulation in the ecodevelopment arena. Therefore Agenda 21 and various conventions and declarations that emerged from the Rio process are perhaps best seen as snapshots of an evolving political process, not as static political outcomes. The Commission on Sustainable Development, like the UNEP itself twenty years earlier, was the result of a compromise among states about what the United Nations could do to interject environmental protection into efforts to produce economic growth.

The United Nations has not exercised a monopoly over efforts to articulate interests related to sustainable development. All developed countries, and many developing ones as well, have their individual programs for environmental protection. Regional organizations such as the European Union also have environmental programs that, when added to efforts to ensure economic growth, produce a combined policy on sustainable development. But as with security and human rights issues, the UN has been used by various actors to articulate a vision of how economic growth can be combined with protection of the environment.

Rule Making

Every society requires a collective procedure to establish rules that differentiate permissible from impermissible behavior. The United Nations plays a central role in this essential rule making for international society—largely through the Security Council, General Assembly, and associated world conferences—but other mechanisms in international society also create rules. Some treaties are made outside the UN system, and some regional organizations make rules. The murky institution of customary international law, which is greatly affected by the behavior of powerful states, also plays a role. But in the final analysis, the UN has a major role in rule making for world politics regarding all three of our issues, to which we now turn in an attempt to appreciate what has been learned about rule making in the past five decades.

Security Rules

Many security rules for world politics have been vague. Neither the International Court of Justice nor the Security Council has specified the distinction between a breach of the peace and outright aggression. Moreover, the term "intervention" has never been authoritatively specified; despite a 1974 General Assembly attempt to define aggression, many ambiguities remain. Moreover, are reprisals legal in peacetime given that the Charter has outlawed the threat or use of force in the absence of an armed attack? Can force be used to implement legal rights? Can a regional organization employ force without prior authorization from the Security Council? These and other questions about security rules have gone unanswered.

Since the end of the Cold War, the Security Council in particular has made a number of decisions that clarify at least some questions about security rule making. The council is sharpening security rules far more than the World Court is. The Court does not normally get the opportunity to pronounce on legal issues related to armed conflict. Most states have regarded security rules as too important to be turned over to fifteen jurists. Therefore, they have not given consent to the Court to rule on these matters. The case of *Nicaragua vs. the United States* (1986) is an exception that proves the general rule (and the wisdom of that judgment was extensively debated). If international security law is to be clarified, it is primarily the Security Council that will do it.

The Security Council in the 1990s gave a very broad interpretation to the scope of Chapter VII of the Charter pertaining to enforcement action in response to threats to and breaches of the peace and acts of aggression. It has said that peace and security issues may arise from human-rights, economic, and ecological situations, not just from the use of force across borders by states. It has even said that humanitarian conditions within a state, even those that do not seem to generate external material effects, may constitute a threat to international peace and security and merit an enforcement action under Chapter VII of the Charter. More recently, it has decided to authorize such action to restore an elected government overthrown by military force. Along the way, the Security Council has specified that individuals in zones of armed conflict have a right to humanitarian assistance, and that to interfere with that right is a war crime for which there can be individual prosecution. The council has also authorized member states to seize the property of a state (Iraq) in order to assist in the implementation of binding sanctions. Under Chapter VII the council has created a war-crimes tribunal for the former Yugoslavia and for Rwanda. These are just a few of the decisions about security rules made by the council under Chapter VII.

If this trend, which is based on agreement among the permanent members, tinues, international security rules will be expanded as well as specified. This e a remarkable and important change, especially given the conventional wis-at much international security law is likely to remain vague because the competing claims of states are rarely authoritatively reviewed by the Security Council or the World Court. In the 1990s the council was clearly doing what it had not been able to do since June 1950, namely, distinguish aggression from self-defense and make use of Chapter VII to organize a legally binding response to threats to and breaches of the peace.

Human Rights Rules

The UN has been codifying rules on internationally recognized human rights since 1948, when the General Assembly adopted the Universal Declaration of Human Rights and also approved the treaty on genocide. Since then, there has been sufficient formal or informal consensus (reflecting an aggregation of interests) to produce numerous treaties, declarations, and resolutions.

Several new developments have happened within the United Nations regarding human rights rules since the end of the Cold War. The Security Council has merged human rights and security rules to a great extent, making decisions under Chapter VII pertaining to peace and security that involved such fundamental rights as the one to adequate nutrition (for example, in Somalia) and freedom from repression (for example, in Iraq). In fact, Stanley Hoffmann has described "international peace and security" as an "all-purpose parachute" (remarks made at a symposium on collective responses to common threats, Oslo, Norway, June 22–23, 1993). In Haiti, the council voted a binding and comprehensive economic embargo on the country during summer 1993 after military elements deposed an elected civilian president. Moreover, the UN Human Rights Commission expanded its rule making even beyond the several dozen treaties and declarations already adopted. The commission took on the complex subjects of the rights of minorities and indigenous peoples.

The 1993 Vienna conference made clear that there was tremendous NGO pressure on all states to continue with UN rule making on human rights. At Vienna there was especially strong demand for further attention to rules on women's rights. Even states not genuinely committed to personal rights found it difficult to withstand combined NGO and state pressure in support of expanded UN rule making. The political situation was such that it was easier for these dissenting states to formally accept rules that they did not really support than to stand up and try to oppose them directly. The Vienna process also indicated clearly that established principles of human rights might not be as universally accepted as many UN and human rights observers had previously thought. The debates in Vienna brought out significant challenges to what in some corners are perceived to be Anglo-Saxon-dominated international norms. Although these challenges were kept at bay in Vienna, they have persisted and are not likely to go away given the turbulent nature of the post–Cold War world order. In this respect, former UN Secretary-General Boutros-Ghali took the unprecedented step of personally opening the annual session of the Commission on Human Rights in Geneva in March 1996, stressing the importance of promoting human rights in all aspects of the world organization's work; his *Agenda for Development* stressed the importance of democratic rights.

Rules for Sustainable Development

Just as the Vienna conference showed the political dynamics of rule making for human rights, the Rio conference illustrated the struggle to make rules on sustainable development. There was less consensus on development at Rio than on human rights at Vienna, at least formally. And there was less decisive action in Rio on rules for sustainable development compared to the establishment of new security rules in Vienna. In fact, although the Security Council has delineated a number of security rules, linking some of these to human rights, the council has not yet directly linked Chapter VII to an environmental threat. Given the armed conflict in the Persian Gulf in 1991, however, with resulting ecological damage from oil wells set ablaze by Iraq, there was a growing demand for making new rules on environmental protection that would apply during war and for considering violation of these new ecological rules a war crime.

The UN Commission on Sustainable Development, recommended by majority vote at Rio and created by the 1992 General Assembly, faces an enormously complicated task. It has to fashion rules on a broad and complicated subject that has proven contentious in every single polity where economic growth and environmental protection have been juxtaposed. For example, President Clinton in summer 1993 found it difficult to establish binding and acceptable rules reflecting a compromise between developmentalists (namely, the logging industry) and environmentalists (namely, those wanting to protect the spotted owl) in the U.S. Northwest. In December 1999 in Seattle, the confrontation between the World Trade Organization and various lobbying groups suggested that lack of consensus on these issues is hardly an American monopoly. The same complicated search for compromise and workable rules bedeviled UN efforts in behalf of sustainable development. Moreover, although the Security Council and the Human Rights Commission are generally held to represent authoritative bodies in their respective fields of security and rights, no such consensual status exists for the new Commission on Sustainable Development. The CSD mandate and scope of authority remain somewhat ambiguous, especially as they relate to the work of the United Nations Environment Programme and the UNDP. This is quite unfortunate given the tenor and substance of the UNDP's annual *Human Development Reports* discussed earlier.

Rule Enforcement

"hat is perhaps most striking about the UN in the 1990s is the extent to which its
'es are passing judgment about the behavior of states under UN-sponsored
which themselves are a reflection of interests articulated and aggregated

through UN channels. The past fifty years reveal important lessons for UN rule enforcement within our three thematic areas.

Enforcing Security Rules

The UN Security Council has clearly eclipsed the General Assembly in the security area, as the Charter originally intended. In the 1990s the locus of supervisory activity concerning state use of force and other security policies was in the council. In one respect matters have not changed since 1945. The Security Council cannot be expected to supervise the permanent members in any vigorous or rigorous way. Each still possesses the veto, which guarantees council impotence when a permanent member's policy is challenged. This is not the result of poor drafting by the Charter's framers but of recognition of the realities of power. No coalition of states could hope militarily to coerce the United States into changing its policies; it is doubtful that any coalition could do likewise against Britain, France, Russia, or China without enormous disruption to world politics. Certainly force could not be used without overwhelming destruction out of proportion to the offense, possibly triggering violations of international law.

Never before in world history, however, has an IGO sought to pass judgment on states' security policies to the extent that the UN Security Council did in the early 1990s. In historical perspective, this was a major experiment. The outcomes constituted a mixed record.

Working closely with the Secretary-General, the Security Council could count a number of successes in supervising various policies in places such as Southwest Africa/Namibia and Central America in the late 1980s and early 1990s. The result was both independence for Namibia and significant steps toward regional peace and national reconciliation in El Salvador and Nicaragua.

From August 1990 the council successfully countered various Iraqi policies that violated international law, primarily because the United States took a very strong interest in resisting aggression against Kuwait and in seeing that council follow-up resolutions were enforced. The council was also successful in ameliorating disorder and starvation in Somalia in 1992 and early 1993, again because the United States decided, for whatever reason, that the situation was intolerable.

At the same time, the Security Council passed numerous resolutions pertaining to the former Yugoslavia that were not implemented. The state members of the council were diplomatically engaged in supervising the policies of the various parties engaged in armed conflict—Serbians, Croats, Bosnians, Bosnian Serbs, Bosnian Croats, and Bosnian Muslims. Those same council members, however, lacked the will to see that the necessary political and material resources were made available to UN forces and representatives in the field. Multilateral diplomacy was divorced from threat or effective use of power, with predictably disappointing results. Serbia's original war aims ended up being the negotiated final solution. Nevertheless, the UN did commendable work in trying circumstances by providing humanitarian relief to many thousands of persons through the activities of the UNHCR, UNICEF, and UNPROFOR.

In Somalia from May 1993, the council and its field representatives through UNOSOM II tried to accomplish what U.S. forces had been unwilling to do under UNOSOM I or UNITAF—namely, to disarm the internal factions that had been threatening civilian life and to protect relief officials. But this task proved difficult given the inadequate training, coordination, equipment, and overall force levels of UN military contingents. Calling the effort an enforcement operation under Chapter VII did not resolve problems in the field, and it was evident that the UN had difficulty in suppressing factions that had long used force to gain their political objectives.

The situation was similar for UNTAC in Cambodia. General elections were supervised in May 1993, but the Security Council found it difficult to fashion a policy that would control the Khmer Rouge while helping competing domestic factions that supported national reconciliation. The United Nations also found itself only nominally in control of key departments in the central government, with much power being exercised apart from UN supervision. The four leading Cambodian factions found it difficult to proceed without UN approval, but the world organization found itself facing great difficulties in making its supervision effective. But even those critical of the UN in Cambodia did not seem to have other viable options, and the largest UN operation to date completed its withdrawal in November 1993 without full peace for Cambodia.

The delayed reactions to genocide in Rwanda and to the ouster of the elected government in Haiti also tarnished the UN's reputation. But in these and other security situations, there was a tendency for the state members of the council to pass resolutions that they were not committed to implementing unless the costs were deemed to be reasonable and the length of the time of an operation short. This attitude damaged the UN's reputation. For example, the credibility of the council was destroyed when it declared "safe areas" for civilians in the former Yugoslavia only to have the fighting parties attack them with impunity. It hurt the UN for the council to create a war-crimes tribunal for the former Yugoslavia but then not to provide adequate staffing for the preliminary investigations or urge IFOR to pursue indicted criminals. The world organization got the criticism, but the real problem was state foreign policy channeled through the United Nations.

Nevertheless, a state that was not a permanent member but that was contemplating action that might be found to be a threat to or breach of the peace had to deal with the possibility that the UN Security Council would find its action in violation of international law and therefore launch some coercive response. The UN's probability of firm reaction was in almost direct proportion to the interest that the United States took in the situation and Washington's willingness to act. This state of affairs was markedly different from the Cold War period, when great-power disagreement guaranteed the lack of a firm council response to peace and security issues, with the partial exception of white-minority rule in Africa (Rhodesia and South Africa).

To be effective, peacekeeping and enforcement operations should be based on unambiguous operational guidelines and procedures. In this regard, the Security Council moved in 1994 to articulate criteria for a variety of important aspects of operational activities, including the initial deployment of forces, ongoing operational reviews, training, command and control, and financing. In addition, effective rule enforcement entails an adequate capacity to act. In the context of the multitude of security-related activities in which the organization is engaged, the United Nations quite simply does not possess this capacity. The world organization is perpetually drained and strained financially to the limits as new tasks are added without the requisite addition of new financial and other resources. In the late 1990s, cumulative debts and arrears hovered around $3.5 billion, or about three times the regular annual budget. As demonstrated clearly in the case of dealing with the crisis in the former Yugoslavia, U.S. officials have shown increasing willingness to "let the UN do it" or to "do it in the name of the UN," but there has not been an equally determined commitment to make certain that the required funds are also forthcoming. In his 1993 address to the General Assembly, President Clinton cautioned that the UN must know when to say no. At that time as well as during the second Clinton administration, this implies that the United States must know when to say yes. Despite a "deal" to pay U.S. arrears in December 1999 that narrowly avoided the loss of the U.S. vote in the General Assembly and a much publicized visit by the Senate's Foreign Relations Committee to the United Nations in January 2000, the future of the UN's capacity to enforce security rules is far from certain.

This uncertainty is reflected in two events that occurred in 1999 and 2000. The crisis in Kosovo was the first, and it showed the old problem that when the Permanent Five members are divided the Security Council cannot be directly or explicitly involved in security operations. Thus the United States led NATO to use military force in modern Yugoslavia outside the council, because Russia and China were not prepared to support such action against Serbia's persecution of Albanian Kosovars. Russia saw itself as the historical protector of the Serbs, and China was worried about UN approval of strong action against a government's treatment of its own citizens. In the second crisis, however, that pertaining to East Timor and Indonesia, the council was able to authorize a deployment of force to ease the transition problems as East Timor moved from unstable internal status to national independence. Russia expressed no opposition, China was willing to defer, and the United States was content with developments since Australia agreed to take the lead on the ground. Facilitating the entire process was political change in Indonesia, which finally (after much destruction and many deaths) led to considerable cooperation between Jakarta and the UN-approved military force. So in the first instance, there was not Permanent Five agreement, and in the second, there was. In the first, the target government (Belgrade) did not give its consent to what was being discussed in the council, and in the second, Jakarta finally did.

Enforcing Human Rights Rules

Since about 1970 the United Nations, principally via the Human Rights Commission, has been more-or-less systematically using embarrassment to pressure states violating UN human rights rules, but it has employed double standards. Before 1970 there was some sporadic UN supervision of rights performance, but only after 1970 did the world organization make this supervision a regular feature of its actions. The realm of essential domestic jurisdiction has shrunk progressively, and the realm of international supervision has expanded.

Small and weak developing countries were the most likely targets of UN human rights supervision, but no state could be guaranteed immunity from diplomatic pressure. It was true that the Expert Committee supervising the UN Covenant on Economic, Social, and Cultural Rights took on the Dominican Republic; the UN Committee on Human Rights supervising the UN Covenant on Civil and Political Rights confronted Uruguay; and the UN Human Rights Commission broke some new diplomatic ground in supervising Guinea-Bissau. But it was also true that more important states such as China, Iran, and Iraq, not to mention Israel, were sometimes targeted for diplomatic supervision.

By the 1990s many states could not be sure that the Security Council would not declare a particular human rights situation a threat to international peace and engage in some type of enforcement. Iraq, Somalia, and Haiti had been so targeted. Bosnia was a case where human rights violations were intertwined with aggression, in the view of the council, and Chapter VII was invoked to deal with both types of issues.

Power still greatly affects human rights issues at the United Nations. The United States and Japan were not as likely as Israel to be pressured about "racial discrimination." Haiti was more likely to be coercively pressured about the denial of political rights than Myanmar (formerly Burma). China could avoid the issue of suppression of Tibetan rights at the Vienna conference, whereas Israel could not so easily avoid the issue of Palestinian rights to self-determination.

Nevertheless, as a historical trend, the United Nations is supervising more rights in more states through more intrusive measures than ever before. Although the world organization's record on supervising human rights paled in comparison with the Council of Europe's, the UN might in some respects approximate the Organization of American States; and the UN did not fare so badly in comparisons with the Organization of African Unity and the Arab League. Many, if not most, states had apparently learned the necessity, if not the benefit, of having the United Nations pass judgment about their human rights performances. During the 1990s, an International Criminal Court was finally approved by UN member states, and special tribunals were created to deal with genocide and other human rights atrocities in Rwanda and Yugoslavia. There remained, however, considerable disagreement about enforcing some human rights via international criminal courts.

Enforcing Rules on Sustainable Development

In this issue area the UN's record on supervision is not only exceedingly complex but also affected by the fact that there have been few agreed-upon rules. True, the ILO monitored labor conditions (usually treated as a human rights question), WHO monitored health conditions (also treated by some as a human rights issue), and UNESCO kept an eye on educational issues.

But on many core issues of sustainable development, the basic rules, as well as the very meaning of the concept, are still being debated and negotiated. Moreover, most sustainable development concerns are treated outside the official framework of the United Nations. For example, the Montreal Protocol on the ozone and related agreements have been negotiated outside the UN, but with some participation by UNEP.

The United Nations has never played as definitive and large a role in monitoring state economic and ecological policies as it has in supervising security and human rights policies. International supervision of economics has been performed more by the World Bank and the International Monetary Fund. The bank in particular has finally incorporated some elements of environmental protection into its decisions about whether a loan project should be funded. It is conceivable in the future that the new UN Commission on Sustainable Development could play a role not only in developing rules (as a reflection of aggregated interests) but also in monitoring and enforcing those rules for the UN system.

Just how the Security Council, the General Assembly, or some other centralized UN body, such as a proposed Economic Security Council, could impose itself on a fragmented UN system, and how such a centralized entity would link to the World Bank and its billions in loan funds, is unclear. Furthermore, there is growing recognition that sustainable development, no matter how defined, entails processes and conditions that lie well outside the scope and domain of interstate relations. It calls for popular participation in decisionmaking processes and project implementation. Sustainable development reaches to the lowest level of social aggregation—local communities, social groups, and individuals. These are elements of sustainable human development and of human security that do not fit well with intergovernmentalism, UN style, and associated assumptions of national state sovereignty and noninterference in "domestic affairs." Indeed, in many ways the worldviews underlying interstate relations, on the one hand, and sustainable development, on the other, do not portray the real world at all. The turbulence that characterizes post–Cold War world politics in this regard will need to be addressed if the CSD is to effectively carry out its various mandates. This task and the way it is handled will foretell much about the future of the United Nations in social and economic areas. Bridging the gap between micro- and macrophenomena is a key to coping with turbulence and for promoting human as well as global security.

Some Final Thoughts

Earlier we discussed the appearance of "good governance" as a topic at the national level for the UN system. At the international level, another concept has emerged, "global governance," whose origins can be traced to a growing dissatisfaction among students of international relations with the realist and liberal-institutionalist theories that had dominated the study of international organization since World War II. In particular, these traditional perspectives failed to capture adequately the vast increase, in both numbers and influence, of nonstate actors and the implications of technology in an age of globalization. We have emphasized in previous chapters the growing network of actors circumscribing the UN's role in all major activities. Thus we would like to conclude with the significance of global governance for the twenty-first century, a subject of growing interest among scholars and practitioners.[15]

The journey to explore the concept has barely begun, and so readers will not be surprised to learn that the nature of global governance is more inchoate than the nature of governance within countries. At the same time that Europe adopts a common currency and moves toward a common defense and security policy, how can the former Yugoslavia implode? James Rosenau, the American academic most closely associated with the notion of global governance, invented the term "fragmegration"[16] to capture the simultaneous integration and fragmentation of societal interactions and authority patterns. Moreover, burgeoning information, communication, market, finance, networking, and business activities are producing a world in which patterns are difficult to discern.

Larry Finkelstein has gone so far as to quip that "we say 'governance' because we don't really know what to call what is going on."[17] In short, analysts are understandably uncomfortable with the traditional frameworks and vocabulary used to describe international relations. However, the nomenclature of "global governance" is akin to "Cold War," which signifies that one period has ended but that we do not as yet have an accurate shorthand to depict the essential dynamics of the new epoch.

In spite of vagueness in ongoing scholarly and policy debates, the application of the notion of governance to the globe was the natural result of mounting evidence that the international system was no longer composed simply of states, but that the world was undergoing fundamental change. Although such actors as the Catholic Church, General Motors, and the International Committee of the Red Cross (ICRC) are hardly new to the Westphalian system, it should be clear to readers by now that the proliferation of nonstate actors and their growing importance and power are a distinctive feature of contemporary world affairs.[18]

Global governance invokes the shifting location of authority. The implications for international action jump from the title of Rosenau's edited volume, with Ernst-Otto Czempiel, *Governance Without Government*. Mobilizing support from the bottom up involves increasing the skills and capacities of individuals and altering the horizons of identification in patterns of global life. Elsewhere, Rosenau characterizes global governance as "systems of rule at all levels of human activity—from the family to the international organization—in which the pursuit of goals through the exercise of control has transnational repercussions."[19]

Globalization is neither uniform nor homogeneous, but it is indisputably accelerating the pace and intensity of economic and social interactions at all levels. Although the history is long,[20] its present manifestation is fundamentally different in scale, intensity, and form from what preceded. As David Held and others have put it, "Contemporary globalization represents the beginning of a new epoch in human affairs [causing] as profound an impact as the Industrial Revolution and the global empires of the nineteenth century."[21] Students and professors, policy analysts and practitioners should not feel uncomfortable about admitting their uneasiness and ignorance about understanding the details of the contemporary political economy, and especially not about the best way to address a bewildering array of global problems.

The logical link between the patterns of governance at the national and global levels lies in solving the collective action puzzle in order to provide public goods. "In both modern domestic political systems and the modern international system, the state has been the key structural arena within which collective action has been situated and undertaken," observes Philip Cerny. And as a result of a multiplicity of interactions, "the authority, legitimacy, policymaking capacity, and policy-implementing effectiveness of the state will be eroded and undermined both within and without."[22] Mark Zacher has summarized the nature of the modest order in today's international economic system in the following way: "In short, without these and other regimes and public goods generated by the UN system, it would truly be 'a jungle out there.'"[23]

But governments and their intergovernmental creations are inadequate. Cerny argues that, as market activity intensifies and economic organization becomes increasingly complex, the institutional scale of political structures is no longer capable of providing a suitable range of public goods. In effect, economic globalization is undermining the effectiveness of state-based collective action. Although the state remains a cultural force, its effectiveness as a civil association has declined significantly. The result may be a crisis of legitimacy. This is not to say that state-based collective action has reached its end, but it is significantly different from what it was in the past.

And at the global level, collective action is still more evasive. Although realists and idealists who analyze international organizations disagree about many issues, they agree that the state system is "anarchic." Whatever the framers of the UN Charter had in mind and whatever John Maynard Keynes and his colleagues imagined at Bretton Woods, nothing like an overarching authority for either the high politics of international peace and security or the low politics of economic and social development has emerged.

In one crucial aspect then, "global governance" is distinct from good or bad governance at the national level. At the country level, a "good" (that is, accountable, efficient, lawful, representative, and transparent) government usually leads to good governance, whereas bad governance is correlated with conspicuously bad government. Although the merits of more-or-less interventionist stances by states can be debated, there is a primary and identifiable sovereign agent at the helm. Prescriptions to improve policy- and decisionmaking flow naturally, albeit controversially, from adjusting the potential contribution of the state as agent.

At the global level, in contrast, we need a term to signify the reality that there has never been a world government, and there undoubtedly will not be one during our lifetime. Finkelstein, for instance, sees global governance as "doing internationally what governments do at home."[24] But his formulation fails to specify the agencies that are supposed to accomplish globally the numerous tasks that governments do nationally. Thus, at both the country and the global levels, governance encompasses more than government. But as there is no government at the global level, of what utility is the notion of global governance? Is it, as Brian Urquhart once quipped, like the grinning but bodiless Cheshire cat in *Alice in Wonderland,* an agreeable notion because it is without substance?

For us, global governance is most usefully seen as a heuristic device to capture and describe the seemingly ever-accelerating transformation of the international system within which the United Nations operates. States are central to it, but their authority is eroding in important ways. Their creations, intergovernmental organizations, are no more in control than they ever were. Local and international NGOs are proliferating and gaining authority and resources. And technological developments are increasing the wherewithal of corporations and criminal groups. Within this context, collective action problems associated with the provision of global public goods have become still more intractable than is their provision in the national setting.[25]

The subtext, here and in the analyses of most proponents, is that multilateral institutions, both universal and regional, should be strengthened. The longing for a monolithic and top-down view of governance for the globe is understandable but seems misplaced in an increasingly decentralized world. At a time when both problems and solutions transcend national borders and there is no likelihood of a central sovereign, the visceral calls from internationalists to strengthen intergovernmental institutions are comprehensible but appear wistful. It would be better to think creatively about ways to pool the collective strengths and avoid the collective weaknesses of governments, intergovernmental organizations, NGOs, and global civil society. Ironically, this is the conceptual and operational challenge for supporters of the United Nations in the face of changing world politics.

Indeed, this was the organizing principle behind the September 2000 Millennium Summit, which Singapore's ambassador to the UN Kishore Mahbubani called "the mother of all summits." Some 150 heads of government participated in an intense series of private and public sessions. But New York's traffic was congested by more than government limosines because of Secretary-General Kofi Annan's effort to reflect the diverse reality of problem-solving in the contemporary world with a "global compact" between the United Nations and representatives of NGOs and business as well as of governments.[26]

In conclusion, we need to reflect again on the primary *raison d'être* of the United Nations, which is the promotion and maintenance of peace and security and—most especially concerning the movement into the new millennium—human security. In this regard, we need to stress the inherent and inextricably linked nature of human security, democratization and human rights, and sustainable human development. The latter is aimed at cumulatively improving and sustaining human security and reducing perceived and actual threats to physical and psychological well-being from all manner of agents and forces that could degrade lives, values, and property. Both sustainable human security and sustainable human development require democracy and the protection of fundamental human rights. In short, enhancing human security is what both development and democracy are about.

The United Nations has always been a blend of ideals and reality.[27] Its Charter represents the ideal goals of international society, a world of peace and justice. Its operation represents the reality of state foreign policies mediated by the views of nonstate parties such as NGOs and independent international civil servants. The UN thus represents both the striving for a better world—more peaceful, with more human dignity and equitable and sustainable prosperity—and the failure to achieve those goals, largely because of shortsighted and self-serving national preoccupations.

After the Cold War there is an opportunity for states to cooperate more through the United Nations. The debilitating competition between Washington and Moscow, between NATO and the Warsaw Pact, between capitalist democracies and authoritarian or socialist states, has been reduced. States have indeed learned to profit from this post–Cold War opportunity, cooperating within the security realm (for instance, in the Persian Gulf and Somalia), the human rights arena (for instance, in Haiti and El Salvador), and the field of sustainable development (for instance, in the Commission on Sustainable Development).

But interstate cooperation via the United Nations clearly has its limits. States learned conflicting things about the wisdom of projecting the UN into armed conflict in places like the former Yugoslavia, into the human rights situation in places like China, and how to handle sustainable development in both the North and the South.

In finally evaluating the successes and failures attributed to the United Nations, we can take a maximalist or minimalist position. If we compare the real record of achievement to the lofty goals stated in the Charter, the UN record is bound to be criticized. If we recognize that UN actions depend heavily on state foreign policy, which is ever sensitive to national interests, and that much of the time the UN is given the difficult problems that states have not been able to solve on their own, then criticism is moderated. In this respect we may do well to conclude with words attributed to Secretary-General Dag Hammarskjöld: "The purpose of the UN is not to get us to heaven but to save us from hell." As Secretary-General Kofi Annan suggested in his inaugural remarks, modesty is undoubtedly a helpful approach in this post–post–Cold War era.

Notes

1. See further J. Martin Rochester, *Waiting for the Millennium: The United Nations and the Future of World Order* (Columbia: Univ. of South Carolina Press, 1993).

2. James N. Rosenau, *Turbulence in World Politics: A Theory of Change and Continuity* (Princeton: Princeton Univ. Press, 1990). The implications of this view for the United Nations are found in his *The United Nations in a Turbulent World* (Boulder: Lynne Rienner, 1992).

3. Ernest R. May, *"Lessons" of the Past: The Use and Misuse of History in American Foreign Policy* (New York: Oxford Univ. Press, 1975).

4. See further Richard E. Neustadt and Ernest R. May, *Thinking in Time: The Uses of History for Decision Makers* (New York: Free Press, 1986).

5. See Cindy Collins and Thomas G. Weiss, *Review of the Peacekeeping Literature, 1990–1996* (Providence, RI: Watson Institute, 1997).

6. Shashi Tharoor, "Forward," in Donald C. F. Daniel and Bradd C. Hayes, eds., *Beyond Traditional Peacekeeping* (London: Macmillan, 1995), p. xviii.

7. See Jay Luvaas, "Lessons and Lessons Learned: A Historical Perspective," in Robert E. Harkavy and Stephanie G. Neuman, eds., *The Lessons of Recent Wars in the Third World: Approaches and Case Studies*, Vol. 1 (Lexington, MA: Heath, 1985), p. 68.

8. Joseph J. Collins, "Desert Storm and the Lessons of Learning," *Parameters* 22, no. 3 (Autumn 1992), pp. 83–95; quote taken from p. 94.

9. Peter M. Haas and Ernst B. Haas, "Learning to Learn: Improving International Governance," *Global Governance* 1, no. 3 (September-December 1995), pp. 255–285, quote at p. 278.

10. For an example of this approach applied to international organizations, see Harold K. Jacobson, *Networks of Interdependence: International Organizations and the Global Political System* (New York: Knopf, 1979).

11. Robert E. Riggs, *US/UN: Foreign Policy and International Organization* (New York: Appleton-Century-Crofts, 1971), p. 298.

12. Ken Roth, "Sidelined on Human Rights," *Foreign Affairs* 77, no. 2 (March-April 1998), pp. 2–6.

13. UNDP, *Human Development Report 1996* (New York: United Nations, 1996), p. 12.

14. David P. Forsythe, *The Internationalization of Human Rights* (Lexington, MA: Lexington Books for the Free Press, 1991), chaps. 4–5.

15. Since 1995 Lynne Rienner Publishers has, in cooperation with the Academic Council on the United Nations System and the UN University, published the journal *Global Governance*. The first issue contained contributions by then Secretary-General Boutros Boutros-Ghali and his Special Representative on Internally Displaced Persons, Francis M.

Deng, as well as articles by Rosenau and three younger academics. The Commission on Global Governance was chaired by Sonny Ramphal and Ingmar Carlsson and published the views of the eminent practitioners in *Our Global Neighbourhood* (Oxford: Oxford Univ. Press, 1995). In addition, see James N. Rosenau and Ernst-Otto Czempiel, eds., *Governance Without Government: Order and Change in World Politics* (Cambridge, UK: Cambridge Univ. Press, 1992); Jan Kooiman, ed., *Modern Governance: New Government-Society Interactions* (London: Sage, 1993); Mihaly Simai, *The Future of Global Governance: Managing Risk and Change in the International System* (Washington, DC: U.S. Institute of Peace, 1994); Meghnad Desai and Paul Redfern, eds., *Global Governance: Ethics and Economics of the World Order* (London: Pinter, 1995); Richard Falk, *On Humane Governance* (University Park: Pennsylvania State Press, 1995); Paul F. Diehl, ed., *The Politics of Global Governance: International Organizations in an Interdependent World* (Boulder: Lynne Rienner, 1997); Martin Hewson and Timothy J. Sinclair, eds., *Approaches to Global Governance Theory* (Albany: State University of New York Press, 1999); and Errol E. Harris and James A. Yunker, eds., *Toward Genuine Global Governance: Critical Reflection to Our Global Neighbourhood* (Westport, CT: Praeger, 1999). In addition, numerous publications from international agencies have used the concept in their titles and analyses. See, for example, World Bank, *Governance and Development* (Washington, DC: World Bank, 1992); and UN Development Programme, *The Shrinking State: Governance and Human Development in Eastern Europe and the Commonwealth of Independent States* (New York: UNDP, 1997).

16. James N. Rosenau, "'Fragmegrative' Challenges to National Security," in Terry Hens, ed., *Understanding US Strategy: A Reader* (Washington, DC: National Defense University, 1983), pp. 65–82.

17. Lawrence S. Finkelstein, "What Is Global Governance?" *Global Governance* 1, no. 3 (September-December 1995), p. 368.

18. For a persuasive discussion, see David Held and Anthony McGrew, with David Goldblatt and Jonathan Peraton, *Global Transformations: Politics, Economics, and Culture* (Stanford: Stanford Univ. Press, 1999).

19. James N. Rosenau, "Governance in the Twenty-first Century," *Global Governance* 1, no. 1 (May-August 1995), p. 13.

20. Emma Rothschild, "Globalization and the Return of History," *Foreign Policy* no. 115 (Summer 1999), pp. 106–116.

21. David Held and Anthony McGrew, with David Goldblatt and Jonathan Peraton, "Globalization," *Global Governance* 5, no. 4 (October-December 1999), p. 494.

22. Philip G. Cerny, "Globalization and the Changing Logic of Collective Action," *International Organization* 49, no. 4 (Autumn 1995), pp. 595, 621.

23. Mark W. Zacher, *The United Nations and Global Commerce* (New York: United Nations, 1999), p. 5.

24. Finkelstein, "What Is Global Governance?" p. 369.

25. Inge Kaul, Isabelle Grunberg, and Marc A. Stern, *Global Public Goods: International Cooperation in the 21st Century* (New York: Oxford Univ. Press, 1999).

26. Kofi, Annan, *"We the Peoples": The United Nations in the 21st Century* (New York: United Nations, 2000).

27. See further Peter R. Baehr and Leon Gordenker, *The United Nations: Reality and Ideal* (New York: Praeger, 1984; rev. ed., Macmillan and St. Martin's Press, 1991).

Appendix:
The United Nations System

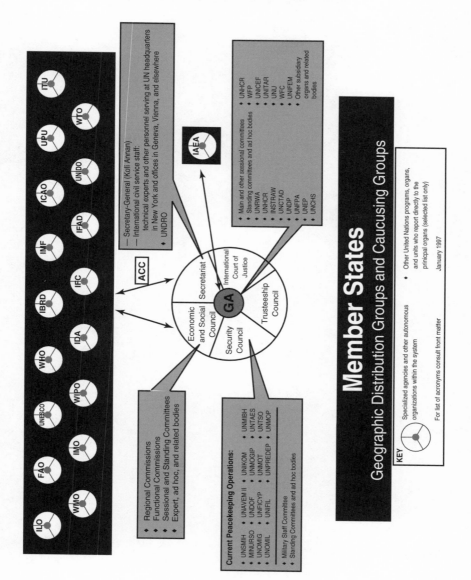

Member States

Geographic Distribution Groups and Caucusing Groups

Organs directly connected to the General Assembly (GA), Security Council, Economic and Social Council, Trusteeship Council, International Court of Justice, and Secretariat.

— Secretary-General (Kofi Annan)
— International civil service staff:
  technical experts and other personnel serving at UN headquarters in New York and offices in Geneva, Vienna, and elsewhere
  ◆ UNDRO

IAEA

Specialized agencies (ILO, WMO, FAO, IMO, UNESCO, WIPO, WHO, IDA, IBRD, IFC, IMF, IFAD, ICAO, UNIDO, UPU, WTO, ITU):

◆ Main and other sessional committees
◆ Standing committees and ad hoc bodies
◆ UNRWA
◆ UNHCR
◆ INSTRAW
◆ UNCTAD
◆ UNDP
◆ UNFPA
◆ UNEP
◆ UNCHS

◆ UNHCR
◆ WFP
◆ UNICEF
◆ UNITAR
◆ UNU
◆ WFC
◆ UNIFEM
◆ Other subsidiary organs and related bodies

ACC

◆ Regional Commissions
◆ Functional Commissions
◆ Sessional and Standing Committees
◆ Expert, ad hoc, and related bodies

Current Peacekeeping Operations:

◆ UNSMIH   ◆ UNAVEM II   ◆ UNIKOM   ◆ UNMIBH
◆ MINURSO   ◆ UNDOF   ◆ UNMOGIP   ◆ UNTAES
◆ UNOMIG   ◆ UNFICYP   ◆ UNMOT   ◆ UNTSO
◆ UNOMIL   ◆ UNIFIL   ◆ UNPREDEP   ◆ UNMOP

Military Staff Committee
◆ Standing Committees and ad hoc bodies

KEY

⊙ Specialized agencies and other autonomous organizations within the system

◆ Other United Nations programs, organs, and units who report directly to the principal organs (selected list only)

For list of acronyms consult front matter   January 1997

333

For Further Reading

Part One: International Peace and Security

The International System and the United Nations

Alger, Chadwick F., ed. 1998. *The Future of the United Nations System: Potential for the Twenty-first Century.* Tokyo: United Nations University Press.

Baehr, Peter R., and Leon Gordenker. 1999. *The United Nations at the End of the 1990s.* New York: St. Martin's Press.

Bailey, Sydney D. and Sam Daws. 1998. *The Procedure of the UN Security Council.* Oxford: Oxford Univ. Press, Third Edition.

Bertrand, Maurice. 1989. *The Third Generation World Organization.* Dordrecht: Martinus Nijhoff.

Boutros-Ghali, Boutros. 1999. *Unvanquished: A U.S.–U.N. Saga.* Mississauga, Ontario: Random House of Canada, Limited.

Bowett, D. W. 1970. *The Law of International Institutions.* London: Stevens.

Bull, Hedley. 1977. *The Anarchical Society.* New York: Oxford Univ. Press.

Childers, Erskine, and Brian Urquhart. 1999. *Renewing the United Nations System.* Upland, PA: DIANE Publishing Company.

Claude, Inis L., Jr. 1984. *Power and International Relations,* 4th ed. New York: Random House.

_____. 1964. *Swords into Plowshares.* New York: Random House.

Commission on Global Governance. 1995. *Our Global Neighbourhood.* Oxford: Oxford Univ. Press.

Diehl, Paul F., ed. 1996. *The Politics of Global Governance: International Organizations in an Interdependent World.* Boulder: Lynne Rienner.

Evans, Gareth. 1993. *Cooperating for Peace: The Global Agenda for the 1990s and Beyond.* St. Leonard's, Australia: Allen and Unwin.

Fawcett, Louise, and Andrew Hurrell, eds. 1995. *Regionalism in World Politics: Regional Organizations and World Order.* Oxford: Oxford Univ. Press.

Feld, Werner J., and Robert S. Jordan. 1994. *International Organization: A Comparative Approach,* 2nd ed. New York: Praeger.

Finkelstein, Lawrence S., ed. 1988. *Politics in the United Nations System.* Durham, NC: Duke Univ. Press.

Franck, Thomas M. 1985. *Nation Against Nation: What Happened to the UN Dream and What the US Can Do About It.* New York: Oxford Univ. Press.

Global Governance. Quarterly journal about multilateral approaches to security, human rights, and sustainable development. Boulder: Lynne Rienner.

Goodrich, Leland, Edvard Hambro, and Anne Patricia Simons. 1969. *Charter of the United Nations.* New York: Columbia Univ. Press.

Gordenker, Leon, ed. 1971. *The United Nations in International Politics.* Princeton: Princeton Univ. Press.

Gregg, Robert W. 1993. *About Face? The United States and the United Nations.* Boulder: Lynne Rienner.

Hinsley, F. H. 1963. *Power and the Pursuit of Peace.* Cambridge, UK: Cambridge Univ. Press.

Hüfner, Klaus, ed. 1995. *Agenda for Change: New Tasks for the United Nations.* Opladen: Leske and Budrich.

Independent Working Group on the Future of the United Nations. 1995. *The United Nations in Its Second Half-Century.* New York: Ford Foundation.

Jacobson, Harold K. 1984. *Networks of Interdependence,* 2nd ed. New York: Alfred A. Knopf.

Joyner, Christopher C., ed. 1997. *The United Nations and International Law.,* 2nd ed. Cambridge, UK: Cambridge Univ. Press.

Karns, Margaret P., and Karen A. Mingst. 1990. *The United States and Multilateral Institutions.* London: Unwin Hyman.

Kaufmann, Johan. 1988. *Conference Diplomacy: An Introductory Analysis,* 2nd rev. ed. Dordrecht: Martinus Nijhoff.

_____. 1980. *United Nations Decision-Making.* Rockville, MD: Sijthoff and Noordhoff.

Kay, David A. 1970. *The New Nations in the United Nations 1960–1967.* New York: Columbia Univ. Press.

Luard, Evan. 1982. *A History of the United Nations: The Years of Western Domination.* London: Macmillan.

Luck, Edward. 1999. *Mixed Messages: American Politics and International Organization, 1919–1999.* Washington, DC: Brookings Institution.

Maynes, Charles William, and Richard S. Williamson. 1996. *U.S. Foreign Policy and the United Nations System.* New York: Norton.

Mingst, Karen A., and Margaret P. Karns. 1999. *The United Nations in the Post-Cold War Era.* (Dilemmas in World Politics Ser.) Boulder: Westview Press.

Muldoon, James P., et al. 1999. *Multilateral Diplomacy and the United Nations Today.* Boulder: Westview Press.

Murphy, Craig N. 1994. *International Organization and Industrial Change: Global Governance Since 1850.* Cambridge, UK: Polity Press.

De Cuéllar, Javier Pérez. 1997. *Pilgrimage for Peace: A Secretary-General's Memoir.* New York: St. Martin's Press.

Peterson, M. J. 1986. *The General Assembly in World Politics.* Boston: Allen and Unwin.

Rivlin, Benjamin, and Leon Gordenker. 1993. *The Challenging Role of the UN Secretary-General.* Westport, CT: Praeger.

Roberts, Adam, and Benedict Kingsbury, eds. 1944. *United Nations, Divided World: The UN's Role in International Relations,* 2nd ed. Oxford: Clarendon Press.

Rosenau, James. 1992. *The United Nations in a Turbulent World.* Boulder: Lynne Rienner.

Ruggie, John Gerard. 1996. *Winning the Peace: America and World Order in the New Era.* New York: Columbia Univ. Press.

South Centre. 1996. *For a Strong and Democratic United Nations: A South Perspective on UN Reform.* Geneva: South Centre.

Thakur, Ramesh C. 1998. *Past Imperfect, Future Uncertain: The United Nations at Fifty.* New York: St. Martin's Press.

United Nations Association of the USA. 2000. *A Global Agenda.* New York: UNA/USA, published annually.

Urquhart, Brian, and Erskine Childers. 1996. *A World in Need of Leadership: Tomorrow's United Nations—A Fresh Appraisal.* Uppsala, Sweden: Dag Hammarskjöld Foundation.

Walters, F. P. 1952. *A History of the League of Nations,* 2 vols. London: Oxford Univ. Press.

Weiss, Thomas G., and Leon Gordenker, eds. 1996. *NGOs, the UN, and Global Governance.* Boulder: Lynne Rienner.

Ziring, Lawrence, Robert E. Riggs, and Jack C. Plano. 2000. *The United Nations,* 3rd ed. Orlando, FL: Harcourt Brace.

Peacekeeping and Collective Security

Alagappa, Muthia, and Takashi Inoguchi, eds. 1998. *International Security Management and the United Nations.* Tokyo: United Nations University.

Ayoob, Mohammed. 1995. *The Third World Security Predicament: State Making, Regional Conflict, and the International System.* Boulder: Lynne Rienner.

Berdal, Mats R. 1996. *Disarmament and Demobilisation After Civil Wars.* Oxford: Oxford Univ. Press. Adelphi Paper no. 303.

Boutros-Ghali, Boutros. 1995. *An Agenda for Peace 1995.* New York: United Nations.

Brown, Michael E., ed. 1996. *International Dimensions of Internal Conflicts.* Cambridge, MA: MIT Press.

Buzan, Barry. 1991. *People, States and Fear: An Agenda for International Security Studies in the Post–Cold War Era.* Boulder: Lynne Rienner.

Chopra, Jarat. 1999. *Peace-Maintenance: The Evolution of International Political Authority.* New York: Routledge.

Collins, Cindy, and Weiss, Thomas G. 1997. *Review of the Peacekeeping Literature, 1990–1996.* Providence, RI: Watson Institute. Occasional Paper no. 28.

Cortright, David, and George A. Lopez, eds. 2000. *The Sanctions Decades: Assessing UN Strategies in the 1990s.* Boulder: Lynne Rienner.

_____. 1995. *Economic Sanctions: Panacea or Peacebuilding in a Post–Cold War World?* Boulder: Westview Press.

Damrosch, Lori Fisler, ed. 1993. *Enforcing Restraint: Collective Intervention in Internal Conflicts.* New York: Council on Foreign Relations.

Damrosch, Lori Fisler, and David J. Scheffer. 1991. *Law and Force in the New International Order.* Boulder: Westview Press.

Daniel, Donald C. F., and Bradd C. Hayes, eds. 1995. *Beyond Traditional Peacekeeping.* London: Macmillan.

Debrix, Francois. 1999. *Re-Envisioning Peacekeeping: The United Nations and the Mobilization of Ideology.* Minneapolis: Univ. of Minnesota Press.

Diehl, Paul. 1993. *International Peacekeeping.* Baltimore: Johns Hopkins Univ. Press.

Downs, George W., ed. 1994. *Collective Security Beyond the Cold War.* Ann Arbor: Univ. of Michigan Press.

Durch, William J. 1997. *UN Peacekeeping, American Policy, and the Uncivil Wars of the 1990s.* New York: St. Martin's Press.

Durch, William J., ed. 1993. *The Evolution of UN Peacekeeping, Case Studies and Comparative Analysis.* New York: St. Martin's Press.

Findlay, Trevor. 1999. *Fighting for Peace: The Use of Force in Peace Operations.* New York: Oxford Univ. Press.

Gordenker, Leon. 1967. *The UN Secretary-General and the Maintenance of Peace.* New York: Columbia Univ. Press.

Hampson, Fen Osler. 1996. *Nurturing Peace: Why Peace Settlements Succeed or Fail.* Washington, DC: U.S. Institute of Peace Press.

Heininger, Janet E. 1994. *Peacekeeping in Transition: The United Nations in Cambodia.* New York: Twentieth Century Fund Press.

Henkin, Louis, et al. 1991. *Right vs. Might: International Law and the Use of Force.* New York: Council on Foreign Relations.

Higgins, Rosalyn. 1969, 1970, 1980, 1981. *United Nations Peacekeeping, Documents and Commentary,* Vols. 1–4. Oxford: Oxford Univ. Press.

James, Alan. 1990. *Peacekeeping in International Politics.* New York: St. Martin's Press.

Knight, W. Andy. 1998. *The United Nations and Arms Embargoes Verification* (Studies in World Peace) Vol. 8. Lewiston, NY: Mellen Biblical Press.

Kühne, Winrich. 1996. *Winning the Peace: Concept and Lessons Learned of Post-Conflict Peacebuilding.* Ebenhausen, Germany: Stiftung und Wissenschaft.

Lyons, Gene M., and Michael Mastanduno, eds. 1995. *Beyond Westphalia? National Sovereignty and International Intervention.* Baltimore: Johns Hopkins Univ. Press.

Martin, Lisa. 1992. *Coercive Cooperation: Explaining Multilateral Economic Sanctions.* Princeton: Princeton Univ. Press.

Otunnu, Olara A., and Michael W. Doyle, eds. Foreword by Nelson Mandela. 1998. *Peacemaking and Peacekeeping for the New Century.* Rowman and Littlefield.

Pugh, Michael, ed. *International Peacekeeping.* Quarterly journal with an exclusive focus on UN military operations.

———. 1997. *The U. N., Peace, and Force.* (The Cass Series in Peacekeeping), no. 2. Ilford, England: Frank Cass.

Ratner, Steven R. 1995. *The New UN Peacekeeping: Building Peace in Lands of Conflict After the Cold War.* New York: St. Martin's Press.

Shawcross, William. 2000. *Deliver Us from Evil: Peacekeepers, Warlords and a World of Endless Conflict.* New York: Simon and Schuster.

Sivard, Ruth Leger. 1999. *World Military and Social Expenditures 1999.* Washington, DC: World Priorities. A useful compendium, updated annually, of information about the costs of war and defense expenditures.

Sutterlin, James S. 1995. *The United Nations and the Maintenance of International Security: A Challenge to Be Met.* Westport, CT: Praeger.

Tow, William B. 1990. *Subregional Security Cooperation in the Third World.* Boulder: Lynne Rienner.

United Nations. 1996. *The Blue Helmets: A Review of United Nations Peace-keeping.* New York: UN Department of Public Information.

Urquhart, Sir Brian. 1987. *A Life in Peace and War.* New York: Harper and Row.

U.S. Congressional Research Office, Joshua Sinai, ed. 1995. *United Nations Peace Operations: Case Studies.* Washington, DC: Library of Congress.

Volker, Paul, and Shituro Ogata et al. 1993. *Financing an Effective United Nations.* New York: Ford Foundation.

Weiss, Thomas G., ed. 1995. *The United Nations and Civil Wars.* Boulder: Lynne Rienner.

———. 1993. *Collective Security in a Changing World.* Boulder: Lynne Rienner.

Whitman, Jim, and Michael Pugh, eds. 1999. *Peacekeeping and the UN Specialized Agencies* (Series on Peacekeeping), no. 4. Ilford, England: Frank Cass.

Zartman, I. William, ed. 1995. *Collapsed States: The Disintegration and Restoration of Legitimate Authority.* Boulder: Lynne Rienner.

_____. 1995. *Elusive Peace: Negotiating an End to Civil Wars.* Washington, DC: Brookings Institution.

Part Two: Human Rights and Humanitarian Affairs

Alston, Philip, ed. 1995. *The United Nations and Human Rights.* Oxford: Clarendon Press.

Anderson, Mary, and Peter Woodrow. 1989. *Rising from the Ashes: Disaster Response Toward Development.* Boulder: Westview Press.

Bennett, Jon, ed. 1995. *Meeting Needs: NGO Coordination in Practice.* London: Earthscan.

Blaustein, Albert P., et al. 1987. *Human Rights Sourcebook.* New York: Paragon.

Clark, Roger S., and Madeleine Sann, eds. 1996. *The Prosecution of International Crimes.* New Brunswick, NJ: Transaction.

Claude, Richard P., and Burns H. Weston, eds. 1992. *Human Rights in the International Community,* 2nd rev. ed. Philadelphia: Univ. of Pennsylvania Press.

Deng, Francis M. 1993. *Protecting the Dispossessed: A Challenge for the International Community.* Washington, DC: Brookings Institution.

Deng, Francis M., and Larry Minear. 1992. *The Challenges of Famine Relief.* Washington, DC: Brookings Institution.

Donnelly, Jack. 1993. *Human Rights and International Relations.* Boulder: Westview Press.

_____. 1993. *International Human Rights.* Boulder: Westview Press.

_____. 1989. *Universal Human Rights in Theory and Practice.* Ithaca: Cornell Univ. Press.

Dunne, Tim, and Nicholas J. Wheeler, eds. 1999. *Human Rights in Global Politics.* Cambridge, UK: Cambridge Univ. Press.

Farer, Tom J., ed. 1996. *Beyond Sovereignty: Collectively Defending Democracy in the Americas.* Baltimore: Johns Hopkins Univ. Press.

Forsythe, David P. 1993. *Human Rights and Peace: International and National Dimensions.* Lincoln: Univ. of Nebraska Press.

_____. 1991. *The Internationalization of Human Rights.* Lexington, MA: Lexington Books for the Free Press.

_____. 1989. *Human Rights and World Politics,* 2nd ed. Lincoln: Univ. of Nebraska Press.

Fukuyama, Francis. 1992. *The End of History and the Last Man.* 1992. New York: Free Press.

Girardet, Edward, ed. 1995. *Somalia, Rwanda, and Beyond: The Role of the International Media in Wars and Humanitarian Crises.* Dublin: Crosslines Communications Ltd. Crosslines Special Report 1.

Gordenker, Leon, and Thomas G. Weiss, eds. 1991. *Soldiers, Peacekeepers and Disasters.* London: Macmillan.

Halperin, Morton H., and David J. Scheffer. 1992. *Self-Determination in the New World Order.* Washington, DC: Carnegie Endowment.

Hannum, Hurst. 1990. *Autonomy, Sovereignty, and Self-Determination.* Philadelphia: Univ. of Pennsylvania Press.

Harriss, John, ed. 1995. *The Politics of Humanitarian Intervention.* London: Pinter.

Heiberg, Marianne, ed. 1994. *Subduing Sovereignty: Sovereignty and the Right to Intervene.* London: Pinter.

Hoffmann, Stanley. 1981. *Duties Beyond Borders.* Syracuse: Syracuse Univ. Press.

Humphrey, John P. 1984. *Human Rights and the United Nations.* New Brunswick, NJ: Transaction Books.

Kent, Randolph. 1987. *Anatomy of Disaster Relief: The International Network in Action.* London: Puster.

LeBlanc, Lawrence J. 1994. *Negotiating the Convention on the Rights of the Child.* Lincoln: Univ. of Nebraska Press.

_____. 1991. *The United States and the Genocide Convention.* Durham, NC: Duke Univ. Press.

Lillich, Richard. 1991. *International Human Rights.* Boston: Little, Brown.

Loescher, Gil. 1993. *Beyond Charity: International Cooperation and the Global Refugee Crisis.* New York: Oxford Univ. Press.

Mayall, James, ed. 1996. *The New Interventionism: United Nations Experience in Cambodia, Former Yugoslavia, and Somalia.* New York: Cambridge Univ. Press.

Minear, Larry, Colin Scott, and Thomas G. Weiss. 1996. *The News Media, Civil War, and Humanitarian Action.* Boulder: Lynne Rienner.

Minear, Larry, and Thomas G. Weiss. 1995. *Mercy Under Fire: War and the Global Humanitarian Community.* Boulder: Westview Press.

Moore, Jonathan. 1996. *The UN and Complex Emergencies.* Geneva: UN Research Institute for Social Development.

Moskos, Charles C., and Thomas E. Ricks. 1996. *Reporting War When There Is No War.* Chicago: McCormick Tribune Foundation.

Newman, Frank, and David Weissbrodt. 1990. *International Human Rights.* Cincinnati: Anderson. A thorough legal textbook.

Newman, Johanna. 1996. *Lights, Camera, War.* New York: St. Martin's Press.

Nolan, Cathal J. 1993. *Principled Diplomacy.* Westport, CT: Greenwood Press.

Omaar, Rakiya, and Alex de Waal. 1994. *Humanitarianism Unbound? Current Dilemmas Facing Multi-Mandate Relief Operations in Political Emergencies.* London: African Rights.

Pieterse, Jan Nederveen, ed. Forthcoming. *World Orders in the Making: The Case of Humanitarian Intervention.* London: Macmillan.

Prendergast, John. 1996. *Frontline Diplomacy: Humanitarian Aid and Conflict in Africa.* Boulder: Lynne Rienner.

Ramsbotham, Oliver, and Tom Woodhouse. 1996. *Humanitarian Intervention in Contemporary Conflict.* Cambridge, UK: Polity Press.

Reed, Laura W., and Carl Kaysen, eds. 1993. *Emerging Norms of Justified Intervention.* Cambridge, MA: American Academy of Arts and Sciences.

Rodney, Nigel, ed. 1992. *To Loose the Bonds of Wickedness: International Intervention in Defence of Human Rights.* London: Brasseys.

Rotberg, Robert I., and Thomas G. Weiss, eds. 1996. *From Massacres to Genocide: The Media, Public Policy, and Humanitarian Crises.* Washington, DC: Brookings Institution.

Schiff, Benjamin N. 1995. *Refugees unto the Third Generation: UN Aid to Palestinians.* Syracuse: Syracuse Univ. Press.

Tolley, Howard, Jr. 1987. *The U.N. Commission on Human Rights.* Boulder: Westview Press.

United Nations. *UN Yearbook.* New York: UN, annual.

_____. 1996. *Human Development Report 1996.* New York: Oxford Univ. Press, annual.

UN High Commission for Refugees. 1995. *The State of the World's Refugees 1995: In Search of Solutions.* New York: Oxford Univ. Press.

Vincent, John. 1974. *Non-Intervention and International Order.* Princeton: Princeton Univ. Press.

Weiss, Thomas G., and Cindy Collins. 2000. *Humanitarian Challenges and Intervention: World Politics and the Dilemmas of Help.* Boulder: Westview Press.

Weiss, Thomas G., and Larry Minear, eds. 1993. *Humanitarianism Across Borders: Sustaining Civilians in Times of War.* Boulder: Lynne Rienner.

Winslow, Anne, ed. 1995. *Women, Politics, and the United Nations.* Westport, CT: Greenwood Press.

Part Three: Building Peace Through Sustainable Development

Sustainable Development

Boutros-Ghali, Boutros. 1995. *An Agenda for Development.* New York: United Nations.

Childers, Erskine, with Brian Urquhart. 1994. *Renewing the United Nations System.* Uppsala, Sweden: Hammarskjöld Foundation.

Clark, W. C., and R. E. Munn, eds. 1987. *Sustainable Development of the Biosphere.* Cambridge, UK: Cambridge Univ. Press.

Hulme, David, and Michael Edwards, eds. 1992. *Making a Difference: NGOs and Development in a Changing World.* London: Earthscan.

Randel, Judith, and Tony German, eds. 1997. *The Reality of Aid 1997–1998.* London: Earthscan. Annual publication by a consortium of NGOs designed to provide a counterweight to the official views put forward by governments and the Organization for Economic Cooperation and Development.

Redclift, M. R. 1987. *Sustainable Development: Exploring the Contradictions.* London: Methuen.

Schmidheiny, Stephan. 1992. *Changing Course: A Global Business Perspective on Development and the Environment.* Cambridge, MA: MIT Press.

Smillie, Ian. 1995. *The Alms Bazaar: Altruism Under Fire—Non-Profit Organizations and International Development.* West Hartford, CT: Kumarian Press.

South Commission. 1990. *The Challenge to the South.* Oxford: Oxford Univ. Press.

Spero, Joan Edelman. 1990. *The Politics of International Economic Relations,* 4th ed. New York: St. Martin's Press.

Susskind, Lawrence. 1994. *Environmental Diplomacy: Negotiating More Effective Global Agreements.* Oxford: Oxford Univ. Press.

Tolba, Mustafa K. 1992. *A Commitment to the Future: Sustainable Development and Environmental Protection.* Nairobi: UNEP.

United Nations Development Program. 1993–2000. *Human Development Report.* New York: Oxford Univ. Press. Annual reports assessing the nature and state of sustainable human development.

World Commission on Environment and Development. 1987. *Our Common Future.* Oxford: Oxford Univ. Press.

Environmental Policy and Institutions

Birnie, Patricia, and Alan E. Boyle. 1992. *International Law and the Environment.* Oxford: Clarendon Press.

Caldwell, Lynton K. 1990. *International Environmental Policy: Emergence and Dimensions.* Durham, NC: Duke Univ. Press.

Gosovic, Branislav. 1992. *The Quest for World Environmental Cooperation: The Case of the UN Global Environment Monitoring System.* London: Routledge.

Haas, Peter M., Robert O. Keohane, and Mark A. Levy, eds. 1993. *Institutions for the Earth: Sources of Effective International Environmental Protection.* Cambridge, MA: MIT Press.

Hurrell, Andrew, and Benedict Kingsbury, eds. 1992. *The International Politics of the Environment.* Oxford: Clarendon Press.

Sierra Club. 1986. *Bankrolling Disasters: International Development Banks and the Global Environment.* San Francisco: Sierra Club.

Stern, Paul C., Oran R. Young, and Daniel Druckman. 1992. *Global Environmental Change: Understanding the Human Dimension.* Washington, DC: National Academy Press.

Environmental Politics

Benedick, Richard E. 1991. *Ozone Diplomacy: New Directions in Safeguarding the Planet.* Cambridge, MA: Harvard Univ. Press.

Carroll, J. E., ed. 1983. *Environmental Diplomacy.* Ann Arbor: Univ. of Michigan Press.

Dahlberg, Kenneth A., et al. 1985. *Environment and the Global Arena: Actors, Values, Policies, and Futures.* Durham, NC: Duke Univ. Press.

Krasner, Stephen. 1985. *Structural Conflict: The Third World Against Global Liberation.* Berkeley: Univ. of California Press.

Lester, James P., ed. 1989. *Environmental Politics and Policy: Theories and Evidence.* Durham, NC: Duke Univ. Press.

Litfin, Karen. 1995. *Ozone Discourses: Science and Politics in Global Environmental Cooperation.* New York: Columbia Univ. Press.

McCormick, John. 1989. *Reclaiming Paradise: The Global Environmental Movement.* Bloomington: Indiana Univ. Press.

Pearson, Charles S., ed. 1987. *Multinational Corporations, the Environment, and the Third World.* Durham, NC: Duke Univ. Press.

Porter, Gareth, and Janet Welsh Brown. 1991. *Global Environmental Politics.* Boulder: Westview Press.

Rowlands, Ian, and Malory Greene, eds. 1991. *Global Environmental Change and International Relations.* London: Macmillan.

Thomas, Caroline. 1992. *The Environment and International Relations.* London: Royal Institute of International Affairs.

White, Rodney R. 1993. *North, South, and the Environmental Crisis.* Toronto: Univ. of Toronto Press.

Index

About the Book and Authors

Gulf War coalition-building. Humanitarian intervention in Somalia, Kosovo, and East Timor. War-crimes tribunals in the former Yugoslavia and Rwanda. International Criminal Court. Development debates in Beijing, Cairo, and beyond. Environmental regime-building in and after Rio. After decades of neglect—and at times ridicule—the United Nations is back, pressing its multilateral agenda forward in the wake of the unilateral, bipolar "bad old days" of the Cold War.

In this nicely thematic and synthetic text, the authors bring the alphabet soup of the United Nations alive from its historical foundations to its day-to-day expanding role in an as-yet-unconsolidated new world order. Students of all levels will learn what the UN is, how it operates, and what its relationships are with the universe of external actors and institutions, from sovereign states to the plethora of nongovernmental and intergovernmental organizations now playing important roles in world politics.

The authors, all of whom have practical as well as academic experience with the UN, show how it has exerted operational and normative influence on issues in three key areas—security, human rights, and sustainable development—even as they make recommendations for improved UN performance in the future.

Well documented and well illustrated, the volume includes the UN Charter and organizational schema, topically organized suggested readings, and photos of UN missions. *The United Nations and Changing World Politics* is essential to a comprehensive and contemporary understanding of the world's leading intergovernmental organization—one that, in the words of Dag Hammarskjöld, may not get us to heaven but could save us from hell.

Thomas G. Weiss is Presidential Professor at The Graduate Center of The City University of New York, where he is codirector of the UN Intellectual History Project and one of the editors of the journal *Global Governance*. Previously, he was research professor and director of the Global Security Program at Brown University's Watson Institute for International Studies. He has also held a number of UN posts (at UNCTAD, the UN Commission for Namibia, UNITAR, and ILO) and served as executive director of both the International Peace Academy and the Academic Council on the United Nations System. He has written or edited some thirty books about international organization related to North-South relations, peacekeeping, economic and social development, and humanitarian action.

David P. Forsythe is the Charles J. Mach Distinguished Professor of Political Science at the University of Nebraska–Lincoln. His research interests include international law, organization, and human rights. He is the author of numerous books and articles, including the recent *Human Rights in International Relations*, *Human Rights and Comparative Foreign Policy*, and *The US and Human Rights*. A former consultant to the International Red Cross, he is now a consultant to the Office of the United Nations High Commissioner for Refugees.

Roger A. Coate is a professor of international organization at the University of South Carolina and has taught at Arizona State University. He has worked in the UN Centre for Human Rights, as a consultant to the U.S. National Commission for UNESCO and the Bureau of International Organization Affairs of the U.S. Department of State, as a member of the HABITAT II Secretary-General's Advisory Panel on Housing Rights, and as head of the International Organization Section of the International Studies Association. His most recent books include *International Cooperation in Response to AIDS* (with Leon Gordenker, Christer Jönsson, and Peter Söderholm) and *United States Policy and the Future of the United Nations*. He was founding coeditor of the journal *Global Governance: A Review of Multilateralism and International Organizations* and currently directs a large transnational collaborative research and professional development program in partnership with the Executive Office of the UN Secretary-General and the United National University.